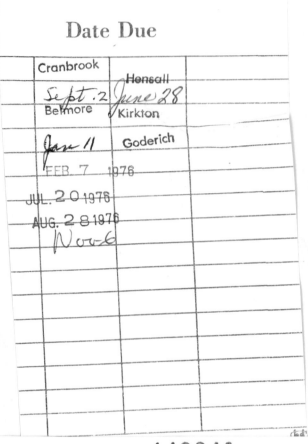

Date Due

Cranbrook	Hensall	
Sept. 2	June 28	
Belmore	Kirkton	
Jan 11	Goderich	
FEB 7 1976		
JUL. 20 1976		
AUG. 2 8 1976		
Nov 6		

Yesterday and Today in

LOVE, WORK, PLAY and POLITICS

Edited by RAYMOND REID

THE CANADIAN STYLE

THE
CANADIAN
STYLE

Fitzhenry and Whiteside Limited
Toronto/Montreal/Winnipeg/Vancouver

Fitzhenry and Whiteside Limited, Don Mills, Ontario
Published simultaneously in the United
States by Paul S. Eriksson, Inc., New York, N.Y.
ISBN No. 0-88902-012-4
          0-8397-1289-8 (U.S.)

Edited by Diane Mew
Production and text design by Arnold Diener & Associates
Jacket design by David Shaw

CONTENTS

Preface

INTRODUCTION

This book is a study of the Canadian character in action, the Canadian way of doing things, the Canadian style. It is based on the belief that there is something unique about that style. It was once said of Lester Pearson that his manner made him instantly recognizable as a Canadian. Without arguing the matter, the point is that someone had the wit to realize that there was a distinctive Canadian personality.

It has long been fashionable, especially for Canadian analysts, to deny this. "There is no such thing as the Canadian identity," they have said. "We are no different than Americans," has been one of the most frequent refrains, usually presented in a regretful tone. Yet, after a few minutes' discussion with Americans, a Canadian soon begins to realize that he is talking from a different set of premises, a different national experience, a different background. He knows he is different and soon discovers that the differences are not merely superficial.

This book, which is really an extended essay, will consider a broad spectrum of Canadian experiences, ideas, fantasies, and attempt to identify those features which are characteristic of us. From the many apparently isolated phenomena, it is hoped that some total picture and understanding of our style will emerge.

To do this, we will examine at first hand the statements which Canadians have made about themselves, their behaviour, their dreams. Comments which others have made about us will also be considered. As compiler and editor, I have provided an interpretive link between the selections, which represent some three hundred years of the Canadian heritage. The interpretation will, of course, reflect my own biases. I think my views are on the right track, but you, the reader, may disagree. From such a meeting of prejudices, some truth may emerge. It should at least prove to be hopefully an interesting, and possibly an amusing, exercise.

The author wishes to thank the North York Public Library for permission to use the Canadian Collection for research, and Mrs. Dorothy Chatwin, Reference and Research Co-ordinator, and Miss Elizabeth Hulse for their generous co-operation and assistance.

Raymond Reid

To Helen

Female and Male

In the Biblical account, God first created Adam and then, from his rib, formed the first woman. The preeminence of the male in western society may be traced to this creation story. Had the Bible been written in Canada, one suspects that order of creation might have been reversed, for in our society the female appears to have an innate superiority over the male. The Canadian woman has long been the object of veneration, respect and fear, and her praises have been sung since the earliest days of our history. The charms of French-Canadian girls in particular have received glowing tributes, as seen in this account written in 1844.

The ladies of Canada possess, in a great degree, that charm for which those of Ireland are so justly famed — the great trustingness and simplicity of manner, joined with an irreproachable purity. The custom of the country allows them much greater freedom than their English sisters; they drive, ride, or walk with their partner of the night before, with no chaperone or guard but their own never-failing self-respect and

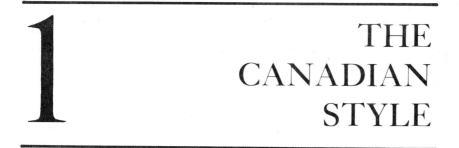

1

THE
CANADIAN
STYLE

innocence. They certainly are not so deeply read generally as some of our fair dames; they enter very young into life, and live constantly in society afterwards, so that they have not much time for literary pursuits; there is also difficulty in obtaining books, and the instructors necessary for any very extensive acquirements. But they possess an indescribable charm of manner rendering them, perhaps, quite as attractive as if their studies had been more profound. . . .

The officers of the army show themselves very sensible to the attractions of the daughters of Canada; great numbers marry in this country; no less than four of one regiment have been made happy at Quebec within a year of the present time. The fair conquerors thus exercise a gentle retaliation on the descendants of those who overcame their forefathers.

English officer's observation, 1844.[1]

Yet the mademoiselles *of Quebec were not alone in their attraction to males.*

The Canadian girls are very attractive, and in many cases very fascinating in their manners. They are free and easy in their deportment when in company, and exhibit very little of that reserve so often found in young ladies in England. American girls carry their freedom and easiness of manner to too great an extent, extreme boldness being the result, but this does not characterize the Canadians; they have the elegance of English girls, with more self-confidence. Quebec is more famed than any other city for its pretty girls, but every town has its share, and some exhibit most beautiful specimens of the sex.

English travellers's comment, 1858.[2]

...There is quite as great a difference between the American women and the Canadian woman as between the men....The Canadian woman is a marked contrast. She is in appearance quite the English-woman —generally a blonde. Canadian ladies are fully as much addicted to out-door pursuits and amusements as are English ladies. Even in the depths of winter they have their daily walks or their snow-shoeing, trabogening, or skating parties. Thanks to this more healthy mode of life, to their robust constitutions, and to their healthy climate, they preserve their good looks to the last. As to the poorer women in Canada they have no Chinamen, negroes, or Irish-women to work for them, and so they are compelled to attend to their own households and dairies, and this seems to agree well with them. Unlike the Americans there seems to be no limit to their families and no end to their good looks, and the middle-aged Canadian women (if such an expression can be applied to the fair sex) present as great a contrast to the worn-out and faded American women of a similar unmentionable age as can possibly be imagined.

J. J. Rowan, *The Emigrant and Sportsman in Canada*, 1876.[3]

...We find in our women practical independence, strongly marked, combined with a demure regard for propriety and form, and partaking in no degree of the crude and vulgar revolt from restraint which begets the female stump orator. The Canadian girl is regarded abroad as a child of Nature. In the literary Mecca of New York she is always first of all "an authority on outdoor sports". At home she may have posed as an authority on Browning and Greek verbs, but to the editors at the point of gravitation she blooms forth as one who has shaken off some of the rusty shackles of social conventions, and revels in the delights of sunlight and breeze. But Canadian girls are something more than irresponsible nympths who are forever basking in the smiles of Nature. In addition to making religions for themselves, some are devoting considerable attentions to the task of being "not like other girls". . . .

The Canadian girl shows a decided aptitude for commanding; there is none of the Anglo-Saxon belief that woman is the weaker vessel. Woman's rights movements make small progress in Canada, because the Canadian woman gets what she wants without let or hindrance: because she has so many privileges, the right to vote on a subject in which she takes little or no interest seems not worth striving for. Canadian legislators are quicker to grant privileges to women than Canadian women are to demand them. The average girl possesses an impulsive force or magnetism that makes its conquests without strife.

It is this quality that is responsible for the fact that, as enquiry has shown, the marriage of Canadian women to Englishmen seldom fails to result in considerable measure of discontent and unhappiness, unless the girl has received her education abroad. . . . The absence in Canada of rigid caste regulations, the diminution of that toadyism to superiors and tyranny to inferiors characteristic of England, and, above all, the freedom from restraint to education, has bred a Canadian independence and breezy self-reliance that assimilated poorly with the English desire to dominate. Miss Canada loves John Bull because he lets her alone. When, however, an Englishman married a Canadian girl— very conscious, we may be sure, of the honor that the son of so glorious a nation is bestowing on a colonist—he is surprised to find that his wife is in the habit of asserting herself with independence and good sense that are exasperating.

Hector Charlesworth, 1893.[4]

My Own Canadian Girl

The demoiselles of sunny France
    Have gaiety and grace;
Britannia's maids a tender glance,
    A sweet and gentle face;
Columbia's virgins bring to knee
    Full many a duke and earl;
But there is none can equal thee,
    My own Canadian girl.

Thy hair is finer than the floss
    That tufts the ears of corn;
Its tresses have a silken gloss,
    A glory like the morn;
I prize the rich, luxuriant mass,
    And each endearing curl
A special grace and beauty has
    My own Canadian girl.

Thy brow is like the silver moon
    That sails in summer skies,
The mirror of a mind immune
    From care, serene and wise,
Thy nose is sculptured ivory;
    Thine ears are lobes of pearl;
Thy lips are corals from the sea,
    My own Canadian girl.

Thine eyes are limpid pools of light,
    The windows of thy soul;
The stars are not so clear and bright
    That shine around the pole.
The crimson banners of thy cheeks
    To sun and wind unfurl;
Thy tongue makes music when it speaks,
    My own Canadian girl.

God keep thee fair and bright and good
    As in thy morning hour,
And make thy gracious womanhood
    A still unfolding flow'r.
And stay thy thoughts from trifles vain,
    Thy feet from folly's whirl,
And guard thy life from every stain,
    My own Canadian girl!

W. M. Mackerachen, 1908.[5]

By contrast we encounter the Canadian male. Explorer, statesman, warrior, hockey player—these roles the Canadian man has been able to handle. But, of his relations with women, very little has been said, and much of it is critical.

When I first arrived I dated several Canadian males, only to find that we were incompatible. On the first date they would take me to dinner and in return, invariably they expected Everything. . . . So now I date men from Australia, England, India, the Philippines—my only rule is: No Canadians. I like them as conversationalists, they're welcome guests at parties in our apartment but that's all. On a date, they frankly scare me.

Young female immigrant, 1971.[6]

. . . a Spanish male is highly romantic in the pursuit of a girl he loves. In Canada, a man's approach is more dignified, and he usually comes right to the point. . . . This is the real difference. The Canadian male is too easily discouraged. He'll ask once, but he never persists. A Mexican can be told "no" 100 times, but he'll return the next night. A Canadian hears one "no" and he gives up forever.

A Mexican girl's view, 1972.[7]

Columnist Richard Needham has long championed the cause of the Canadian girl, mainly by pointing out the deficiencies of her prey. The mythical adventures of Ariadne as she searches for love clearly illustrate Needham's message. It would appear that the problem of finding an ideal man is well nigh insoluable in Canada.

She went out with men who furtively slipped a copy of The Sensuous Woman into her purse when she wasn't looking. She went out with men who smoked not just between courses but between mouthfuls. She went out with men who when they were in some public place, kept staring at and commenting on other women. She went out with a man who bought her flowers in Simpson's basement, and was warmly greeted by the clerks, and explained to her, "I'm about their best customer."

She went out with men who yawned when they saw her to her doorstep. She went out with men who telephoned her from a party just to say hello. She went out with men who said, "Of course I love you; now shut up and let me watch the football game." She went out with men who said, "What color is your hair really?" and "Don't be silly, I prefer my women fat."

She went out with men who tried such pitches as "I can just tell that inside you, there's a warm, passionate woman waiting to be let out," and "So you've trouble sleeping at night? I think I can help you," and "Don't be too quick to judge me by other men, I am sincere, and wish only your happiness. By the way, do you live alone?"

She went out with men who used the swizzlestick to clean their fingernails; with men who liked getting up at seven on Saturday mornings; with men who made her take a shower before and themselves took a shower after. She went out with a man who on their first date said, "Now don't get any wrong ideas, baby, I'm not the marrying kind." She went out with a man who was too good to be true, and accordingly wasn't.

She went out with men who wrote her love letters in disappearing ink. She went out with men who used expressions like "anyhoo" and "happenstance" and "humdinger" and "jim-dandy". She went out with men who talked about N.Y. and Chi and Frisco and Vegas and going to dear old London on Bo-ack.

She went out with a political writer who bewildered her with expressions like hawk, dove, clout, image, profile and credibility. She went out with a newspaper copy chief who kept telling her the difference between flout and flaunt, between infer and imply, between careen and carom, between titillate and titivate, giving him up when he insisted on demonstrating the difference between prone and supine.

She went out with a hippie who attempted to throttle her with his love beads; with a peacenik who boasted to her about the number of pigs he had clobbered; with a philosophy professor who had stomach ulcers and a nervous tic and terrible domestic problems, and made stormy scenes in restaurants if the waitress brought the wrong order.

She went out with men who told her she was the first, and with men who told her she was the 41st. She went out with a man who revealed that he had had 12½ previous amours and when she looked puzzled, explained, "The telephone rang." She went out with men who referred to newspaper and magazine articles as write-ups.

She went out with men who complained to the waiter that the Vichysoisse was cold; with men who winked as they told the hotel clerk, "Same room as usual"; with men who said, "I brought a razor and toothbrush along just in case"; with men who corrected her grammar in public; with men who referred to cars and the weather as "she".[8]

The poor Canadian male has even been subjected to a rating of his qualities as a lover.

The only reason for dealing with the French-Canadian lover as distinct from the English-Canadian lover is that the French-Canadian lover *is* distinct from the English-Canadian lover. It has been repeatedly noted that when a French-Canadian man buys you flowers, and wines and dines you, he expects to go to bed with you. This may or may not be true, but an English-Canadian seldom buys you flowers, or wines and dines you, and he still expects the same thing.

The French-Canadian thinks of flowers, perfume, wine and soft music as a prelude to love. He has another distinct advantage, he speaks the language of love, which means that he speaks a language in which plain old seductive phrases sound like promises of love eternal. French-Canadian men *like* women and you can tell it by the way the girls in Montreal and Quebec dress; you can tell that the French-Canadian girls like men by the way they go so freely and gaily with them into dining-rooms, cocktail bars and motels.

Herein lies the reason why Montreal is such a popular tourist city with the other inhabitants of Canada. Everybody goes to Montreal. Statistics show that it is the only Canadian city where sooner or later everybody goes. Everyone is curious about Males and Females who really *like* each other. But stampedes, exhibitions, reversible falls and Peace Towers are of interest to only a few.

The English-Canadian, when wooing, talks about cars and business, about the business cycle, the stock market quotations and the effects of the last election on the stock market. The French Canadian presses his knee against the girl's, looks into her eyes and murmurs something about "feminine essence . . .".

When an Anglo-Saxon Canadian opens a car door for a girl, he runs all the way round the front of the hood for fear of touching her; but a French Canadian leans across a girl, saying softly "Excusez moi ..." presses against her and looks down the front of her blouse. This whole operation is symbolic of the difference in his attitude towards women. When he finally takes her to bed with him, he undresses her, bit by bit, with murmurings and sighings, interspersed with sweet nothings. The other Canadian, in the same prelude to romance, will phone Room Service to bring up some ice, or will straighten his pants over the back of the chair so that he won't look mussed when he leaves. ...

There are many reasons why the Canadian male cuts a poor figure as a lover; his cold Anglo-Saxon qualities, his Puritanical conscience and his jealous, possessive wife, work together against his endeavours to fit himself into the image of the Great Lover, and he himself still embodies the old love-on-the-run tradions of the *coureur-de-bois* and fur-traders who partially make up his background, and who passed down to him some of their attitudes towards love and sex. As a result, the Canadian lover has no understanding of a woman's unquenchable need for Dalliance. He fully expects to pop in during the afternoon for a few hours, make love, have a few words about the state of his business affairs, grab a cup of coffee, and run off to the next appointment, leaving his mistress feeling unsatisfied and slightly chilled, even though the love-making interlude included a rare orgasm.

Michelle Bedard, *Canada In Bed*, 1969.[9]

Formidable Females

Is the Canadian woman superior to the man? Even in the history of our military achievements, a woman first gained renown. In October 1692, fourteen-year-old Madeleine de Verchères suddenly discovered that her village was under attack and that forty Iroquois were pursuing her personally.

I ran for the fort, commending myself to the Holy Virgin. The Iroquois who chased after me, seeing that they could not catch me alive before I reached the gate, stopped and fired at me. The bullets whistled about my ears, and made the time seem very long. As soon as I was near enough to be heard, I cried out, *To arms! to arms!* hoping that somebody would come out and help me; but it was of no use. The two soldiers in the fort were so scared that they had hidden in the blockhouse. At the gate, I found two women crying for their husbands, who had just been killed. I made them go in, and then shut the gate. I next thought what I could do to save myself and the few people with me. I went to inspect the fort, and found that several palisades had fallen down, and left openings by which the enemy could easily get in. I ordered them to be set up again, and helped to carry them myself. When the breaches were stopped, I went to the blockhouse where the ammunition is kept, and here I found the two soldiers, one hiding in a corner, and the other with a lighted match in his hand. "What are you going to do with that match?" I asked. He answered, "Light the powder, and blow us all up." "You are a miserable coward," said I, "go out of this place." I spoke so resolutely that he obeyed. I then threw off my bonnet; and after putting on a hat, and taking a gun, I said to my two brothers: 'Let us fight to the death. We are fighting for our country and our religion. Remember that our father has taught you that gentlemen are born to shed their blood for the service of God and the King." ...

I assembled all my troops, that is to say, six persons, and spoke to them thus: "God has saved us to-day from the hands of our enemies, but we must take care not to fall into their snares to-night. As for me, I want you to see that I am not afraid. I will take charge of the fort with an old man of eighty and another who never fired a gun; and you, Pierre Fontaine, with La Bonté and Gachet (our two soldiers), will go to the blockhouse with the women and children, because that is the strongest place; and, if I am taken, don't surrender, even if I am cut to pieces and burned before your eyes." ...

I may say with truth that I did not eat or sleep for twice twenty-four hours. I did not go once into my father's house, but kept always on the bastion, or went to the blockhouse, to see how the people there were behaving. I always kept a cheerful and smiling face, and encouraged my little company with the hope of speedy succor.

We were a week in constant alarm, with the enemy always about us. At last Monsieur de la Monnerie, a lieutenant sent by Monsieur de Callières, arrived in the night with forty men. ... As soon as I saw Monsieur de la Monnerie, I saluted him, and said, "Monsieur, I surrender my arms to you." He answered gallantly, "Mademoiselle, they are in good hands." "Better than you think," I returned. He inspected the fort, and found everything in order, and a sentinel on each bastion. "It is time to relieve them, Monsieur," said I; "we have not been off our bastions for a week."[10]

Madeleine was certainly an awe-inspiring teenager, but she does not stand alone in the gallery of Canadian heroines. Think of our sports champions who have gained success in international competition. The names of males are few compared to nubile females such as Barbara Ann Scott, Marilyn Bell, Nancy Greene, Karen Magnussen. How, for instance, is a Canadian male to feel when he meets someone like Mari-Lou MacDonald?

Mari-Lou MacDonald has a recurring problem at parties. She's attractive and beautifully dressed, tall and slender, and looks very much like the fashion model she is. Naturally some of the men are attracted to her and—booze-encouraged—start trying to impress her. And for a lot of young men that means making a big thing about their prowess at sports. That's when the trouble begins.

Because the more dangerous the sports feat is, the greater are the chances that Mari-Lou has done it, and done it better than any man in the room.

"I'm afraid that really gets to them," she says. "A man just doesn't like to think that a woman can do something that's risky or dangerous better than he can."

After the initial surprise, the cocktail party chatter turns to just what she can do, and eventually the men learn that she is also a professional stunt girl in movies and television.

"All right," says a well-built, deeply tanned man, taking a hearty drink of scotch and a long pull on his cigarette, "so what do you do apart from the odd fall or fight sequence?"

"Oh, everything," says Mari-Lou with that bright instant smile that all models seem to have. "I'm a licensed pilot; I'm the former, undefeated Canadian women's sky diving champion; I'm a balloonist and a motorcyclist; I ride, everything from equestrian to rodeo to bronco-busting; I race cars; I scuba dive, sail, swim, walk on the wings of airplanes; I skate; I ski on both snow and water; I've done falconry and, oh, lots of stunts."

And then, even more threatening to their masculine self-image, the men discover that Mari-Lou is not only the best stunt girl in North America but possibly the best in the world.

That's the moment when things begin to sour and the men retire in a huff to shore up their battered egos.

"Then," says Mari-Lou, "after a while, one of them will come over to me and ask: 'Do you play golf?' And he's not joking, he's deadly serious about it. They feel they've just got to come up with something that I can't do."[11]

In 1972 the suspicion that Canadian females are superior to males was confirmed by a scientific study!

In Canada, women no longer can be called the weaker sex. Pound for pound, Canadian women are stronger than Canadian men up to the age of 40. In almost every age group women score more than 20 percent higher than men in a key fitness measurement called VO2, which is the ability to take in and utilize oxygen during effort. . . .

This alarming assessment of the fitness of Canadians in the '70s emerges from a four-year study just completed by Lloyd Percival's Fitness Institute of Toronto. In a $25,000 program Percival administered exhaustive tests to 4,421 men and 1,675 women between the ages of 18 and 70 who enrolled at his institute. . . .

"Perhaps the most surprising discovery to emerge," said Percival, "was the comparative weakness of the Canadian male compared to the female. Basically, men should be 50 per cent stronger than women, yet we found that proportionately, pound for pound in body weight, women were stronger than men in every age group up to the age of 40."

Bob Pennington, 1972.[12]

And what does this do to our relations?

Canadian males seem afraid of women. At cocktail parties guests soon isolate into groups of one sex; at dances the women are granted territorial rights to one side of the hall. Until reaching Canada I had never heard of the custom "boys' night out," which still seems a disgusting sort of habit. For example, the men in my office were always puzzled when I declined to join them for lunch. Of course I wasn't interested. I preferred a young woman as my lunchtime companion.

European immigrant, 1972.[13]

Another writer commented on the effects of a "woman-dominated" society.

Indeed, part of the general superficial friendliness of the urban Canadian in business may well come from this woman-dominated background. There is about it something of the camaraderie of the prison camp or of the recreation break in jail. In all the male sessions with drinks, in clubs, at the ball game, or on the curling rink, there is that underlying anxiety; What, they seem to say, can the enemy be thinking up for us now? At least let us enjoy our freedom while we can.

It is all a great pity. It is not for nothing that traffic with woman was once described as playing with fire, for how true it is that they make both good servants and poor masters. Women need some stimulus before they will exert themselves to please; in North America the stimulus has gone, for, on level terms, man is a poor match for woman. He dreams, and imagines that success in business somehow secures his independence. Women dominate the home. They allow sexual relations to become either a manifestation of their productive urge or a form of gymnastics. Romance is an excitement to be enjoyed vicariously, at second-hand, not to be sought, still less built up, in the home. The male is not to be wooed; he is to be received. The furnishings of the North American home do not suggest long nights of bliss. The emphasis is on the sanitary fittings; a bed is sold as guaranteeing a good night's sleep. Instead of planning how to entertain her husband, the wife seeks to master the conventions of contract bridge, and is there any more pathetic sight in the world than four women clad as for golf striding down the fairway?

Ernest Watkins, *Prospect of Canada*, 1954.[14]

And yet the Canadian male yearns for the girls, for their approval, for their affection. Never given to elaborate demonstrations of affection, or great works and songs of love, the male occasionally commits to words his longings, hope and, sad to relate, his disappointments.

Last summer we had lassies here
    Frae Germany—the hurdies, O!
And troth I wot, as I'm a Scot,
    They were the bonnie hurdies, O!

There was Kate and Mary, blithe and airy,
    And dumpy little Lizzie, O!
And ane they ca'd the Kangaroo,
    A strappin' rattlin' hizzy, O!

They danced at nicht in dresses light,
    Frae late until early, O!
But oh! their hearts were hard as flint,
    Which vexed the laddies sairly, O!

The dollar was their only love,
    And that they lo'ed fu' dearly, O!
They dinna care a flea for men,
    Let them coort hooe'er sincerely, O!

They left the creek wi' lots o' gold,
  Danced frae oor lads sae clever, O!
My blessins' on their "sour krout" heads,
  Gif they staw awa for ever, O!

                    Cariboo Gold Miner, 1866.[15]

Woman hunger

I have felt the woman-hunger of the lonely northern wilds,
  I've dealt in dreams that shack walls couldn't hold;
Through the lonely nights of summer, and the winter's long, long days,
  I've read of maids as novelists have told,
And the girls on the magazine covers, the new year's almanac,
  And the mail house catalogue, have framed my mould.

It comes most any sort of time, but strikes the hardest in
  Those drear nights of the never-ending kind,
When there's only you in vastness—nought to do but make up dreams,
  And ponder on the seasons put behind.
And anything can rouse it when you're sick and lorn and blue—
  A writer's picture, and your dream's enshrined.

I've dreamed just how 'twould be to have a wife with breakfast on
  When I come in from the barn all caked in ice;
A woman's face above the table right across from me,
  And grub I haven't had to cook up twice;
Someone to fetch me slippers when I come in wet from chores,
  This junk-shed straightened out and fixed up nice;

A woman to turn toil to joy, and pain mirth for her sake,
  To fill my soul again plumb full of vim;
A partner always ready with a willing heart and head,
  When the bowl of trouble's running o'er the brim;
A friend to soothe and comfort when it gets the best of me,
  A comrade when the prairie lights grow dim.

There when as I mix the batter for the flapjacks
on the stove,
And icicles drop sizzling from my cheeks,
I laugh, and softly curse myself for all the wasted hours—
Through night-made visions toiling daylight rips;
The homestead is a place of facts, of teeming Things-that-are—
I've had so many dreamings torn in strips.

And those pure-souled, brain-shaped women are far from this lonely
shack,
Far from this tousled room, this medley life,
This haggy, ragged being, with bronzed visage, rough, unshaved.
Far from the burdens of a homestead's strife.
There's so many men far better—yet a Man's soul dwell in here,
And man, God-built, ordained to crave for wife.

And there's a voice e'er ready in the lonesome, lingering hours—
"A woman's love is compassless as sky;
The pioneering women, mothers of the new-born lands,
Are the purest gems, God-given to fortify.
And twin-souls is no fable, in the woman-hunger hours
There's somebody sighs with you as you sigh.

Homesteader, 1900[16]

Summer's Girls

Girls, you're all wonderful,
you who deny yourselves
meals, live in cheap rooms,
simply to drape your young bodies
in colours that spill down your limbs,
press your breasts, etch your thighs,
all the pigments of Easter eggs
splashing the morgue streets
with summer's Easter.

Girls, we're unworthy of you,
drab males in blues and grays.
The deep life within you
sweeps by us madly
like cars at a speedway,
and as we watch, fascinated,
you turn to wave at us,
gathering us up
in your whirlwind race
we never quite understand.

Raymond Souster, 1968.[17]

Plea for my Lady

You won't let me kiss you?
Me?

Lady, you must be joking!
Lady, you must be mad!

Who put the agony in my lips
as though they had sucked
for a thousand years
on a prickly pear?

Who taught them
to want yours
with such a fever?
On crowded thoroughfares
of the city
I feel my mouth pulled
towards wherever you are.
Mariners need a compass:
you are my lodestar

Of what use are my hands
if you won't let them caress you
My arms, if they can't embrace you?
O my whole frame's
become a piece of useless junk

The season that lovers
and worms wait for
is here
but your disdain
has sewn up all my senses
with invisible threads
I'm blind to green buds
dead to lilac smells
deaf to all birdsongs

O lady, my cries
are wilder
than those Abelard shrieked
that wild night
they plucked out his stones

Lady, let me have your lips
Lady, let my hands caress you
Lady, let me embrace you
O lady, lady, lady, lady.

Irving Layton, 1971[18]

With an Independent Air

A certain independence, closely approaching outright disrespect for authority, or just plain ornery behaviour has been noted in Canadians. Perhaps it was the influence of the frontier which encouraged the development of such an attitude. Certainly, in the nineteenth century, new arrivals and visitors commented on the often disturbing behaviour of Canadians.

And here I would observe, before quitting this subject, that of all follies, that of taking out servants from the old country is one of the greatest, and is sure to end in the loss of the money expended in their passage, and to become the cause of deep disappointment and mortification to yourself.

They no sooner set foot upon the Canadian shores than they became possessed with this ultra-republican spirit. All respect for their employers, all subordination is at an end; the very air of Canada severs the tie of mutual obligation which bound you together. They fancy themselves not only equal to you in rank, but that ignorance and vulgarity give them superior claims to notice. They demand the highest wages, and grumble at doing half the work, in return, which they cheerfully performed at home. They demand to eat at your table, and to sit in your company, and if you refuse to listen to their dishonest and extravagant claims, they tell you that "they are free; that no contract signed in the old country is binding in 'Meriky'; that you may look out for another person to fill their place as soon as you like; and that you may get the money expended in their passage and outfit in the best manner you can.

Susanna Moodie, *Roughing It in the Bush*, 1871.[19]

You would be surprised to see how soon the new comers fall into this disagreeable manner and effectation of quality, especially the inferior class of Irish and Scotch; the English less so. We were rather entertained by the behaviour of a young Scotchman, the engineer of the steamer, on my husband addressing him with reference to the management of the engine. His manners were surly, and almost insolent. He scrupulously avoided the least approach to courtesy or outward respect; nay, he even went so far as to seat himself on the bench close beside me, and observed that "among the many advantages this country offered to settlers like him, he did not reckon it the least of them that he was not obliged to take off his hat when he spoke to people (meaning persons of our degree), or address them by any other title than their name; besides, he could go and take his seat beside any gentleman or lady either, and think himself to the full as good as them.

Catharine Parr Traill, *The Backwoods of Canada*, 1846[20]

I was much struck at Prescott — and indeed all through Canada, though more in the upper than in the lower province — by the sturdy roughness, some would call it insolence, of those of the lower classes of the people with whom I was brought into contact.

Anthony Trollope, *North America*, 1862. [21]

No tipping waiters, no feeing porters; their spirit of independence forbids them to take any remuneration from any one but their master. They hold themselves in every bit as good a position as the visitor on whom they wait; *he* looks upon *them* as of equal station with himself. No grades, no classes, no rank. We in England are totally unable to realize this great levelling principle, but it crops up in Canada as it does in the States, at every turn you take. You will meet it in the railway officials, who will quietly tell you to carry your bag yourself; you will find it in the chambermaid, who will answer the bell or not, just as she pleases, and if you politely suggest, that you rang, will coolly reply that she is "quite aware of it", you will notice it everywhere in being addressed as "Mister"—none but niggers will call you "Sir"—and find that no request made of you is ever preceded by "if you please," no act of civility on your part followed by "thank you". . . .

[And] then there is such a delightful air of perfect independence and respect for anything or anybody, an amount of self possession which is quite charming; and yet a certain civility withal, but rude and unpolished, as I should hardly have expected it in a district where the population is considerably more than half of it of French extraction.

George Tuthill Barrett, *Out West*, 1866.[22]

> I love this land of forest grand!
> The land where labour's free;
> Let others roam away from home,
> Be this the land for me!
> Where no one moils, and strains and toils,
> That snobs may thrive the faster;
> And all are free, as men should be,
> And Jack's as good's his master!

Alexander McLachlan, 1900.[23]

The Canadian approach is demonstrated in a traditional anecdote from World War I.

Sentry: 'Alt, who goes there?
Reply: Scots Guards.
Sentry: Pass, Scots Guards.

Sentry: 'Alt, who goes there?
Reply: The Buffs.
Sentry: Pass, the Buffs.

Sentry: 'Alt, who goes there?
Reply: Mind your own God-damn business!
Sentry: Pass, Canadians.[24]

*In the increasingly organized and bureaucratic society of the twentieth
century, it becomes more difficult to be one's own man. But, even
in that most disciplined of all activities, professional football, the Canadian spirit is noticeable.*

Canadian football players react differently to the type of discipline
and hardrock stuff that is given out by the Head Coaches in pro football.
Canadian ball players are not that well disciplined. The Coach knows
the difference, it's noticeable. The Canadians don't have the brainwashing
program yet that they do in the States. So Canadian ball players are
notoriously weaker ball players in overall ability, even though they have
the physical potential. They don't have the conditioning. They don't have
the training, the indoctrination....

The ball player has been conditioned and conned and cowed over the
years by Head Coaches, certainly if he is an American ball player, to
take the word of the Head Coach as Law. When the Head Coach speaks,
God speaks.

When the Head Coach tells you to Leave That Pussy Alone, Son,
the ball player obeys. "Yes, Coach."

The Canadian ball player, because of his lack of years of conditioning
by Head Coaches, may do the very best thing. He may laugh at the
man. The odd Canadian ball player may stand there and tell the Head
Coach to fuck off, and laugh.

LaVerne Barnes, *The Plastic Orgasm*, 1971.[25]

*The Canadian disrespect for authority, especially authority which is
conceived to be in error, was never so amply demonstrated as in the
Canada-Soviet hockey series of 1972. Who will ever forget Phil Esposito's
verbal attacks on the referees, or Jean-Paul Parise swinging his stick*

in fury at the referee, or Alan Eagleson giving his famous one-armed salute to the Russian officials? One can almost pity the harassed West German referee, Josef Kompalla.

Ten more such games and I would age several years. I am very glad that I got back home uninjured.

The conduct of the Canadian professionals on the rink had little to do with sports. . . . They play very crudely, purposely using foul methods that endanger the lives of their rivals. If a match does not go well for the Canadians, they blame the referees. In my opinion, the transoceanic professionals behaved in a scandalous way.

They went so far as to attack my colleague, Franz Baader. When we were on board a plane bound from Moscow to Prague, the Canadians pelted Baader with cucumbers and food leftovers.

One gets an impression that it would suit the Canadians best to play games without referees so that they could do all they like.[26]

Crude? Boorish? Barbaric? Perhaps. Yet it may have been good for the Russians and other Europeans to see that we do not tolerate incompetent or biased authority. We have had no Hitlers, Stalins, Mussolinis; we simply wouldn't put up with such nonsense. Could it be that by attacking authority, and forcing it to back down, Team Canada struck a blow for freedom behind the Iron Curtain?

God Bless the Government

Although they like to assert their independence against authority, Canadians have never been shy about asking the government to do things for them. They have eagerly allowed their government to subsidize business and cultural activities. Our great national enterprise, the Canadian Pacific Railway, would not have been built without vast government aid; private industry has often turned to the government to bail it out of trouble; those great individualists in any society, artists and writers, gladly welcome their annual Canada Council grants; even the hit "sexploitation" film of 1969, Valerie, was partially financed with government funds. In recent years, government money has been used for increasingly interesting purposes.

. . . I had this great idea for an Opportunities for Youth program project but I blew it . . . on the application I accidentally put down South Pole instead of North Pole . . ."

TOWN FOOL GETS $3,500 BURSARY

The Canada Council has awarded a $3,500 bursary to Vancouver's town fool, declaring that many people consider him to be making "a serious contribution to the self-awareness of the entire community."

Polish-born Joachim Foikis, 26, has revived the ancient tradition of town fool and is making it his vocation, the staid government cultural agency said Monday in announcing the award.

The council decided upon the award at a serious meeting on April Fool's Day.

Mr. Foikis discovered his vocation as a fool on St. Valentine's Day last year, and since then has been a familiar figure in Vancouver's downtown courthouse square, the council said.

"Dressed in traditional fool's motley, he has nursery rhymes for the children and metaphysical riddles for adults."

Married and the father of two young children, he has unsuccessfully sought official recognition and an annual stipend from the Vancouver city council.

He applied for the Canada Council grant by letter stating that his purpose is "integrating art and life."

The council which distributes federal government funds available for the support of arts, letters and social sciences, put its award in the category of an arts bursary.

These go "to artists in the earlier stages of their professional careers who would benefit from a period of free work or study" the council said.

Ottawa Citizen, April 2, 1968

Canada Council grants; Local Initiatives Program grants; Opportunities For Youth grants; the list grows and a new style of life and work emerges.

At Rochdale, a $24,570 LIP grant was received by the THOG foundation for the Arts to employ 15 people "to produce a kaleidoscoped history of Canada employing music, dance and mime." The production will be presented free at several Metro high schools.

Commune-Ication Collective received a $14,835 grant to employ six people to operate a switchboard providing information to youngsters on legal aid, housing, food co-ops, health clinics, hostels and jobs.

GRANT TO SATANISTS

Brewery receives $39,000 LIP grant

OTTAWA (CP-Special) — One of the first grants under a special section of the Local Initiatives Program has gone to Formosa Spring Brewery in Barrie.

The brewery received about $39,000 to employ 16 people in developing a 60-acre recreation and conservation area at Barrie. In the House yesterday Manpower Minister Robert Andras said $10-million was being held for the special section which deals with special applications.

Another recipient is Bondar-Clegg, an Ottawa geochemical Laboratory, which will get $60,000 to employ 34 people in testing water in Lucerne, Que.

The grants are made to private companies or individuals to create employment on the condition that there is no financial gain and that the projects are aimed at community betterment.

$15,060 grant given to create comic book of Canadian history

Ottawa gives $46,250 grant to help senior citizens go bird watching

Senior citizens' studies of the environment, tours of Parkdale by artists, and women's lib groups get support in $1,400,000 of new grants announced by the Federal Government.

Under another program, $46,250 has been awarded to a Toronto group called Ecological Education. Its aim is to "involve senior citizens" in bird conservation and mating habits, bird watching, care

publication about dental health for the elderly.

Under the same New Horizons program, the Lakeshore Retirees Action Group was awarded $8,065 for a program set up by the Humber

Homosexuals' group given federal grants

A Manpower con... yesterday it had given ...602 Local Initiatives ... (LIP) grant to a ... homosexual group.

...kesman also con... that a $23,000 grant ...he federal program ...ven to the Process ...of the Final Judg... ...alled by some a "Sa... group because its

members believe Satan must be loved to fulfil Christ's injunction to "love thine enemy."

Despite criticism, Prime Minister Pierre Trudeau insisted in Toronto yesterday that the grants are given "to people who say, 'We can make work and so do some good to the society.'"

But Trudeau promised an

open-line radio show caller who complained about what he called "devil worshippers" that "I sure will look into it."

The Community Homophile Association of Toronto, a group of admitted homosexuals, plans to operate a 24-hour distress centre with its money.

George Hislop, director of

Drama producer ridicules system after receiving grant of $40,000

SOUTH OF ST. JAMES TOWN WINDFALL
$574,000 in LIP, OFY grants

'These aren't handouts with no strings attached; these are tough jobs...' LIP regional director

Grants that raised a storm mean jobs for 93,000 in '73

Quit earlier job to avoid garnishees
Man uses his first LIP pay cheque to launch his own bankruptcy

LIP grant pays this man $160 weekly salary

Ontario considering direct financial aid or making movies

JOBLESS TO GET PRIORITY
Another $85 million for LIP grants

OFY grant to tell readers how to rob, steal, kill

OTTAWA — (Special) — A Toronto newspaper that told readers how to rob, steal and kill.

A Toronto "research foundation" receiving $18,700 for a farm project and leaving behind a shambles.

A Toronto youth community keeping no records of work but paying out $25,800 in Federal funds for wages.

These were some of the Federal Opportunities For Youth and Local Initiative Program grant projects criticized by Auditor-General Maxwell Henderson yesterday in his last annual report.

$2,733,000 goes to arts

The Canada Council today announced grants totalling 733,000 to 10 arts organizations.

The St. Lawrence Centre eatre company receives 25,000 for its 1973-4 sea... . Also for next season.

the National Ballet receives $660,000; the Grands Ballets Canadiens of Montreal receives $330,000; and the Canadian Opera Company receives $415,000, with an additional special grant of $35,000 to produce the Canadian opera Heloise and Abelard.

The Shaw Festival gets $80,000 for this summer's season; the National Theatre School gets $505,000 for its 1973-4 operations; and the Vancouver Opera Association gets $118,000 for three productions next season. Other grants go to the Vancouver Art Gallery ($170,000), the Edmonton Art Gallery ($50,000) and the magazine Arts/canada in Toronto ($115,000).

Homosexual group awarded another LIP grant

O Handmade Paper received $13,946 to employ eight people producing special handmade paper for artists, printers and writers. It is hoped the group will become self-supporting when the LIP funds run out May 31. . . .

People for Ecological Action received $29,123 to hire 10 people to recycle garbage, especially cans and non-returnable bottles.

The Inner City Puppet Theatre got $9,255 so five people could produce and present puppet shows three times a week in hospitals and schools throughout Metro. The group will also train children to work with puppets.

Globe and Mail, March 2, 1972.

> *Has the Canadian government realized some great truth; that it is actually possible to make people free and more independent with gifts of public money? The views of two young Canadians, male and female, on receiving unemployment insurance, are instructive.*

Unemployment really is a good wage, people can live on it really well. I didn't find time heavy on my hands. I found life more meaningful. I found I could start doing things. I had time to talk to people, time to read, time to understand myself. I could just relax and go to beaches when I felt like it. I had a wonderful time.[27]

Look, my friends and I are the products of technology—the new leisure class. I've worked. I've had a job (for six months) with the Toronto Board of Education and I've been a personnel officer. I didn't fancy either job as a life's occupation.

We take time, and we relish time, and while we don't aspire to a more luxurious lifestyle than our parents, we are the aristocracy of the century. If people thought more and stopped putting us down because they think we *should* be working, then I think we'd be appreciated as the people of the future.[28]

> *And Prime Minister Trudeau reinforced the suspicion that the government is leading us into a new style of life.*

Perhaps more jobs is not the first thing we want in the long run. Perhaps it's more wealth with more leisure and less jobs, less hours of work for less people.

I say that the most sacred law is that a man who lives in society should be able to enjoy his own possibilities to the maximum, but work is not perhaps the way to do it.

Prime Minister Trudeau, 1972.[29]

The Easy-Going Canadian

A Canadian has been defined as someone who does not play for keeps.

W. Kilbourn, *A Guide to the Peaceable Kingdom*, 1970.[30]

Let us look at the case. On the American side, the people are all life, elasticity, buoyancy, activity; on the Canadian side we have a people who appear subdued, tame, spiritless, as if living much more under the influence of fear than hope. Again: on the American territory we behold men moving as if they had the idea that their calling was to act, to choose, to govern—at any rate to govern themselves; on the Canadian soil we see a race, perhaps more polite than the other, but who seem to live under the impression that their vocation is to receive orders, and obey. Then, on the American side, you are placed in the midst of incessant bustle, agitation; the hotels are filled, coaches are in constant movement, railroad trains passing and repassing with their passengers, while men of business are seen pushing their concerns with impassioned ardour. On the Canada shore we have comparatively still life; delicate, genteel, formal. Moreover, on the American territory, all along the shores of the lakes, the country is being cleared, houses and villages built, works put up, incipient ports opened, and trade begun. On the Canada shore, unbroken forest appears for miles, while the small openings which have been made present themselves to view in a very infantine and feeble state of progress.

Visitor's comment, 1849.[31]

I could not enter Canada without seeing, and hearing, and feeling that there was less of enterprise around me than in the States—less of general movement, and less of commercial success. In the meantime, I return to my assertion, that in entering Canada from the States, one clearly comes from a richer to a poorer country. When I have said so, I have heard no Canadian absolutely deny it; though in refraining from denying it, they have usually expressed a general conviction, that in settling himself for life, it is better for a man to set up his staff in Canada then in the States. "I do not know that we are richer," a Canadian says, "but on the whole we are doing better and are happier."

Anthony Trollope, *North America*, 1862.[32]

English Canadians are far more like Americans than they are like French Canadians or Englishmen. But there are subtle differences. Canadians take their work more calmly and their pleasures more sadly. High-pressure salesmanship never threatened to blow off the cylinder heads in Canada. High-pressure radio announcing is not favored, as one announcer discovered when he tried it during the Moose River Mine disaster in Nova Scotia some years ago. Canadian theatre audiences are among the world's coldest. A political convention in the United States bears the same relation to a political convention in Canada as bedlam bears to a cemetery.

J. MacCormac, *Canada—America's Problem*, 1940.[33]

American companies in Canada try like the devil to put top Canadians into top roles. They train fellows. The men won't take the responsibility. You have to put in long hours if you want to succeed. Canadians won't do this—they want the same money as an American gets, but they just don't want to work hard and they can't make decisions or gamble.

Canadians seem to be happier than Americans. At least they're more contented and more balanced. They don't hemorrhage if an order is slow getting out and, after all, they argue, is one late order worth an ulcer?

Americans' comments, 1963.[34]

To Americans traveling in Canada for vacations, or working in business, the surface of life seems much like home, but they discover differences in point of view and the tempo of living. Canadians are more conservative than Americans, slower and more cautious in action. They instinctively resist the dynamic self-confidence of their neighbors' spirit and perhaps emphasize British elements in their thoughts and life in order to counteract the overwhelming influence of the American way.

Anne Merriman Peck, *The Pageant of Canadian History*, 1963.[35]

There seems to be less optimism, less faith in the future, less willingness to risk capital or reputation. In contrast to America, Canada is a country of greater restraint.

K. Naegele, *Canadian Society*, 1961.[36]

HOCKEY NIGHT IN CANADA
FOR
THE RUGGED CANADIAN

In December 1970, Maclean's Magazine reported results of a survey which indicated that Canadians rejected success in terms of wealth, fame, power. Canadians, the report said, valued most highly qualities of trust, honesty, sincerity, love and ability to get along with others.

There are probably thousands of Canadians engaged in high-pressure pursuits who would violently disagree with the foregoing analysis. The view that Canadians do not like to go full-out is, however, supported by our record in international athletic competitions. Our Olympic record of gold or any other medals is weak. Every time another Olympic competition is completed, and we depart with few laurels, the voices of concern are raised. In 1952 the editor of the Canadian Sport Monthly *viewed the situation with alarm.*

Looking hard at us, I should say that we, as a nation, are far more adept at being "Monday Morning Quarterbacks" in sport than at playing anything very well. We have our specialties, but we don't very often surprise anybody by doing better than expected. That's because the theory of "study and sacrifice" to become great at sports is not part of our make-up. Canadians generally speaking are "party athletes", eyeing always the "blowout" at the end, showing only desire to win when the event is at hand, and begrudging any hour before midnight that we have to give up just to be rested for the next day of play. This is a national characteristic—not just an idle observation.[37]

The disappointing showing of Canadians in the Winter Olympics at Sapporo in 1972 led to a new awareness of our failings. The disappointed manager of the ski team offered his views on the disaster.

It's bred into us in Canada. If their mothers didn't put food on the table, most Canadian kids wouldn't eat.

I'd hate like hell for our guys to get into a war. We'd lose in the first day.

Not enough of our kids are willing to sacrifice to make the top. If they're mediocre, they're happy."[38]

The Prime Minister himself also viewed with alarm.

The lifestyle which so many Canadians have chosen for themselves—to be sports spectators rather than participants, to drive instead of to walk, to use our increasing leisure time in passive activities rather than active ones, is contributing to an increasingly unhealthy population.[39]

> *Naturally the government felt that it must take the responsibility for correcting the situation. To fight laziness and to get Canadians fit, Sports Participation Canada was launched under the direction of Philippe de Gaspé Beaubien.*

Again and again Philippe de Gaspé Beaubien brings his fist down hard on the desk, the silver letter opener jumping with each blow.

"FAT!" he shouts (Wham). "We're FAT!"

"We're TIRED! (Wham). We're LAZY! (Wham). We're SLUGGISH! (Wham).

"We don't like to COMPETE! (Wham). We don't like to FIGHT! (Wham). We don't like to get INVOLVED! (Wham).

"We'd better do something SOON! (Wham). The situation is ALARMING! (Wham).

And then—lips curling, eyes narrowing, head tilting forward, Philippe de Gaspé Beaubien, brilliant, wealthy, hard-driving scion of a blue-blooded Montreal family, honors graduate from Harvard University in business administration, owner of a small TV and radio empire, working brains behind Expo '67, delivers the ultimate blow.

"The AMERICANS! The Americans are more fit than CANADIANS![40]

The Wealthy Canadians

> *Ask an American to name the wealthy men in his nation's history and he will have no difficulty in narrating the list: Carnegie, Rockefeller, Morgan, Ford, Getty, Hughes. A Canadian would find difficulty in matching the list. Our men of wealth and power lack the flamboyancy and excess of American tycoons; they are men who control quietly and discreetly; they are the kind of men portrayed by Hugh MacLennan in his novel* Two Solitudes.

At precisely two minutes to nine-thirty on Monday morning, Huntly McQueen stepped out of his Cadillac town-car and entered the Bank Building in Saint James Street. He was dressed in a dark suit, a black coat, a black hat, a dark blue tie very large in a winged collar. In the tie he wore a pearl pin.

He passed through a pair of bronze doors, was saluted by the ex-sergeant of Coldstream Guards who stood there in livery, and entered a marble atrium as impersonal as a mausoleum. He joined a group of middle-aged and elderly men waiting for an elevator at the far end of the atrium. They were all dressed exactly like himself. Nods passed between them, they stepped into the elevator, shot each other a few more discreet glances as though to make certain that nothing important had happened in their lives over the weekend, then stared straight ahead as the cage moved upward.

On the second floor Sir Rupert Irons got out. He had a heavily hard body, was square in the head, face, jaws and shoulders; his hair was parted in the middle and squared off to either side of his perpendicular temples. His face was familiar to most Canadians, for it stared at them from small, plain portraits' hanging on the walls of banks all the way from Halifax to Vancouver. Even in the pictures his neck was ridged with muscles acquired from a life-long habit of stiffening his jaw and pushing it forward during all business conversations.

On the fourth floor MacIntosh got out. He shuffled off toward his office, a round-shouldered, worrying man who carried in his head the essential statistics on three metal mines, two chemical factories, complicated relationships involving several international companies controlled in London and New York, and one corset factory.

On the seventh floor Masterman got out, to enter the offices of Minto Power. Although Minto harnessed the waters of one of the deepest and wildest rivers in the world, there was nothing about Masterman to suggest the elemental. He was a thin, punctilious man with a clipped moustache, a knife-edge press in his dark trousers, and a great reputation for culture among his associates in Saint James Street. He was one of the original members of the Committee of Art. He also belonged to a literary society which encouraged its members to read to each other their own compositions at meetings; he was considered its most brilliant member because he had published a book called *Gentlemen, the King!*. The work was an historical record of all the royal tours conducted through Canada since Confederation.

One floor higher, Chislett got out: nickel, copper and coal, a reputation for dominating every board he sat on, and so great a talent for keeping his mouth shut that even McQueen envied it.

The elevator continued with McQueen to the top floor. The thought crossed his mind that if an accident had occurred between the first and second floors, half a million men would at that instant have lost their masters. It was an alarming thought. It was also ironic, for these individuals were so remote from the beings they governed, they operated with such cantilevered indirections, that they could all die at once without even ruffling the sleep of the remote employees on the distant end of the chain of cause and effect. The structure of interlocking directorates which governed the nation's finances, subject always to an exceptionally discreet parliament, seemed to McQueen so delicate that a puff of breath could make the whole edifice quiver. But no, McQueen smiled at his own thoughts, the structure was quite strong enough. The men who had ridden together in the elevator this morning were so sound they seldom told even their wives what they thought or did or hoped to do. Indeed, Sir Rupert Irons was so careful he had no wife at all. They were Presbyterians to a man, they went to church regularly, and Irons was known to believe quite literally in predestination.[41]

> "Sound" men—respectable, quiet, anonymous. The more power they wield, the less publicity they seem to attract. Canada's best-known millionaire, E. P. Taylor, long a folklore symbol of wealth, is said to "just make it" into the list of the fifty wealthiest men in this country. K. C. Irving of New Brunswick, until recently one of the most powerful feudal barons in Canada, was almost completely unheard of by the masses. There are, of course, more flamboyant business types who have become well-known and gained a certain notoriety. Some of the more outrageous members of this group such as "Honest Ed" Mirvish and "Bad Boy" Lastman can not be seriously taken as figures of national importance. But three men do stand out—Lord Beaverbrook, Jack Kent Cooke, Roy Thomson—and they all left Canada to seek opportunities for their business zeal and imagination. Roy Thomson of Fleet, is one of these mavericks whose style is not quite right for the Canadian community of wealth.

Roy Thomson is a man no one can deny. The Scots yielded their national newspaper to him, the *Scotsman*. The English sold him their sovereign daily, *The Times*. The other day he flew around the world and stopped one day in Bangkok. He showed me both that city's dailies, saying "They're mine!" He sweeps up ownership of newspapers across the world. . . .

He also collects titles. The president of Lebanon couldn't resist pinning the Commandership of the Order of Cedar on his breast. Our gracious Queen, one of whose favorite subjects he is, I gather, made him a baron, despite Lester Pearson.

He wanted to be Lord Thomson of Toronto. Canada wouldn't go for that, or allow him to keep his Canadian citizenship, if he were to become a British peer. So, he became Lord Thomson of Fleet (the London street where the newspapers come from) and a British citizen.

Businesses fall into his hands. He acquired an airline. He's just started an incredibly cheap tourist air lift all over the world (3,000,000 tourists in this first year of operation). During the morning I was with him, he chased a wily Arab all over the Middle East (by phone), trying to collect a million pounds.

He gave me his usual patter, "Anyone can do it. Just three secrets to the trick; One, seeing the opportunity—this is part luck, like being there, and part training; two, seizing it—this is confidence or courage; and three, having the money or the credit to pull it off."

Daniel Cappon, 1971.[42]

Below these figures lies a group not so wealthy and powerful, but still significant enough to rank as an "upper upper" class. Here, background and community influence may be more important than financial standing in determining status, but the same conservative life style persists.

This is the "social register" class, the Canadian equivalent of aristocracy. Its members display a minute interest in genealogies and take great pride in their distinguished ancestry. They try to be very exclusive and, as far as possible, keep their marriages within the clan. In rural communities, they are likely to be gentlemen farmers, with great estates, model farms, and a type of living patterned after the nobility of England. . . .

The basic values of this class are to uphold the family reputation, to reflect the excellence of one's breeding, and to display a sense of community responsibility. The members try to create an impression that wealth has little bearing on their social pre-eminence. Rather, it is the gracious, leisurely way of life they have achieved as a result of their innate good taste and high breeding. Their reference group is the British upper class. Their clothing shows strong British influence, and British sports, such as sailing, polo, and riding, are their favorites.

As a rule, the upper-upper class families are oriented to the past, and tend to be highly ritualized in their behavior. They often live in big, old houses, sanctified by historic traditions. Dining arrangements, and even gatherings of the immediate family in the living room, are stylized. The child is trained to a code of behavior appropriate to his position as a member of the distinguished lineage.

Their consumption patterns do not reflect a desire for status symbols. Their position is so secure that there is no need to live ostentatiously. They tend to avoid mass-produced, mass-marketed goods, and spend their money on such items as paintings, sculptures, stamp collections, old maps, rare books, and the like. Also, they are not heavy purchasers of durable goods. Many of their belongings are inherited. It is rare indeed to find an upper-upper couple who cannot set up their first home completely from ancestral furniture and wedding presents.

N. K. Dhalla, *These Canadians*, 1966.[43]

For those who cannot attain the great wealth of a Thomson, Irving or Taylor, there are positions which bring money and the chance to live the good life, in the proper environment. It seems natural for them to band together in protective ghettoes—British Properties in Vancouver, Rosedale and Forest Hill Village in Toronto, and Westmount in Montreal. The name "Westmount" has symbolized the perfect residential community for those who have made their money and are secure in their social prominence.

I've been working for some weeks now on a little song about Westmount, that separate municipality of 38,000 people set down inside Montreal. It begins like this:

> In Westmount we are good to us,
> Good to us,
> Good to us,
> In Westmount we are nice—
> And who are we nice to?
> We're nice to us!

I use the word "we" because from May 1 to today my family and I have been in an apartment in Westmount. Now, alas, our time in Montreal ends and I go on a few weeks' holiday before returning to my normal beat in Toronto.

Living here has been like residing inside a myth. For years I'd heard and read about this peculiar enclave. From a distance one had got the impression that it was stiff, formal, snobbish, very Anglo-Saxon, very self-enclosed.

Curiously enough, most of this is true. The Anglo-Saxon part is not—at least not anymore. There are many French Canadians in Westmount now, and there are enough Jews to support a first-class delicatessen. But the other stories can hardly be described as unfounded slanders.

Take the public library, for instance. The Westmount Public Library is for Westmount people, nobody else. In order to get a card you must prove residence, and you do this with a letter from either your bank manager or a Westmount property owner.

The Westmount Public Library has an unlisted telephone number. The librarians say this is because they haven't the staff to answer questions on the phone, but I suspect it's just part of the screening process to keep out foreigners. After all, you can't show your library card over the phone, and *anybody* might call up and get free information.

Or take the Westmount swimming pool. There too you must prove residence. When you do so you get a little plastic card with your photograph baked into it. You show this every time you go for a swim. They don't want people lending their cards to outsiders.

When you swim, incidentally, you are well protected. It is a small pool but there are three lifeguards at all times, watching the people intently. One time a kid swimming beside me was using a kind of dog paddle in the deep end. The lifeguard called down to him that he wasn't to do that, he was to use the crawl as he'd been instructed to do. In the Westmount swimming pool, you don't step out of line.

Westmount has no slums, no hippies, and no other visual disturbances. It has carefully manicured parks—Westmount Park itself has not only a wading pool, first-class children's equipment, and a giant checkerboard, but also a tiny artificial stream and a tiny artificial waterfall.

Much of Westmount seems built on an enormous scale. The churches are very large and very substantial, and the houses up on the hill look like castles. (Among the property owners there, I understand, the servant problem is crucial.) There are some streets on a more modest scale, and a few of these are being given the town-house treatment so familiar in Toronto. Westmount, in fact, is what Rosedale would be like if it included the town-house district and a shopping centre and had a local government of its own.

Everybody goes first class in Westmount, even the YMCA. The Y summer day-camp for children organizes frequent expeditions, like other day-camps; but they aren't the ordinary kind of factory visits. They go to other towns, like Granby, to see the zoo; one time this summer they went a hundred miles to see Upper Canada Village. That's style.

Westmount residents generally are the sort of people who would like to have their children in private schools. Some can manage this, but not all. As compensation the Westmount public schools try to act as much like private schools as possible. From kindergarten on, little boys must wear white shirts and ties, and girls must wear standard black tunics.

At least a hint of the Quiet Revolution has reached the Westmount schools; French is now taught in all grades, for instance. But they haven't *quite* got the message. One day last spring my daughter came home from her grade-one class and alarmed her parents by singing, right through, "The Maple Leaf Forever". (Do you recall the words—all about Wolfe the conquering hero planting firm Britannia's flag and so on?)

We had a little difficulty explaining to her that in 1967 we Canadians don't talk that way, and that it isn't really a very good idea to sing that song on a public bus in the city of Montreal. Why even Torontonians *know* that much.

Robert Fulford, 1967.[44]

Some Thoughts, Pleasant and . . . Unpleasant?

Every nation has its peculiar national characteristics. . . .And my own experience was that the following are the three most noticeable characteristics of Canadians, though I do believe that you have to actually live in the country in order to observe them in their proper perspective.

1. A lack of a sense of humor, particularly in that they are unable to laught at themselves.
2. A degree of personal, individual thriftiness, or frugality, of the type which one associates with the proverbial (that's figurative not actual) Scotsman.
3. An individual and national inability to look problems in the face and to do something about them. They prefer to ignore them hoping that they will go away.

B.R. Myers, *North of the Border*, 1963.[45]

Despite everything, however, I think we can begin now to detect some of the special characteristics common to all Canadians, and add them up to something.

First, and most obvious, is our national humility. We are a people bounded on one side by the northern lights and on the other, by an inferiority complex just as vivid, a people distracted by the mossy grandeur of the old world from which we came and by the power, wealth and fury of our American neighbours. We are the last people to realize, and the first to deny, the material achievements of the Canadian nation which all the rest of the world has already grasped and envied. Self-depreciation is our great national habit.

This is curious, when you come to think of it, because so many of us are of British origin. A few days ago a scholar from India wrote in the London *Times* that the English consider their primary national vice to be hypocrisy, but he said. "I must insist on first things first. The root and beginning is self-admiration, and hypocrisy only its most distinguished product." Now that's an interesting epigram but its reception in England is *more* interesting. In Canada we would resent it, but the English loved it. They have had so much experience, they are so sure of themselves, that they can laugh at the impudence of outsiders. We don't laugh because we lack any self-admiration, and we're not very good at hypocrisy, either. We are hurt by the foreigner's criticism because we have a sneaking suspicion that it must be true, a suspicion that would not occur to an Englishman. Never has there been a people in all history which has accomplished so much as the Canadian people and thought so little of it. An Indian scholar won't find self-admiration here. He'll find self-apology written in big black letters across our Canadian map—no, not in big letters. We write everything small if it's Canadian.

This, perhaps, lies close to the root of another national characteristic —we are a conservative and steady people hardly daring to believe in our own capacity in the more complex affairs of statecraft, afraid to test that capacity too far with new systems and experiments. The Canadian patience at a political meeting (a significant little test, if the glummest), the most stolid and dead-panned ever known—a collection of dull and sceptical haddock eyes to daunt the boldest politican; and our politicians truly reflect us in their stodgy competence, their unvarying pedestrianism, their high ability, their positive terror of colour and flair.

Bruce Hutchison, 1948.[46]

One of the national illusions of Canadians is that nothing can be done without an ample supply of statistics. When we feel we are running short, we appoint another Royal Commission to compile a few more volumes. We believe, as a group, that the Dominion Bureau of Statistics is the chief source of fuel for the clear frame of nationalism. No public speech is complete without statistics, in order to show that twenty-five years or so ago Canada was a nation of only 11,000,000 poor, unenlightened individuals with a paltry Gross National Product of only a little more than three billion dollars, accumulating to the credit of a labour force of less than 3,500,000 persons of brawn and brains.

B. Richardson, *Canada and Mr. Diefenbaker*, 1962.[47]

I consider it not unfair to suggest, however, that if some Canadians think some Americans brash and loud, most Americans think Canadians generally are not only quiet and standoffish on occasion but also—let's be frank about it, rather dull and often very drab. Even an overseas visitor to North America may detect the contrast with the friendly, talkative habits of the curious American which he finds among reserved Canadians in trains, in cafes, and even in some private homes. American women, moreover, find a sharp contrast in the apparent readiness of their Canadian sisters to leave public life in many forms to their husbands and to their brothers.

F. Alexander, *Canadians and Foreign Policy*, 1960.[48]

It is wrong to say that Canadians have no distinctive national characteristics; what about our national custom of Keeping Down With the Joneses? In other countries people keep up with the Joneses; they vie with one another in the acquirement of showy and prestige-giving possessions. But the crafty Canadian always wants his neighbours to think that he has less money than he really has. He under-dresses, for the possession of more than two suits might suggest affluence and a desire to seem glorious in the eyes of men. His wife probably has a fur coat, but she wears it to do the shopping, and to sweep off the stoop, so that it is really just a hard-wearing overall, and not a token of wealth. He eats good food, but he likes it to be disguised, so that even the tooth-test sometimes fails to reveal how good it is. It is only when he goes on a holiday to the USA that he splurges, takes suites in hotels, gives huge tips to hirelings, and drinks pearls dissolved in wine. At home he likes the neighbours to think that he is just keeping out of jail.

Robertson Davies, *Marchbank's Almanack*, 1967.[49]

Who Are We?

So runs the Great Canadian Riddle. It has become the magnificent obsession of writers, historians, statesmen and disc jockeys. We Canadians have been overly preoccupied with the question of our identity; and we have always been disappointed because we never got the answer we were looking for.

We have always hoped that one day it would be possible to define a Canadian in the way one could define an Englishman, German, Frenchman, American. So far our plea has not been answered, nor does it seem likely that it will be answered in the way we want. We have been looking for unity in our identity, and all we have been able to see is diversity. Because we do not perceive unity, we somehow sense failure in ourselves and in our nation. We have failed, we feel, to achieve the ultimate goal of all respectable nations—a unified, homogeneous population with a clear identity:

> *"One voice, one people, one in heart,*
> *And soul, and feeling, and desire!"*[1]

THIS
QUESTION
OF IDENTITY

There was, however, a time in our history when we caught the vision of such a possibility. It came in the years immediately following Confederation and found its expression in the enthusiasm associated with the birth of the new dominion of Canada. The search for a common Canadian identity began in the movement known as Canada First. George Denison, one of its founders, tells of the men whose meetings in 1868 gave rise to Canada First.

We were five young men of about twenty-eight years of age, except Haliburton, who was four or five years older. We very soon became warm friends, and spent most of our evenings in Morgan's quarters.... These meetings were the origin of the "Canada First" party. Nothing could show more clearly the hold that Confederation had taken of the imagination of young Canadians than the fact that, night after night, five young men should give up their time and their thoughts to discussing the higher interests of their country, and it ended in our making a solemn pledge to each other that we would do all we could to advance the interests of our native land, that we would put our country first, before all personal, or political, or party considerations.... It was apparent that until there should grown, not only a feeling of unity, but also a national pride and devotion to Canada as a Dominion, no real progress could be made towards building up a strong and powerful community.... History had taught us that every nation that had become great, and had exercised an important influence upon the world, had invariably been noted for a strong patriotic spirit, and we believed in the sentiment of putting the country above all other considerations, the same feeling that existed in Rome, "When none was for a party; when all were for the State". This idea we were to preach in season and out of season.

George T. Denison, *The Struggle for Imperial Unity*, 1909.[2]

From those meetings, and the idealism which inspired them, the young men, Denison, poet Charles Mair, Toronto lawyer William Foster, Maritime lobbyist Robert Haliburton, and author Henry Morgan went forth to spread their idea of Canadian identity.

...The old Norse mythology, with its Thor hammers and Thor hammerings, appeals to us—for we are a Northern people—as the true out-crop of human nature, more manly, more real, than the weak marrow-bones superstition of an effeminate South.

William Foster, 1871.[3]

We are not Britons. We are the descendants of Britons, but we are sons of the New World, cherishing fondly the traditions of the old world, but feeling that here "old things have passed away, and all things have become new."

Robert Haliburton, 1870.[4]

Lest some mistake the true intent of Canada First, the following address was published in 1871.

Fellow Countrymen:

In addressing you thus early respecting a movement which has been successfully inaugurated in Toronto to promote the growth of a Canadian national sentiment and to secure Canadian unity, we recognize the necessity of freeing that movement from the effects of misconception as well as of wanton misconstruction. . . .

Our motto, "CANADA FIRST," is said to admit of various interpretations—fertile imaginations have almost proved that. Some profess to see in it, Annexation; others, Independence; others, Know-nothingism. The meaning attached to it by us may be gathered from the following expressions of opinion, which will serve to show that the motto is not necessarily ambiguous and has not been misapprehended by all:—

"...What reason exists why when Englishmen, Irishmen and Scotchmen give their whole hearts to their respective countries, we in Canada should not place our own land first, and so act and speak as though we felt proud—as we have a right to be—of the name of Canadian. We have a country in which any people might glory, we have a future that is dazzling in its promise; all we need is a sentiment which shall break down all provincial and sectional distinctions, which shall make us feel not as Ontarios or Quebeckers, Nova Scotians or New Brunswickers, but as Canadians—proud of our country as a whole."—Hamilton Times.

"And this is the feeling we want more of in our Dominion—a feeling of Canadianism. Are we to be forever jabbering about our respective merits as Englishmen, Scotchmen, Welshmen, French and Germans; as Irish Catholic and Irish Orangeman? We have heard a great deal too much of this stuff talked. It is time that all classes of our population, whether born here or elsewhere, whatever their creed or country, should consider themselves, above all, Canadians. It is from this standpoint that we bid God-speed to those who, in Toronto or elsewhere, are endeavouring to foster in our midst a national Canadian spirit."—London Advertiser.

It has been alleged that we desire to create antagonism between native born Canadians and Canadians by adoption. The contrary is the fact. Our earnest desire is to do away with all invidious distinctions of nationality, creed, locality or class, and to unite the people of the Dominion, as Canadians, through affection for and pride in Canada, their home.

W. A. Foster, *Canada First*, 1890.[5]

Although Canada First did not last long as an organized crusade, its concept of a distinctive Canadian identity was not lost. The need for a common identity was felt most strongly in the years around the turn of the century. Canada had opened up its interior to immigrants who came by the thousands, not only from the old stand-bys—the British Isles and the United States—but from strange lands to the east. Clifford Sifton, the minister of immigration, might well say, "I think a stalwart peasant in a sheep-skin coat, born on the soil, whose forefathers have been farmers for ten generations, with a stout wife and a half-dozen children, is good quality." But there were others who found much to fear in the onslaught of the newcomers.

Canada today faces the greatest immigration problem that has ever confronted any nation. . . .Of the Anglo-Saxon we are not in the least afraid, but when we consider that last year over twenty-one per cent of all the incomers to Canada were non-Anglo-Saxon, who can not speak our language, have no sympathy with our ideals, and are foreigners in every sense of the term, then we begin to understand what a task is ours as a nation. One man out of every five who lands on our shores is a foreigner. He comes here with a foreign tongue, foreign ideals, foreign religion, only a mere caricature of religion, with centuries of ignorance and oppression behind him, often bringing with him problems that the best statesmen of Europe have failed to solve.

Rev. W. D. Reid, 1913.[6]

Over this country are thrown little pools of that flood of European immigration that grows through Winnipeg, to remain separate or be absorbed, as destiny wills. The problem of immigration here reveals that purposelessness that exists in the affairs of Canada even more than those of other nations. The multitude from South or East Europe flocks in. Some make money and return. The most remain, often in inassimilable lumps. There is every sign that these lumps may poison the health of Canada as dangerously as they have that of the United States. For Canada there is the peril of too large an element of foreign blood and traditions in a small nation already little more than half composed of British blood and descent. Nationalities seem to teach one another only the worst. If the Italians gave the Canadians of their good manners, and Doukhobours or Poles inoculated them with idealism and the love of beauty, and received from them British romanticism and sense of responsibility! . . .But they only seem to increase the anarchy, these "foreigners", and to learn the American twang and method of spitting.

Rupert Brooke, *Letters From America*, 1916.[7]

The melting pot means that instead of the pure race from which we have come, we shall have a mongrel race, and this mongrel race is making itself known in Canada as a result of the immigration we have had.

Andrew Macphail, 1920.[8]

The United States are welcome to the Hungarians, Poles, Italians and others of that class; they are, as a rule, wretchedly poor, make very poor settlers, and bring with them many of the vices and socialistic tendencies which have caused such trouble to their hosts already. Renewed efforts should . . .be made by our government to induce more of the hardy German and Norwegian races to remain here.

Dominion Illustrated, 1891.[9]

So long as Britons and northwestern Europeans constitute the vast majority there is not so much danger of losing our national character. To healthy Britons of good behaviour our welcome is everlasting; but to make this country a dumping ground for the scum and dregs of the old world means transplanting the evils and vices that they may flourish in a new soil. . . .

The granting of the franchise to these groups only serves to encourage corruption in political matters, endangering the interests of good government. The serious character of the problem may be stated thus: if we do not Canadianize and Christianize the new-comer, he will make us foreigners and heathen on our own soil and under our own flag. If British institutions mean anything they stand for the championship of Christian civilization.

The Canadian Courier, 1914.[10]

The man whom Canada needs is strong and healthy, preferably young enough to be readily adaptable to new conditions, sound in mind and well taught, trained and educated. The man she desires most of all is one of the good blood of the British Isles, imbued with love for the old flag of the Empire, and for the ancient traditions of his race; one who will help in the building up of Canada on the same lines as those on which the work has been begun—as a free British nation within the Empire; one, in short, who is adapted by heredity, education and previous history to understand this ideal of nationhood, and to take his place in the furtherance of it.

Good British immigrants are the more needed—to aid in leavening the whole lump—because today Canada is the goal for people of many races and languages, who, in most instances, have everything to learn of the institutions and the ideals of the nation, which...they will soon be helping to mould.

Emily P. Weaver, *Canada and the British Immigrant*, 1914.[11]

The fear of the "foreigner" was extended to Americans who, although they had the advantage of speaking English, were known to have other undesirable characteristics.

The non-religious character of the American invasion presents a serious difficulty in attempting missionary work. It is true that some of those settlers from the south are loyal supporters of Christian churches, but the great majority are indifferent to religion and enslaved by money-making, diligent in business, but God is not in all their thoughts. They come from districts of the United States that fifty years ago were largely neglected by all the Protestant Home Mission Societies and they were reared in a materialistic atmosphere. As a consequence more than three-fourths of the territory between the Mississippi River and the Pacific Coast is practically churchless, Sabbathless, Godless, lawless. Now if the Christian people of Canada do not wish to see repeated on the fair map of our Dominion those black spots, the irreligious communities that have distressed the most earnest Christian worker in the United States, the Gospel message must be proclaimed to the progressive American settlers. First things must be placed first so that spiritual riches may rise above material wealth.

Desirable the American settlers are with one exception—the Mormons, a name that carries a Bluebeardish horror. They are a deadly menace to this country if allowed to carry out their tenets.

C. J. Cameron, *Foreigners Or Canadians*, 1913.[12]

It was traditional in Canada to fear that American settlers would either try to Americanize us, or work as a disloyal element within Canada to bring about union with the United States. The following statement by H. A. Kennedy in his book New Canada and New Canadians, *written in 1907, shows that Americans were more "assimilable" than previously thought.*

There is a hope cherished in some quarters of the United States that these American emigrants to Canada, if lost for a while to the Republic, will by-and-by use their power to bring the Dominion under the Stars and Stripes. Well, the future is a free field for the prophets. So far as my experience goes, the Americans in Western Canada are perfectly content with the political institutions they have adopted, and certainly not inclined to act as missionaries of the annexation doctrine. They have personally annexed as much of the country as they want. Those Americans who are afflicted by the thought that the whole continent is not ruled from Washington appear to have stayed at home, and their emigrant kinsmen seem rather glad of it. "How are you going to vote?" one of the new-comers was asked. "I don't care which side," said he with brutal candour. "What I want to vote for is to keep them darned Yankees out! " . . .

An old Scottish-Canadian, who has watched the Americans closely ever since their invasion of the West began, says; "You'll find exceptions, of course; but taking them all round they're as well behaved a lot as any of us, and they're a great people for a new country like this—far ahead of our old-country folk. They come right in with a tent, and plough up a big slice of land before they bother about putting up even a shack to live in. You can always tell an American settler by the way he begins. Yes, *sir*, they're a great people!"[13]

There was another element in Canada, much smaller in numbers than the "men in sheepskin coats", but potentially more dangerous. This was the Asiatic population—Chinese, Japanese and Indian—which was developing on the West Coast. The 1907 Anti-Asiatic riots in Vancouver led to the preparation of the following report by William Lyon Mackenzie King, the deputy minister of immigration.

. . .That Canada should desire to restrict immigration from the Orient is regarded as natural, that Canada should remain a white man's country is believed to be not only desirable for economic and social reasons, but highly necessary on political and national grounds. . . .

It is clearly recognized in regard to emigration from India to Canada that the native of India is not a person suited to this country, that, accustomed as many of them are to the conditions of a tropical climate, and possessing manners and customs so unlike those of our own people, their inability to readily adapt themselves to surroundings entirely different could not do other than entail an amount of privation and suffering which render a discontinuanace of such immigration most desirable in the interest of the Indians themselves. It was recognized, too, that the competition of this class of labour, though not likely to prove effective, if left to itself, might none the less, were the numbers to become considerable ...occasion considerable unrest among workingmen whose standard of comfort is of a higher order, and who, as citizens with family and civic obligations, have expenditures to meet and a status to maintain which the coolie immigrant is in a position wholly to ignore.[14]

> *The fear of the oriental reached its zenith during the Second World War with the forcible detention and dispersion of Japanese-Canadians living in British Columbia. But it is doubtful if statements concerning Chinese and Japanese citizens and immigrants have ever been harsher that those made in the 1920s and 1930s.*

Canada has never sought colonists from Asia. Following out her policy of encouraging people of a ready assimilable type, Canada felt that any great influx of Asiatics would tend to endanger the type of civilization that Canadians feel is best adapted to their needs.

Japanese immigration has been regulated under a Gentleman's Agreement whereby the entrance of Japanese into Canada is kept within limits agreed upon by the two Governments and regulated by Japan. In a word, it is now limited to 150 annually.

K. A. Foster, *Our Canadian Mosaic*, 1926.[15]

> *Magazine articles also trumpeted the authors' fears of immigrants who were "unabsorbable aliens" with "deep differences in moral outlook and philosophy" from white Canadians, and whose acceptance of a lower standard of living created unfair competition for the Canadian workingman.*

"Will Canada Go Yellow?"
"Shall We Bar The Yellow Race."
"The Oriental Threat."
"Can Canada Do Without The Immigrant?"
"British Columbia's Racial Problem."[16]

THE REAL CHINESE GIANT.

One point clearly emerges from all this concern about immigrants, whether they were "inassimilable lumps" from Eastern Europe, irreligious Americans, or Orientals. What was desired was apparently a uniform Canadian identity. There was even a definition of the ideal Canadian, although it might be presented in a negative way. A Canadian was one who understood, practised, and protected the proper ideals, traditions, loyalties, morals and laws, most of which were, of course, British in origin. He was English-speaking, and thus able to participate in fulfilling the above duties. He possessed the qualities of hardiness and vigour which were associated with "northern races."

La Survivance

This approach completely overlooked or deliberately ignored the presence of the French in Canada and gave them no part to play in creating a Canadian identity. Indeed, it seemed to assume that they too would eventually be assimilated. The threat of assimilation and destruction of their traditional identity was not new to the French. They had encountered that possibility at the time of the Conquest in 1763 when, for a few years, the British had contemplated turning Canada into a typical British colony. However, the anglicization of Canada was soon regarded as both unjust and impractical, and was abandoned. The French felt secure in their religion and culture.

Then, in 1839 the spectre of assimilation rose again in the words of Lord Durham. This English lord made recommendations to his government concerning the future of the French.

. . .I entertain no doubts as to the national character which must be given to Lower Canada; it must be that of the British Empire; that of the majority of the population of British America; that of the great race which must, in the lapse of no long period of time, be predominant over the whole North American Continent. Without effecting the change so rapidly or so roughly as to shock the feelings and trample on the welfare of the existing generation, it must henceforth be the first and steady purpose of the British Government to establish an English population, with English laws and language, in this Province, and to trust its government to none but a decidedly English legislature. . . .

. . .The English have already in their hands the majority of the larger masses of property in the country; they have the decided superiority of intelligence on their side; they have the certainty that colonization must swell their numbers to a majority; and they belong to the race which wields the Imperial Government, and predominates on the American Continent. . . .The French Canadians, on the other hand, are but the remains of an ancient colonization, and are and ever must be isolated in the midst of an Anglo-Saxon world. Whatever may happen, whatever government shall be established over them, British or American, they can see no hope for their nationality. . . .

. . .The language, the laws, the character of the North American Continent are English; and every race but the English (I apply this to all who speak the English language) appears there in a condition of inferiority. It is to elevate them from that inferiority that I desire to give to the Canadians our English character. . . .

There can hardly be conceived a nationality more destitute of all that can invigorate and elevate a people, than that which is exhibited by the descendants of the French in Lower Canada, owing to their retaining their peculiar language and manners. They are a people with no history, and no literature. . . .

In these circumstances, I should be indeed surprised if the more reflecting part of the French Canadians entertained at present any hope of continuing to preserve their nationality. . . .

Lord Durham's *Report*, 1839.[17]

For the French these sincerely ominous words created resentment and qualms concerning the future.

Yet with the coming of Confederation in 1867, the French once again felt secure. It was believed that in the union of the British North American colonies there would be an assured place for French identity. Some French Canadians saw in Confederation the only hope for French survival in North America.

. . .the annexation of Canada to the United States . . .is a question which must be examined when discussing that of Confederation, because it is one of the alternatives offered to us, and out of which we have to make a selection. . . .Let us profit by the example of the French race in the United States, and enquire what has been the fate of the French in Louisiana? What has become of them? What has become of their language, their customs, their manners and their institutions? . . .

. . .What we desire and wish, is to defend the general interests of a great country and of a powerful nation, by means of central power. On the other hand, we do not wish to do away with our different customs, manners and laws; on the contrary, those are precisely what we are desirous of protecting in the most complete manner by means of Confederation.

Under the new system there will be no more reason than at present to lose our character as French or English, under the pretext that we should all have the same general interests; and our interests in relation to race, religion and nationality will remain as they are at the present time. . . . Not only indeed did we assure ourselves of that protection, but the provinces who were parties to the Confederation desired it also. All local interests will be submitted and left to the decision of the local legislatures."

Hector Langevin, 1865.[18]

. . . if union were attained we would form a political nationality with which neither the national origin, nor the religion of any individual, would interfere. . . . We could not do away with the distinctions of race. We could not legislate for the disappearance of the French Canadians from American soil, but British and French Canadians alike could appreciate and understand their position relative to each other. They were placed like great families beside each other, and their contact produced a healthy spirit of emulation. It was a benefit rather than otherwise that we had a diversity of races.

George Etienne Cartier, 1865.[19]

Somehow the promise of Confederation did not live up to French expectations. Instead of a cultural partnership in which the French "fact" would be protected, Confederation brought a series of blows directed against French Canada. The crushing of the Riel uprisings, the execution of Louis Riel, the action against separate schools in Manitoba, the restrictions against French language instruction in Ontario—all were seen as part of some plot to destroy the French identity. And when English Canadians spoke of their desire for a homogeneous Canadian identity, the suspicion was confirmed.

The French reacted with a determination to survive as a distinct identity. There developed the concept of "Fortress Quebec", where French culture would alone be safe; the outside world was increasingly pictured as hostile territory. A new school of French-Canadian historical thinking arose, headed by Abbé Lionel Groulx. Canadian history, since the Conquest of 1763, was seen as a struggle by the French to maintain their identity in the face of sinister Anglo-Saxon onslaughts against the French language, religion and culture. Abbé Groulx portrayed the story in the following passage.

This germ of a people was one day profoundly stricken in its life; it was constrained, paralysed in its development. The consequences of the Conquest weighed heavily upon it; its laws, its language were hamstrung; its intellectual culture was long hobbled; its system of education, deviated in some of its parts, sacrificed more than was fitting to English culture; its natural domain was invaded, leaving it only partially master of its economic forces; its private and public customs were contaminated by the Protestant and Saxon atmosphere. . . .

This evil of the Conquest was aggravated after 1867 by the evil of federalism. . . . Our particular situation in the federal alliance, the isolation of our Catholic and French province amidst eight provinces in majority English and Protestant, the imbalance of forces which ensued, sometimes increased by the hostile policy of some rulers, led federal legislation little by little towards principles or acts which endangered our fundamental interests. The political system of our country, such as it is by way of being applied, leads not to unity but straight to uniformity. The dominant ideas at the present time at the seat of the central government tend to restrict from year to year the domain of the French language, to undermine secretly the autonomy of our social, religious, and even political institutions.

Abbé Groulx, 1921.[20]

Other Canadiens, *notably Henri Bourassa, also emphasized the survival interpretation of Canadian history.*

. . . If French ideas, if the French language, if the French civilization has some chance of survival in America, it will not be because of some more or less cordial and more or less durable understanding between France and England; it will be because of the ultimate triumph of the battle which French Canadians have waged for a hundred and fifty years for the maintenance of these ideas, this language and this civilization. . . .

Henri Bourassa, 1916.[21]

With vigour the French Canadians stated that their language and culture must not, and would not, be surrendered to those who proposed a uniform Canadian identity.

We have a right to our national existence as a race apart, and woe to any man who will try to deprive us of it. But we must not in any way molest our brothers whose racial origins or religious creed differ from our own. We must claim our rights with firmness, but not aggressively. We must energetically oppose everything which tends to destroy our national character, but we must respect in others the rights that we demand for ourselves. There is no longer any question of fighting enemies weapon in hand, but of competing as a race with brothers in the fields of education, labour, and honesty.

Honoré Mercier, Premier of Quebec, 1890.[22]

The goal of those who hope to create a great homogeneous Canadian entity from the Atlantic to the Pacific, composed of all the British North American colonies, also has some captivating aspects. Nonetheless, we find this object frightening and horrifying because we see all too clearly that its achievement would be detrimental to French Canada.

J.P. Tardivel, 1904.[23]

...we deserve better than to be considered like the savages of the old reservations and to be told: "Remain in Quebec, continue to stagnate in ignorance, you are at home there; but elsewhere you must become English."

No, we have the right to be French in language; we have the right to be Catholics in faith; we have the right to be free by the constitution. We are Canadians before all; and we have the right to be as British as anyone. And we have the right to enjoy these rights throughout the whole expanse of Confederation.

Henri Bourassa, 1912.[24]

...A history now three hundred years long, the nearly complete possession of the soil by a determined race, the profound imprint that this race has given it by its original manners and institutions, the special status reserved for it by all the political constitutions since 1791, have made of Quebec a French state that must be recognized in theory as well as in fact.

Abbé Groulx, 1921.[25]

1. That the French language, recognized as an official language in the Canadian Parliament, should be similarly treated in all parts of the country, because it has rights acquired in virtue of treaties and of the Constitution.

...

6.   That there should be an end of the belief that national unity can be secured only by unity of language; that the law of the strongest should no longer be enforced against us.

7.   That good understanding between the two great races which predominate in Canada should be established on the basis of a knowledge of the two official languages.

Proposals of La Presse, 1918.[26]

Could there be any middle ground between the French desire to preserve their unique identity and the viewpoint which sought a common identity? French Canadians proposed a compromise out of which might come a definition of Canadian identity.

Our own nationalism is a Canadian nationalism founded upon the duality of races and on the particular traditions which this duality involves. We work for the development of a Canadian patriotism which is in our eyes the best guaranty of the existence of the two races and of the mutual respect they owe each other. . . .

The nation that we wish to see develop is the Canadian nation, composed of French Canadians and English Canadians, that is of two elements separated by language and religion . . . but united in a feeling of brotherhood, in a common attachment to the common fatherland.

Henri Bourassa, 1904.[27]

Tied together as the branches of the same tree, the various races that dwell in Canada today must accept this community of existence. The interests of Canada, our common fatherland, must dominate interests of race and caste. We must not forget, we the citizens of this country who are called upon to become a great people, that if we are French, English, Scots, and Irish, we are also Canadians, and that this title must satisfy our pride as well as our legitimate ambition. We descend from the world's strongest races. Our destiny is not to perpetuate antiquated hatreds on this continent, but to build here a great nation whose future is bright in the designs of Providence.

Honoré Mercier, 1890.[28]

We wish both elements to conserve the characteristic traits of their race, their traditions, their language, their literature, and all their aspirations which are compatible with the moral and political unity of the Canadian people. We wish that the one should become more Canadian than French, and the other more Canadian than English. Let each group derive from its country of origin the ideas, advances, and developments necessary to the conservation of its particular patrimony, intellectual or moral; but each must also have enough patriotism, intelligence, and generosity to subordinate its particular tastes or prejudices to the exigencies of national unity.

In other words, we oppose equally French colonialism, in the world of ideas, and English colonialism in the world of politics and facts; we wish that both give place to a Canadian nationalism, both English and French, sharply distinct in the elements proper to the two races and their particular genius, but harmoniously united in the research of a common ideal, made up of Canadian traditions, rooted in the Canadian soil, and having no other object than the moral and material greatness of the Canadian fatherland.

Henri Bourassa, 1915.[29]

The Canadian identity was seen as a duality of two races, a partnership which would be unique and truly Canadian. The idea of uniformity, one language, one culture, one people, was rejected. Such a view staggered many English-speaking Canadians. It seemed to prevent forever the development of a true Canadian identity. It was denounced as being provincial, and accused of sacrificing the development of a true Canadianism on the altar of French and Quebec interests. To this charge, Israel Tarte made the following observations.

...The French-Canadian population do not belong, if I may speak that way, to the same civilization as their fellow-countrymen of English origin. The French genius is not the same as the Anglo-Saxon genius. We are French, you are English. Would you permit me to add that we are Canadians to the fullest extent of the word while, on many occasions, you are more British than Canadians. If there is any trouble in future, the trouble will come out of that difference.

Israel Tarte, 1900.[30]

This was a legitimate observation. Perhaps it was not the French desire for survival but rather the tendency of the English-speaking Canadian to hearken unto the "old country", which hindered the development of a Canadian identity. It could be suggested that English-speaking Canadians have often been British and not Canadian in thought, and loyalty.

For myself I am a true Briton. I love the old land dearly. I am **glad** that I was born a British subject; a British subject I have lived for **three** score years and something more. I hope to live and die a British subject. I trust and hope that my children and my grandchildren who have also been born British subjects will live their lives as British subjects, **and** as British subjects die.

Oliver Mowat, Premier of Ontario, 1891.[31]

One may say that the Englishman in Canada is English before he is Canadian; to tell the truth he has never ceased to be English and would be surprised if anyone took him for anything else. His allegiance, in so far as British nationalism has a territorial allegiance, lies outside the country; politically his heart is far away, somewhere in the north-west of Europe in some corner of the British Isles.... At heart, though he does not always admit it, he had a "colonial" mentality. Apart from the liberties which he prizes like the rest of his compatriots, he has no wish for a new nationality, which to him could not replace the elementary pride in being English. In case of war he would react immediately as a "Britisher", and would rush to the flag—to the British flag. We all know English people of this type, for they are the same the world over.

The attitude of the English Canadian is different, for he is first of all a Canadian, and feels that he is distinct from the English. We must admit that he does not like them, and is always running them down.... But we must be careful here—this Canadian who does not like the English loves England, and, moreover, he clings to the British tie, to the British connection.

André Siegfried, 1937.[32]

A poem in the Ontario school reader of 1925-1935 gave its readers an interpretation of Canadianess.

The Canadian

I never saw the cliffs of snow,
    The Channel billows tipped with cream,
The restless, eddying tides that flow
    About the Island of my dream.
I never saw the English downs
    Upon an April day,
The quiet, old Cathedral towns,
    The hedgerows white with may.

And still the name of England,
      Which tyrants laugh to scorn
Can thrill my soul. It is to me
      A very bugle-horn.

J. E. Middleton.[33]

The respect and affection for Britain in the Second World War was understandable. Still, it is an interesting comment on our sense of identity that the following poem should have the place of honour in a Canadian book of wartime verse entitled Voices of Victory.

Canada Speaks of Britain

This is that bastioned rock where dwell the Free,
      That citadel against whose front in vain
Storm up the mad assaults of air and sea
      To shatter down in flaming wreck again.

This, this is Britain, bulwark of our breed,
      Our one sure shield against the hordes of hate.
Smite her, and we are smitten; wound her, we bleed.
      Yet firm she stands and fears no thrust of fate.

Stands she, and shall;—but not by guns alone,
      And ships and planes and ramparts. Her own soul
That knows neither to bend nor break,—her own
      Will, hammered to temper,—keeps her whole.

She calls. And we will answer to our last breath.—
Make light of sacrifice, and jest with Death.

Charles G. D. Roberts.[34]

In Canada, America's Problem, *written in 1940, John MacCormac saw the continuing strength of the old country ties.*

In Canada, to be "disloyal" means to be disloyal to Great Britain. Such a crime as disloyalty to Canada scarcely exists. A Canadian may with utter safety impugn the motives of a Canadian government. He may deplore his country's attitude in this or that matter of foreign or domestic policy, disparage her part, or doubt her future. Few will answer him and none will question his right to revile or even despair. But let him challenge the expediency of her present relations with Great Britain and he will bring a hornet's nest about his ears. Let him, for instance, argue that Canada's security depends in the last analysis upon the Monroe Doctrine rather than upon the British Navy and he will provoke a swarm of angry editorials in Canadian newspapers and a myriad indignant letters to their editors.

It will be worse for him if he attacks the policy and still worse if he assails the motives of any British Government. If he does he may be denied space in many influential Canadian newspapers and he will certainly be denied the facilities of the Canadian Broadcasting Corporation.[35]

> *It might be noted that the great Canadian patriotic songs of the Second World War were, "There'll Always Be An England", and "The White Cliffs of Dover"*

The Mosaic Myth

> *So here we had the situation: on one side, a desire for a homogenous population united by a common language and common ideals; on the other a French population determined to survive as a separate cultural and language identity; and in the middle, "inassimilable lumps" who maintained their ethnic identities against both English and French influence.*
>
> *If nothing else, Canadians are political realists. If our ideals cannot be met in a practical manner, then we adjust the ideals to realities. We could not satisfy the dream of a unified identity, so we adjusted the dream and renamed it the "Canadian Mosaic". The Mosaic Myth, almost reluctantly, and perhaps with a feeling that it was a temporary measure, put aside the dream of a common identity, and accepted the fact of diversity.*

How colourless it would be if the world was inhabited by people who had the same tastes, talked the same language, and—more frightening still—thought the same way. We in Canada have learned to respect this truth. As new-comers arrive from other lands we invite them to become citizens when they qualify, and to assume the duties of citizenship, but we are happy to have them make their individual contributions to Canadian life through the culture they bring with them. Our aim is not standardization, sameness. As I have already suggested, our unity is not that of the melting pot. It is based on a recognition and harmonization of differences.

Vincent Massey, 1959.[36]

The present population of Canada is roughly, one-third of Anglo-Saxon stock, one-third of French stock and one-third of many racial groups. There is no Canadian race. We have never had a melting-pot policy toward newcomers. We have never tried to fashion them into one, and only one, mould. Rather we have rejoiced in and we have been strengthened by their special contributions.

Sidney Smith.[37]

Beneath their work the moral core of Canadian nationhood is found in the fact that Canada is a monarchy and in the nature of monarchical allegiance. As America is united at bottom by the convenant, Canada is united at the top by allegiance. Because Canada is a nation founded on allegiance and not on compact, there is no pressure for uniformity, there is no Canadian way of life. Any one, French, Irish, Ukrainian or Eskimo, can be a subject of the Queen and a citizen of Canada without in any way changing or ceasing to be himself.

W. L. Morton.[38]

I know a very clever man, an articulate, alert, highly intelligent professor who, after he'd lived two years in Canada, asked me, "Why does there have to be another country up here at the top of North America?" He was from the U.S., of course, and he was ready to make the mass assumption that there was no reason imaginable to live in a way different from the way people live in the States. The tendency of U.S. history has been to sink the minority in the mass — all but the one minority that won't go down, the Negroes. In Canada, the minorities — whether cultural, religious, ethnic, whether Bluenoses, Spud Islanders, Italians, Ukrainians or, God knows, French — have always and utterly refused to assimilate. And *that*, in reply to my professor friend, is why there's another country at the top of North America. This country offers an alternative life style to people who do not want to share in the benefits and deficiences of mass society. . . .

Hugh Hood, 1967.[39]

To these fine sentiments historian Arthur Lower adds a more hard-headed comment.

The notion that is sometimes heard about Canada being a "mosaic", rather than a "melting pot" like the United States, is not the product of hard thinking. No one in Canada would contemplate with equanimity a dozen little racial enclaves separated from the general community. The only reality there is in such vague nonsense is the fact that, Canadian national symbolism not yet having developed far, the new-comer has not been called upon quite as forcibly to conform publicly. Since we have had no George Washingtons to make "Farewell Addresses", children of foreign parentage do not have to learn "Farewell Addresses" by heart.

A.R.M. Lower, *Canadians in the Making*, 1958.[40]

Symbols that Divide

Lower's observation concerning the undeveloped state of national symbolism in Canada is worthy of consideration. Other nations have symbols which unite their people; in Canada our symbols, songs, heroes, flags, have served mainly to divide. The search for a suitable Canadian anthem, which required more than a century for its fulfilment, is a case in point. "God Save The King" or "Queen", which until recently brought Canadians crashing to their feet in movie theatres and hockey arenas, was really the Royal Anthem. Even confirmed monarchists had to admit, albeit reluctantly, that it was not a distinctively Canadian anthem. Most English-speaking Canadians held out for "The Maple Leaf Forever", written by Alexander Muir in 1867.

In days of yore, from Britain's shore,
    Wolfe the dauntless hero came,
And planted firm Britannia's flag
    On Canada's fair domain.
Here may it wave, our boast, our pride,
    And, joined in love together,
The Thistle, Shamrock, Rose entwine,
    The Maple Leaf forever!   [41]

French Canadians could hardly be expected to embrace such sentiments. Instead, they sang "O Canada", sometimes, it was rumoured, in place of "God Save The King"! Such behaviour was incomprehensible to many English Canadians. Still, there were some of Anglo-Saxon descent who could see the reason and justice for preferring "O Canada."

...Did you ever hear a company of French-Canadians sing "O! Canada"? Did you ever observe the effect of asking a company of English-Canadians to sing "The Maple Leaf"? The sentiment of "O! Canada" may not be all-embracing enough, possibly because it has too much of the Cross in it. But it is Canada that the verses laud. The words may be sung by any Canadian who venerates the Cross without feeling that he is a stranger to their throbbing soul. In Quebec the children and old people sing it with equal fervour. They know every syllable of it. To hear them is to receive a kindred thrill to that which comes when the sons of Wales, among their immemorial hills, wake the echoes with "Land of my Fathers," and when the daughters of Alsace exult in "The Marseillaise."

What congregation of English-Canadians can spontaneously, unanimously, sing all of "The Maple Leaf"? It is the best we have; but its lines are not known to the English as "O! Canada" is known to the French. It alludes to the senior Canadians only in a boastful reference to the conquest. It forgets that Wolfe appropriated what others had begun. The shamrock, thistle and rose entwine; but there is no historical implication which Canadians who are neither Irish, Scotch nor English can equally acclaim. It is a colonial song. It can never be the truly national anthem for the typical Canadian, when he is announced to his international brethren.

Arthur Hawkes, *The Birthright*, 1914.[42]

Time has solved the problem. "O Canada" is now accepted as the national anthem, although some old-stock Canadians are displeased that it has replaced "God Save The Queen", and are convinced that it was imposed upon Canada by French Power. The words of "O Canada" are presented here for those Canadians to whom they are unfamiliar.

O Canada! Our home and native land!
True patriot love in all thy sons command.
With glowing hearts we see thee rise,
The True North strong and free!
From far and wide, O Canada, we stand on guard for thee.
God keep our land glorious and free!
O Canada, we stand on guard for thee,
O Canada, we stand on guard for thee.

Heroes as symbols of national pride and identity are also absent in our traditions. Once again, the basic duality in Canada is at fault. Jean-Charles Falardeau reveals how his education in Quebec gave him a viewpoint completely opposed to impressions an English Canadian might gain from his exposure to history.

I was born in Quebec City where non-French people were and still are so few in number and geographically and socially concentrated in such a self-segregated minority that one could, as I did, spend all one's younger and later years without even noticing them. My earliest, blurred recollection of reference to "les Anglais" is associated with the teaching of Canadian history at the parochial school. The English were to be hated for the "déportation des Acadiens." The real heroes of the Seven Years' War were the French. Montcalm and Lévis overshadowed the touching image of the valiant, poetic Wolfe. The English régime climaxed in the "révolte des patriotes de 1837-8." From this event, we shifted to a colourless Confederation era in which neither teachers nor pupils were interested....

...The little jingle of Canadian history which I had learned at the primary school was orchestrated, at college, into a Beethoven-like, devastating concerto in which the French soloists were the admirable protagonists in a duel against endlessly renewed English furies. The heroes of my history of Canada then were Papineau, Chénier, Mercier, Bourassa. The 24th of May was celebrated as "le jour de Dollard," not as Victoria Day. The writings of the Abbé Groulx were the stock-in-trade for our rhetorical essays. I had a fairly good geographical idea of my country. I had no idea whatsoever of what life was like outside Quebec. The "English-Canadians" were the descendants of those who had crushed the Papineau rebellion, had hanged Riel, had approved the Canadian participation in the Boer War, and had imposed conscription in 1917.

Jean-Charles Falardeau, *Roots and Values in Canadian Lives*, 1960.[43]

But such differences were nothing compared to the fury which would be unleashed over the flag. Since 1763 the Union Jack has flown in Canada, and there have been Canadians to whom the idea of any other emblem was unthinkable. The Union Jack symbolized the British heritage of liberty; it showed our links with the Empire and Commonwealth; it confirmed our unique position as a free monarchy in the American continent; it was the flag under which Canadian soldiers fought and died. In song and verse Canadians confirmed their allegiance to the Union Jack—the Flag.

Raise the flag, our glorious banner,
O'er this fair Canadian land,
From the stern Atlantic Ocean
To the far Pacific strand.

Raise the flag with shouts of gladness,
'Tis the banner of the free!
Brightly beaming, proudly streaming,
'Tis the flag of liberty.

E. G. Nelson, 1909.[44]

Rumours of closer ties with and possibly annexation to the United States, caused this song to be written in 1877.

Shall we break the plight of youth
    And pledge us to an alien love?
No! we hold our faith and truth,
    Trusting to the God above.
Stand Canadians, firmly stand
Round the flag of Fatherland.[45]

Generations of Canadian school children would solemnly intone the following poems on important occasions, especially Victoria Day—the 24th of May.

The Colours of the Flag

We'll stand by the dear old flag, boys,
    Whatever be said or done,
Though the shots come fast, as we face the blast,
    And the foe be ten to one—
Though our only reward to be the thrust of a sword
    And a bullet in heart or brain.
What matters one gone, if the flag float on
    And Britain be Lord of the main!

Ontario Teachers' Manual, 1915.[46]

The Union Jack

It's only a small piece of bunting,
    It's only an old coloured rag;
Yet thousands have died for its honour,
    And shed their best blood for the flag.

It's charged with the cross of St. Andrew,
    Which, of old, Scotland's heroes has led;
It carries the cross of St. Patrick,
    For which Ireland's bravest had bled.

Joined with these is our old English ensign,
    St. George's red cross on white field;
Round which, from Richard to Roberts,
    Britons conquer or die, but ne'er yield.

Ontario Teachers' Manual, 1915.[47]

"Ne'er yield" became the watchword of those determined to maintain the flag which was under attack. The assault came not only from French Canadians for whom the Union Jack would always be a British, not a Canadian symbol, but from other native Canadians of both British and European background who sought a more Canadian identity.

By the end of the Second World War there was a definite growth of opinion favouring a distinctive Canadian flag. We had come the route from colony to fully independent nation; we had played an important part in the war; we were accepting new responsibilities in the United Nations and postwar world. Perhaps it was time for us to put aside symbols of our childhood as a nation, and state, by choosing a flag, our manhood.

Some Canadians say that Canada should not have her own flag but that she should use only the Union Jack or the red ensign with the Canadian emblem in the fly. They say that it was the flag of their forefathers and is good enough for them. They say that the Union Jack is the flag of the British Empire or, worse still, of the British Commonwealth of Nations, but it is not. It is the flag of the United Kingdom only and when flown officially outside that country asserts possession or ownership by the United Kingdom, or when flown by individuals asserts patriotism to the United Kingdom. Real Canadians say that their country should have a national flag that asserts possession and ownership by Canada and, when flown by individual Canadians, would assert patriotism to Canada. The claims of those who wish to have the Union Jack or the red ensign, then, are supported by their wish to show their patriotism to the United Kingdom and not by any wish to show patriotism to Canada.

The demands in the press, during the sittings of the Flag Committee, for a flag which has the Union Jack in it shows very clearly that there are many persons in Canada who cannot be considered as patriotic Canadians for their patriotic sentiments are in favor of the United Kingdom, instead of being in favor of their own country.

T. S. Ewart, *A Flag For Canada*, 1947.[48]

Such was one view, which enraged traditionalists. Other Canadians, who accepted the need for a flag, believed that any new emblem would have to bear the stamp of our solution to most problems, compromise.

Tired but happy, I have emerged from my studio with the design for the new Canadian flag. It wasn't easy, believe me, to strike the compromise between the traditional heraldry of both French and English Canada, while maintaining integrity of concept and avoiding annoying those who don't want a new flag at all.

But I think I've got it:

A red-and-blue beaver, rampant on a field of white, with a comic-strip bubble coming out of the mouth in which are contained the first few notes of "Alouette."

To be on the safe side I have shaped the beaver's tail so that it looks like a maple leaf to English-speaking Canadians and a fleur-de-lis to French-speaking Canadians. (See the rather poor reproduction accompanying this article.)

This flag avoids many of the pitfalls of previous designs. For one thing, it cannot be hung upside down accidentally, as can the Union Jack and the Stars and Stripes. Upside down the beaver is clearly standing on his head. Since it is unlikely that a beaver would be whistling "Alouette" in this position, only the densest of decoration committees would fail to right it before the annual dinner.

Another advantage of this flag is that it doesn't include a lot of historical devices whose derivation is hard to remember. For example, the Union Jack is made up of the crosses of St. George, St. Andrew and St. Patrick, but I had to look this up in the encyclopedia to be sure. A person doesn't need an encyclopedia to recognize a beaver. Unless, that is, he lives in

My gift to the nation—the Canadian Flag.

a part of the world where the beaver is unknown, in which case he may take it for a large rat. There is no point in worrying about these ignorant foreigners, however.

The flag also avoids a representational design like the Stars and Stripes, whose forty-eight stars will be hopelessly jumbled when Hawaii is given its statehood. This is why I rejected an earlier design of mine made up of ten beavers gnawing on a large maple leaf. You never know when you're going to get more beavers. . . .

Eric Nicol, *Shall We Join the Ladies*, 1955.[49]

Eric Nicol's comments were more cynical than funny. What with politicians shilly-shallying, pressure groups demanding retention of traditional symbols, flag design contests, there was every possibility that some horror would emerge as our national symbol. We were saved from this by something which Bruce Hutchison sensed when he wrote Canada: Tomorrow's Giant, *in 1957.*

Something strange, nameless, and profound moves in Canada today. It cannot be seen or labeled, but it can be heard and felt—a kind of whisper from far away, a rustle as of wind in prairie poplars, a distant river's voice, or the shuffle of footsteps in a midnight street. It is less a sound than a sense of motion.

Something moves as it has never moved before in this land, moves dumbly in the deepest runnels of a collective mind, yet by sure direction toward a known goal. Sometimes by thought, more often by intuition, the Canadian people make the final discovery. They are discovering themselves.

That passion of discovery which once sent birchbark canoes down unmapped waters, pushed railways across the Rockies, and dragged men to the frozen sea turns inward to explore a darker terrain. The nation labors in the travail of self-discovery and, by this labor, proves that it is in truth a nation, the home of a people. . . .

The Canadian whose father accepted Canada as a spiritual dependency of some external power is thinking of it now solely as a nation in its own right. Though the nation is diverse, confused, self-centered, a little dizzy and smug from success at the moment, it is essentially whole. It has become cognate and organic. The Canadian knows, better than his father knew, that he belongs to it and no other.[50]

Something was moving in Canada. The people knew it, and the politicians sensed it. The Liberals led by Lester Pearson took office in 1963 under a pledge to establish a distinctive Canadian emblem. By 1964, Prime Minister Pearson was determined to put forward a flag bearing the Maple Leaf. In May of that year he went into the lion's den of the opposition to the flag—the Royal Canadian Legion Convention in Winnipeg—to present his views.

When I went overseas in 1915, I had as comrades in my section men whose names were Cameron, Kimura, English, Bleidenstein, DeChapin, O'Shaughnessy. We didn't fall in, or fall out, as Irish Canadians, French Canadians, Dutch Canadians, Japanese Canadians. We wore the same uniform, with the same maple leaf badge, and we were proud to be known as Canadians, to serve as Canadians, and to die, if that had to be, as Canadians. I wish our country had more of that spirit today, of unity, "togetherness," and resolve; the spirit that was shown by Canadians in time of war when the survival of our country was at stake. Well, the survival of our country as a united and strong federal state is at stake today. . . .

What we need is a patriotism that will put Canada ahead of its parts; that will think more of our future destiny than our past mistakes; that rejects emphatically the idea that, politically, we are, or should become, a federation of two associated states—some kind of prewar Austria-Hungary. We should have none of such separatism or of petty, narrow nationalism of any kind. . . .

. . .we are all, or should be, Canadians—and unhyphenated, with pride in our nation and its citizenship, pride in the symbols of that citizenship.

The flag is one such symbol. . . .

I believe that today a flag designed around the maple leaf will symbolize —will be a true reflection of—the new Canada. Today there are five million or more Canadians whose tradition is not inherited from the British Isles, but who are descendants of the original French founders of our country. There are another five million, or more, who have come to Canada from other far-away lands, with a heritage neither British nor French. I believe that a Canadian flag—as distinctive as the maple leaf in the Legion badge—will bring them all closer to those of us of British stock and make us all better, more united, Canadians. . . .

But I want to add this, ladies and gentlemen, that while I am concerned about this whole question of national symbols, national anthem, national flag, and all they mean to our country, I am even more concerned with making Canada the kind of country—with freedom, economic security, social justice, and opportuinity for all—over which we will be proud to have our flag fly.

People are more important than emblems.[51]

You're selling Canada to the pea-soupers!

A legionnaire's reaction.[52]

We have a despairing feeling that this insipid flag, instead of promoting national unity, will produce only an indifferent response. . . .Whatever may be said about the use of the maple leaf as a Canadian emblem in the past, it has never gained anyone's vigorous allegiance, and it involves no commitment to the human fact of Canada.

Canadian historians' letter to the Prime Minister.[53]

The fight was carried to Parliament; there were furious debates, predictions of doom, hearkenings of past allegiance, and bitter personal insults. In the end, the flag bearing the maple leaf was adopted as the national flag of Canada. The official flag-raising ceremony took place on Parliament Hill and Lester Pearson delivered the formal inaugural address.

If our nation, by God's grace, endures a thousand years, this day, the fifteenth day of February 1965, will always be remembered as a milestone in Canada's national progress. It is impossible for me not to be deeply moved on such an occasion or to be insensible to the honour and privilege of taking part in it.

There are many in this country who regret the replacement of the Red Ensign by the Red Maple Leaf. Their feelings and their emotions should be honoured and respected. But I am sure, now that the decision has been made by the representatives of the Canadian people in Parliament assembled, that all Canadians, as good patriots, will accept that decision and fly with pride our national flag.[54]

Newfoundland will continue to fly the Union Jack if we are the last place on earth to do so.

Joey Smallwood.[55]

Newfoundland now flies the Union Jack as the official flag of the Province.·

Towards New Definitions of Identity

All that we have seen and heard has led us to the conviction that Canada is in the most critical period of its history since Confederation. We believe that there is a crisis, in the sense that Canada has come to a time when decisions must be taken and developments must occur leading either to its break-up, or to a new set of conditions for its future existence. We do not know whether the crisis will be short or long. We are convinced that it is here. The signs of danger are many and serious.

Royal Commission on Bilingualism and Biculturalism, 1965.[56]

These grim words referred to the great crisis of the 1960s, when the long-smouldering economic, political and emotional discontent of French Canada emerged first as the "Quiet Revolution" and then burst forth as separatism. A vital part of that discontent concerned the French identity and its role in Canada. French Canadians were saying: "If, with our language and culture, we are not accepted as Candians everywhere in Canada; if, as French Canadians we cannot share in the opportunities throughout Canada, then perhaps we should reconsider our position in Confederation. If complete fulfilment of our identity involves separating from Canada, then so be it!"

Prime Minister Pearson responded to the crisis by appointing a Royal Commission on Bilingualism and Biculturalism. That commission, in its studies and reports, left no doubt where it stood on the question of identity.

Our terms of reference make it clear that the Canadian Confederation should recognize the principle of equality between English-speaking and French-speaking Canadians. This concept of equal partnership is the mainspring of our terms of reference.[57]

From evidence so far accumulated, it appears to us that English-speaking Canadians as a whole must come to recognize the existence of a vigorous French-speaking society within Canada, and to find out more about the aspirations, frustrations and achievements of French-speaking Canadians, in Quebec and outside it. They must come to understand what it means to be a member of a minority, or of a smaller partner people, and to be ready to give that minority assurances which are unnecessary for a majority. More than a century ago, Sir John A. Macdonald wrote to an English-speaking friend: "Treat them as a nation and they will act as a free people generally do—generously. Call them a faction and they become factious." They have to face the fact that, if Canada is to continue to exist, there must be a true partnership, and that the partnership must be worked out as between equals. They must be prepared to discuss in a forthright, open-minded way the practical implications of such a partnership. . . .[58]

We recommend that English and French be formally declared the official languages of the Parliament of Canada, of the federal courts, of the federal government, and of the federal administration.

We recommend that the provinces of New Brunswick and Ontario themselves declare that they recognize English and French as official languages and that they accept the language régimes that such recognition entails.

We recommend that bilingual districts be established throughout Canada and that negotiations between the federal government and the provincial government concerned define the exact limits of each bilingual district.

For the federal capital area we recommend: a) that the English and French languages should have full equality of status throughout the area; b) that all services should be available at all levels of public administration in the two languages.

We recommend that the right of Canadian parents to have their children educated in the official language of their choice be recognized in the educational systems, the degree of implementation to depend on the concentration of the minority population.[59]

> *The federal government accepted the concept that Canada was a partnership of two cultures and languages. Through the Official Languages Act, it set out to make bilingualism and biculturalism work. But the implications of bilingualism and biculturalism have not been accepted by everybody, either on the intellectual, emotional, or practical levels.*

I find myself unable to think that there is anything very special in Canada about a man being French, of French derivation. So what! He's of Ukrainian, of Russian derivation, of Portuguese derivation, of Scottish, of Irish derivation. So what! . . .

I don't believe that Canada ought to be two races, that special rights ought be held by two races, English and French. I don't accept that. I don't think that either English-speaking Canadians, or French should have any special rights.

I think that the province of Quebec, not French people, but the province

BY SID BARRON

of Quebec, should have all the rights that were guaranteed her, that are unmistakably named in the constitution of Canada. They should have these rights. It would be intolerable to touch them. Rights must remain enshrined.

These rights are not the rights of being a sort of co-equal nation within Canada with the English-speaking Canadians. I don't accept that. I don't believe it was ever intended for one moment.

Joseph R. Smallwood, *Peril and Glory, 1966.*[60]

On July 1, 1972, a nationally televised outdoor concert on Parliament Hill in Ottawa was presented almost completely in French. A small tempest blew up over the incident; some English newspapers asked indignantly why the emphasis was so heavily on the French language; others suggested that the nation had once again been polarized, perhaps deliberately, by the Secretary of State who was responsible for the production. Prime Minister Trudeau commented rather tartly on the reaction.

I think the July 1 incident is a good issue for us because if English-speaking Candians could wax so indignant, and I believe rightly . . .they should remember that for 100 years French-speaking Canadians have been exposed to celebrations heavily based on the English side.[61]

Unilingual civil servants have not been pleased by the government's bilingual policy.

If you dig you'll find more the 90 per cent of the non-French civil servants at all levels are waiting to punish the government—more particularly, Trudeau, Pelletier and Drury, for their bulldozing tactics, for the waste in human and material resources, for all the abuses.

It doesn't matter much what you do in government today as long as it is done bilingually.

You can get away with anything if you have a French name—poor work, extended lunch breaks and all the rest.

All things being balanced, the contract usually goes to Quebec.

Non-French supervisors are fearful of disciplining French employees. The non-French initiate: the French translate.

Managers are driven up the wall by French language classes, several mornings or afternoons a week, regardless of the work pile. Since the managers seldom have an opportunity to use it, they forget it almost as fast as they learn it. . . .

Civil servant, 1972.[62]

We are going to make sure it [the bilingual program] is accepted, because we feel we have the support of the great majority of Canadians.

Prime Minister Trudeau, 1972.[63]

The Third Force

We respectfully acknowledge the fact that the problem is primarily with the two founding races, the French-speaking Canadians and the British Canadians, but over the years a third force, a vital force, has emerged and this force must be recognized.

Royal Commission on Bilingualism and Biculturalism, 1965.[64]

In all the talk of bilingualism, where would the third force, those Canadians of origin other than French or English, fit in?

Our Canada is no longer made of two founding races, or should I say floundering races, but through immigration is made up of numerous races, and our real problem is to blend them into one Canada, not two or more.

Royal Commission on Bilingualism and Biculturalism, 1965.[65]

What image of Canada would do justice to the presence of these varied ethnic groups? This question preoccupied western participants especially, and the answer they often gave was "multiculturalism", or, more elaborately, "the Canadian mosaic". They asked: If two cultures are accepted, why not many? Why should Canada not be a country in which a multitude of cultural groups live side by side yet distinct from one another, all contributing to a richly varied society? Certainly, it was stated, the mosaic idea was infinitely preferable to the "melting pot".

Royal Commission on Bilingualism and Biculturalism, 1965.[66]

The unrest and disagreement of the two founding nations of Canada have brought a new challenge to the Poles in this country. The time has arrived for them to closely examine their position and to decide on a course of action for the future. They can become neither English-Canadians nor French-Canadians, but must remain as they are, Canadians of Polish origin.

Under no circumstances can they take sides in the dispute between the two major elements in this country, but rather must strive to form a bridge between them. They cannot accomplish this on their own, so they must unite with other ethnic groups and together form a balance and a unifying force that will help to build a stronger Canada—a Canada where every ethnic group will retain its cultural identity, sentiments, and pride in its heritage; a Canada where each ethnic group will integrate voluntarily rather than forcibly, bringing its best value to the common cultural treasure house.

William Boleslaus Makowski, *History and Integration of Poles in Canada*, 1967.[67]

If the French people think that they lost a lot of their rights since Confederation, what should the Indian say? They lost the whole land. ...As soon as an Indian wants to succeed in Canadian life he must assimilate....

Indian chiefs, 1964.[68]

In 400 years many people have taken physical things from us... and now there is a cry from my people north and south of the border. Give us back our heritage.

Walter Currie, Ojibwa Indian, 1972.[69]

The way of the Indian has been a downward trail ever since the White Man first came to upset our long standing social organization. Our religion and our dances nave been suppressed, much of our culture forgotten. The old way of life, the customs and traditions, the authority of the chiefs, the family discipline, all these have had to change as we tried to adapt to the White Man's way.

Chief John Albany, Coast Salish, 1963.[70]

They are using education to destroy the Indian life style.

They are trying to teach my children to go out in the world and grab as much as they can. They make the people selfish. This is so far different from the way of Indian culture, when people lived for the group.

They say they are offering the best possible life and they can't understand why we reject it. But if they were only tolerant enough to see that there are other ways that people are happier living.

No matter how much it hurts, they have to squeeze us in a mold whether we fit or not. I think this is why there is so much hurt in

IN FRENCH OR ENGLISH

society. People are being squeezed out of shape. I think a lot of the people in mental hospitals are a direct result of that.

That is how they are hurting the Indian—stripping him of his Indianness. There is only one thing that produces an Indian and that is his culture. . . .

Our concern is not motivated by sentimentality. There are real and practical reasons why I desire not to see Indianness pass away. I suppose you could say that the value that resides in Indianness is that it stands in contradiction of every value and view held by the dominant society—that society and life-style that has proven itself so harmful to mother earth and all her children.

Alex Jamieson, Iroquois, 1971.[71]

The Final (?) Word on Identity

"We want to survive." All the hopes for a common Canadian identity have been shattered against that instinct which seems to thrive in Canadians. No matter what the background, there has always been determined resistance to a uniform identity which would destroy or dilute an earlier heritage.

Duality, diversity, mosaic, biculturalism—these are the words which classify our style, and they are hardly calculated to stir men's souls. We have had no cries of "United We Stand, Divided We Fall", or "Ein Volk, Ein Reich . . .". Yet in failing to achieve the nineteenth-century dream of national identity, we have avoided the pitfalls and disasters of nationalism gone mad. Perhaps by our muddling we have created something sensible, unique, and truly Canadian.

In 1971 the Canadian government announced a policy known as multiculturalism. In recognizing the Canadian style of nationality, it pronounced what may well be the definitive statement on our identity.

. . .One of man's basic needs is a sense of belonging, and a good deal of contemporary social unrest—in all age groups—exists because this need has not been met. Ethnic groups are certainly not the only way in which this need for belonging can be met, but they have been an important one in Canadian society. Ethnic pluralism can help us overcome or prevent the homogenization and depersonalization of mass society. Vibrant ethnic groups can give Canadians of the second, third, and subsequent generations a feeling that they are connected with tradition and with human experience in various parts of the world and different periods of time. . . .

The sense of identity developed by each citizen as a unique individual is distinct from his national allegiance. There is no reason to suppose that a citizen who identifies himself with pride as a Chinese-Canadian, who is deeply involved in the cultural activities of the Chinese community in Canada, will be less loyal or concerned with Canadian matters than a citizen of Scottish origin who takes part in a bagpipe band or a highland dancing group. Cultural identity is not the same thing as allegiance to a country. Each of us is born into a particular family with a distinct heritage: that is, everyone—French, English, Italian and Slav included—has an "ethnic" background. The more secure we feel in one particular social context, the more we are free to explore our identity beyond it. Ethnic groups often provide people with a sense of belonging which can make them better able to cope with the rest of society than they would as isolated individuals. Ethnic loyalties need not, and usually do not, detract from wider loyalties to community and country.

Canadian identity will not be undermined by multiculturalism. Indeed, we believe that cultural pluralism is the very essence of Canadian identity.[72]

There is Ontario patriotism, Quebec patriotism, or Western patriotism, each based on the hope that it may swallow up the others, but there is no Canadian patriotism, and we can have no Canadian nation when we have no Canadian patriotism.

Henri Bourassa, 1907.[1]

...It is important and obvious that in Canada there are two or three (some say five) distinct Canadas. Even if you lump the French and English together as one community in the East, there remains the gulf of the Great Lakes. The difference between East and West is possibly no greater than that between North and South England, or Bavaria and Prussia; but in this country, yet unconscious of itself, there is so much less to hold them together. The character of the land and the people differs; their interests, as it appears to them, are not the same.

Rupert Brooke, 1916.[2]

3 MY FELLOW CANADIANS

...It is trebly divided—between a West and an East, and a French and an English, in addition to the New World and the Old World division of loyalty.

Wyndham Lewis, 1941.[3]

As a people we don't like each other very much. We tend to feel that our region is being screwed by some other region. Ontario people, for instance, think Montreal gets too much of Ottawa's attention. Quebec people tend to think Ontario is the cause of Quebec unemployment. Westerners think Toronto is robbing them. Maritimers think that central

Canada is ignoring them. People in Northern Ontario think people in Southern Ontario don't care about them.

The Canadian style, as expressed in regionalism, tends to be suspicious, narrow, nasty, even paranoid.

Robert Fulford, 1971.[4]

> As a nation we are fragmented by history, geography, economics and emotion. Our provinces grew out of colonies which were founded at different times, by diverse groups of people, under varied conditions. They grew separately, and developed distinctive styles of life and loyalties. Confederation was an attempt to forge a nation out of the isolated colonies, and create a national identity to which provincial and regional allegiances would be subordinated. We have not succeeded in completely fulfilling this dream. Often Confederation seems to have strengthened, rather than lessened the local loyalties. For it has created situations which have led to feuds between the regions, provinces and peoples of Canada. And towards their fellow Canadians, our people have expressed sentiments ranging from gentle, insulting humour to outright hatred. An examination of the basic duels shows that they have been well-defined by years of diligent practice.

West versus East

Western Canadians, typically, are famed for their hospitality.[5]

Once I picked up a hitch-hiker out west and when I told him I was from the east he got right out of the car.[6]

Toronto is still a cold city to me—and I'm not talking about the weather. I got off the train this morning and asked for directions. No one would answer me. Is this Toronto's hospitality?[7]

> These statements illustrate both the myth and the reality of Western attitudes. Westerners really believe that they are friendly to strangers. They are indeed renowned for hospitality, but only towards fellow Westerners. Towards Easterners, especially Ontarians, and particularly Torontonians, they exhibit resentment and hostility. On meeting an Easterner, a Western Canadian will firmly grasp him by the arm, and in aggressive tones tell him how much more friendly Westerners are to strangers than are Easterners.

Westerners like to believe that the East is unfriendly. It gives them an immense pleasure to relate tales of inhospitable reception in the East, the smug East, the puritan East. One suspects that Westerners would be unhappy if they received a friendly greeting upon arrival in the East. Sometimes the expectation of a hostile reception achieves the level of paranoia. In 1952, when the Edmonton Eskimos arrived in Toronto to play the Argonauts in the Grey Cup game, it was deemed necessary to take certain precautions.

The Esks will drink only Edmonton water carried in special containers while they are in the east. They will eat only Edmonton steaks and loaves of Alberta bread and other food to be flown to Toronto daily.[8]

That Grey Cup game incidentally was the last to be won by an Eastern team for many years. The Western squads began to dominate football, a situation which was seen by some as a sign of Western social, cultural and moral superiority. Analytical articles explained how Western emphasis on team play, solid fundamentals, disciplined work habits, had beaten, and would continue to beat the Eastern teams which emphasized flashy but basically unsound tactics and whose members played for their individual glory.

Beneath the myths exist a solid foundation for the West's dislike of the East. The West has always felt that it has been dominated economically by the powerful moneyed interests of Eastern Canada, and that, in the clutch, its interest will inevitably be sacrificed to Eastern Industry and Money. In My Discovery of the West, *written in 1937, Stephen Leacock described the essence of Western discontent.*

...all the grievances of the West focus on Winnipeg. All the ills of all the provinces and all the parts of them press on Winnipeg. It is therefore in connection with the fate of Winnipeg that one finds a common ground for setting together all this "Bill of grievances" now drawn up by the people of the West against the so-called "money power" of the East. The West, that is to say, has an idea that there is a thing in the East called the "money power" which piles up money in the East as the moon piles up the tides, and leaves the West in low water with the dry shoals sticking out. The West has a further idea that the "money power" has created an ingenious contrivance called the tariff from which the East gets all the benefit and the West none; which compels the farmer on the prairies to buy all the things he needs for his work,—implements

and tractors,—or needs for his life,—motors, clothes, boots, shoes,
everything,—at high prices; while just south of him across an imaginary
line, another set of farmers, situated otherwise just as he is, buy the
same things at much lower prices. From this promised land the Western
Farmer is shut out.[9]

> *Protective tariffs for Eastern industry, high freight rates, low prices
> for wheat, higher costs of manufactured goods—these have been the
> traditional complaints of the West; and, just as traditionally, they seemed
> to have been ignored by governments whose power rests on the support
> of the central provinces of Canada. In the 1970s a new wave of Western
> protest arose with apparently serious intent. Out of the West came
> sounds not just of complaint, but of separatism and revolt.*

The West is not a carbon copy of any other region in Canada or the
U.S., despite wholehearted attempts to make our cities just that. The
West is not a carbon copy of the East, nor is it an extension of American
society.

The West wants to preserve its independence, to create opportunities
for involvement and fulfillment, to develop its own social and cultural
institutions, to give expression to its distinctiveness.

It is a distinctiveness which is worth preserving; which makes the West
in its own particular way just as different and just as much entitled to
special status as any other province or region in Canada. The federal
government's perversion of the federative principle is doing much to
perpetuate the alienation of the West. The West wants the right to develop
freely, creatively, and in its own style. To secure this right the West
has been, and will be, prepared to revolt.

Owen Anderson, Executive Assistant to the Premier of Alberta, 1971.[10]

> *In their talk of revolt, Westerners found a new focus of discontent
> to add to the old complaints.*

The tie that binds western Canada together from the Lakehead to the
Pacific is fear and distrust of "the East."...

Throughout the West, it is now dogma that French-speaking Quebec
has been able to extort favored treatment from Ottawa. This is a source
of intense jealousy.

It is reinforced by the belief that French-speaking Quebec politicians
dominate the Trudeau cabinet.

No matter how well one is prepared for it, the depth and intensity of this resentment still shock. In four weeks in western Canada, I don't think that I heard a single favorable comment about the federal government. And many people went out of their way to complain. . . .

There is no sympathy among westerners for the difficulties encountered by Trudeau and his Quebec colleagues as they attempt to maintain a federalist position in a nationalist Quebec.

If western Canada made some attempt to understand Quebec in the '60s, the prevailing emotion now is impatience. No one in the West any longer asks, "What does Quebec want?" The question has been replaced by a statement: "Let them go".

Peter Desbarats, 1971.[11]

. . .the creation of a French language television station in Edmonton—where fewer than six per cent of viewers list French as their mother tongue but almost eight per cent of the viewers list German and eight per cent Ukrainian as their mother tongue—says some interesting things about the determination of the federal government to push a bilingual policy on all parts of the country, regardless of local needs or circumstances. It also says some interesting things about who is influential in this country and who is not. . . .

The *major* opposition to the "pro-French" movement of national policy over the past decade came from Westerners who had nothing in particular against the French—they simply resented Ottawa's imposition on their style of life and their habits when Pierre Trudeau suggested that at least a substantial minority of people outside the Ontario border should have special language facilities, special schools, and special language rights not available to other ethnic groups that were at least as numerically important in their communities as the French, if not more important.

John J. Barr, *The Unfinished Revolt*, 1971.[12]

Maybe I'm a bit of a bigot or not properly informed, but I'm slightly prejudiced against the attitudes of Quebec and the obviously special treatment that is being given to Quebec within Confederation.

Westerner, 1971.[13]

I would rather go for a holiday in the western or southwestern United States than in eastern Canada. I've had the misfortune to visit Quebec on several occasions and I feel that I'm not wanted there.

Westerner, 1971.[14]

When Solange Chaput Rolland, a sensitive and distinguished French-Canadian lady, visited Winnipeg, she encountered one form of Western hospitality.

We have spent our first evening in Winnipeg with some old friends and they startled us with their views on Quebec and on Canada.

"What has Canada done to make us proud of being Canadians?"

"Why should nine provinces be made to change their attitudes and their way of life for the sake of one?"

"Quebec is pushing too hard and we won't cater to you."

"Language is the only link we have with other Canadians."

This peculiar conversation, I was told hours later, was intended to "provoke my reaction". I have none. Tonight, I am, as the boxers say, punch-drunk.

Solange Chaput-Rolland, *My Country, Canada or Quebec?* 1966.[15]

1971 saw the birth of the Western Canada party whose aim was better Western representation in Ottawa. The president of that party had some interesting views concerning the "Quebec Question".

He believes that the people of Quebec are being held back by leaders who are forcing them to speak French. It all started when the "high mucky-mucks" came over from France, looked at the land, then decided to import serfs to work it. The best way to keep the serfs in line was to keep them ignorant and the best way to keep them ignorant was to keep them from speaking English, the language of commerce in North America.

"If a secret ballot were allowed on being able to learn English in Quebec," he said, "you'd have a resounding 'yes' because the ordinary people in Quebec want to learn English so they can get out and become part of this country. They're hampered because of their language.

"If you want to know how this country is changing, pick up the telephone and phone Ottawa. But I'd suggest you have someone who's bilingual because you're going to be answered in French. And if you get a wrong number the voice that comes on is going to come on in French."[16]

Western protest gathers force in attacks upon Eastern "cultural domination". In a letter to the editor of Saturday Night, *a westerner gave vent to long-standing frustration.*

Sir: I have faithfully subscribed to each new Canadian periodical that has appeared because I believe in supporting home industry. However, each of these either starts out as or quickly becomes, a strictly "Ontario" or Eastern Canada publication. Every so often a pundit takes a trip via Air Canada across from Ontario to British Columbia and then writes a learned article on "This Great Canada of Ours," touches lightly on maybe Winnipeg, Calgary, Vancouver, Victoria, Edmonton, then breathes a sigh of relief that he is back in the smog of great Toronto. Is Saskatchewan not still a part of Canada? Do we not have capable reporters in Western Canada who can paint a true word picture of this land and maybe mention some of the cities and places that are as unknown to Torontonians as the top of Mount Everest.

In your last issue there is a learned article by Tom Hendry, "The Canadian theatre's sudden explosion." Not a single word of the Globe Theatre in Regina or any other company in Saskatchewan. Maybe you should send some missionaries out to this backward area and show some compassion for the poor benighted natives.

If you really want to find out about "separatism" in English-speaking Canada, have one of your staff spend some time in Western Canada. We are very close to Montana and there is beginning to be a strong undercurrent of thought that we should be considering joining with the U.S.A. rather than simply be handy people who are forced to buy "Canadian." If we are to be vassals let's be more comfortable vassals![17]

In February, 1973, Western television producers presented a brief decrying the tyranny of Eastern control of the Canadian Broadcasting Corporation.

It has been evident for many years that western Canadians feel little or no relationship to the CBC English TV network—to them it is an eastern thing, a Toronto parochial organization pretending to be able to interpret Canada to Canadians.

Events of political and social significance to western Canadians are ignored in favor of stories on the striptease joints of Yonge Street.[18]

It's time to stop being ruled by the Toronto rat's nest of the CBC.[19]

Manitoba Liberal leader, I.H. Asper echoed the complaint.

He was tired of seeing every CBC program being produced in the

East. And when the corporation paid any attention to the West, there was always a mouth organ wailing, breezes blowing through the wheat and the picture of a rustic farmer.

We're always portrayed as some sort of backwoods people.[20]

> *In the 1970s, the West suddenly and gleefully discovered that it too held power in the form of natural resources, especially oil and gas. Premier Lougheed of Alberta commented on the significance of that situation.*

So many times in Confederation and the history of Canada, the West, and Alberta in particular, we have been the ones seeking—we haven't been the ones holding the cards, if you like. We now do hold the cards in terms of energy.[21]

> *When Lougheed announced that Eastern consumers of natural gas would have to pay more than Albertans, a cry of outrage came from the East. Fellow Westerners supported Lougheed to the hilt.*

Listen, we have been paying above world prices for years for what is produced in Ontario behind a tariff wall.

If what is produced in Ontario is sold at higher than world prices in Western Canada, then I think that what is produced in western Canada...natural gas, is not going to be sold at low world prices.to the consumers in Ontario. You can't have it both ways.

James Richardson, Western representative in the federal cabinet, 1973.[22]

...the West's patience is nearing an end after 100 years of exploitation at the hands of an independent Eastern Canadian industrial society. . . .The action by Alberta is only the tip of the iceberg of Western anger.

Manitoba Liberal leader I. H. Asper, 1973.[23]

> *That the West's anger is legitimate, and seriously purposeful, can be seen in Prime Minister Trudeau's reaction. These words, remember, came from a man who is not beloved in the West, who once said, "Why should I care about your wheat?", and whose party's strength in the West was annihilated in the 1972 federal election.*

I want to understand the West. Without this understanding, we as Liberals will cease to be a national party. . . .Tell us what you want."

Prime Minister Trudeau, 1973.[24]

British Columbia: The Promised Land

To the native of the prairies Alberta is the far West; British Columbia the near East.

Edward A. McCourt, *Canada West in Fiction*, 1949.

It will be noticed that British Columbia is not considered part of Western Canada. There are those, both British Columbians and other Canadians, who would not even consider it part of Canada. "Beyond Canada" has often been the extended version of B.C. British Columbia stands by itself, a strange contradiction in Canada, for it is neither East nor West. It is the haven of those who, having escaped from the regions east of the Rockies, immediately discard all emotional ties with the original homeland and devote their loyalty to the Promised Land. British Columbia is the home of politicians who behave in eccentric fashion. Its climate, at least in the southern regions, is un-Canadian. One reads that British Columbians are irritated by snow-tire ads which come via TV stations controlled by snow-bound souls east of the Rockies.

British Columbia was not an original member of Confederation. She joined in 1871, with the understanding that a transcontinental railway would be built to link the Pacific coast with the east. This union was not the result of a great love affair, and British Columbians did not throw themselves wholeheartedly into the marriage.

I say that the United States will probably ultimately absorb both this Colony and the Dominion of Canada. . . . No union between this Colony and Canada can permanently exist, unless it be to the material and pecuniary advantage of this Colony to remain in the union. . . . The people of this Colony have, generally speaking, no love for Canada; they have but little sentimentality, and care little about the distinctions between the form of government of Canada and the United States.

Therefore no union on account of love need be looked for.

J. S. Helmcken, 1870.[25]

True Loyalty's to Motherland
And not to Canada,
The love we bear is second-hand
To any step-mama.

British Columbia slogan, 1870.[26]

...I remember when I came to Canada twenty-three years ago, some British Columbians corrected me rather sharply when I casually referred to them as "Canadians". "We are not Canadians", they said to me, "we are British Columbians."

James Cappon, 1911.[27]

His contempt for Canadians was paralysing. Your British Columbian old-timer can stand the Britisher if he does not "put on too much style"; but he thinks the Canadian—by which he means Eastern Canadian—too mean to live. The Canadian retaliates by calling him a shell-back. It is very curious how the British Columbian prefers the Englishman to the Canadian of the Eastern provinces.

Douglas Sladen, *On the Cars and Off*, 1895.[28]

Despite the aloofness of British Columbia towards Confederation, there has been little of the deep resentment which has characterized attitudes of other Western provinces. Certainly there have been clashes between B.C. and the federal government over the use of natural resources, and resentment concerning "Quebec Power". But B.C. has not suffered economically in Confederation. There is no paranoia in the Pacific province, but rather a feeling of confidence and a belief that B.C. could "go it alone" if necessary. An interview with Paddy Sherman, editor of the Vancouver Province, *reveals this attitude.*

"Is B.C. separatist?"

"No. There is no question of our leaving Canada, but if the political situation became too tense, we might seek the status of a dominion allied with the British Commonwealth. We owe nothing to the rest of Canada. Our population comes chiefly from England, the United States, and European countries. We are pragmatists here; we seldom ask why we must do this or that, but *how* we can do it."...

"You are British Columbians first, then."

"Every province is the same," observes Sherman. "We become real Canadians in times of crisis, during a war or to offset an economic recession. Then we wake up to our Canadian identity. Here we lead a privileged life; we are able to golf, ski, sail, climb mountains, garden, ten months every year. Philosophical discussion is not popular in B.C."

Solange Chaput Rolland, *My Country, Canada or Quebec?*, 1966.[29]

Here we come to the essence of B.C. regionalism—its pride in the climate and scenery. Somehow a native British Columbian assumes that there is a connection between the natural beauty of his environment and his own moral worth. Newcomers from less well-endowed regions beyond the mountains must recognize the connection and pay homage to it. An Easterner should register awe at the sight of the mountains, fear at crossing the Capilano suspension bridge, and humble envy of gardens in Victoria. To read Bruce Hutchison is to understand much of the British Columbian mystique.

Let me come to British Columbia in the spring, in the lush first days of April. Let me go to bed in the frozen prairies and wake among the green maple leaves, the swelling catkins, the uncurling ferns, and the blossom of old orchards beside the railway. Or blindfold me and stand me on the rear platform of the train and I will tell you, by the smell and the very feel of the air, when we pass through Golden and Revelstoke, when we reach the sagebrush country of Kamloops, when we are breathing the brave stone smell of the Fraser canyon and the meadow airs of the Chilliwack Valley. Every station and siding, every brook and field and little farm I would surely recognize by instinct, though I were blind. This is our own incomparable land.

Better still, let me steal in by night, lying, sleepless, on a lower berth, watching the moonlight skim the Thompson, the velvet hills of the Dry Belt, the lights of lonely farm houses, the bands of cattle staring at the passing spectacle of the train, and the mare with her new foal gazing from the meadow. Let me lie there and see the billows of smoke playing among the stone cliffs, and the dark, calm mass of forests and the awful bulk of the canyon at Hell's Gate.

Then, as dawn breaks, the canyon widens suddenly and there are the fields of the Pacific coast, deep green, rank, overgrown, and succulent, each with its own mountain in the corner. There are the wild currant blossoms dripping red and smelling of all the Aprils of the ages, the fierce growth of bracken, the white plumes of elderberry, and everywhere the hungry forest, marching back, with scouts of fern and alder, with shock troops of fir and hemlock, upon the settler's clearing. There in the broadening river are the great rafts of reddish cedar, the sea gulls roosting on them with wise and ancient look. There at last is the ocean and the unreal, flat shape of ships, the smell of the salt water, and the mountains dropping into it at a single leap.

BY SID BARRON

Wild and upheaved, and forever changing, forever new, is this land. What hopes our fathers had for it! This was a land fit for men to live in, not just to struggle and exist in—men who had bleached in the prairie suns and frozen in the prairie winters, men who had stifled in the crowded, used-up air of eastern cities and the old world, men who wanted to be alone and free.

Bruce Hutchison, *The Unknown Country*, 1948.[30]

That is the attitude which makes British Columbians so irritating and explains why an item such as the following is greeted with glee in the East.

Still on the west coast, a Toronto lawyer met a Vancouver friend in the Georgia Hotel coffee shop last week at 10 p.m. The friend ordered a small steak, the Toronto lawyer asked if the place was licensed, found that it was and ordered a beer. His Vancouver friend said, "You must realize that we are getting pretty big-time out here. We've got lots of liquor licenses, Kosygin's here tonight and the Montreal Canadiens played here yesterday." Just then the waitress arrived with my lawyer friend's beer, "Do you want a glass?" she said.

The Toronto Sun, 1972.[31]

Ontario versus Quebec

This is the classic confrontation in Canadian history, the longest-standing feud, and the conflict with the deepest significance for the nation. It has pitted the two largest and most powerful provinces against each other as champions of opposing religious, languages, loyalties and politics. In the great crises which have threatened our unity, the Riel affair, the Boer War, Conscription in World War One and Two, Protestant, English-speaking, "Loyal" Ontario has battled Catholic, French-speaking, "Nationalistic" Quebec; and so often the original problem changed its complexion until it became a struggle to see whose will would prevail—Ontario's or Quebec's.

The feud can be traced back to 1841 when Upper Canada (Ontario) and Lower Canada (Quebec) were joined together by the British government and compelled to live as partners with equal political representation. Within a few years Upper Canada began to feel constrained by a partnership which appeared to be dominated by the French-speaking

population of Lower Canada. George Brown, the editor of the Toronto
Globe, *became the staunch defender of Upper Canada's "rights", and
lashed out at the Lower Canadians.*

THE GLOBE is the unflinching advocate of REPRESENTATION BY
POPULATION. By the present iniquitous system, Lower Canada sends
the same number of Representatives to Parliament as Upper Canada,
although Upper Canada has THREE HUNDRED THOUSAND SOULS more than
Lower Canada, and contributes SEVEN DOLLARS to the general revenue
for every THREE DOLLARS contributed by Lower Canada! By this system
of injustice and the unanimity with which the French Canadians act
together, the Representatives of the Lower Section not only administer
the affairs of their own Province, but control those of Upper Canada
as well; they not only select their own public men for the highest positions
of State, but they have placed in the Cabinet and maintained there, year
after year, as the Representatives of Upper Canada, men who possess
not the confidence of the people of Upper Canada, but who on the contrary
have been repeatedly condemned by large majorities of the Upper Canada
members. With a constitution professedly based on the principle that
the will of the majority should prevail, the minority is thus enabled to
rule the Upper Province, in direct hostility to the popular will.

George Brown, 1861.[32]

*These complaints of "minority domination" were merely a prelude to
harsher and more violent statements. Confederation removed many of
the minor irritations of living together, for Ontario and Quebec were
allowed to go their way as separate provinces. But tranquillity was
ruptured by the 1870 and 1885 Riel rebellions which brought into
focus racial and religious prejudices and hatreds. The most incredibly
virulent statements appeared in Ontario newspapers.*

Ontario is proud of being loyal to England.

Quebec is proud of being loyal to sixteenth century France.

Ontario pays about three-fifths of Canada's taxes, fights all the battles
of provincial rights, sends nine-tenths of the soldiers to fight the rebels,
and gets sat upon by Quebec for her pains.

Quebec, since the time of Intendant Bigot, has been extravagant, corrupt
and venal, whenever she could with other people's money, and has done
nothing for herself or for progress with her own earnings.

Quebec now gets the pie.

Ontario gets the mush, and pays the piper for the Bleu carnival. . . .
Hundreds of thousands of dollars are spent in maintaining the French
language in an English country.

Ontario is getting sick of it.

Ontario taxpayers are about to take a tumble.

An anti-French party is springing up in all the Provinces except Quebec.

As the Republicans said, after the war of secession, "if we are to have
a solid South, we must have a solid North."

If we in Canada are to be confronted with a solid French vote, we
must have a solid English vote.

If Quebec is always to pose as a beggar in the Dominion soup kitchen,
she must be disfranchised as a vagrant.

If she is to be a traitor in our wars, a thief in our treasury, a conspirator
in our Canadian household, she had better go out.

She is no use in Confederation.

Her representatives are a weakness in Parliament, her cities would
be nothing but for the English speaking people, and to-day Montreal
would be as dead as the city of Quebec but for Anglo-Saxons, who are
persecuted and kept down by the ignorant French. . . .

We are sick of the French Canadians with their patriotic blabber and
the conspiracies against the treasury and the peace of what without them
might be a united Canada. . . .

With Quebec holding the balance of power Canada isn't safe a moment.

The constitution, or the British North America Act, which is our alleged
constitution, must be altered so as to deprive these venal politicians of
their powers or else Confederation will have to go.

As far as we are concerned, and we are concerned, and we are as
much concerned for the good of Canada as any one else, Quebec could
go out of the Confederation to-morrow and we would not shed a tear
except for joy.

If Ontario were a trifle more loyal to herself she would not stand
Quebec's monkey business another minute.

Toronto *Evening News*, 1885.[33]

[The people of Ontario] see the French language, French history, French
sentiment and French philosophy instilled into the minds of Canadian
children in the schools of Quebec, while allegiance to Rome and Pontifical
infallibility are steadily inculcated in the churches and homes.

Can the people of Ontario submit any longer in silence? Could but
the heroes who rose that glorious September morning long ago on the

Plains of Abraham before the astonished gaze of Montcalm and his troops return for one brief day to the scene of their brilliant achievements, with what thunder tones would they arouse to united thought and action the men of Ontario? Let Ontario's sons view with shame the position their Province holds in Confederation....

The Week, 1885.[34]

Such bitterness helped Ontario "win" its case, politically and legally. Louis Riel was found guilty of treason and hanged; and there seemed no doubt that this represented a victory of Ontario and the Ontario viewpoint over Quebec.

No further domination, said Upper Canada, Riel's head or yours. *No further French Domination, said the Orangemen: Riel's head or yours.*
In the end the old chief gave in, and the gallows, the hideous gallows was built deep in the far off wilderness of the West. The rest is known.

Le Monde, Montreal, November 20, 1885.

He shall hang though every dog in Quebec bark in his favour.

John A. Macdonald, 1885.

At the moment when the corpse of Riel falls through the trap and twists in convulsions of agony, at that moment an abyss will be dug that will separate Quebec from English-speaking Canada, especially Ontario.

Israel Tarte, 1885.[35]

That "abyss" was dug and has continued to divide Ontario and Quebec almost to the present day. For Quebeckers, the outcome of the Riel affair was proof that, in a showdown, the rights of Quebec would be sacrificed. The feeling grew that Quebec stood alone, not only against Ontario, but against all of English-speaking Canada. It was reinforced during later political crises when results showed that it was eight provinces against one. There also developed a belief that Quebec was not a province like any other province, but that it had a special mission— that of protecting the rights of French-Canadians wherever they might be in Canada. If the rights of the French-Canadian language and culture were threatened, the rights of Quebec were threatened. Thus, when the separatist Marcel Chaput spoke bitterly of the inferior position of French-Canadians in Confederation, he demonstrated the pent-up frustrations of Quebec concerning its own position in Canada.

He is a Canadian, but he is also a French-Canadian.

His country is the whole of Canada, but he is accepted only in Quebec.

He is told that he belongs to the great French civilization, but simultaneously he hears someone speak of "those damned Frenchmen."

He is forced to be bilingual; the others are unilingual.

He hears nothing but praise at school and elsewhere for the beauty of the French language; he is obliged to learn English.

He is told that Canada is a country which united two cultures; he has difficulty getting service in west Montreal if he uses French.

He thinks he speaks an international language; people snarl out "Speak White" in his face.

He enters the French university only to study from American text books.

He is told all about national unity, but he is ordered: "Stay in your province."

He hears people insist that Canada is an independent country; every day he sees another country's queen on his coinage and on his stamps.

He is told that his province is the most wealthy; it is always in his province that there is the most unemployment.

He is told that he is eligible for any position, but he is hampered by the extra obligation of bilingualism.

He is roused to Canadian patriotism, but all he hears played is God Save the Queen.

He sees the fleur-de-lis waving from all the flagpoles on the twenty-fourth of June; a week later he sees the Red Ensign waving over his town-hall.

He is incited to rid himself of his inferiority complex; then he hears someone assert that he is not mature enough to govern himself.

He is urged toward self-respect, and as his emblem he is given a sheep.

Marcel Chaput, *Why I Am A Separatist*, 1962.[36]

The feeling that "it's them against us" was revived again in the federal election of 1972. While the rest of Canada severely chastised Pierre Trudeau and the Liberal party, Quebec continued its support and made it possible for Trudeau to form a minority government. The failure of the rest of Canada to verify Quebec's choice by supporting Trudeau was seen as a blow against Quebec and "French power".

La Presse views the significance of the 1972 election

I watched the election with friends. Most were not Trudeau fans. Yet, as the election results from the rest of Canada came in, there was little elation in their reaction. At one point, as Conservative Leader Robert Stanfield, awkward in the victor's role, struggled to say a few words in French, a French-speaking colleague listening to him said, "Well, at least he won't have to speak French anymore."

As the evening continued, people whom I knew to be separatists, and others strong federalists, suddenly found themselves agreeing. It was one of those special moments of awareness, where a common condition over-rides long standing differences and conflicts. It became quite apparent to all of them that English Canada had decided to detach itself once again from the problems of its troublesome and demanding partner."

Ann Charney, 1972.[37]

One thing is sure. For the time being at least French-Canadian influence in Ottawa has been curbed again.

This represents ·a real victory only for the extremists on both sides—separatists in Quebec...and the English-speaking separatists who have always pretended that the French Canadians were a vanquished people with no special rights outside their own reserve.

I believe that in the immediate future the choice lies to a very large extent with English-speaking Canadians. Do they want to participate more actively in the building of a strong Canada or are they prepared to let our country be destroyed by extremism?

Maurice Lamontagne, 1972.[38]

Despite Quebec disappointment at the result of the 1972 election, recent years have witnessed an interesting entente *between Ontario and Quebec. Officially and emotionally Ontario has accepted the French fact and the implications of bilingualism to a degree which would have been unthinkable twenty years ago. The two provinces have found themselves allied against the federal government and against the demands of less favoured provinces. It would be naive to assume that all is sweetness and light, but the bitter racial and religious tensions of the past appear to have disappeared.*

There is, however, one feud which remains in force—Montreal versus Toronto. Their long-time commercial, hockey and "cultural" rivalry has usually ended with Montreal coming out on top although, with the exception of hockey, Torontonians would claim new superiority.

... AND MAKE THE GRASS GROW GREEN

A TORONTO VIEW

But Montreal has something no other city in Canada can claim—Mayor Jean Drapeau. The praises sung to his glory indicate that Montreal is still far ahead in the struggle for supremacy.

It is perhaps extreme to describe Mayor Drapeau as a film flam man. Master strategist would be better. There's no more revealing illustration of his genius than the way he extracted federal government approval of the funds-raising schemes which, he says, will finance the '76 Olympics.

Jim Proudfoot, 1973.[39]

A hue and cry arose over Drapeau's plans to hold the 1976 Olympics in Montreal. His opponents roared that the taxpayers of Canada would end up paying the sum of $500 million to get Drapeau and Montreal out of hock. Even Westerners joined with Torontonians in criticizing the potential tax cost and the whole rationale of the Olympics. Drapeau won, of course, as we all knew he would. His persuasive tongue cast a magic spell over Ottawa and he came away with permission to sell "souvenir coins" to finance the Olympics. What will be Drapeau's next major coup?

The Martimes versus Canada

Nowhere in Canada is the feeling of regionalism so strong as in the Maritimes. Local pride and loyalty is deeply ingrained in the hearts of the people of these provinces, which are the oldest English-speaking settlements in Canada. It is perhaps in Nova Scotia that one sees the strongest evidence of provincial patriotism—a patriotism defined by the Grand Old Man of Nova Scotia, Joseph Howe.

Boys, brag of your country. When I am abroad, I brag of everything that Nova Scotia is, has, or can produce; and when they beat me at everything else, I turn round on them and say, "How high does your tide rise?"[40]

In 1964 the American observer Edmund Wilson noted the continuing vitality of Nova Scotian independence.

...Nova Scotia regards itself, in fact, as more or less a country in its own right, much closer to maritime New England than to the prosperous

Scottish business world of Montreal. The Nova Scotians are likely to refer to the rest of the now rather misnamed "Dominion" as "Canada" or "Upper Canada." I am told that there is even on the island of Cape Breton a kind of Cape Breton nationalism which makes a distinction between its own inhabitants and the rest of the population of Nova Scotia.[41]

Returning to the province in 1967, historian George Rawlyk found that Nova Scotian nationalism was as strong as ever.

In late June I returned to Nova Scotia from the "fleshpots of Upper Canada." Within a few days of my arrival, I seriously wondered whether Nova Scotia's major Centennial project had been the revival of the "Repeal Movement" and the concomitant growth in intensity of anti-"Upper Canadian" sentiment. Almost the first thing I heard on the radio was an impassioned attack on the federal government by a former Halifax Conservative MP. He denounced Ottawa for spending millions of dollars to provide ice-breaker service for various St. Lawrence ports, thereby assuring the further decay of Halifax as an ocean port. He also questioned the spending of vast sums of federal money on further improvements on the Welland Canal while Nova Scotia continued to be an economic backwater of despair. He concluded his emotional address by declaring that the time had come for all true Nova Scotians to take the initiative and save their own province from the indifferent if not hostile Ottawa Liberal administration. The banner of "Repeal" had apparently been raised once again in Joseph Howe's province and Sir Charles Tupper once again was without question spinning wildly in his grave!

The following day, before I had time to recover fully from the virulence of the radio broadcast, I heard this strange fragment of conversation while researching at the Public Archives of Nova Scotia, "I did not know how he would use the material—so I was particularly careful—you know he might have been an Upper Canadian."[42]

"Upper Canadians" are the dark cloud in the Maritimer's sky, be he Nova Scotian, New Brunswicker, or Prince Edward Islander. A "Canadian" is one who comes from either Quebec or Ontario, those foreign countries to the West. Though nominally and legally part of Canada, the Maritime provinces have never really given their complete emotional devotion to the nation outside the provincial boundaries. In the beginning they did not want to be part of "Canada". In the 1860s, when the plan of uniting the British North America colonies was first

*being seriously considered, the voices of Maritimers were raised in protest.
On a voyage from England in 1866, a young woman named Isabella
Moore encountered a typical Nova Scotian viewpoint.*

A gentleman from Nova Scotia who sits opposite us at table by no
means agrees with cousin Jack that it would be a splendid thing for all
the British American colonies to unite. He growled into his claret again
and again and said confederation would bring no joy to Nova Scotia.
Nova Scotia would be swamped. And as for the whole idea, it was a
monstrous one and its nature would be a "thing of shreds and patches,"
neither monarchy or republic, an unnatural thing altogether. He pounds
on the table and gets purple in the face and leaves us very abruptly
whenever the subject comes into conversation, which it, of course, very
frequently does.[43]

*Newspapers in New Brunswick and Prince Edward Island echoed the
apprehension of Nova Scotia.*

A Legislative or Federal Union of the three Provinces may be practicable,
but of the whole of the North American Colonies, we consider it neither
feasible or desirable, at the present period. The Candian people know
too little about us; they have been so busy building up their own country;
snarling over their own political bones; righting their many provincial,
party and local grivances that they have not had time to look at their
neighbours . . . or to see if their interests and those of the lower Provinces
are precisely the same. . . . There is another impediment—Canada at
present is too far away from us.

Chatham *Gleaner*, 1864.[44]

The majority of the people are under the impression that Confederation
would ruin the Island. They have been told that if the Island should
be united with the other Provinces, under a Federal Government, the
people would be heavily taxed—that they would be marched away to
the frontiers of Upper Canada to fight for the Canadians; and that the
completion of the intercolonial Railroad would bring the produce of Canada
to St. John and Halifax, and thus injure the farmers of P.E. Island. Firmly
believing that all these evils would come upon them were they to enter
the Confederation the people, with but few exceptions, are unanimous
in the cry "away with Confederation—we will have nothing to do with
it."

The Charlottetown *Islander*, 1865.[45]

In spite of resistance, Nova Scotia and New Brunswick became part of the Dominion of Canada in 1867. Prince Edward Island remained aloof until 1873. The pressures of practical necessity, and the skilful manipulations of politicians such as Charles Tupper in Nova Scotia and Leonard Tilley in New Brunswick brought the Maritimes into Confederation. The caution of most Maritimers, and the resentment and hostility of many, was evident in the public reaction to Confederation.

In Pictou and New Glasgow, the display of flags by Confederates was meagre; and as an offset might be seen quite a number of flags upside down and half-mast, with several black pennants, and a black flag. Only one or two stores were closed. . . .No church-bells were rung, no salutes were fired, no congratulations were offered on the birth of the "infant monster Confederation," those who rejoiced did so politely, not desiring to insult the body of their countrymen who look upon the day as a dark one for Nova Scotia.

Eastern Chronicle, 1867.[46]

Of the first of July celebration in the city, we have stated fairly that it was a failure...in the country districts there was seen nothing but evidently earnest mourning. The flags in many localities were flying at half mast or upside down; crape was worn by many, and the burial of Nova Scotia thus fittingly honoured.

Halifax *Novascotian*, July 8, 1867.

You were a free people...but you are free no longer.

Eastern Chronicle, 1866.[47]

"Father, what country do we live in?"
"My dear son, you have no country, for Mr. Tilley has sold us all to the Canadians for eighty cents a head."

Andrew R. Wetmore, 1865.[48]

We are sold for the price of a sheepskin.

Joseph Howe, 1866.[49]

On Tuesday, whether for weal or woe, Prince Edward Island became a province of the Dominion of Canada. At 12 o'clock noon, the Dominion flag was run up on the flag staffs at Government House and the Colonial Building, and a salute of 21 guns was fired from St. George's battery and from H.M.S. *Sparta* now in port. The Church and City bells also rang out a lively peal, and the Volunteers under review at the City Park, fired a *feu de joie*. So far as powder and metal could do it there was for a short time a terrible din. But among the people who thronged the streets there was no enthusiasm. A few moments before 12, Mr. Sheriff Watson stepped forward on the balcony of the Colonial Building and read the Union Proclamation. He was accompanied by two ladies and about half a dozen gentlemen. The audience below within hearing distance consisted of three persons, and even they did not appear to be very attentive. After the reading of the Proclamation was concluded, the gentlemen on the balcony gave a cheer but the three persons below . . .responded never a word.

The Patriot, July 3, 1873 (Prince Edward Island)

Before Confederation, the Maritimes were prosperous communities, with an economy built on timber, shipbuilding, fishing and sailing. Unfortunately, a new era of iron and steam was to render obsolete much of the Maritime skills and resources. Their prosperity declined; Confederation and the "Canadians" were regarded as the villains. The 1870s and 1880s witnessed the growth of a "Maritimers Rights" movement directing its tirades against the enemy.

. . .I don't wish to be on friendly terms with Canada. I hate her and her politicians, and all who sympathize with her in her accursed policy of enslaving a few people. . . .

. . .What Ireland is to Britain—what Poland is to Russia,—that Nova Scotia will be to Canada,—a smoldering fire ready to burst out when the crisis comes.—And if I mistake not the signs of the times, that crisis is approaching, and the time of our deliverance is near. May we not be wanting in our duty!

Dr. E. L. Brown, 1871.[50]

The people of Nova Scotia know the Ontario or Quebec man but we know him principally in the shape of the commercial traveller. He comes here to sell, but he buys nothing but his hotel fare and in this respect he makes a rather ostentatious display. He is usually a genial enough sort of person, has a diamond ring, smokes fair cigars, "sets them up with the boys" in an off-hand way, and generally conveys the impression that in his own estimation he is a very superior being, whose condescending patronage it is a great privilege to enjoy. He spreads himself periodically throughout this province, in number he equals the locust and his visit has about the same effect. He saps our resources, sucks our money and leaves a lot of shoddy behind him. He has been able—at least the people whose agent he is—to have laws passed that compel us to buy his wares or submit to a tremendous fine, if we purchase from John Bull or brother Jonathan.

Halifax Morning Chronicle, 1886.[51]

That if it be found impossible, after negotiations...to secure the co-operation of the respective Governments of the sister provinces in withdrawing from the Confederation and entering instead into a Maritime Union, then this Legislature deems it absolutely necessary that Nova Scotia, in order that its railways and other public works and services may be extended and maintained...its industries properly fostered; its commerce invigorated and expanded; and its financial interest placed upon a sound basis, such as was the case previous to Confederation, should ask permission from the Imperial Parliament to withdraw from the Union of Canada and return to the status of a Province of Great Britain with full control over all fiscal laws and tariff regulations within the Province, such as prevailed to Confederation.

W. S. Fielding, Premier of Nova Scotia, 1886.[52]

"Repeal" of Confederation as a solution became a Maritime slogan which would rise again, as it did in the 1920s in this plea by a Nova Scotian politician.

Restore our province as an independent, self-governing British dominion, make us once more free and independent in the matter of trade and commerce, competent to protect ourselves sanely and wisely from the products of Ontario and Quebec as well as other lands, then there would undoubtedly be a great revival in business and local manufacturing in this province. Instead of decreasing, as at present, our population would increase. In a comparatively short time, in my opinion, we would have a million people in Nova Scotia. Farming would become remunerative. Manufacturing, commerce and foreign trade would quickly and actively develop. Enterprise would flourish. Distributing houses, banks and other institutions would quickly spring up.

H. W. Corning, 1923.[53]

The shattering of Confederation ties is no longer a serious possibility, if indeed it ever was. But the demand for a better deal, a fairer share of prosperity, and more reasonable attidues by a government controlled by central Canadians continues unabated.

Now, we are Canadians and we want to remain Canadians, and over the years we have got this situation.

. . .Our taxes are double what they are in Ontario. In fact the municipal taxes and the provincial taxes are double. That is not all. We, for instance, buy a car in the Atlantic Provinces. Everybody has a car. It is no longer a luxury to have a car. It is a necessity of life. We buy a car which is manufactured in Ontario. We pay $300 to $400 more than the resident of Ontario has to pay for a car, just to buy it.

Premier Robichaud, 1969.[54]

And people have to live generally on a lower standard, which means to say that some little youngster that is going to be born tomorrow night, or tonight, or at daylight tomorrow morning, somewhere east of that line, north-south line in Quebec, or anywhere east of that in Quebec and in the four Atlantic Provinces—some little baby is going to be born tomorrow morning of whom you may say that a Court has condemned that Canadian baby to an inferior existence, food not so good, home not so good; schools not so good, hospitals not so good, roads not so good, municipal services not so good. That child is condemned, as though a Court had done it, to an existence inferior to the Canadian average, certainly the Ontario average.

Premier Smallwood, 1969.[55]

There are many things that we Prince Edward Islanders reflect upon. We are too much wedded to our Canadian association ever to think of fulfilling our destiny in any other way. We are Canadians to the core, but we ask that although we are the smallest among the provinces we still be regarded as a province and that the rights which appertain thereto never be neglected or forgotten by the powerful governmental machinery here in Ottawa.

Prince Edward Island Member of Parliament, 1972.[56]

We are all Canadians. Just because we aren't like someone from downtown Toronto, it doesn't make us any less Canadian.

Maritimer, 1972.[57]

To be blunt, it seems as if certain segments of opinion in central Canada, having achieved the benefits of industrialization for themselves, now wish the Atlantic Provinces to forego the industrialization they never had, in the interests of maintaining an ill-defined Canadian economic independence. . . .

We tend not to make any distinction between investment that comes from central Canada, the United States or other foreign countries, regarding it all, somehow, as "foreign".

Atlantic Provinces Economic Council Brief, 1972.[58]

Newfies Never Die

Hurrah for our own native isle, Newfoundland!
Not a stranger shall hold one inch of its strand!
Her face turns to Britain, her back to the gulf.
Come near at your peril, Canadian wolf!

Ye brave Newfoundlanders who plough the salt sea
With hearts like the eagle, so bold and so free,
The time is at hand when you'll all have to say
If Confederation will carry the day.

Would you barter the rights that your fathers have won,
Your freedom transmitted from father to son?
For a few thousand dollars of Canadian gold,
Don't let it be said that your birthright was sold."

Newfoundland campaign song, 1869.[59]

Newfoundland is practically more remote from the principal parts of Canada than from Britain itself, and has never had any political, and only minor commercial, connection with the former — a connection which is entirely cut off by the sea for nearly six months of the year, during which there can be no communication with Canada, except through the territories of a foreign power — the United States of America.

The inhabitants of this colony would desire to see this island always retained separately by Britain, as its ocean fortress and military outpost in this part of the world, whatever might be the future destiny of the colonies of the mainland. . . . The colony has no community of interests with Upper or Lower Canada, and little with the other maritime provinces.

Newfoundland Petition, 1867.[60]

The people of Newfoundland shrink from the idea of linking their destinies with a Dominion in the future of which they can at present see nothing to inspire hope, but much to create apprehension.

Newfoundland House of Assemblies, 1870.[61]

Newfoundland was able to avoid the jaws of the "Canadian wolf" until 1948. In that year, the vigorous efforts of Joseph Smallwood, who believed passionately that Newfoundland's destiny lay in union with Canada, brought Newfoundland into Confederation. The event, however, was not without anger or heartbreak on the part of many Newfoundlanders.

Don't vote Confederation, and that's my prayer to you,
We own the house we live in, we own the schooner too;
But if you heed Joe Smallwood and his line of French patois,
You'll be always paying taxes to the men at Ottawa.

Anti-Confederation Ballad, 1948.[62]

On this day of parting, sad nostalgic thoughts arise,
Thoughts to bring the hot tears surging to the New-
  foundlanders' eyes;
Thoughts that bring to mind the story of the struggles of the
  past,
Of the men who built our island, nailed its colours to the
  mast;
Those who lost the fight for freedom have the greater pride
  this day,
Though their country's independence lies the victim of the
  fray.
They have kept *their* faith untarnished, they have held *their*
  honour high,
They can face the course of history with a clear and steadfast
  eye;
They will have their day of sorrow, but will ever take the
  stand,
As the staunch and faithful servants of a well-loved Newfoundland.

Albert Perlin, 1949.[63]

As with other Maritimers, the Newfoundlander found it difficult, if not impossible, to consider himself a Canadian.

From the time of our arrival in Newfoundland to the moment of departure, there was no questioning that Americans were held in greater favour there than fellow Canadians. In a way, I resented this, yet it is impossible to really be affronted by the attitude of a Newfoundlander to a guest, for he is always genuinely courteous and hospitable with real honesty. He treats you at all times as a human being and not as a representative of anything or anybody. Though we often felt the lack of a close bond between mainland Canadians and Newfoundlanders, never for a moment were we made to feel a lack of bond between us *as persons.*

Dorothy Henderson, *The Heart of Newfoundland.*[64]

"You come from Canada?" I am asked upon my arrival. "My son goes to Canada to school," continues someone else. An islander is a Newfoundlander first, then a Canadian. Where have I heard this point of view before?

Solange Chaput-Rolland, *My Country, Canada or Quebec?*, 1966.[65]

Such attitudes should come as no surprise. The Newfoundlander cannot forget his roots. The "Mainland" and "Mainlanders" will never replace the heritage of his beloved island. If he leaves Newfoundland, he goes reluctantly, as an exile, knowing he will have to endure Newfie jokes told by crass Mainlanders. But being a Newfoundlander makes up for such oppressions.

Oh love I'm bound for Canada
Dear Sally we must part
I'm forced to leave my blue-eyed girl
All with an aching heart
To face cold-hearted strangers too
All in a foreign land.

Newfoundland Ballad.[66]

So distinctive is the Newfoundland type that it is only with the greatest difficulty that one may translate it in foreign terms or communicate it even to Canadians. When a half-dozen of us Newfoundlanders gather together in Toronto to smoke and yarn, the foreign born, if he happen to be invited to the company, finds himself only on the fringe of the charmed circle.

The conversation, once it has lapsed into dialect, is a closed book to him. He may know that haggis is a Scottish dish, or a particular hybrid of stew is Irish, but has he ever eaten brewis? No. His palate for dried cod is limited to a few tasteless fillets which the proprietor of a meat-and-fish store in the city claimed to have been cut from genuine cod. Has he ever eaten whorts? No, only blueberries—a fundamental error. Or bake-apples or capillaire or partridge berries? Never heard of them. Had he ever been stimulated by the smell of kelp after a north-easter had lashed the shores—a tonic like strychnine to the blood? Or by the smell of caplin three days after the tonnage had been deposited on the cabbage beds? No. Then he was for ever excommunicate, a stranger to the true faith. How did he pronounce the name of the country? With the accent on the second syllable. That was enough, the final heresy.

And for the rest of the evening, while our friendly alien tilted his head over the back of an arm-chair and dozed, we reminisced about Newfoundland dogs, the departure and return of the sealing and fishing fleets, the Gargantuan meals of flippers in the spring, partridge coveys, the size of the trout we almost landed, school thrashings, snow-drifts, fore-and-afters, the late arrival of trains and steamers, and the stories of old salts who knew life as it was in the sixties and seventies. . . .

These are the light and happy memories of Newfoundland, the casual ones which belong to the excursions from the main highway and which form the usual subject of chat when a few of the native-born are grouped around a stove.

E. J. Pratt, 1936.[67]

Now I know that we don't talk like you Mainlanders.
And I know that we're the victims of your jokes.
And I know that you all think we're Goofy Newfies,
And that we all belong in fishing boats. . .
. . . So go on and call us Goofy Newfies.
Laugh aloud when you hear us speak.
We'll just sit back and enjoy living.
And chug-a-lug that good old Newfie screech.

Newfie boy, Newfie boy
I was born one and I'll be one when I die
And I couldn't care less
If my English ain't the best
I'm proud to be a Newfie boy.

Songs by Roy Payne, Newfoundlander, 1970.

With such rivalries how have we been able to survive as a nation? It would be foolish to underestimate the intensity of our regional and provincial differences. It will be necessary to right the wrongs of the past, to fight economic disparity, to unify the peoples of Canada.

But it is possible that beneath the resentment and hostility there lurks an underlying affection of Canadians for each other. Perhaps any unity we have is based on a love-hate relationship. What would a Westerner do without the East to dislike; how could Ontario exist without the comforting challenge of Quebec; could a Maritimer be content without Upper Canadians to blame for his ills; would Quebec be happy without the feeling of being persecuted; without Canada how could a British Columbian feel superior?

These feelings make life tolerable for us. They are part of the great Canadian Game which every real Canadian understands. We all know the rules, the correct prejudices, the appropriate reactions. We would be disappointed if a fellow citizen from a different region failed to play the game. And if the game gets rough we can hardly pick up our sticks and leave. Does anyone seriously believe that Western, or Maritime, or Quebec, or B.C. separatism is desirable or possible? We have lived, and can live with our differences. In fact, we may have no other choice.

The Land and the Canadian Imagination

Although Canadians have been hesitant and reluctant nationalists with an aversion to showing affection towards their fellows, there is one area where they have been unabashedly emotional, and that is in their attitude towards the land. Most Canadians have a love affair with the land, even if the romance is not fully consummated but remains a fantasy. For what Canadians say and believe about the land is not always based on actual experience but results from constant exposure to the myth that there is some mystic link between Canadians and their land. Writers, poets, artists and professional nationalists have established this belief, and reinforced it until it has become a traditional part of Canadian folklore. One of the most important elements of the myth is the conviction that in the land alone is to be found the true meaning of the Canadian identity. This view we may call the "Hutchison Thesis", for it is in Bruce Hutchison's eloquence that the theory is most effectively presented.

THIS
LAND
OF OURS

If any stranger would know the Canadian mind, let him look first at the land of Canada.

The land, more than anything else, has shaped the mind. We are too young to be fully shaped by history, too remote from one another to be shaped by any abstract theory. But we hold the land jointly, its beauty, illimitable distance, and healing silence. The land lives for all of us in that hidden, wordless region where nations are darkly fashioned and a people is born.

Our eyes see and our racial mind remembers the mountains, the plains, the forest, the lakes, the rivers, and the seacoast. Our ears are tuned to the sounds of the land, to trees under the wind, grain whispering in summer dawn, the song of birds, the nighttime boom of frogs, the hum of insects, the click of ax, and the crunch of footsteps in the snow. We remember the sound of water as it moves across the land, the brook's gurgle and the river's deeper voice in the darkness, the lap of waves on the inland beach, the pound of surf on the sea rocks, the splash of trout or salmon, the swirl of paddle, and the boy's shout in the swimming hole.

These things enter through the eye and ear, but within the racial mind they are distilled and compacted beyond the measurement of knowledge.

The land can be reckoned in area, topography, and wealth. No man can reckon its power in the Canadian's subconscious. It is ours, won through long struggle, broken, tilled, and reaped through three centuries of toil. Its image—so large, inexpressible, and fair—overtops our divisions and unites us, by a common possession, in the Canadian creaturehood.

Bruce Hutchison, *Canada, Tomorrow's Giant*, 1957.[1]

Hutchison does not stand alone in his analysis. His view is supported both by the clear, analytical mind of the historian, and the creative imagination of the poet.

Canada, with its divisions of race, presents no common denominator in those profundities which normally unite, in race, language, religion, history and culture. If a common focus is to be found it must come out of the common homeland itself. If the Canadian people are to find their soul, they must seek for it not in the English language or the French but in the little ports of the Atlantic provinces, in the flaming autumn maples of the St. Lawrence valley, in the portages and lakes of the Canadian Shield, in the sunsets and relentless cold of the prairies, in the foothill, mountain, and sea of the West and in the unconquerable vastness of the North. From the land, Canada, must come the soul of Canada.

Arthur Lower, *Colony to Nation*, 1946.[2]

Between Two Furious Oceans

You have asked me an enormous question;
You have looked at me with all
The bitter wistful yearning that
Uncertainty brings to young eyes;
You have asked me, "What am I?
• • •

You are the quiet bays and the lonely shadows of the firs;
The vast green acres blanketing the wide Alberni hills,
Hemlock and cedar and spruce . . .proud with everlasting green;
Cold blue glaciers, spilling their life into roaring Atlin creeks;
Meadows in the clouds and valleys mute with solitude;
Sun-bright arbutus islands of the Gulf of Georgia; oaks,
Golden broom and meadow larks and the mournful cry of
    gulls.

You are the Rocky Mountains, white with the snows   of
    centuries,
Eternal rocks that rise in columned ranks to meet the dawn,
The sunset and the frigid moon; you are the canyon walls,
Loud with ferocious rivers, and the still, imperious lakes,
Cobalt and sapphire, emerald and violet, and under the
    starlight, black
With the secrets of the western night; you are the mountain
    goat,
Poised, majestic and alone upon the barren crag,
And below, deep woods, blue grouse and grizzlies and the
    sombre moose.

You are the reckless foothills clambering down the eastern
    slopes;
The winding Bow, the dusty Badlands and the Sweetgrass
    buttes;
The flat immenseness of the prairies, blue with unbounded
    space.

You are the heaving lakes, the rolling, greenjacketed hills
Of Stormont and Dundas; roaring Niagara and the swift
Cold current of the Ottawa, hedged with silver birch;
The stately St. Lawrence and the rugged hills that stretch
    into the vast
And friendless wilderness of Porcupine and Kirkland Lake.

You are the dainty meadows and the lazy dappled streams
Of Joliette; the cool sweet whisper of Laurentian breezes;
The river willows and the gracious elms; chipmunk and beaver
And the antlered deer; the green windswept curve of Gaspé's
    loin,
Its sanded coves, white capes and beaches, and their curling
    waves.

You are the maple groves that undulate, mile upon mile,
Over the wave-like hills of the Maritimes, mantling them
With rich green in summer, kindling them with a million fires,
Blazing with consuming crimson golden lights like beacon
  flames
To proclaim the season's death when crackling autumn days
  explode,
Leaving them black and naked in the waning year, tracing
Their lonely fingers against the leaden sky and the forbidding
  ocean.

                                              Dick Diespecker.[3]

*The theory has a long and honourable history in Canada. The latter
part of the nineteenth century even witnessed an interesting fling with
a racist vision. There were some Canadians who saw in our land and
climate a purifying element which would mould us into a hardy and
distinctive race, a special breed with a promising destiny.*

A constitution nursed upon the oxygen of our bright winter atmosphere,
makes its owner feel as though he could toss about the pine trees in
his glee.

                                          Lord Dufferin, 1878.[4]

The atmosphere is highly purified, joyous and clear, and charged with
ozone—that element which is mysteriously associated with soundness
of mind and body.

                                           Charles Mair, 1891.[5]

...the most virile nation on this continent will be to the north of the
great lakes.

                                      Dr. William Osler, 1904.[6]

If the world lasts long enough there is a glorious future in store for
Canada. The northern countries and the hardy northern races possess
an energy and a vitality which in all times have enabled them, in the
long run, to win the race and go ahead of their Southern rivals.

    John J. Rowan, *The Emigrant and Sportsman in Canada,1876.*[7]

We are the Northmen of the New World.

R. G. Haliburton, 1869.[8]

Though we may smile at the naiveté of these sentiments, especially since our ozone-charged air has not allowed us to go ahead of our "Southern rivals", it would be well to remember that many prominent Canadians, even today, profess to discover a special quality bred in Canadians by their land.

Every time I travel across the country I am moved anew by the Canadian landscape. It is not a homely landscape for the most part. This is no place for the lover of languid airs, and soft yielding flesh. It is a northern country, warmed only obliquely by the sun, a country of cold winters and long nights. Half the continental land-mass is occupied by thick, bony plates of Precambrian rock, so ancient it predates organic life. Most of the rest is a dwarfing sweep of prairie, or a convulsion of fresh, jagged mountain peaks, still creaking upwards. No one, I am convinced, can live with such a geography and climate without being shaped by them.

Canadians have also had to deal with other forces beyond their control; economic forces, cultural forces, and perhaps most of all the thoughtless expansionism of our neighbour to the south. But out of these unique circumstances has been forged a special Canadian character, a Canadian tradition, a Canadian way-of-life—in fact a Canadian identity.

John C. Parkin, 1971.[9]

We should be grateful that our country is of heroic size. How commonplace it would be to live in a small one...If we were deprived of our vast spaces we should be without much of our challenge. Even more we should have lost that essential quality which is part of us all and which makes us different from others. Rupert Brooke wrote that he was most impressed with the "fresh loneliness" of Canada. He wrote that "the soul—or the personality—seems to have indefinite room to expand." Blair Fraser understood the wilderness which is Canada when he wrote of "the vast empty land in which for more than three centuries a certain type of man has found himself uniquely at home.". . .

Of all the changes which will come to Canada in the next generation, therefore, we must prevent, surely, any of a sort which will diminish the essential beauty and lonely nature of this country. For if that beauty is lost, or if that wilderness escapes, the very nature and character of this land will have passed beyond our grasp. Denied an opportunity to breathe the brisk freshness of an Atlantic gale, to view the unbelievable glory of a Prairie sunset, to feel the overwhelming silence of a northern lake, we would no longer be Canadians...this was expressed...by a Canadian Indian called Saltatha. He is recorded as having said to a priest:

"My father...you have told me that heaven is very beautiful. Tell me now one more thing. Is it more beautiful than the country of the musk-ox in summer when sometimes the mist blows over the lakes and sometimes the water is blue and the loons cry very often? That is beautiful, and if heaven is still more beautiful my heart will be glad and I shall be content to rest there until I am very old."

We are a particular breed, we Canadians. We hail from many sources but we have a common destiny: it is to perpetuate the character of this land and to share the benefits that result. Canada is not a country for the cold of heart or for the cold of feet. For those who qualify, the rewards exceed those of any other country. Indeed, as Saltatha suggested, they approach those of heaven itself.

Prime Minister Trudeau, 1970.[10]

The land has not only caused writers to compose rapturous phrases and politicians to make significant speeches, it has also inspired what has probably been the only original Canadian contribution to the visual arts. Lawren Harris, one of the Group of Seven artists who established a distinctive Canadian style, describes the motivation which directed their work in the 1920's and 1930's.

Canada was then, as it still remains, a long, thin strip of civilization on the southern fringes of a vast expanse of immensely varied, virgin land reaching into the remote north. Our whole country is cleansed by the pristine and the replenishing air which sweeps out of that great hinterland. It was the discovery of this great northern area as a field of art which enticed and inspired these painters....

They began to realize how far this country of Canada was different in character, atmosphere, moods, and spirit from Europe and the old land. It was a country which evoked a response free from all preconceived ideas and rule-of-thumb reactions. It had to be seen, lived with, and painted with complete devotion to its own character, life, and spirit, before it yielded its secrets. For only great devotion can achieve real insight and arrive at a full meaning.

All this was something completely new to Canadians. It was something which the vast majority of our people, most if not all of our art lovers and critics, simply did not understand. Art to them was no more than a decoration, a pleasant distraction, a social cachet, not a way of life. Too often they confused mere prettiness with real beauty. They did not know their own country. They did not know its spirit as a transforming power. They did not think of the arts as a living, creative force in the life of a people. They had no other idea than that of accepting the crumbs from the richly laden table of European art and culture.

Nevertheless a native art movement had come into being, an art movement which had its source, growth and life in a direct, first-hand, and continuous experience of a native scene unknown to most Canadians except as geographical names. And the men of this movement, the Canadian painters, explored the whole land: Georgian Bay, Algonquin Park, the Laurentians, Northern Ontario, the north and south shores of the Gulf of St. Lawrence, Algoma, the north shore of Lake Superior, the Nova Scotian coast, the Rocky Mountains, and the Canadian Arctic from Labrador to Kane Basin. . . .

We had commenced our great adventure. We lived in a continuous blaze of enthusiasm. We were at times very serious and concerned, at other times hilarious and carefree. Above all we loved this country and loved exploring and painting it. Emerson once wrote "Every great and commanding movement in the annals of the world is the triumph of enthusiasm." Please do not think that we had any idea of leading a great and commanding movement; but we did have enthusiasm. We began to range the country and each one of us painted hundreds of sketches. The love of the country and our irrepressible ardour commenced to infuse something new into our work.

Lawren Harris, 1948.[11]

Emily Carr was to find personal inspiration in the work of the Group of Seven. Her diary entries not only show how she was influenced by their achievments, but also reveal the spiritual exultation she felt in her own relationship with the land.

Thursday, November 17th, 1927.

Oh, God, what have I seen? Where have I been? Something has spoken to the very soul of me, wonderful, mighty, not of this world. Chords way down in my being have been touched. Dumb notes have struck chords of wonderful tone. Something has called out of somewhere. Something in me is trying to answer.

It is surging through my whole being, the wonder of it all, like a great river rushing on, dark and turbulent, and rushing and irresistible, carrying me away on its wild swirl like a helpless little bundle of wreckage. Where, where? Oh, these men, this Group of Seven, what have they created?—a world stripped of earthiness, shorn of fretting details, purged, purified: a naked soul, pure and unashamed; lovely spaces filled with wonderful serenity. What language do they speak, those silent, awe-filled spaces? I do not know. Wait and listen; you shall hear by and by. I long to hear and yet I'm half afraid. I think perhaps I shall find God here, the God I've longed and hunted for and failed to find. Always He's seemed nearer out in the big spaces, sometimes almost within reach but never quite. Perhaps in this newer, wider, space-filled vision I shall find him.

Jackson, Johnson, Varley, Lismer, Harris—up-up-up-up-up! Lismer and Harris stir me most. Lismer is swirling, sweeping on, but Harris is rising into serene, uplifted planes, above the swirl into holy places.

November 12th, 1932.

Listen, this perhaps is the way to find that thing I long for: go into the woods alone and look at the earth crowded with growth, new and old bursting from their strong roots hidden in the silent, live ground, each seed according to its own kind expanding, bursting, pushing its way upward towards the light and air, each one knowing what to do, each one demanding its own rights on the earth. Feel this growth, the surging upward, this expansion, the pulsing life, all working with the same idea, the same urge to express the God in themselves—life, life, life, which *is* God, for without Him there is no life. So, artist, you too from the deeps of your soul, down among dark and silence, let your roots creep forth, gaining strength. Drive them in deep, take firm hold of the beloved Earth Mother. Push, push towards the light. Draw deeply from the good nourishment of the earth but rise into the glory of the light and air and sunshine. Rejoice in your own soil, the place that nurtured you when a helpless seed. Fill it with glory—be glad.[13]

> *In the midst of all this rapture, it is wise for Canadians, now and then, to be brought back to reality. Are we really a hardy northern race on intimate and loving terms with the land? In "The Authentic Voice of Canada", Robert Fulford offers an alternate view.*

"We are the people who survived the hard land," writes a bitter, angry correspondent. "We are the descendants of the people who cut the trees to plant a crop, froze to death in the winter, were eaten alive by bugs in the summer, fished in the streams as free men...

"That is Canadian culture; not this mincing, aping pseudo-European has-been stuff you call Culture with a large C."

I recognized the tone of voice and the ideas behind it as soon as I opened the letter. This was my regular communication from The Authentic Voice of Canada. The authentic voice writes to me often. The letter always comes from a different person, and the wording is always different; but the theme is constant. My correspondent always insists that he (or, as in this case, she) speaks for the true Canada, while I speak for something false, alien, effete, and shallow.

When the letter is postmarked west of Ontario, then the conflict is described as West (tough, solid, hockey-playing) versus East (soft, undependable, ballet-loving). When it comes from a rural address, my correspondent tells me that country people are honest and true whereas city people are decadent. In this case the writer of the letter—who for some reason doesn't want her name used—lives in Toronto.

"My definition of culture," she writes, "is what a nation represents, its past, present and hopes for the future. Your definition of Canadian culture seems to be Art."

But art in this country, she says, is meaningless. Ballet, symphonies, art galleries—these things matter so little to Canadians that they have to be shoved down our throats by committees of rich women with nothing else to do.

"We are CANADIANS," she writes, "a hardy pioneer, if you like, rustic people, not a bunch of...court fops, or dainty ladies doing a minuet. We are of the land, the rocks, the rivers, the mountains, the sea.

"We are not displaced Europeans, trying to ape what we left behind. We are the people who left Europe because it was decadent and dead. We rejected the American way and we still reject it."

She goes on to say that the Stratford Festival is phony. What is really Canadian is hockey, football, trotting races, camping.

"This is what being a Canadian is; the embodiment of all the inner strengths it takes to live in this land, in which only the strong can survive."...

The idea that nature, outdoor life, and Canadian history are on one side of a great divide, and art on the other, is of course nonsense. Canadian writing, painting, music, and dances—they are all, at some point, on intimate terms with the landscape. I have a friend who has won national prizes as both a paddler and an abstract artist; his life is a particularly striking example of a constant factor in the culture of Canada.

BY SID BARRON

On the other hand, of course, Canadian art—like Canadian life—is increasingly urbanized. And here I find myself, when I receive these authentic-Canadian-voice letters, almost intimidated. I've never lived anywhere but in cities, and never wanted to. At this point I begin stuttering about how "my people" (as they say) have been in this country for more than a century, and I may even throw in my great-aunt whose husband was shot by Big Bear's braves in 1885. But of course that means nothing; what matters is who you are now, not where your family lived then.

So I telephoned my correspondent, prepared to be put down once again by pure, native Canadianism. Who could she be? A female bush pilot? A teacher of Eskimos in the Arctic? The wife of a wheat farmer at least? None of these, it turned out. She moved to Toronto forty-five years ago, and she's lived here ever since.

Robert Fulford, 1965.[14]

The Call of the North

"The North is always there like a presence; it is the battleground of the picture without which Canada would not be Canada."

André Siegfried.[15]

Nowhere is the relationship between man and the land so elemental as in the North. There, there is no middle ground. Man either accepts the inhospitable expanse of land and learns to live in harmony with it, or he perishes. Man does not change the North; the North moulds man. It is here that a remarkable people, the Eskimo, learned to accept the North on its terms and survive. A short passage from a story told by Comock illustrates how his people, the Inuit, live in harmony with the land. At this point in his tale, he and his band have just completed a day's journey.

"Ae," said everyone. And the dogs sank into the snow, too tired to fight, and they buried their noses between their paws and let the snow-smoke drift over them, and while our women sat in the shelter of our sleds and nursed the small children, Annunglung and I went off with our snow knives and harpoons, and by good luck we found along a crack in the ice a deep drift of snow. We cut out a block of snow. The edges cut sharp and did not crumble and then we cut out block after block and built our igloo.

The dogs between sleep kept watching us and when we had built our igloo and from the inside cut out the door and crawled out, they were all around us howling for their seal. I had to use my long whip to keep them away, and then our wives crept inside and they were all smiling for they were away from the burn of the cold, and they lit our seal-oil lamps and put our willow mats and deerskins down while the children chewed their pieces of raw seal. Outside we gave our dogs their meat, and then they bedded themselves in the snow in the shelter of the sleds and the igloo, and let the snow cover them again. Annunglung and I went inside, and our wives cut seal meat and filled our mouths, and we said the night was full of good signs, though there were growls now and then running through the ice, growing louder and louder as they came toward us, and sounding in our ears like Nanook the bear rushing toward the spear, but I said, "Never mind, there is always growling from the sea." So we fell asleep, cold though our igloo was, as a new igloo always is when there is no wind.

When I awakened I was happy, for our ice window was blue, and by that I knew that there was no snow-smoke in the air. My head wife made fire in her willow down, and she blew it into a flame and lit the lamp. "Look at our children, Comock," she said, "they are warm." There were little smokes rising from the deerskin robes under which they slept.

Comock, 1912.[16]

Another Eskimo, Nuligak, recalls how his people passed the long Artic night when he was a boy in the 1890s.

During the period of darkness, the Inuit hardly left their igloos. When the days shortened and the sun was but a little dot on the horizon, the Inuit from the surrounding area would assemble at Kitigariuit for the winter festivities.

Brown bear skins were stuffed to appear alive, and the heads were ingeniously made to produce grunting sounds. White bears were also stuffed, and the paws and claws made to move. As soon as the sun had left the sky the merry-making began. In those days these holidays took the place of Christmas and New Year festivities. The day was spent watching wrestling matches and eating. As deeper darkness set in, we children would not dare leave the igloo: we were afraid of the bears!

The village had a Chief to organize things and launch the games. This Chief was quite old. When night fell the children squatted on the sleeping platform of the igloo, afraid of the brown and white bears. Suddenly

someone would shout "Aaa!" "Bears" would enter through the katak in
the floor, while the Inuit sang amusing songs. Since I was very little,
I did not memorize them.

Once the bears were gone, the Inuit would challenge each other in
tug-of-war contests; tugging at someone's arm was another way to prove
one's strength. Another game was called *Orsiktartut*, they-make-a-loop.
Two ropes were fastened to the vault of the igloo. Someone sitting on
the floor would grasp the ends of the ropes and raise himself from the
floor. Once raised, he must bring his hands under himself and sit on
them. Then he was to return to his first position without touching the
floor, and begin all over again. Some would do this five times in a row,
while others could not raise themselves from the floor at all. It was not
easy. At the end there was a champion! . . .

During the times of merrymaking that were the night festivals a host
of interesting and amazing things was shown. There was such an
abundance of meals, games and things to admire that these sunless weeks
sped by as if they had been only a few days.

As the sun reappeared and the gatherings were close to an end, we
ended our festivals with dart shooting. The dart, there was only one,
was balanced by little wings made from a duck's tailfeathers. It flew
straight and true. It was carried to each contestant by the one who had
made it. The target was a little piece of caribou fat (tunu) thinned out
and formed into the shape of a candle, about four inches long and an
inch and a half in diameter. It was set in the middle of the floor. The
igloo was large and the onlookers many. Men, women and children were
all admitted. Someone would set up a prize and another would aim for
the target. The greater the stake, the higher the interest rose. Peals of
laughter echoed all around. The winner, the one who hit the target,
was in turn expected to put up a prize for the next contestant.

Thus ended the last game of the kaivitjvik, the time of dancing and
rejoicing which began with the departure of the sun and ended with
its return.

I, Nuligak, 1966.[17]

> *The Eskimo lived in harmony with the land, but there came a new*
> *breed who sought to conquer the North and to take from it. For them*
> *the North would always be a challenge, a cruel and hostile environment,*
> *with no pity. These were the men who inspired the writing of R.W.*
> *Service, poet of the Yukon and the gold rush.*

The Law Of The Yukon

This is the law of the Yukon, and ever she
    makes it plain:
"Send not your foolish and feeble; send me
    your strong and your sane.
Strong for the red rage of battle; sane, for I
    harry them sore;
Send me men girt for the combat, men who
    are grit to the core;
Swift as the panther in triumph, fierce as the
    bear in defeat,
Sired of a bulldog parent, steeled in the
    furnace heat.
Send me the best of your breeding, lend me
    your chosen ones;
Them will I take to my bosom, them will I
    call my sons;
Them will I gild with my treasure, them will
    I glut with my meat;
But the others—the misfits, the failures—I
    trample under my feet.
Dissolute, damned and despairful, crippled
    and palsied and slain,
Ye would send me the spawn of your gutters—
    Go! take back your spawn again.

Robert W. Service, *Songs of a Sourdough*, 1907.[18]

The North has called all types of men—explorers, prospectors, adventurers—and men with a touch of madness in them. In 1924, James Charles Critchell-Bullock, who had ostensibly gone to the Barren Lands to write, study and photograph the flora and fauna, found himself alone in a dug-out cave.

Alone this Christmas Eve on the Barren Lands of the Sub-Arctic of America, when those outside are contemplating the morrow with hearts full of happiness and pleasurable excitement. Alone in a dug-out beneath the sand and snow when but one thousand miles away homes are alight with fairy lights and decorated with those little frills pertinent to

Christmastide. Alone in this awful shack of continual discomfort with its subsiding walls and crazy roof likely at any moment to fall and entomb me in a living grave. Alone with sufficient wood to make only one more fire. Alone with a dying dog whose foot is stinking with the decay consequent on frost bite. Alone with but the howl of the blizzard outside to cheer me and the thoughts of peace and happiness and the faces of loved ones coming to mind only to remind me more and more of my deep loneliness. . . .

Now again it is becoming cold and although half past four in the afternoon I must roll myself in the blankets and wait seventeen hours for the return of daylight. Thank goodness I have my health. Were I to lose it for a single day, were I to injure myself with a fall or cut myself with an axe my plight indeed would be serious. For a few days at least I can struggle on now, but unable to move with a damaged leg or with broken health, short indeed would be my shrift. Let it be known, however, that I have won so far and I will not abandon my task. Nothing now would induce me to leave for the comforts of civilization, till all is accomplished.[19]

> *The poems of Service, the stories of men such as Critchell-Bullock, the legends of Eskimos and Mounties, have created a myth about the North which Canadians have accepted as reality. Although we are a northern nation, we still reject the presence and opportunity of the Arctic. Farley Mowat has commented on this aspect of the Canadian approach to the North.*

This North, this Arctic of the mind, this frigid concept of a flat and formless void of ice and snow congealed beneath the impentrable blackness of the polar night, is pure illusion. Behind it lies a lost world obscured in drifts of literary drivel, obliterated by blizzards of bravado and buried under an icy weight of obsessive misconceptions. The magnificent reality behind the myth has been consistently rejected by Canadians since the day of our national birth and is rejected still. Through almost a century the Far North has meant to Canadians either a nightmarish limbo or an oppressive polar presence looming darkly over southern Canada and breathing icily down our necks. During most of that century the handful of people who called themselves Canadian were engrossed in the occupation of the apparently limitless spaces on the souther fringes of the country. When that space was finally circumscribed and its limits reached, Canadians did not look northward to the challenge of the unknown half of their share of the continent. The northern myth seemed more than they could face, even as it had in the past. They shunned it then—they shun it still. . . .

Only since the early 1950's have southern Canadians begun to glance over their shoulders northward. As yet only a handful have made the effort to penetrate to the reality behind the myth and to actually go north, not to make a quick buck and then flee south as if the very hounds of hell were on their heels, but to attempt to make themselves integral parts of a gigantic and exiting world spurned by the nation that pretends to own it.

Farley Mowat, Canada North, 1967.[20]

Although it may have been ignored, the North has not escaped the advantages of modern culture and technology.

Eskimo Hunter
(New Style)

In terylene shirt and suspenders
sun glasses and binoculars
Peterborough boat and Evinrude motor
Remington rifle with telescope sight
making hot tea on a Coleman stove
scanning the sea and shore for anything
that moves and lives and breathes
and so betrays itself
one way or another
All we need in the line of further equipment
is a sexy blonde in a bikini
trailing her hand thru the sunlit water
maybe a gaggle of Hollywood photographers
snapping pictures and smoking
nationally advertised brands
Like bwana in Africa
pukka sahib in Bengal
staked out on a tree platform
a tethered goat underneath wailing
Papa Hemingway's bearded ghost on safari
or fishing for giant turtles in Pango Pango

Maybe it is phony
(and all we're after is seal)
but over the skyline
where the bergs heave and glimmer
under the glacier's foot
or down the fiord's blue water
        even under the boat itself
anywhere the unhappened instant is real blood
        death for someone or some thing
        and it's reassuringly old fashioned

Al Purdy, 1968.[21]

Bush Country

The Lonely Land

Cedar and jagged fir
uplift sharp barbs
against the gray
and cloud-piled sky;
and in the bay
blown spume and windrift
and thin, bitter spray
snap
at the whirling sky;
and the pine trees
lean one way.

A wild duck calls
to her mate,
and the ragged
and passionate tones
stagger and fall,
and recover,
and stagger and fall,
on these stones—
are lost
in the lapping of water
on smooth, flat stones.

This a beauty
of dissonance,
this resonance
of stony strand,
this smoky cry
curled over a black pine
like a broken
and wind-battered branch
when the wind
bends the tips of the pines
and curdles the sky
from the north.

This is the beauty
of strength
broken by strength
and still strong.

A.J.M. Smith, 1943.[22]

This land of beauty, of lakes, bush, rock, can do strange things to man. It is here that the Windigo lurks; that incredible force which seizes hold of men and leads them to do the unspeakable.

On the northern shores of Lake Nipigon there once lived an Indian trapper by the name of Windigo.

There came a particularly cruel winter, cruel both for Windigo and for all the living creatures around him. It was so cold that the air crackled and the game vanished. Windigo had to go further and further from his cabin in search of food, and he became hungrier and hungrier as he tracked wearily back each day empty-handed.

Eventually, for his mere subsistence, he was forced to drink a brew made from the bark of a tree. When even this was depleted, he was weak, hungry, cold and crazed with fear. In desperation, he prayed to an evil spirit for help.

His call was not unanswered. He had a dream, and in his dream an evil spirit promised to help him by bestowing him with supernatural powers.

When Windigo awoke from his dream, he saw that it was a clear, cold night with a full moon. He was still suffering biting pangs of hunger, but he was suddenly no longer weak or tired.

With enormous swift strides he walked south and soon approached a distant Ojibway village about a hundred miles from his home. His eyes blazed as he gave three blood-curdling yells, which so terrified all the Ojibways in the village that they fell down in a faint. No sooner had they fainted than they were all turned into beavers by Windigo's evil sorcery.

At last Windigo had enough food to eat, so he began to devour the beavers one by one. As he was eating them, he began to grow taller and taller; first as tall as a wigwam, then bigger than the trees, then taller than the highest mountains, until his head was high above the clouds. The bigger he grew, the hungrier he became. So, when he had eaten all the beavers in the village, Windigo went away in search of more food.

Ojibway Legend.[23]

Anyone may fall under the Windigo spell and become tormented by a hunger satisfied only by human flesh. In 1660, Fathers Drueilletes and Dablon reported a case involving some Saulteux Indians.

Those poor men (according to the report given us) were seized with an ailment unknown to us, but not very unusual among the people we were seeking. They are afflicted with neither lunacy, hypochondria, nor frenzy; but have a combination of all these species of disease, which affects their imaginations and causes them a more than canine hunger. This makes them so ravenous for human flesh that they pounce upon women, children, and even upon men, like veritable werewolves, and devour them voraciously, without being able to appease or glut their appetite—ever seeking fresh prey, and the more greedily the more they eat.

Jesuit Relations.[24]

Even in this century, the Windigo psychosis prevails.

This is a story of a young man named Shaywayko and his parents. They went back into the bush to hunt and snare rabbits and they stayed there for quite a while. One day when his father was away looking after these snares, his mother said to him, "My son, I want to ask you if you would kill your father when he comes back," and he said, "All right". He waited along the road for his father and when his father came, he shot and killed him, and they ate him up. He had a sister older than himself, and brothers and sisters younger. His older sister helped him while he killed his younger brothers and sisters, and ate them up too. His mother was the last one they ate. They did not eat them all up, but they ate all the good parts. When they had nothing more to eat, Shaywayko told his sister that they would go away and try to find some Indians (to eat); so they went. When night came they stopped, and he got so hungry that he killed his sister and ate some of her.

Modern Ojibway Account.[25]

The early French explorers and settlers also fell under the spell of the lonely land. For them it was not the terror of Windigo but the freedom and challenge of the forests. Many young men entered the woods as coureurs de bois, *free fur traders.*

The journeys they undertake; the fatigues they undergo; the dangers to which they expose themselves, and the efforts they make, surpass all imagination. . . . They love to breathe a free air, they are early accustomed to a wandering life; it has charms for them which make them forget past dangers and fatigues, and they place their glory in encountering them often.

P.F.X. de Charlevoix, *Journal of a Voyage to North America,* 1761.[26]

Unfortunately, the influence of the bush helped to create one of the earliest moral crises in Canada. In 1685, the Marquis de Denonville reported on the seriousness of the situation.

It seems to me, Monseigneur, that the place from which it is necessary for us to give an account of the disorders that are taking place is not only the woods, but the settlements. These disorders do not stem only from the youth of the country but from the freedom which parents and governors have given to the young people in letting them spend time in the woods on the pretext of hunting or trading. This, Monseigneur, has reached such an excess that from the time children are able to carry a gun, fathers cannot restrain them and dare not anger them. Imagine, then, the evils which can arise from such a way of living. . . .

A fashion of dressing, nude like the savages, not only on carnival days but on all days of feasting and debauchery, has been treated with leniency and as a joke. All these practices tend only to attract the young people to the manner of life of the savages, and to associate with them and be forever libertines like them. I cannot tell you, Monseigneur, the attraction that all young people have for this life of the savage, which is to do nothing, follow every whim and be removed from all control.

For a long time it has 'been considered a very good practice to visit the savages in our settlements in order to accustom these people to live like us and become instructed in our religion. I perceive, Monseigneur, that just the opposite has taken place, for instead of becoming accustomed to our laws, I assure you that they have given to us everything they have that is most wicked and have taken for themselves only that which is bad and vicious in us.[27]

> *The* coureurs de bois *were succeeded by the voyageurs who crossed the great expanse of rivers, lakes and forests to reach the prairies. The sheer exhilaration of their life is seen in the reminiscences of an old voyageur in 1825.*

I have now been forty-two years in this country. For twenty-four I was a light canoe man. . . .No portage was too long for me; all portages were alike. My end of the canoe never touched the ground till I saw the end of it (the portage). Fifty songs a day were nothing to me. I could carry, paddle, walk, and sing with any man I ever saw. . . .No water, no weather, ever stopped the paddle or the song. I have had twelve wives in the country; and was once possessed of fifty horses, and six running dogs, trimmed in the first style. I was then like a Bourgeois, rich and happy: no Bourgeois had better dressed wives than I; no Indian chief finer horses; no white man better harnessed or swifter dogs. . . .I wanted for nothing; and I spent all my earnings in the enjoyment of pleasure. Five hundred pounds, twice told, have passed through my hands; although now I have not a spare shirt to my back, nor a penny to buy one. Yet, were I young again, I should glory in commencing the same career again. I would spend another half-century in the same fields of enjoyment. There is no life so happy as a voyageur's life; none so independent; no place where a man enjoys so much variety and freedom as in the Indian country. Huzza! Huzza! pour le pays sauvage![28]

> *For the modern Canadian, the lonely land exercises a different kind of a spell: the urge to flee to it on weekends or vacation, to build a cottage in it, to hold it for his own.*

For the plain fact is that the Canadian will not summer anywhere except beside a lake. It does not matter much how large the lake is, nor how clean, nor what sort of odours emanate from it. A lake is a lake. The fish may have been all fished out years and years ago. The water may have gone down and down, as a result of the denudation of the surrounding forest, until acres of ill-smelling morass separate the settlement from its water-frontage. It does not matter how far it is. . . .

It gives a man status to be able to tell his business associates that he was up at two that morning in order to come in from his weekend with the family in the Laurentians or Muskoka. He boasts about the wonderful air that blows across the lake at two in the morning, and the superb colours of the sunrise across the mountains, and the constant plash-plash of the leaping fish. . . .

I have mentioned that it does not matter how large the lake is. This brings us to another peculiar characteristic of the mind of the Canadian lake-dweller. Merely to dwell alongside a lake is good, but it is not everything. The true ideal of summer residence is to OWN a lake, so that you may dwell by it and nobody else can. This does not imply any selfishness or lack of neighbourliness on the part of the lake-dweller; on the contrary, the man who owns his lake will spend hundreds of dollars of money and months of time taking everybody he knows up to his lake and feeding them every luxury that the express companies will ship to him from the city. It is not that he is unwilling to share the use of his lake, or the fish in his lake, or the summer breezes off his lake, or the music of the frogs in his lake, or the iron-tinctured drinking water of his lake, or anything else that is therein. What he wants is to be able to walk all round the blessed thing and say to himself: "This is mine. If I liked I could drain it dry and nobody could stop me."

B. K. Sandwell, *The Privacity Agent.*[29]

Prairie

I wonder about us.

You meet your fellow Canadian and, as you talk, you come to feel he's a lot like you—solid, intelligent, knowledgeable, salt of the country and a credit to the nation—until he learns you are from the prairies.

"Went through there once," he says. "Miles of it," he says, "Flat as a goddam board."

At that point, Canadian unity goes down the drain.

He's right in one sense, but the perspective is all wrong. It's like seeing in one dimension, no breadth, no depth, just length.

You can't "see" prairie without using every sense the good Lord gave you. You have to stop, close your eyes, wait, then smell its warming wetness in spring, the leaf burn of autumn, the oven of summer, the star cold of winter, touch stubble, feel the caress of sweet clover, the bite of sawgrass.

Maybe it's stronger out there, but you come to realize you don't really "see" anything unless you understand the real world is a perceptive whole you must sense with every facet of your being. If we remembered this more often we might stop being a unidimensional nation, we might even learn that no matter who your neighbor is, it's a beautiful, beautiful land.

Hugh Lorren, 1971.[30]

Is is strange how some modern Canadians react to the prairie with distasteful shudders, for the earliest arrivals on the plains had a completely different impression. They revelled in the space, the beauty, and the adventure of the prairie.

The unending vision of sky and grass, the dim, distant, and ever-shifting horizon; the ridges that seem to be rolled upon one another in motionless torpor; the effect of sunrise and sunset, of night narrowing the vision to nothing, and morning only expanding it to a shapeless blank; the sigh and sough of a breeze that seems an echo in unison with the solitude of which it is the sole voice; and, above all, the sense of lonely, unending distance which comes to the *voyageur* when day after day has gone by, night has closed, and morning dawned upon his onward progress under the same ever-moving horizon of grass and sky.

Sir Francis Butler, 1869.[31]

The river *Saskatchawine* flows over a bed composed of sand and marl, which contributes not a little to diminish the purity and transparency of the waters, which, like those of the Missouri, are turbid and whitish. Except for that it is one of the prettiest rivers in the world. The banks are perfectly charming, and offer in many places a scene the fairest, the most smiling, and the best diversified that can be seen or imagined: hills in varied forms, crowned with superb groves; valleys agreeably embrowned, at evening and morning, by the prolonged shadow of the hills, and of the woods which adorn them; herds of light-limbed antelopes, and heavy colossal buffalo—the former bounding along the slopes of the hills, the latter trampling under their heavy feet the verdure of the plains; all these champaign beauties reflected and doubled as it were, by the waters of the river; the melodious and varied song of a thousand birds, perched on the tree-tops; the refreshing breath of the zephyrs; the serenity of the sky; the purity and salubrity of the air; all, in a word, pours contentment and joy into the soul of the enchanted spectator. It is above all in the morning, when the sun is rising, and in the evening when he is setting, that the spectacle is really ravishing. I could not detach my regards from that superb picture, till the nascent obscurity had obliterated its perfection.

Gabriel Franchère, 1812.[32]

In October the herds of bison began their leisurely march towards the wooded section of the country, near the foothills of the Rockies. And what a sight it was to see a drove of thousands moving majestically a few steps, then pausing for a mouthful or two of grass—another few paces, another mouthful, and so on—always travelling in the one direction. When spring came in the following year they would turn tail on the wooded areas and make again for the open prairie.

The joys of the hunt! Soon I was to learn its routine. A sort of rhythm pervaded it. The vast plains teemed with herds of *les animaux*, as my half-breed friends called them, or as the Crees named them—*Mus-toos-wuk*. The captain for the day would give the order for a run. You'd saddle your mount, parade out in a slow canter till a convenient mound or hill hid the hunters from their quarry, dismount to offer a short prayer, remount and await the captain's word to "let loose". Sure then it was every man for himself—a quick rush on the unsuspecting herd, each hunter singling out his particular animal.

Crack, crack went the guns! Or, if Indians were in the group, you'd hear the twang of bow-string and the hiss of the arrow as it sped to and found its mark. Now the grunt of the buffalo as he toppled headlong! (If his wound was not mortal, care was needed, for a wounded buffalo was a dangerous animal.) Then on after another and another till you had enough or your horse was tired.

Then back you would ride to your kill, dismount, spread the fallen monarch. Out would come the razor-sharp knife and in an incredibly short time the beast would be skinned, cut up, and ready for the carts that had been driven on the field by the womenfolk. And back to camp you'd go.

There were dangers, for wounded animals might turn on you or your horse step into a badger hole and tumble you out of your little running-saddle. But the hunter is blind to danger in the excitement of the chase.

John Kerr, 1872.[33]

For the Indians of the Plains—Cree, Assiniboine, Blackfoot, Piegan, Blood—the buffalo hunt was the great central event. But when the food supply was assured, the men of the tribes faced a new challenge.

Then it was incumbent upon every able-bodied man, under the code of honor of the time, to make an annual or bi-annual or even more frequent foray for horses and scalps. These trips generally took place in the spring and fall. With the melting of snow and ice in spring, or the making of the same in autumn, parties large and small would be made up. Each with lariat and a few pairs of moccasins, and, if possessed of a gun, with as much ammunition as he could obtain, or armed with bow and quiver full of shod arrows, in the dead of night these men would start for the enemy's country, depending on sustaining life by the chase on their way. Journeying on, sometimes by day and sometimes by night, fording rapid streams and swimming wide rivers, what signified the breaking up of the season or the plunge into ice-cold water of river and swamp to them? These must be considered trifles. By and by, when the enemy's presence is felt there will come the weary watching and waiting, amid cold and hunger, for cunning and strategy are now pitted the one against the other, and endurance and pluck must back these up or the trip will be a failure. One, two, three hundreds of miles of steady tramping, with your camp always facing in the direction of where your enemy is supposed to be. Every day or night the scouts, making thrice the distance covered by the party, keep up their constant effort to discover and forestall counter war-parties, or to find the enemy's camp; and when this is found sometimes to hang for days on its movements, and, following up, watch for a favorable spot and time either to make a charge or to steal in under cover of storm or darkness and drive off bands of horses. Then in either case to start for home, and push on regardless of weather so long as men and horses will hold out.

After a successful raid those long runs for home were great tests of horse-flesh and human endurance. With scaled ledge, blistered feet and weary limbs, and with eyes heavy for want of sleep, these men, now exultant with victory, would vie with each other in the race for camp. A lazy man assuredly had no place in such trials of endurance and of hardship. Furthermore, upon the men and boys of the camp devolved the care of the horses. The herding and guarding of these gave many a weary tramp or ride, and many a night in cold and storm, without sleep or rest. And finally, the constant need of protecting their camps from the wily enemy was a source of permanent worry, and always rested as a heavy responsibility upon these men.

John McDougall, *Pathfinding on Plain and Prairie*, 1898.[34]

The settlement of the prairies began with a trickle in the 1870s and developed into a flood by the 1900s. On the prairies the settler experienced a new environment, new sensations and, sometimes, terror.

This has been a hard day. The most terrible prairie fire that we have ever seen has swept across the country and we have been fighting it all day. . . .

. . . None of us had ever seen anything like it, and we had seen many· prairie fires. As you know, a prairie fire burns in the form of a wedge, with the headfire at the point. Here the heat had created a whirlwind, in which the flames danced like mad demons, leaping and whirling in an insane fury and racing along almost as though the fire had been following a train of gunpowder. As the fire advanced, the draft which it created, added to the swift breeze already blowing, was tremendous, and the rush and roar of the flames sounded much like the roar that accompanied the hailstorm last year.

The smoke was dense but we could see the bright flames of the headfire as they approached the guard. The guard might as well not have been there, for the flames leaped over it instantly. The heat, roar and smoke were so terrific that Lathrop and I took to our heels and ran out into the soft water pond as fast as our legs would carry us. It was lucky for us that we were so near the pond. The fire passed quickly and we were safe in the water, but we were alarmed about Papa, for he was left with the oxen and the pony and we were afraid that he might be rash enough to try to fight the headfire. If he had done so, I really believe that he would have perished.

It is strange how helpless some people are and what foolish things they will do in times of danger. When the Willis family saw the fire coming toward them, they went three miles to meet it and to start a backfire. The backfire, with three miles before it in which to gather head, became a raging headfire, beat them back to their own place and burned their barn with its contents to the ground.

Alberta settler, 1909.[35]

Gumbo is the bane and the saviour of Manitoba. It is a rich argillaceous mould or loam formed by the lake deposits and forest growth of ages, and resting upon a clay sub-soil. Its dark colour is due in part to the long accumulation of the charred grasses left by annual prairie fires and the collection of decayed vegetable and animal matter. But it is literally a profusion of stored-up wealth. It will grow grain; it will grow food for cattle; and it will go on like that for years to come without rotation of crops or without fertilizer. But as a roadway for vehicular traffic, Westerners will tell you that it is a "fright". They will tell you, in order that you may understand something of the glutinous sticking properties of gumbo, the story of the man who was one day out on the prairies with an ox and wagon. The wagon became hopelessly stuck, and he left it in the mud, unhitching the ox and returning home. That incident occurred some time ago. Every month or so, the young man went back to the spot, and tried to salvage his wagon. The years have flown by, but the man has never lost heart. He is determined to have that wagon, unless old age overtakes him and he is compelled to renounce the work in favour of his sons.

Thomas Wilby, *A Motor Tour Through Canada*, 1914.[36]

A Hard Land

The prairie is a land of extremes which subject body and soul to severe tests. And yet the Westerner often talks with a touch of pride in the disasters which befall him, as if glorying in the challenges. 1936 was a year in which all possible calamities came together.

"Never before and never since has western Canada lived through such a year! Beginning in the first week of January and continuing for two solid months without even the semblance of a break, an unbelievable cold spell held the West in its grip. It was the year Winnipeg earned its reputation as the coldest city of its size in the world, though it wasn't even as cold as Edmonton that February....

The week of February 11 to 17 was probably the coldest week ever experienced by large groups of civilized people anywhere. On February 16 it was -51° at Edmonton, -54° at Regina, -43° at Saskatoon, -36° at Calgary, and -40° everywhere in between. . . .

For two months, half a million farm people huddled around stoves and thought only of keeping warm. If food supplies ran low, they ate less. Only when fuel reached the vanishing point would they venture to town for a load of relief coal. By 1936 there was relief coal and relief food for anybody who needed it, and it was available for the asking, but it was available in town, and for many farmers town was eight or ten miles away.

The wait for moderation seemed interminable. Thousands of farm families lived permanently in their kitchens, bringing in their mattresses at night to be near the heat from the cook-stove. To augment their coal supplies, they gathered the celebrated buffalo chips—cow dung that had dried in the sun and hardened to a burnable consistency. Bags of weed seeds from straw stacks were mixed in with soft coal, as another way of stretching fuel supplies.

James H. Gray, *The Winter Years.* [37]

Then came the summer of the great heat wave.

By Dominion Day, ninety-degree temperatures were the rule between Winnipeg and Lethbridge. At Foremost, it reached into the nineties every day but three for the next six weeks. At Willow Creek, in south-western Saskatchewan, it went about 100° on thirteen days in July. The heat not only covered the Great Plains, it fastened a deathly grip on Ontario and the Great Lakes as well. . . .

What made the heat intolerable was the way the wave built. Every day was hotter than the previous day, with heavier haze and more dust. At the end of the first week in July, people were taking pillows into the down-town parks in Winnipeg and Regina in an effort to get some rest. In the down-town tenements, beds were deserted as the inhabitants stretched out on floors, on verandahs, and on lawns. But there was no escape. Swarms of mosquitoes and crickets made sleeping out of doors almost impossible in Winnipeg. In Regina even mosquitoes would have been welcome, for their presence would have meant there was water some place. The only visible sign of water in Regina was the circles of moisture around the trees on Victoria Street; the city saved the trees by hauling water in fire trucks.

The Manitoba peak was reached on July 11 when the temperature reached 108° in Winnipeg, 110° in Brandon, and 110° at Morden. During the third week in July, it went over 100° every day everywhere in the south country of Saskatchewan and Alberta. In Winnipeg, the weather story was bigger even than the provincial election. A dozen people died daily from heat prostration, and soon we were reporting the deaths of dogs, cats, and canary-birds.

James H. Gray, *The Winter Years.*[38]

With the heat came drought and the terrifying dust storms, the "black blizzards".

The morning is usually fine and clear, with maybe just a gentle breeze blowing. We farmers are all out in the fields ploughing, seeding, summer fallowing—doing any one of a score of jobs and duties that fall to the farmer's lot where the soil will produce. The breeze comes on just a little stronger, and a few small particles of soil start to drift gently along the top of the cultivated land. These tiny soil particles soon loosen up other little particles. Very soon, with the increasing wind, the whole surface of the field is gently sifting along, always moving, always gathering fresh momentum by rapidly increasing volume. There is nothing spectacular yet. But wait—away off to the northwest a heavy black cloud is forming between sky and earth. Black, yes, black as night. It sweeps towards us rapidly at forty, fifty, sixty miles an hour. We turn, each individual one of us, looking for the nearest shelter. Teams are unhooked as quickly as possible, and if no stable room is near turned with their heads away from the storm. Those of us with tractors either make for shelter or stay with the machines as long as possible. . . . The air gets colder. The huge black wall is now only a mile away. A minute, and with a blast like the roar of a thousand lions it is upon us. We are alone in a sightless mass of hurtling soil, stinging sand and thumping clods. We lose all sense of direction. Unless one happens to be within hand's reach of a fence progress in any calculated direction is almost impossible. We can only stand buffeted by the blows of a thousand hammers, or drift helpless, smoking, blinded. This is the black blizzard.

For hours the tortured soil is torn and ravished until the storm ceases. Then we look out on the fields which we have tilled. They are as smooth as if polished by a giant plane. Here and there a few wheat plants, stricken, stand on roots still remaining in the hard subsoil. With to-morrow's sun they will probably fade and die. Millions in rich top soil is gone forever. That is the black blizzard, the most appalling thing in nature.

Alberta farmer, 1936.[39]

They said, "Sure, it'll rain next year!"
When that was dry, "Well, next year anyway."
Then, "Next—"
But still the metal hardness of the sky
Softened only in mockery.
When lightning slashed and twanged
And thunder made the hot head surge with pain
Never a drop fell;
Always hard yellow sun conquered the storm.
So the soon sickly-familiary saying grew,
(Watching the futile clouds sneak down the north)
"Jest empties goin' back!"
(Cold laughter bending parched lips in a smile
Bleak eyes denied.)

Anne Marriott, *The Wind Our Enemy*, 1939.[40]

Winter: The Great Canadian Challenge

It is true there is no want of wood to guard against the cold, which very soon becomes extreme and encroaches greatly on the spring. But it is, however, something extremely shocking not to be able to stir out of doors without being frozen, at least without being wrapt up in furs like a bear. Moreover, what a spectacle is it to behold one continued tract of snow which pains the sight and hides from your view all the beauties of nature? No more difference between the rivers and fields, no more variety; even the trees are covered with snow-frost, with large icicles depending from all their branches under which you cannot pass with safety. What can a man think who sees the horses with beards of ice more than a foot long, and who can travel in a country where, for the space of six months, the bears themselves dare not show their faces to the weather? Thus I have never passed a winter in this country without seeing someone or other carried to the hospital who was obliged to have his legs or arms cut off on account of their being benumbed and frozen.

Pierre Charlevoix in New France, 1708.[41]

It was a cruel winter. No white man in the country had ever known any like it, and if the Indians did, it was only through legends ancient and incredible. It began early in November with a blizzard which made the world one great glare of white—an Arctic landscape as bleak as the imagination can depict or reality furnish. For weeks that stretched into agonizing months, the cold was unbroken, varying only in intensity, and always merciless. Storm followed storm, until it became hard to believe that warm breezes had ever waved green grasses back and forth where now the north wind piled the snow into forbidding drifts. It seemed difficult to remember the summer, and it seemed folly to hope for spring. Much of the time the sky was a great white frost-cloud, like a vast reflection of a plain of snow. And if the eye sought relief from its cruel light it met the relentless glare from below, until sight seemed an illusion, and earth met sky in an unreal horizon but a few feet away. Or, when the sun shone, it was like a cold copper disk, far down in the southern sky, giving light without warmth, as though its mission were to enable the world to see its misery. And, on clear nights, the Northern Lights played back and forth among a million stars, a vast kaleidoscope of swiftly changing color and awe-inspiring beauty.

It seemed that almost every living thing that had been able to escape had gone, but occasionally, the weird, dismal howl of a coyote broke the silence of the frosty night, or a great white owl flitted silently over the snow, like a lost spirit in a hell of cold. Long before the cold had broken, it had taken its full toll. I remember the cattle at the ranches on the Ribstone flat, and at Caseley's ranch. One by one they had dropped in the feed-lots, pitiful, frozen lumps of clay. And I saw them frozen and standing in the deep snow like statues, as though waiting for a kinder day to grant them the privilege of lying down. I saw them in the Ribstone Coulee, black spots in the snow, or piled in rows along the fences against which the storm had driven them, and beyond which they could not go.

The seasons come and go. There have been other winters—there will be many more. But no one who knew this one will be able to recall it without a shudder, or to think of it other than as a long ordeal of cold and death and desolation.

Alberta farmer on the winter of 1906-1907.[42]

Thanks to a long and uninterrupted stay abroad I was able to escape six Canadian winters. Thus it was not without some anxiety that, back home once again, I faced the prospect of January for the first time in six years.

It was not so much the physical cold that I feared (for I was well aware of the efficiency of central heating in our houses) as much as the doping of the spirit, that strangulation or crushing of the soul under the weight of the opaque snow. . . .

. . . The fear I felt at the thought of returning to the Canadian winter was fear of firemen who extinguish the fire burning beneath the snow and ice, a fear of the mortifying silence of these snow-bound spaces, the fear of winter as absence, of winter as an excuse for inaction, of winter as an alibi, as confession and penitence, as a refuge for a bad conscience, as an escape, as a scapegoat for our inability to exist.

Pierre Trottier, 1963.[43]

The old-time Canadians must have been a hardier breed than the present-day lovers of comfort, for they seemed to ignore the rigours of winter and concentrate upon the joys of that season. Whether they were sincere, or simply trying to make the best of a bad thing is not known, but there is a ring of sincerity in their words.

The snow of Canada is a source of both pleasure and profit. Young and old, especially the former, hail with delight the first approach of the winter's snow. There is more real merriment in Canada in Winter than in Summer, although in both seasons the Canadians are a very happy people.

"You may well, indeed, refer with pride to Canada as your home, for in no country in the world that I have ever visited, have I seen so many happy and contented homesteads, or so few signs of destitution or distress." —Lord Dufferin.

The winter sports, such as tobogganing, snow-shoeing, skating, sleigh-riding with a tandem team, a spanking span, or a four-in-hand, is something to be experienced, not adequately described. Wrapped in warm robes, with agreeable companions, dashing away up hill and down across frozen rivers and lovely lakes, or over the plain, or through evergreen groves, along the hill-sides,—but you must come and see and know for yourself.

Reverend D.V. Lucas, *All About Canada*, 1882.[44]

But now it is winter in the city, and the mountain wears the patriarchal snow that befits it, and the heaven the church-spires point to shines very clear and cold above them, and the great river vexes itself under strong bonds. Winter in the city, and that mad, merry time of the winter when its sober inhabitant putteth away from him his sobriety, and his dignity, and his ulster, and his boots, and goeth forth in a spirit of unaccountable hilarity, a blanket-suit and moccasins, his snowshoes on his shoulder, his toboggan trailing after him, to do homage to the King of the Carnival.

Sara Jeanette Duncan, 1887.[45]

A fair American visitor to Quebec last Summer said to me, "How do you manage to live here in Winter?" "Madam," I replied with mock gravity, "as soon as the last tourist has departed, we all take to the woods, build ourselves igloes and go into hibernation. We do this because of the scarcity of Americans, upon whom we mainly subsist, but we're going to change all that by bringing the American here in winter. No igloe hibernation once they arrive."

"Really," she answered, "come to think of it, I have been devoured with kindness since my arrival, and if a winter visit should have half the warmth of welcome that has made my summer stay so agreeable I'll come back next winter to get thawed out the first cold spell we have in New York."

From a residence now of sixteen years in Quebec, I dare the statement that it is now the most alive little city on the continent in the winter season. When the last ship goes down to the sea at the end of November, and the first big snow storm has covered the ground to a depth of five or six inches, the city and country awaken to a new life. With the close of navigation much of the commercial activity of the city ceases and people give themselves up to the enjoyment of the winter with the ardor of children let loose for a long holiday. The clear cold begets outdoor activity, and the amusements of the day and night are mainly those that take men and women into the open air.

G. M. Fairchild, *My Quebec Scrap-Book*, 1907.[46]

Canada is colder than the British Isles in winter, still I doubt very much if the natives of Canada would prefer an English winter to their own. In fact, I have been in Toronto in winter when we were having typical English weather—muggy and rainy and muddy. Were we glad? Certainly not. Everyone was complaining bitterly, and Canadian-born and British-born alike felt aggrieved because they were not having the cold, dry, frosty, sunny winter they considered themselves entitled to as Canadians. . . .

The last New Year's day I was in Toronto, the thermometer was about ten degrees above Zero, and I went to High Park in West Toronto, to see the people on the toboggan slides. A great crowd of happy young folk were having boisterous fun and fine sport on the steep icy slopes where the sleighs and toboggans, some of them with a crew of eight, flew like the wind for a good half-mile. The winter in Ontario certainly has its compensations. What glowing faces peeping out from fur collars, or bright woollen mufflers! What merry laughter! A bright cold day, the sun shining gloriously, and not a cloud visible. How the snow glittered! How beautiful the pine trees looked, their branches bent with their loads of snow, glittering like a good old-fashioned Christmas card.

British immigrant in early 1900.[47]

In the midst of all this happiness appeared the viper of temptation—the lure of gentler climates to the south. Could it actually be possible to escape winter? As early as 1909 Florida, where lay the fountain of youth, was beckoning to Canadians. One writer, perhaps with an eye to the future, detected this disturbing trend and spoke out against it.

Some of our citizens now and again cast longing eyes toward Florida, fancying that in that land of perpetual sunshine more pleasure can be experienced than in our own land, possessing the four seasons clearly and distinctly defined. It is quite a mistake. This beautiful Ontario of ours presents, as the seasons flow along, a variety of contrasts in scenes and foliage which the warm climates know not of. Our springs are incomparably finer and pleasanter than anything down south, and our foliage is greener and cleaner than hot countries can show. Our summers are just hot enough to give us a taste of what hot weather really is, and make us long for the russet fall season, with its golden grains, and red-cheeked fruits, and delightful sombre days, when our atmosphere becomes veritable champagne in itself, followed by the forest pictures of bright colours as the frost touches the foliage. Our bright, crisp, clear, cold and jolly sleighing is life-giving to the uttermost human extremity, and we would not have a warm, muddy, rainy winter if we could. Then comes our spring season, just the interlude, as it were, between winter and summer, when the old drifted snow banks are disappearing, and this is the season which gives us the "sugaring-off", which cannot be duplicated anywhere out of our North American continent.

Thomas Conant, *Life In Canada*, 1903.[48]

The plea failed. Modern Canadians flee by the thousands to the sunny lands of Florida and the Caribbean. Perhaps, however, there is a feeling of guilt at having deserted the challenge of a Canadian winter. Scott Young explored the psychology of the winter emigrés.

Galoshes!

New Smyrna Beach, Fla.

That was a devastating blow Zena Cherry dealt to the cause of lolling around and going to seed when she wrote recently, "My idea of hell would be a winter in Florida."

All up and down the sunny beach from Miami to St. Augustine little knots of Globe and Mail subscribers gathered to stand ankle-deep in the surf and morosely hitch up their shorts while they asked themselves, "Where have we failed?"

One gentleman here at New Smyrna was so upset that he went to the trunk of his car and got the shovel that he'd needed to get out of his driveway a few weeks ago, when he still thought that going to Florida was a good idea. He went out in front of his beach house and began shovelling sand. "This is more like it," he cried.

However, when he followed this up by carrying out a 50-pound bag of salt to sprinkle on what he said were slippery places, some college girls who were playing touch football in tiny bikinis became alarmed and moved their game to another part of the beach. Whereupon some more level-headed Canadian males towed him out to sea and sank him.

Putting on my Enquiring Reporter beanie with the propeller on top, I went out to interview people on their reactions to Zena Cherry's opinion.

First I approached the manager of a large condominium, feeling that as a Floridian he would have a balanced, neutral view. "Do you feel that Canadians who come here for the winter go through hell?" I asked.

"Just the first day or two," he said. "They come here sort of frantic, it always seems to me. I've had them undress right in the parking lot and go straight into the ocean. They get here at noon, by three o'clock they're sunburned and by four o'clock they have colds. I've always thought they act irrational, like people who are running away from something. Say, what is, or are, galoshes?"

"Like rubber snakeboots, but they buckle or zip up the front. Why?"

"I thought it meant something like cheers, or prosit, or skol. Every Canadian who comes in here, first he buys a bottle and then he gets another bunch of Canadians and they all say to each other, "Galoshes!" and then they all laugh and get stoned. . . .

Scott Young, 1972.[49]

Will Spring Never Come?

There comes a time when every Canadian knows in his soul that winter is going to last forever, that he will never again smell warm earth, or feel the hot sun on his flesh. Indeed he may wonder if he has ever experienced such pleasure. Then come the first days of Spring. Spring, alas, is not to be trusted, for it holds out a promise which is so often unfulfilled. Our despair and sense of betrayal find expression in the works of our poets.

New Brunswick

All breath is crystal spinning in the air,
the only warmth that strokes this friendless cold,
and winter is the season that we share,
shut out and young or shut away and old.
The very dung behind the cattle freezes,
the wind insults the face like a sprung branch,
who can condemn the exile if he seizes
an icicle and thrust it like a lance

into his heart? Oh, Christ our faith is strong
that winter lasts forever, being long.

Alden A. Nowlan, 1961.[50]

Winter

Winter, by whom our stumbling feet were caught
Who held us long in iron chains of cold,
Winter has turned reluctantly at last,
Unfastened the sharp snares and soberly
Moved like a dream up slopes and over hills,
breathing a last cool sigh before he went.
Winter has gone. The marsh-hawk and the crow
Follow relentlessly his backward step.
Now you would think that spring must take his place,
Heal up the wounds, breathe freedom on the earth,
Throw all her singing on the barren air.
I tell you, no: we must be captives still
Who watch each other with the winter's look,
Touch with his hand, speak with his bitter breath.

Dorothy Livesay.[51]

Snow In April

Over the boughs that the wind has shaken,
   Over the sands that are rippled with rain,
Over the banks where the buds awaken
   Cold cloud shadows are spreading again.

All the musical world is still,
   When sharp and sudden, a sparrow calls,
And down on the grass where the violets shiver,
Through the spruce on the height of the hill,
Down on the breadths of the shining river
   The faint snow falls.

Last weak word of a lord that passes—
   Why should the burgeoning woods be mute?
Spring is abroad in the spring grasses,
   Life is awake in the robin's flute.
But high in the spruce a wind is wailing.
   And the birds in silence arise and go.
Is it that winter is still too near
For the heart of the world to cast out fear,
When over the sky the rack comes sailing
   And suddenly falls the snow?

                                        Marjorie Pickthall, 1925.[52]

*And yet spring does finally come. Mordecai Richler caught the excitement
of that magic moment when we know that spring, in truth, has arrived.*

To understand what a fine place Montreal is when spring is coming
you must know the winters that come first. Chill grey mornings; sun
bright in the cold noon sky but giving off no heat to speak of; skies
darkening again early in the afternoon; long frosty nights with that
window-banging wind whipping in burning hard from the north, pushing
people before it like paper, making dunes and ridges that hurt the eye
to look at on the mountain snows, burning children's cheeks red and
cutting like a knife across flat frozen ponds. Old men blowing on their
wrinkled hands, boys with blue lips and women with running noses all
huddled up and knocking their feet together in the bitter cold waiting
for liquor commissions to open and banks to shut, late dates, streetcars. . . .

So when the first rumours of thaw reach the city everybody is glad. That first rumour, coming towards the end of February, is usually hidden away in the back pages of newspapers. It says that two government icebreakers, the *d'Iberville* and the *Ernest Lapointe*, have started poking their way down the frozen St. Lawrence towards Montreal. That's a while before the NHL hockey playoffs, and most people on the streetcars are talking about how the players are moving slow because of the heat. The resorts up north stop advertising themselves as the St. Moritz or Davos of Canada: they begin to talk of the sun, their pamphlets saying how so many happily married couples first fell on their beaches. That first thaw is a glory. The big snow heaps on Fletcher's Field and a whole winter's caboodle of snowmen begin to shrivel and shrink away. Giant sweepers roar up and down the streets wiping a winter's precautionary sands off the pavement. You can make out chunks of yellow grass here and there like exposed flesh under the shrinking slush that still sticks to the flanks of Mount Royal. Occasionally it snows: but noon comes and all the gutters are gurgling again. There is a green, impolite smell to the streets.

With the first thaw the change takes hold: there is a difference to everything, the difference between a clenched fist and an open hand. The kids get out on their roller-skates and make most side-streets a hazard. Belmont Park opens, so do the race tracks. Ships steam into port from Belfast and Le Havre and Hamburg and Liverpool and Archangel and Port-of-Spain. NDG organizes softball teams, the ladies of Westmount plan their flower-shows, and the Jr. Chamber of Commerce sets aside one week as Traffic Safety Week. The man who reviews books for the *Star* will say that spring is here but J.P. Sartre is without that traditional Gallic charm, and young writers aren't cheerful enough. But best of all is St. Catherine Street on an April evening. Watch the girls, eh, their hair full of wind, as they go strolling past in their cotton print dresses. Men, sporting smart suits and spiffy ties, waving enticingly at them. See the American tourists having a whale of a time frantically, a Kodak strapped to one arm and a lulu of a wife to the other. . . . Kids wandering in and out of the crowds yelling rude things at girls older than themselves. . . . Sports fans clustering at corners waiting for the *Gazette* to appear. . . .

In parks, playgrounds, and on Mount Royal, tattered men with leather faces loll on benches, their faces upturned to the sun. Maiden aunts hopeful again after a long winter's withering knit near to baby carriages which hold the children of others. Come noon, lovers freed from the factory sprawl on the green mountainside while the children tease and the tattered men watch laconically and the maiden aunts knit near to baby carriages that hold the children of others.

Everybody is full.

Mordecai Richler, *Son of a Smaller Hero*, 1965.[53]

It's my feeling that Canadians work very hard and are tremendously efficient, but as a Trinidadian would say: Where is the fun?

Pearl Cameron, from Trinidad, 1971.[1]

Where, indeed, is the fun? A strong strain of puritanism has always existed in the Canadian character. To us, there has seemed something unsound, perhaps even evil, about hearty enjoyment of the pleasures of life. Discipline. Control. Regulation. These are the guidelines which have dominated Canadian society, and certainly its authorities. The attitudes which for so long have dominated us were summed up by a very sincere gentleman, Charles Durand, in 1897.

Once as a young man (away back in 1830, perhaps earlier,) I thought I would become a cigar smoker. It made me sick at first, as it always does, and I went to bed for a day. I persisted in it, however, until I found it injured me, caused excessive spitting, etc., hence I at once broke it off. Some people think it renders them more social and helps them to think, as some orators think brandy or wine increases their eloquence;

5

OUR

PLEASURES

but it is all imaginary. Why should it? It may give a temporary stimulus, which becomes a stupor afterwards. Did such smokers and drinkers ever ask themselves how it is that dumb beasts—the lion, the tiger, or deer, and birds, the ostrich and eagle, or the mocking-bird, and thrush—can endure great fatigues, exhibit great strength, and sing beautifully on mere cold water? How is it that the fish can exist in water, or the flowers look so lovely in the dews of heaven? Never, my young friends, girls or boys, use either of these poisons. . . .

The drinking habit is bad, the use of tobacco worse, visiting theatres is not so bad, but leads to waste of time, frivolous thoughts, and too often to immorality. I have visited theatres in my life, although not very often, and I never received any real benefit, but have always seen the evil of them. We suppose we are to live again in a future state, then let us only do what will make us happy here and in another world.

Charles Durand, *Reminiscences of Charles Durand*, 1897.[2]

The Men of God

The Canadian approach to pleasure owes much to the influence of the clergy in this country. Jesuit martyrs, Methodist circuit riders, Northern missionaries—all were aggressive men and women of conscience who sought to bring about a more perfect world through the purification of men's souls. Their efforts to correct and improve human behaviour contributed much to the social improvement in Canada. But, at times, their zeal could be a nuisance. Baron Lahontan, who visited Montreal in 1685, found the activities of the local clergy extremely frustrating.

...here we cannot enjoy ourselves, either at Play, or in visiting the Ladies, but 'tis presently carried to the Curate's ears, who takes public notice of it in the Pulpit. His Zeal goes so far, as even to name the Persons: and since he refuses the Sacrament of the Holy Supper to Ladies of Quality, upon the most slender Pretences, you may easily guess at the other steps of his Indiscretion. You cannot imagine to what a pitch these Ecclesiastical Lords have screw'd their Authority; They excommunicate all the Masks, and wherever they spy 'em, they run after 'em to uncover their Faces, and abuse 'em in a reproachful manner; In fine, they have a more watchful eye over the Conduct of the Girls, and married Women, than their Fathers and Husbands have. They cry out against those that do not receive the Sacrament once a month; and at *Easter* they oblige all sorts of Persons to give in Bills to their Confessors. They prohibit and burn all the Books that treat of any other Subject but Devotion. When I think of this Tyranny, I cannot but be inrag'd at the impertinent Zeal of the Curate of this City. This inhumane Fellow came one day to my Lodging, and finding the Romance of the Adventures of *Petronius* upon my Table, he fell upon it with an unimaginable fury and tore out almost all the Leaves. This Book I valued more than my Life, because 'twas not castrated; and indeed I was so provok'd when I saw it all in wreck, that if my Landlord had not held me, I had gone immediately to the turbulent Pastor's House, and would have pluck'd out the Hairs of his Beard with as little mercy as he did the Leaves of my Book. These Animals cannot content themselves with the studying of Mens Actions, but they must likewise dive into their Thoughts. By this Sketch, Sir, you may judge what a pleasant Life we lead here.[3]

*Even more formidable were the Methodist circuit riders who brought
the Word and the Wrath of God to the isolated pioneer communities.
These men were not to be trifled with and they exercised a profound
influence on their flock.*

Hezekiah Calvin Wooster was received on trial in 1783, and Daniel
Coote in 1794. These two offered their services for Canada and were
accepted. . . . The way in which divine power often manifested itself under
Wooster's preaching was very remarkable. Once at a quarterly meeting
on the Bay of Quinte circuit, just as Wooster began his sermon, a man
in the front of the gallery began to swear profanely, and otherwise to
disturb the congregation. The preacher appeared to take no notice until
he was in the midst of his sermon, when suddenly fixing his eyes on
the profane man, he pointed his finger at him, and stamping with his
foot, cried with great energy, "My God, smite him!" Instantly the man
fell as if shot through the heart, and such a sense of God a presence
and power came down upon the congregation that on every hand sinners
cried for mercy, while the saints shouted for joy.

G. F. Hayter, *History of Methodism in Canada*, 1862.[4]

At a later period came the camp meetings, and these were at times
scenes of the most intense excitement. The sermon, and it was the real
old-timer with plenty of brimstone in it, was followed by singing, and
during the singing sinners were urged to advance to the penitent bench.
"Come Sinners to the Gospel Feast" and "Blow Ye the Trumpet Blow"
were among the favourite hymnal appeals to the ungodly. The fierce
urge of the sermon and the passionate call of the singers stirred the massed
audience to a state of indescribable excitement. I have seen people literally
fall over each other while the anguished wails of repentant sinners mingled
with the voices of the singers and weird sound of the wind in the tree
tops.

The most exciting time of the kind I ever experienced was at an indoor
revival, held by a man named Beale, at Orono in 1843. This man warned
the assembled hundreds to prepare for the end of the world, which he
declared was then at hand. One man actually tried to climb a stovepipe
on the way to heaven and one woman went raving mad.

W. L. Smith, *The Pioneers of Old Ontario*, 1923.[5]

*Methodism eventually became less dramatic in the presentation of its
message. But it continued to brook no compromise with the forces of*

evil—drink, cigarettes, dancing, card-playing, stage plays, horse-racing, sexual dalliance. If there was anything as influential as the stern Methodist clergy on the formation of the Canadian puritan psychology, it was the surfeit of Scots in this country.

The Mark of the Scot

Alexander Mackenzie—explorer; William Lyon Mackenzie—fighter for freedom; John A. Macdonald—Father of Confederation: only three of thousands of Scots who have penetrated every part of Canada. And wherever they went, the Scots influenced the very soul of this nation.

...men of Scottish origin have proved their claim to the foremost place among those who have laid the foundations of Canadian nationality. The splendid intellectual and moral gifts of the race have lost nothing by transplatation to the alien soil, but have rather become strengthened by the strenuous conflict and pressure of unaccustomed social conditions, and the action and reaction of new forces. . . . The strong religious instincts, the keen moral perceptions, the resolute will, tireless energy, and acute logical faculty of the Scot, tempered and modified by the qualities of the people who share our national heritage, will enter very largely into the fibre of the coming race.

W. J. Rattray, *The Scot in British North America*, 1880.[6]

He is hardworking, honest, extrovert, not given to melancholy, or poetry, thinking of art in terms of decoration and sport in terms of physical fitness. Utilitarians, practical, reasonable men, except when under the influence of a strong passion, like that brewed in an Orange Lodge. Not strongly humorous in the mass, not particularly adventurous on the average. They are bankers, engineers, and technicians. They have little interest in women, save for sex, and little interest in Leisure, save as a rest from work."

Ernest Watkins, *Prospect of Canada*, 1954.[7]

The Scottish bourgeoisie of the cities believe that the chief aim in life is to work very hard and make money, and that an artist is a weakling and trifler; if he devotes all his time to his work, he becomes one of the very worst things that it is possible to be in British Canada—a man without a regular job."

Edmund Wilson, *O Canada*. 1964.[8]

The Scotch are prominent above all other people for their observance of the Lord's Day. I do not suppose that there is a race on the face of the earth whose progress has been more remarkable, whose influence is more widely extended, that has made a better figure in science and literature and material advancement than the Scotch people. They inhabit a little country, with a limited population, but the leaven of their influence has reached the ends of the earth; it is felt in this Dominion, in the United States, in every British colony, and in proportion to their number their influence is vastly greater than that of any other race on the face of this globe. It is not because of the superiority of the race or of any natural advantage, but it is in consequence of their stability of character, firmness and persistency in adhering to their rules in regard to religious matters, especially Sabbath observance, a characteristic which they have displayed during the last two hundred or three hundred years.

John Charlton, *Speeches and Addresses*, 1905.[9]

Sunday, Dreadful Sunday

A Canadian who visits the United States almost never fails to be surprised, shocked almost, by the roaring commercial hub-bub of the American Sabbath; for a distinctive characteristic of Canadian life has been the protection of the Sabbath day from the foibles of human activity. The origins of our "closed" Sundays, and the "blue laws" which enforced them, go back to the early day of New France.

...the *Curé* of Pointe-Levy, having exposed to us that there is an abuse committed continuously in his parish, which he cannot remedy no matter what remonstrances he makes to the inhabitants who, without reason and without his permission, use their carts (for business) on Holy days and on Sundays, and by this contravene with impunity the commandments of God. . . .

We forbid all the inhabitants of the parish . . . as well as of all parishes in this country, to use their carts on Sundays and on Holy days without the permission of their *curés* and, in case of contravention, permit all militia officers to seize the goods which are loaded on the said carts . . .

The Bishop of New France, 1708.[10]

In 1834 a Toronto city ordinance laid the foundation of "The Toronto Sunday"—that symbol of purity and goodness which would confound and amuse all Canadians.

Any person who shall on Sunday do any servile work, or labour, (works of piety, charity, and necessity excepted) or buy or sell, or show forth, or expose for sale, any Goods, Wares, or Merchandize, or any other thing shall forfeit a sum not less than five shillings nor exceeding fifteen shillings for each offence, in the discretion of the Magistrates convicting, but it shall be lawful to sell Milk, until nine o'clock in the morning, and after four o'clock in the afternoon.[11]

In 1903 the Regina Standard commented approvingly on Ontario's Sunday laws.

The Act of 1845, which is the only Operative Sunday law in Ontario, now declares it to be unlawful to transact business, exercise any worldly labor or calling, tipple or permit tippling in any inn, tavern, grocery or house of entertainment, hunt or fish, or play at ball or any other noisy games on Sunday. That is going a big way toward providing for the protection of the rest day.[12]

Westerners have always been smug in their condemnation of Toronto and Ontario piety. But the reminiscences of James Gray, a native of Winnipeg, showed that Ontario was not alone in its fight against evil.

. . .Winnipeg suffered through what must have been the most restrictive Sunday on the continent. It took fifteen years of intermittent agitation before the operation of streetcars on Sunday was finally approved in 1906. A suggestion that Sundays might be made less austere by permitting concerts of sacred music was roundly attacked by a Presbyterian zealot. So formidable did the Protestant clergy become when aroused that Manitoba was well into the Jazz Age before its government had the courage to override their opposition to Sunday trains to the Lake Winnipeg beaches. It was almost as if a puritanical Sunday was the weekly revenge the clergymen took on the public for its refusal to join in their crusades against the brothels and bars.

James H. Gray, *Red Lights On The Prairies,* 1971.[13]

And the defence for restrictive laws? John Charlton, one of the founders of the Dominion Lord's Day Alliance, set forth one argument in 1905.

Now, sir, we have in all parts of the world at the present time labour troubles and unrest; we have to-day 200,000 miners on strike in the United

States; we have an army of disaffected men marching on to Washington; we have bomb-throwing in almost every capital of Europe; we have society trembling on the verge of great social upheavals; and we are all standing in dread of the changes that may speedily come. . . . The remedy for all these difficulties lies in the application of Christian principles, which will make better masters and better men. Unless these principles are applied, these social upheavals will continue. And the first step to take in applying them is to recognize God's law, that the Sabbath Day is to be remembered and kept holy, and the labourer is to secured in the possession of his right to enjoy that day as a day of rest.

John Charlton, *Speeches and Addresses*, 1905.[14]

The Reverend W. A. Mackay in his book How To Succeed, *which appeared in 1900, gave his support to the cause.*

. . . The present is an intensely materialistic age, when, in the mad rush after gain and worldly pleasure, home life is at a low ebb, the religious education of the young sadly neglected, and the sanctity of the Sabbath trampled under foot. We would seek to combat this dangerous tendency of our day by exhibiting men born and reared in homes where God was honored, the children instructed in the Scriptures, and the Sabbath observed as holy unto the Lord and honorable.[15]

The efforts to protect the Sabbath at least have given Canadians a subject for humorous comment. In a satirical glance at the Toronto Sunday, Lister Sinclair described the arrival of a fictional newcomer.

So he came at last to Toronto, the great teeming city of eastern Canada; the swarming, seething tumultuous sky-scraper-ridden heart of Ontario! Toronto; the wealthiest city in the Dominion, its sidewalks paved with gold and obscured by an endless throng of eager, excited, happy, bustling people!

Only he happened to arrive on a Sunday.

He walked out of the huge echoing Union Station, and out into Front Street. Not a soul as far as the eye could see. Not a sound except the dust falling on the silent queue of corpses hidden away in the bowels of the Union Station still waiting for a cab. So Charlie started to walk. He trudged past the Customs and Excise Building down there by the station, bowing three times, of course, as he passed the Department of Income Tax. Then he turned up Yonge Street, stretching away straight as an arrow (and about as wide) all the way up to Hudson Bay, the Arctic Circle and North York.

So he came through, the hollow empty streets of the city that nobody loves, with all the eyes of Toronto peeping in horror at the man who dared to walk up Yonge Street on a Sunday; till at length he came to Queen's Park, where he curled up for the night cradled in the stern bronze lap of Her Late Majesty Queen Victoria, who was not amused.[16]

> But, by the 1970s, things had changed. Sunday football games were played in Vancouver; streetcars operated on Sunday in Winnipeg; and Toronto, yes, Toronto, enjoyed Sunday beer.

Well, whadda-ya-know! They finally opened a pedestrian mall on Yonge Street and the people arrived in droves. Not only that, but they actually served b-e-e-r in sidewalk cafes on a Sunday! And, did the earth shake and the skies darken and avenging bolts of lightning descend from above? Not a bit of it. The sun continued to smile benignly down upon the good people of Toronto actually enjoying themselves on a Sunday. There have been whispers, in the past, that we occasionally enjoyed ourselves on a Saturday. But never on a Sunday! Why, I was a young man before I discovered that anyone anywhere ever enjoyed himself on a Sunday. It was during my first trip to England that this sensational revelation occurred. . . .

I believe that was the first time I ever saw anyone drink an ale outdoors in a public place on a Sunday without nervous twitches and uneasy sidelong glances. Because that is the Canadian way of life and particularly the Toronto Canadian way of life. . . .

. . .Do we have such horrible drinking laws in Canada because Canadians are such terrible drinkers, or are Canadians such terrible drinkers because we have such horrible drinking laws? Perhaps, with the gradual relaxation of the liquor laws here and there, we'll be able to find out.

Bruce West, 1971.[17]

The Beer Parlour Syndrome

I had travelled extensively before arriving in Canada a few years ago and I was frankly shocked to note the contrast between the general orderliness of the Canadian lifestyle and the sordidness of all but a few of the taverns which I have had occasion to visit.

By inclination I am only a one or two draught drinker, but even if I were tempted to indulge further, the sight of those men in despair idly whiling away their time until oblivion sets in—it's too much; I pay and leave.

One has the impression of a system, perhaps orginally conceived as a way of providing the working man with a place where he could buy a glass of beer or two at a reasonable price, which has gone horribly wrong.

Letter to the Editor, 1972.[18]

Whether because of, or in spite of the liquor laws, Canadians are usually hard drinkers. Men in from some arduous job in the bush would consider they had a good week-end in town if they bought several crates of beer and consumed the lot in an hotel bedroom. On one occasion when lumberjacks, paid off from a camp, hit Vancouver, a novel party took place. Men drinking in one hotel room heard their friends having a lively time in the next room. In order to join in they knocked a hole in the wall. Since all the rooms on the top floor were occupied by lumbermen soon there was not a wall left intact, and the horrified manager discovered a new passageway parallel to the original corridor.

There are strict laws against having opened bottles in automobiles. I once travelled with a Canadian who regularly every fifty miles drove off the highway and furtively drank a mixture of beer and whiskey. I also had an exciting ride with a woman who drove her Ford faster than any car she saw in front of her, weaving in and out of the traffic with one hand on the wheel and the other on a bottle. Her three children were trained to look out of the back window for any overtaking "mounties".

An Englishman's impressions, 1966.[19]

These comments are mildly typical of the statements which visitors and Canadians have made concerning those most puritan restrictions of all—our liquor laws. It has been fashionable to criticize these regulations and to blame them for excesses involved with alcohol. Yet hearty drinking has a long and honourable history in Canada. The tradition was established in the pioneer communities of the 1800s.

At a logging bee in those old times whiskey was ever present. All the settlers in the locality would invariably turn out and help at the logging. Wonderful stories they tell of logging an acre of land in an hour and a half by three men and a yoke of oxen. Old men to-day tell me that they were mere lads then, and were the "whiskey boys" at these loggings. Whiskey was partaken of by the bowlful, and no ill effect seemed to follow from it. If a man were to drink one-half the quantity of whiskey to-day he would be more than drunk, and sick on the morrow. It must be that the whiskey of those days was better than the modern stuff.

Thomas Conant, *Life In Canada*, 1903.[20]

In a rural Scottish community of Ontario, the McIntyre House was the rallying point for drinkers. John Galbraith recalled the social significance of that establishment.

The effect of alcohol on different races is as remarkable as it is invariable. An Englishman becomes haughty; a Swede sad; an Irishman sentimental; a Russian fraternal; a German melodious. A Scotchman always becomes militant. It was on Saturday night that the Scotch gathered at the McIntyre House to make merry and seek one another's destruction. Whiskey bottles were emptied and used as weapons; sometimes the bottom was knocked off to make a better impression on the thick epidermis that so admirably protected the average clansman. Boots and even furniture were also used, although on gala occasions the furniture was removed. On a Sunday after one of these festivals, men would be in poor condition from Port Talbot to Campbellton and from Iona Station nearly to West Lorne. . . .

Finally, there was the gala evening—it must have been about 1910—when one of the Campbells who inhabited the country north and west of town mounted the bar and announced his intention of avenging, once and for all, the insults that had been heaped on the Clan Campbell ever since it has fought on the wrong side at Culloden a hundred and sixty-five years before. He specifically promised to lick any man who lived between Lake Erie and the Michigan Central Railway. A score leaped to the challenge; the Campbells rallied round. It was a glorious struggle. The outcome was indeterminate although it was said that the Campbells acquitted themselves well. Next morning a half-dozen clansmen were still stacked like cordwood in the livery stable back of the hotel. None was seriously hurt.

John Kenneth Galbraith, *The Scotch*, 1964.[21]

An old-timer in Ontario commented on the effects of drink in the 1860s.

The drinking habits of the people were in keeping with the number

of taverns from which liquor was supplied. Fighting was a natural consequence of this excessive drinking. Liquor flowed with special freedom during
elections, and fists and sticks formed the ultimate argument in the political
controversies of the day. Nor were elections the only cause of quarrels.
An incident of an international character once occurred at the old Tyrone
tavern at the corner of the fifth. An American lumber firm (the Dodge)
was engaged in cutting pine from our old place for the mill that was
then in operation at Belle Ewart. The firm had a number of Americans
in its employment and one night a fight began at the tavern between
the Americans and a number of Canadians. The former soon got the
worst of it and were driven for shelter to their camp across the way.
There was one negro in the American party, and he came in for some
of the hardest knocks. People say that after the scrap was over, it was
hardly possible to tell which was his face and which was the back of
his head. If a white man had received such a pounding, his head would
have been reduced to a pulp. A few years ago when Wightman Goodfellow
tore down the old tavern, bloodstains, resulting from this and other fighting, could still be seen on the walls. . . .

Nor was the consumption of liquor confined to taverns. At almost
every store a pail of liquor and a cup stood on the counter and all comers
were at liberty to help themselves. No logging-bee could be held without
an abundant supply of the same sort of refreshment, and, after the bee
was over, men fought or danced as fancy moved them—provided they
were not by that time too drunk to do either.

Where did the money come from to pay for all the liquor consumed?
It came from the sweat-stained dollars that should have gone to the creation
of homes; women were robbed of their due, and children of their heritage,
that liquor sellers might wax fat. I have been told that the man who
kept the old Tyrone tavern at the fifth, was able to supply his boys
with two or three watches each from among those that had been left
in pawn for liquor. Nor was this all. Many a good farm was drunk
up over the bar in the old days and the owners and their children were
forced to begin life over again in a new location.

W. L. Smith, The Pioneers of Old Ontario, 1923.[22]

*Such evidence gave fuel to the temperance movement which gathered
strength at the turn of the century. This vigorous campaign was aided
by a basic stability in the Canadian population which rejected excess.
Visitors and newcomers to Canada frequently commented on the strength
of self-discipline in Canadians.*

From liquor, however, the Canadian farmer abstains. He has become temperate without coercive law, and for him prohibition is an impertinence. He is altogether a moral man and a good citizen, honest, albeit close, as indeed he needs to be, in his dealings. He supports his minister and his schoolmaster, though both perhaps on a rather slender pittance. Such is the basis of society in British Canada.

Goldwin Smith, *Canada and the Canadian Question*, 1891.[23]

There are a great many
HOTELS AND SALOONS IN MONTREAL
To the latter the citizens are very much opposed, and although hotels are useful, and as American and Canadian society is constituted they are even necessary, still their drink-selling license ought to be restricted, as well as that of their less important neighbours. I am very glad to say that drinking is not looked upon as the correct thing, and that drunkards, high and low, are generally treated with contempt, and serve them right, for, if a man is so corrupt or diseased that for the sake of gratifying his appetite he will sink below the level of the beast, such a man cannot be a good citizen or a good Christian. As a rule the
NATIVES ARE VERY TEMPERATE

Peter O'Leary, *Travels in Canada and U.S.*[24]

A British workman seems to think it is his bounden duty to consume all the beer he can get. . . .
In Canada this is not the case. Large districts are entirely without places where beer is sold, and even where it is not so, where people can get what they choose to drink, they do not soak themselves in beer. If anyone did, he would be looked on as a very black sheep indeed, even by his mates; would not be trusted, and would not be employed.

Edward Roper, *By Track and Trail*, 1891.[25]

Temperance won. Prohibition in its various forms came to most of Canada during or shortly after the Great War. In Canada however, it lacked the notoriety of the American experiment, and within a decade most of the laws forbidding the sale of alcoholic beverages were repealed. In their place remained a general distrust of the drinking public, firm government control over sale and consumption of alcohol, and the creation of the "beer parlour", that place where the disreputable drank in shabby surroundings. L.A. MacKay paid bitter homage to these customs in the following poem.

Frankie Went Down to the Corner

Ontario's such a respectable place;
Drinking's no crime, but it's still a disgrace,
So hide us away behind curtain and screen
While we stealthily go through the motions obscene
    In a manner genteel, correctly genteel,
Secret and stuffy, but always genteel.

Let us drink upon land, as we smoke in a train,
In places as airy and light as a drain,
Let us scuttle for cover, like bugs under shelves,
Lest people should think we're enjoying ourselves.
    Oh no, we're genteel, we're grimly genteel
(To be seen drinking gaily is far from genteel).

Though our neighbours all say, with a sneer and a snicker,
We're not man enough to stand up to our liquor,
Three cheers for the tables! A man on his feet
Can carry much less than slumped in a seat.
    Besides, it's genteel, it's very genteel;
Beer served at a table's completely genteel.

But of course if a restaurant ask us to dine
It's immoral to order a bottle of wine
—But wait! Are there six standard beds in the house?
Then away with dull care! We're all set for a souse
    For then it's genteel (beds make it genteel),
Though drunk and dyspeptic, we must be genteel.

And we can't allow music, or people might think
Our pleasure's not limited solely to drink.
So musicians may starve, but they must not appear
In the sinister presence of bottles of beer.
    For that isn't genteel, it's far from genteel;
Only a gurgle is really genteel.

"Bar" is a nasty, a horrible word.
"Taprooms" and "taverns" and "pubs" are absurd;
Give us a name with a resonant boom,
A respectable name like "Beverage Room".
  Shabby genteel, shabby genteel,
Ontario's bound to be shabby genteel.

L. A. MacKay, 1936.[26]

In the 1970s, a new joie de vivre *appears to have replaced the sense of shame associated with drinking. Liquor laws have been modified; the British pub atmosphere appears in more of our taverns; one may sing and even dance without being hurled out the door as a troublemaker. Advertisements on the publicly owned CBC now may show wholesome young people enjoying beer in pleasant surroundings. One wonders where it will all end.*

And What of the Pleasures of the Flesh?

The influence of Presbyterianism and Methodism has notoriously worked in Canada to discourage the practice of the arts, and, except in the rather sporadic and sometime brutish Scottish way, the enjoyment of the fleshly pleasure.

Edmund Wilson, *O Canada*, 1964.[27]

Sex pours over us in imported culture, but the culture we make ourselves is close to sexless. There is a strain that runs through what we make, from high culture to low, that blatantly denies sexuality. (Did you notice, for instance, the girls chosen to perform at half time during the Grey Cup?)

Our historic culture heroes—say, the Group of Seven—come across in the books about them as earnest Boy Scouts, far more interested in canoemanship than bedmanship. Other cultures glory in the sexual exploits of their artists; but to write about the sex life of a Group of Seven member (and, it is whispered, they actually did have sex lives) would be close to sacrilege.

A Ph.D thesis on "Sex and the Canadian Novel" would be as short as a book on night life in St. Catharines. Fifteen years ago, in a critical article in the Tamarack Review, Alan Brown said that in Hugh MacLennan's Two Solitudes, "sex...is introduced with a hollow sound as of the distant shunting of CNR frieght cars." Exactly. Sex for MacLennan was something that happened somewhere over the horizon, seldom if ever in the foreground. The same might be said about most of our other serious novelists.

In those 15 years not much has changed. It's true that Irving Layton has established a reputation based partly on the celebration of sex in his poetry, but it is the very boyishness of Layton's approach—the feeling, again and again, that he's just now discovering these things—that sets his work apart so clearly and stamps it as so distinctly Canadian. You have the sense that he thinks he invented sex, in the way that Richard Needham invented women.

. . .Canadian culture, French as well as English, suffers from Puritan inhibitions; and these affect even those writers who believe they have long since cast off the religions which gave force to those inhibitions.

Robert Fulford, 1971.[28]

John Galbraith had something to say about the inhibitions which have been inspired by the Scotch influence in Canada.

. . .We were taught that sexual intercourse was, under all circumstances, a sin. Marriage was not a mitigation so much as a kind of license for misbehavior and we were free from the countervailing influence of movies, television and John O'Hara. Among the rougher element of the community, after the weather, the wisdom of selling cattle and the personality of the schoolteacher had been touched upon, conversation would often be taken over by one or another of the acknowledged masters of salacious detail. However, in contrast with other cultures, no one ever boasted of his own exploits, presumably because there was no chance he would be believed. More often a shy or especially puritanical participant would be accused of fornication with some highly improbable lass. Interest would center on the way he denied it. The charge would then be repeated, and coupled with more graphic, though even more imaginary detail, and a pleasant hour or two would thus be whiled away. Members of the more prestigious clans never participated in such pastime. In our family we would have been visited by a Jovian wrath had it been known that we even listened. The mere appearance of my father at a neighborhood gathering would turn the conversation back to crops.

An important feature of an austere education in such matters is that it need influence only one of the two people involved to be fully effective. And uncertainty as to the state of conviction of the other person, plus the moral consequences of miscalculation, can be a powerful deterrent. One such experience had a durable effect on me.

At some time during adolescence, I encountered a novel by Anatole France which made unlicensed sexual transactions, especially if blessed by deep affection and profound' mutual understanding, seem much more defensible than I had previously been allowed to suppose. It was summer and I was deeply in love. One day the object of my love, a compact golden-haired girl who lived on Willey's Sideroad, a half mile away, came over to visit my sisters. They were away and we walked together through the orchard and climbed onto a rail fence which overlooked a small field between our place and Bert McCallum's. Our cows were pasturing on the second-growth clover in front of us. The hot summer afternoon lay quiet all around.

With the cows was a white bull named O.A.C. Pride, for the Ontario Agricultural College where my father had bid him in at an auction. As we perched there the bull served his purpose by serving a heifer which was in season.

Noticing that my companion was watching with evident interest, and with some sense of my own courage, I said: "I think it would be fun to do that."

She replied: "Well, it's your cow."

John Kenneth Galbraith, *The Scotch*, 1964.[29]

English Canadians generally consider their French brothers and sisters to be more lascivious in their attitudes to sex. Yet, as has been suggested, puritanism can live even in French Canada. In his book La Guerre, Yes Sir!, *Roch Carrier illustrated the results of a strict religious upbringing. The hero, Bérubé, has just accompanied a prostitute to her room and now faces the moment of truth.*

The girl was before him, naked. She had kept on her brassiere, which was full to bursting. She held out her arms to Bérubé who was incapable of getting up, of leaping towards the naked girl, of seizing her in his arms, of clutching her violently and throwing her on the bed. Bérubé felt completely weak, as if he had had too much to drink. In his head he heard a tick-tock like a drumbeat. "Always, never," repeated the monstrous clock which had marked the hours of his childhood, the clock of hell which throughout eternity would say "always, never"; the damned are in hell for ever, they never leave. "Always, never." Under the clock Bérubé saw the viscous caverns of hell where serpents climbed, mingled with the eternal flames. And he saw the damned—naked, strangling in the flames—and the serpents. "Always, never": the clock of his childhood beat out the measure, the clock of eternal damnation for those who go naked and those who touch naked women; "always, never," sounded the clock and Bérubé had to beg, "Do you want to marry me?"[30]

Despite these restraints which run deep in our culture, there have been occasions when Canadians have pursued the fleshly delights with vulgar exuberance. The year of 1814 in Halifax was one of those times.

The upper streets were full of brothels. Grog-shops and dancing-houses were to be seen in every part of the town. A portion of Grafton Street was known as Hogg Street from a house of ill fame kept by a person of that name. The upper street (i.e., Brunswick or "Barrack" Street) was known as "Knock Him Down Street" in consequence of the affrays and even murders committed there. No person of character ventured to reside there; nearly all the buildings were occupied as brothels for the soldiers and sailors. The streets of this part of the town presented continually the disgusting sight of abandoned females of the lowest class in a state of drunkenness, bareheaded, without shoes, and in the most filthy and abominable condition.

Thomas Akins, 1814.[31]

Even more spectacular were the years around the turn of the century when the West was opening up. In his book Red Lights on the Prairies, *James Gray described those boisterous times.*

...historians have managed to create the illusion that the West was settled by monks, eunuchs, and vestal virgins, interested only in debating such ethereal issues as free trade, the Manitoba Schools question, and discriminatory freight rates.

No such society could ever have turned prostitution into a major industry, as it clearly was in Winnipeg where 200 women were employed in the forty-eight McFarlane Street and Annabella Street brothels, in Calgary which once boasted three segregated areas, and in Edmonton where the brothels spilled over from Kinistino Street in all directions. How many girls plied their profession on the prairies can hardly be estimated. In Winnipeg police magistrate Daly once complained that there were hundreds of streetwalkers there. One Edmonton madam, in 1914, put the number of practising prostitutes at between 400 and 500. Another regarded this as a gross exaggeration and said there were hardly more than forty or fifty brothels in town. Both figures may well have been accurate, for in one raid in 1909 the Edmonton police picked up 28 girls and 64 men in one house of ill fame where sex and gambling were provided as a joint enterprise. Regina, Moose Jaw, and Lethbridge all had their segregated areas although they functioned on more modest scales than those in the larger centres.

...By the summer of 1910 the Winnipeg red-light district had degenerated into a massive orgiastic obscenity. The sky-rocketing Winnipeg population, coupled with the tremendous floating population, kept the district on a twenty-four-hour shift all through the summer. Though it was isolated from the main part of the city, it was only five minutes by streetcar or ten minutes on foot from the C.P.R. station. As many of the customers had already tarried in the Main Street saloons, it was only to be expected that they would arrive in the district somewhat foggy about precise addresses. So it was common for householders some distance removed from the brothels to have their meals and their sleep interrupted by ruffians bursting in looking for prostitutes. Men exposing themselves to women and children on the streets was an almost continual occurrence. Citizens who sought to protect their women from abuse were often painfully assaulted by the drunks who ranged through the district in groups. A woman testified that one afternoon three men entered her home on Higgins Avenue (some distance from the red-light district) and, assuming she was a prostitute, threw some money on the table and started tearing off her clothes. She escaped to the street and a nearby factory where her husband worked. Another resident complained of being awakened at five o'clock in the morning by the whooping and hollering of a couple of whores who were chasing each other around the block on horseback, naked, as he said, from knees to hips.[32]

> *This frenzy, however, was peripheral to the mainstream of Canadian interest. It took place in a "boom-town" atmosphere; it was bawdy, crude, and barbarous, and was ended (or at least removed from open view) by an indignant public. The 1970s have witnessed a revival of the boisterous interest in sexual activities. Never before have the opportunities of fulfilling sexual fantasies been made so flagrantly available.*
>
> SEX SHOP'S TIP FOR LOVERS:
> JUST SMELL LIKE AN APRICOT

If The Garden, a sex shop opening to the public here today, is any indication, it seems you have to smell like an orchard to get the girls these days.

Soaps with erotic flavors such as honey-banana, cucumber, lemon and lime or avocado-apricot were on display for about 40 curious reporters invited to a preview yesterday.

There were books that tell you what to do, how to do it, when and where to do it and who with. No one explains why.

Billing itself as North America's first sex shop, The Garden is located in the downtown area's boutique belt.

Owner Ivor Sergent calls it "a daring innovation, something new for North America."

The shop sells powders, lotions, salves, sprays, gels and creams guaranteed to make "you and your partner more appreciative and responsive to each other." There are 32 kinds of multicolored prophylactics.

The three-room sex supermarket features a check-out line like your neighborhood grocery store.

On a shelf above the cash register there are potency drugs, not guaranteed, however, to make you potent because of drug laws. Among the items is Vitamin E, Vitamin B12, golden pollen, and Korean ginseng, which according to the label, has been used by Korean men for 5,000 years.

There are "risque magazines and games" to set the mood and other apparatus—such as a water bed cover with sexy sheet—to get you merrily on your way.

The Toronto Star, November 19, 1971.

Yet in all of this there seems to exist the "naughty little boy" atmosphere. Are these pleasure palaces, movies, sex shops, indicative of a deep and healthy delight in sex? Or are they just fads, imitations of the western world's infatuation with naked bodies, which will soon be replaced by a return to indifference?

Festive Rituals

On Grey Cup Day, the best football team in the East meets the best football team in the West to battle for the Grey Cup. While this is going on, football fans all over the country will be holding Grey Cup parties. The night before the game, of course, the Grey Cup Dinner will be eaten, the Grey Cup Dance will be held, and Miss Grey Cup will be chosen. Together these events are known as Grey Cup fever or Grey Cup madness. And it all began in 1948 when an exuberant band of Calgarians escorted their team into Toronto.

Union Station Stampeded
As Calgarians Roar In

Toronto was "westernized" today in nothing flat.

That loud noise your heard from Front St. wasn't the rumble of mighty locomotives. It was barnyard music—in Union Station, of all places. Yep, podner, a square dance was in progress.

The Stampeders Special, bearing 400 grid fans from you-know-what city for you-know-what game, drifted quietly into Toronto at 8:23 a.m. ....After that there was so much racket no trains were on schedule and if they were no one cared. . . .

The Calgary enthusiasts swept down the station runways in a solid bloc and Toronto citizens—who were stoically about to begin their day's work—were appalled to see a little army of 10-gallon hats push through the main rotunda—and beneath the hats were cowboy shirts and spurs and other western regalia.

The shrill yells of the cowpunchers echoed through the quiet station almost the instant the special train pulled in. Red shirts, yellow shirts, pink shirts, green shirts, high-heeled boots, spurs, lovely western lassies, were all there in colorful confusion. A parade formed up at the side of the train and with banners of "Stampede 'Em Calgary" in the lead, the fans moved off to the station proper.

In the foyer the west took over the eastern end, and proceeded to call a square dance. A trio, accordion, guitar and violin, of youthful "cowpunchers" supplied the music. Passengers and visitors stood amazed as the staid station rocked and vibrated to the music and stamping feet. . . .

Several waitresses from the station restaurant who were watching the demonstration, suddenly found themselves the centre of attraction. Tall, husky men of the west spied the girls and helped them to take part in the dancing.

Amid the bystanders, with a broad grin on his face, stood Mayor McCallum. "They really put on a show, don't they?" he said. "I'm glad I'm not here officially, it's more fun just to stand and watch. Toronto has never seen anything like this.[33]

Those were pretty big doings for 1948. In the years which followed,

*the rites of Grey Cup Day were increased and refined until they attained
the structure described by Bob Hesketh in 1958.*

That Grey Cup:
Canada's Annual
Touch of Madness.

On Sunday Morning, November 30th, Vancouver will wake up with
a hangover to end all hangovers.

Cautiously opening one red eye to greet the arrival of a new day,
thousands of people, each with a throbbing headache and an upset stomach,
will rue Grey Cup day and solemnly swear off.

One year later, to the day, thousands will make the same pledge in
hotel rooms in Toronto where the 1959 game will be played.

The Grey Cup hangover plays no favorites. Suffering from it will be
bankers from Toronto, financiers from Montreal, secretaries from
Saskatoon, oil men from Calgary, dry goods salesmen from Winnipeg
and plumbers from Medicine Hat.

During the Grey Cup, westerners will wear white Stetson hats. Wealthy
westerners will wear boots that Gene Autry wouldn't be caught dead
wearing. Easterners will wear anything that tickles their fancies and,
being easteners in the west, will also feature an air of smug complacency.

Wives, temporarily freed as if by some special licence from the burden
of being wives, will flap their eyelashes at eligible and ineligible males.
Husbands will do likewise with eligible and ineligible females in thousands
of hotel-room parties where nobody needs an invitation and everybody
needs a drink.

Black eyes will be worn along with split lips as badges of honor. Wads
of money will change hands, exchanged by those who knew they had
a sure thing—that this was the year for the west to win or this was
the year that the east couldn't lose.

If Vancouver law enforcement officers adopt the same routine they
followed the last time this city was honored with this civilized riot in
1955, the doors of the major hotels should be barricaded by midnight.
Pictures will be taken down from the walls, chandeliers put in safe storage.
If the Hotel Vancouver emerges as fortunately as it did in 1955, only
about $500 damage will have been done.

Outside, the streets will be littered with ticker tapes, a memento of
the previous day's Grey Cup parade which should be viewed by about
200,000. In the jails there may be a few black-jacketed hoodlums who
have crawled out of the woodwork looking for trouble.

Windows will be broken, parking meters smashed, decorations stolen, women chased, toes trod and shins barked.

It all comes under the heading of good clean fun.[34]

And what is the social and cultural significance of Grey Cup Day?

During the broadcast of the game Saturday, Edmonton's streets were strangely silent and almost deserted. It was almost as if an air raid alarm had sounded, warning the citizens to take cover. Business almost came to a standstill as practically everyone huddled over radios in stores, offices, and homes.

Grey Cup Day, 1954.[35]

...the Grey Cup classic has become much more than a game. It is an annual celebration in which sports fans from all over the country can meet to get to know each other.

Toronto Star editorial, Grey Cup Day, 1956.[36]

A man standing with six friends kissed a girl so thoroughly in the basement of the Royal York that two policemen turned their heads in embarrassment.

Grey Cup Day, 1959.[37]

This is a night when you can feel unity in Canada.

Mayor Given of Toronto, Grey Cup Dinner, 1965.[38]

With a short run, Prime Minister Pierre Trudeau made a 25-yard kick to launch the 1970 Grey Cup game, 15 yards short of his 40-yard kickoff in the 1969 game.

Grey Cup Day, 1970.[39]

It's a corporate festival atmosphere like Santa Claus....It proclaims a way of life that goes to the very heart of the people.

Marshall McLuhan, Grey Cup Day, 1971.[40]

No service will be provided at this bar to any Calgarian on a horse.

Sign in Hotel Vancouver, Grey Cup Day, 1971.[41]

Hockey: The Ultimate in Canadian Pleasure

There are those who claim that hockey is not merely a sport, but the essence of Canadian culture. Our obsessive love affair with hockey goes back a long way. As early as 1894, Lady Aberdeen, the wife of the Governor General, observed the characteristics of hockey, the strange blend of violence and art, which not only explain its appeal to Canadians, but also· say something about our character as a people and nation.

Went this evening with all our party to witness one of the championship hockey matches between Ottawa & Montreal. The latter expected to win, but were beaten by 5 to 1. This game appears to be a most fascinating one and the men get wildly excited about it. But there can be no doubt as to its roughness, and if the players get over keen & lose their tempers as they are too apt to do, the possession of the stick & the close proximity to one another gives the occasion for many a nasty hit. Tonight one man was playing with his nose badly broken & the game had twice to be stopped, once because a man got hit in the mouth & the other time because one of the captains was knocked down unconscious & had to be carried out. When he recovered consciousness he came out & played again, but the amount of risk even in the ordinary way seems to be scarcely compensated for by the game—at least so it appears to some spectators at any rate. There are many men & boys here in Ottawa who practically live for hockey. It must be said that it is beautiful to see the perfection of skating that is involved in the playing of the game—the men simply run on the ice as if they were on the ground.

Lady Aberdeen, 1895.[42]

Skill, stamina, physical courage—these are the demands that hockey makes upon its willing warriors. Hockey does not build character; it is a test of character—and for many Canadians it is the crucial test of manhood.

You can't lick 'em on the ice if you can't lick 'em in the alley.

Conn Smythe.[43]

I shudder to think what would have happened to the Canadian World War II effort if we had depended on track and swimming participants instead of mannish hockey players.

Stan Obodiac, 1970.[44]

"... we were all just having coffee and Mrs. Haroldson claimed Mrs. Wilson's boy Clarence deliberately boarded and cross-checked her son Ricky in last night's Peewee game ... and they started fighting in the corner and ..."

Organized hockey brings out the best in young boys and the worst in some parents according to a group of "hockey mothers" from Etobicoke....

Each has seen or heard of mothers physically attacking coaches and shouting obscenities at players....

"The women are more vicious than the men. You just have to look at their faces in the stands," said Betty Moffatt of Tallon Rd.

"It's difficult to keep calm when a mother yells at her son to 'get' your son," she said. "No wonder some mothers turn around and haul off at each other."

The *Toronto Star*, January 24, 1972.

The lengendary Eddie Shore exhibited all the qualities which could be asked of any hockey player.

He gave no quarter and he asked none. One night in 1929, Montreal Maroons deliberately set upon him. A long-reaching jab with a stick-blade tore open his cheek. Another sliced his chin. He was hammered, pounded, cut; and just at the end, a Maroon player cut across Shore and deliberately gave him a sickening smash in the mouth, which knocked out several teeth and felled the Bruin in his tracks. He was carried off, and five minutes later, his wounds temporarily doctored, he was standing silently beneath the showers. Expecting an outburst, I said, "Rough going, Eddie." Through bloody, swollen lips he answered laconically. "It's all in the game. I'll pay off."

Henry Roxborough, *The Stanley Cup Story.*[45]

The hockey hero then, embodies all that we admire and in the hero we find fulfillment of our desires. To trifle with the true hockey hero is to challenge the Canadian psyche. In 1955, N.H.L. President Clarence Campbell dared to do just that, and brought the wrath of the people down not only upon himself, but upon the city of Montreal. In March of that year, Maurice "The Rocket" Richard, the superb and fiery star of the Montreal Canadiens, was involved in an explosive incident in which he struck another player with his stick and punched an official. This followed an earlier case of Richard assaulting an official. Campbell suspended Richard for the remainder of the season, including playoff games. In his book Fire-Wagon Hockey, *Andy O'Brien described the events which followed the suspension.*

The National Hockey League headquarters was deluged by crank calls. Several threatened anonymously to "kill Campbell." One caller pledged to dynamite the Gibraltar-like Sun Life edifice. Grocery chains were amazed at the shoppers' venom directed at Campbell's soups—although the link with the NHL prexy was a matter of name only.

Fans jammed the Forum lobby to announce that they would never again attend a hockey game there. Others called to say they wouldn't even follow the NHL via television. One woman warned the Forum that she would be among a specially organized one thousand fans "who will be there tonight to protest."

Loyal line mate Elmer Lach helped feed the flames with; "They always tried to get the Rocket and now they finally have."

Coach Irvin flatly tagged the suspension "an injustice."

In Ottawa, the Progressive-Conservative member for Three Rivers, Leon Balcer, attempted to inject the suspension issue on a "question of privilege." The Liberal benches yelled for "Order!" and Speaker René Beaudoin ruled it out of order.

At the Forum that night of March seventeenth, the angry-mob feeling oozed from the walls as we entered. Campbell had said, in reply to questions, that he would be going to the game. Later when Mayor Jean Drapeau criticized him for going, Campbell blew his top. A former combat officer who had been assigned to serve on the prosecution staff at the Nuremberg war crime trials and an ex-NHL referee to boot, he snorted; "Does the mayor suggest I should have yielded to the intimidation of a few hoodlums?"

It was a nasty sight; throughout the first and only period of the game, Campbell and his fiancée Phyllis (now Mrs. Campbell) sat under a shower of eggs and assorted debris. When the period ended, a black-jacketed hoodlum rushed to Campbell's seat and hit him twice before running off. The other hoodlum had the tear-gas bomb, also meant for Campbell, but it went off prematurely in the promenade a short distance away.

The smoke billowed up to the Forum roof and people ran gasping for the exits. The lobby was soon filled with coughing, weeping fans. The public address system finally announced that the game had been forfeited; the crowd pouring from exits on all sides of the Forum seemed to flow around to the front of the building on St. Catherine Street. Now the hoodlums took over amid the dense crowd of people who were mainly standing around "just to see the fun."

The "fun" extended to shattering windows in front of the Forum as well as windows of stores located there. Then the mob marched eastward on St. Catherine Street, breaking more windows, upsetting cars, roughing up bystanders and looting jewelry stores. The damage estimates soared above one hundred thousand dollars.[46]

A Matter of National Pride

Until 1954 Canadians took for granted their superiority in hockey. The defeat of the East York Lyndhursts by an upstart Russian squad in the international tournament led to shock, despair, concern in Canada.

In 1955, the Penticton V's, champions of the Canadian Hockey Association, set out for the international competition in Germany to restore Canadian hockey honour. It was only natural that the voice of Hockey Night in Canada, Foster Hewitt, should fly to Europe to broadcast the game which, as one newspaper stated, was "To Be Carried to All Parts of the Civilized World".

When I arrived at the scene of the game I was soon aware that this was to be much more than just a hockey match; indeed it had become so important politically that some Europeans who could speak English implored me to use any influence I might possess to ensure that the Russians would be not only beaten but clobbered. Naturally my voice or my desires weren't going to score goals; I might shout "He shoots! He scores!" but I couldn't put the puck in the net. The hopes of friends and allies keyed me up to such an excited pitch, however, that as I proceeded to the rink on that eventful Sunday afternoon the butterflies in my stomach were enjoying a great game of tag.

Foster Hewitt, *Hockey Night in Canada*, 1961.[47]

Hewitt need not have worried. Canadian honour was avenged in a most fitting and satisfying way.

WHOLE SOVIET TEAM DEPRESSED

ONE THROWS SKATES OUT WINDOW

CLOBBER RUSSIANS 5 TO 0

PENTICTON V'S REGAIN

HOCKEY TITLE FOR CANADA

Krefeld, Germany, March 7—Better hockey games have been played by better players before more people, but it is safe to say no game ever meant more to so many Canadians—yes and to so many Europeans too—as this 5-0 shellacking which Canada gave Russia here yesterday in the sardine-packed ice stadium. For Canadians from coast to coast at home and for the thousands of Canadian expatriates on this side of the ocean it was incidental that the prize was a silver cup worth $100 or less at any hockey shop.

This prestige was the stake for which the two teams were battling. For generations they had boasted that hockey was Canada's game. Then suddenly folks were saying, "But doesn't Russia hold the world's championship?"

The political implications had been too obvious since Canada lost this European version of the world title last year at Stockholm. Airline crews told the Canadians here that news reels of last year's final was still running up until a few months ago at Czechoslovakian theatres. Canada resented the fact that the outcome of a hockey game was used for propaganda purposes.

This was the background against which the Canucks clobbered the red-suited Russians yesterday and left them a completely subdued band of athletes. Although they are a splendidly conditioned bunch of men—the result of months of preparation—the Russians were out on their feet at the end. The big man of their club—although you couldn't prove it by Canadian standards—Wsewolod Bobrow probably summed up the situation as neatly as was possible after the game. Asked for his comment, Bobrow said, "You saw it. What is there to say?". Pavel Korotkov, head man of hockey in Russia, was unhappy over the showing of his team, but he added; "Never have we encountered such strong opposition."

Milt Dunnell, *Toronto Daily Star*, March 7, 1955.

The great victory of 1955 satisfied our sense of justice, but the Russians quickly regrouped. Except for a Canadian victory in 1961, the Russians have dominated Olympic and international tournaments for the last seventeen years. Denied the right of playing her "best" players, who were the professionals of the National Hockey League, Canada withdrew from world tournaments in 1970, until such time as she could play her best against the Russians. And for years Canadians have had to endure the needling of Anatoly Tarasov, the seemingly eternal coach of Russian championship teams.

Our will training is based on Soviet principles of ethics and culture, while Canadians put winning first, honor and solidarity among sportsmen a distant second.

Tarasov, 1968.[48]

I will speak frankly: it seems to me the fear of losing is the only reason for refusing to play us. How strange. Canadian professional hockey is proud and touchy. Canada is the birth place of this tremendous game. You invented it and you always want to be the best. Prove it, then, in honest battle.

Tarasov, 1969.[49]

Your players are good on a technical level and can do all kinds of things with the puck, but don't you think at the same time you're playing very primitive hockey?...Let them stick to their type of game. Later the Canadian professionals will change their style after meeting the Europeans.

Tarasov, 1972.[50]

The Big Showdown

HOCKEY—PROPOSED CANADA-RUSSIA GAMES—

REPRESENTATIONS TO NATIONAL HOCKEY LEAGUE

RESPECTING USE OF PLAYERS

Mr. Mark Rose (Fraser Valley West): Mr. Speaker, in the absence of the Minister of National Health and Welfare perhaps I might direct this question to the Acting Prime Minister. Since there is considerable interest across the land in the proposed series between NHL players and a Russian team, and in view of the fact there is some evidence that certain United States based teams are reluctant to allow their Canadian players to participate, is the government considering making representations to the NHL headquarters in Montreal, expressing official Canadian support for this series?

Hon. Mitchell Sharp (Acting Prime Minister): Mr. Speaker, I do not know whether it will be necessary to make any such representations, but I can assure the hon. member that the Canadian government is very much in favour of games between the Russians and the Canadians to see who really is the best in the world.

Hansard, April 21, 1972.[51]

And so it came to pass in September 1972 that Team Canada went forth to do battle with the Russians. At stake was more than a hockey series. Our victory, we knew, and hoped, would demonstrate more than our superiority in hockey. Team Canada held Canada's pride and worth as a nation in its hands. Red Berensen, a player on Team Canada, saw the true significance of the series which was to begin on Saturday, September 2.

On Saturday night, Canada will be a very united country. All regional differences will disappear and the various peoples who make up Canada will be cheering as one voice.

I doubt very much if one single Canadian will be cheering against Team Canada. Differences based on nationality or religion or any of those petty things which sometimes get in the way of this country's development will be forgotten.

This series will get attention all over the world. We've always said hockey was our game, something of value that was unique for Canada. This is the first real chance to prove it and show the world something about our country.[52]

Disaster! It is still painful to think of that first game—an unbelievable 7-3 victory for the Russians. When Canada rallied to win the second game 4-1, the former Prime Minister Lester Pearson said, "We can hold our heads up again." But a tie in Winnipeg, a defeat in Vancouver, bloody and futile battles with the Swedes, and a Russian victory in Moscow threw despair into Canadians. Incredibly, we won three games in Moscow, to win the series. And our troops returned home to receive their laurels from a grateful public.

This was more emotional than winning the Stanley Cup. A Stanley Cup's for your team and your city, but beating Russia is for your country.

Phil Esposito, Team Canada.[53]

You're standing on the greatest country in the world right here.

Mickey Redmond, Team Canada.[54]

You have shown the whole world that Canadian athletes—when they receive support—demonstrate courage, determination and vigor to compete against anyone on equal terms.

Man-for-man, Canadian athletes have the skill and the determination to beat anyone.

Prime Minister Pierre Trudeau.[55]

"When I scored that final goal, I finally realized what democracy was all about."

Paul Henderson, Team Canada scorer
of series winning goal.[56]

But, my God, it was close!

Team Canada's success transforms Réné Levesque and his fellow separatists into ardent Canadian nationalists.

Hockey showdown with the Russians

Canada, Russia to clash in 8-game hockey series

Shattered myth

'Now we know who's got the better team'
Phil Esposito praises the Soviet players

Help send Bobby Hull to Russia

Sinden analyzes loss:
Soviets 'never let up'

Trudeau intervenes
in Hull rhubarb,
wants him to play

HL prestige hits rock bottom in Stockholm

am Canada's play 'criminal'
r envoy in Sweden says

**Team Canada declares
war on spear-carrying
Swedes**

Canada ties series with 4-3 triumph

COME ON CANADA!

It's do-or-die day
for Canada, Soviets

**There's more at stake
than the game itself**

NEVER IN DOUBT!

Revolution Is not our Style

The mental climate of English Canada in its early formative years was determined by men who were fleeing from the practical application of the doctrine that all men are born equal and are endowed by their creator with certain unalienable rights amongst which are life, liberty, and the pursuit of happiness....In Canada we have no revolutionary tradition.

Frank Underhill, *In Search of Canadian Liberalism*, 1960.[1]

There was no revolutionary tradition in Canada, no glorification of force as a means of winning freedom and release. Moreover, the Canadian nation had been fashioned in a spirit of cautious defensiveness as a means of preserving what might at any moment be snatched away. All of this led to an innate suspicion of violence, and a tendency to equate the exuberant and the expansive with the empty and the vulgar.

Claude Bissell, 1962.[2]

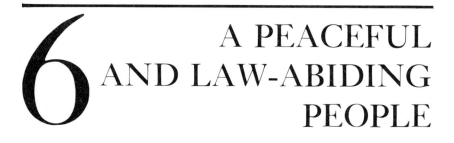

6 A PEACEFUL AND LAW-ABIDING PEOPLE

The October Crisis of 1970 was to shock Canadians into re-examining this traditional image of themselves and their nation. Not only did it bring into focus those fundamental beliefs which Canadians cherish, but also it confronted us with the dilemma of reconciling the maintenance of law and order with the protection of individual rights and liberty. It was to be an interesting case study of Canadian attitudes towards revolutionary and violent political activity. The crisis came to light on October 5, 1970, with the kidnapping in Montreal of a British diplomat, James Cross.

I was dressing in my bathroom when I heard a ring at the door bell downstairs. I heard a second ring a few minutes later, and I heard voices. I took no notice as I thought the maid was answering the door.

Then a man came into the bedroom and pointed a pistol at me and told me to get down on the floor. He made me turn, lie on my face. He called downstairs to one of his friends and a second man came up armed with a sub-machine gun, driving in front of him the maid who was carrying her child.

The first man kept the maid and child and my wife under control in the bedroom. I might add that our dog had jumped up on to the bed and he told my wife to hold the dog. Otherwise, he would shoot it.

The second man took me into the dressing room, dressed me, allowed me to say goodbye to my wife and took me downstairs, where there was a third man also armed with a sub-machine gun.

They threw a raincoat over my shoulder, took me out down the steps to a car which had a taxi sign on the roof, and there was a fourth man sitting at the wheel of the car. I was pushed into the car down between the seat at the back and covered up with a rug.

We drove for about five minutes, then we stopped at a garage or building of some sort. I was taken out of the car, told to keep my eyes closed and a gas mask was put on my head, in which the eye pieces had been painted out.

I was then driven for approximately 20 minutes and taken out of the car in the garage, led upstairs into a room, where I spent the next 60 days.

James Cross, 1970.[3]

Through this move, the Front de liberation du Québec wants to draw the attention of the world to the fate of French-speaking Quebecois, a majority which is jeered at and crushed on its own territory by a faulty political system (Canadian federalism) and by an economy dominated by the interests of American high finance, the racist and imperialist "big bosses." . . .

Thousands of Quebecois have understood, as did our ancestors of 1837-38, that the only way to ensure our national as well as economic survival is total independence.

The Front de liberation du Québec supports unconditionally the American blacks and those of Africa, the liberation movements of Latin America, of Palestine, and of Asia, the revolutionary Catholics of Northern

Ireland and all those who fight for their freedom, their independence, and their dignity.

The Front de liberation du Québec wants to salute the Cuban and Algerian people who are heroically fighting against imperialism and colonialism in all its forms, for a just society where man's exploitation by man is banished.

However, we believe that the only really true support we can give these people moving, towards their liberations is to liberate ourselves first. . . .

We shall overcome!

Front de liberation du Québec.

FLQ communique, October 6, 1970.[4]

> *The boldness of the kidnapping and the brazen communique of the FLQ with its further demands for $500,000 ransom money and the freeing of "political prisoners" came as a stunning blow to Canadians. Violent actions by the FLQ were not unknown up to this point; mail boxes had been dynamited, banks robbed to acquire funds for further activity, and armouries raided for weapons. But the kidnapping injected a new and more ominous note into the story of FLQ terrorism. The government rejected the demands of the kidnappers, although it did offer to grant them safe conduct to a foreign country in return for James Cross's freedom. At this point a further incredible note arrived from the FLQ.*

In the face of the persistence of the governmental authorities in not complying with the requirements of the FLQ and in conformity with Plan 3 established earlier to provide for such a refusal, the Chenier financial cell has just kidnapped the Minister of Unemployment and Quebec Assimilation, Pierre Laporte.

The minister will be executed Sunday evening at 10 PM if between now and then the ruling authorities have not responded favourably to the seven demands set forth following the kidnapping of Mr. James Cross. Any partial acceptance will be considered as refusal. . . .

We shall overcome.

Front de liberation du Québec.

FLQ Chenier cell communique.[5]

> *Two kidnappings within a week! Canadians were befuddled by this strange turn of events which was beyond our experience and by the*

un-Canadian tone of the notes with their strange references to foreign causes. We were shaken, possibly panic-stricken, and certainly fearful of the ominous organization which was able to strike with impunity.

The government, taking no more chances with the FLQ which had now proved itself to be deadly serious, called troops in to guard the federal ministers' homes in Ottawa. The sight of armed soldiers in the streets of a civilized Canadian city was the occasion for a dramatic T.V. confrontation between a reporter and Prime Minister Trudeau. Trudeau reacted not with the guarded caution we have come to expect of our politicians, but with the anger which he shared with thousands of his fellow Canadians.

T.V. REPORTER: Sir, what is it with all these men with guns around here?

TRUDEAU: Haven't you noticed?

REPORTER: Yes, I've noticed them. I wondered why you people decided to have them.

TRUDEAU: What's your worry?

REPORTER: I'm not worried, but you seem to be.

TRUDEAU: So if you're not worried, what's your...I'm not worried.

REPORTER: I'm worried about living in a town that's full of people with guns running around.
. . .

TRUDEAU: Yes, well there are a lot of bleeding hearts around who just don't like to see people with helmets and guns. All I can say is, go on and bleed, but it is more important to keep law and order in the society than to be worried about weak-kneed people who don't like the looks of...

REPORTER: At any cost? How far would you go with that? How far would you extend that?

TRUDEAU: Well, just watch me.

REPORTER: At reducing civil liberties? To what extent?

TRUDEAU: To what extent?

REPORTER: Well, if you extend this and you say, OK, you're going to do anything to protect them, does this include wire-tapping, reducing other civil liberties in some way?

TRUDEAU: Yes, I think the society must take every means at its disposal to defend itself against the emergence of a parallel power which defies the elected power in this country and I think that goes to any distance. So long as there is a power in here which is challenging the elected representative of the people, I think that power must be stopped and

I think it's only, I repeat, weak-kneed bleeding hearts who are afraid to take these measures.[6]

> *This emotionally charged exchange was followed within a few days by a calmer message to the nation. It was a significant statement by Trudeau. In it he interpreted clearly what he felt was the mood of the nation, summed up much of our political philosophy towards radical methods, and gave a straightforward account of the drastic measures which were to be employed reluctantly to fight the menace.*

I am speaking to you at a moment of grave crisis, when violent and fanatical men are attempting to destroy the unity and the freedom of Canada. One aspect of that crisis is the threat which has been made on the lives of two innocent men. These are matters of the utmost gravity and I want to tell you what the Government is doing to deal with them.

What has taken place in Montreal in the past two weeks is not unprecedented. It has happened elsewhere in the world on several recent occasions; it could happen elsewhere in Canada. But Canadians have always assumed that it could not happen here and as a result we are doubly shocked that it has.

Our assumption may have been naive, but it was understandable: understandable because democracy flourishes in Canada; understandable because individual liberty is cherished in Canada.

Notwithstanding these conditions—partly because of them—it has been demonstrated to us by a few misguided persons just how fragile a democratic society can be, if democracy is not prepared to defend itself, and just how vulnerable to blackmail are tolerant, compassionate people.

Because the kidnappings and the blackmail are most familiar to you, I shall deal with them first.

The Governments of Canada and Quebec have been told by groups of self-styled revolutionaries that they intend to murder in cold blood two innocent men unless their demands are met. The kidnappers claim they act as they do in order to draw attention to instances of social injustice. . . .

To bow to the pressures of these kidnappers who demand that the prisoners be released would be not only an abdication of responsibility, it would lead to an increase in terrorist activities in Quebec. . . .

If a democratic society is to continue to exist, it must be able to root out the cancer of an armed, revolutionary movement that is bent on destroying the very basis of our freedom. For that reason the Government, following an analysis of the facts, including requests of the Government of Quebec and the city of Montreal for urgent action, decided to proclaim the War Measures Act. . . .

The War Measures Act gives sweeping powers to the Government. It also suspends the operation of the Canadian Bill of Rights. I can assure you that the Government is most reluctant to seek such powers, and did so only when it became crystal clear that the situation could not be controlled unless some extraordinary assistance was made available on an urgent basis. . . .

The police have therefore been given certain extraordinary powers necessary for the effective detention and elimination of conspiratorial organization which advocate the use of violence. These organizations, and membership in them, have been declared illegal.

The powers include the right to search and arrest without warrant, to detain suspected persons without the necessity of laying specific charges immediately, and to detain persons without bail.

These are strong powers and I find them as distasteful as I am sure you do. They are necessary however, to permit the police to deal with persons who advocate or promote the violent overthrow of our democratic system.

In short, I assure you that the Government recognizes its grave responsibilities in interfering in certain cases with civil liberties, and that it remains answerable to the people of Canada for its actions. . . .

Canada remains one of the most wholesome and humane lands on this earth. If we stand firm, this current situation will soon pass. We will be able to say proudly, as we have for decades, that within Canada there is ample room for opposition and dissent, but none for intimidation and terror.

Prime Minister Trudeau's TV Message, October 16, 1970.[7]

That there was a crisis no one denied; that the methods used by the terrorists were despicable was agreed; but that the imposition of the War Measures Act, with its reduction of liberties, was a necessary solution was not so easily conceded. The voices of the Opposition rose to attack the Government's methods.

I say that the government's action today is an action of panic. In the hysteria which people feel, the government may, as the Prime Minister has said, get many letters and calls approving what is being done. But

I predict that within six months, when the Canadian peoples have had time to reflect on what has happened today—the removal of all the protection and liberties presently on the statute books of Canada, a country placed under the War Measures Act, regulations introduced allowing persons to be detained for 90 days without a chance to prove their innocence—when that day comes, the Canadian people will look on this as a black Friday for civil liberties in Canada.

Hon. T. C. Douglas.[8]

I ask the government even now to withdraw this resolution, bring in a bill and let members of this House give effect to bringing about changes in the Criminal Code to cover the situation rather than take away from Canadians something which is dearer than life itself—their civil rights, their right to live their lives as they will and not to be denied their constitutional freedoms without which life would cease to have any interest.

Hon. John Diefenbaker.[9]

Since when has repression solved anything? I challenge the Minister of Justice and any other spokesman for the government to give the House one single example in the history of the western world where repression has accomplished the preservation and reintroduction of order. It never has and it never will. I hope with all my heart that I am wrong, but the result of this action in Quebec will be that a good many of our young students in that province will look upon those apprehended in the middle of the night as heroes and martyrs.

Hon. David Lewis.[10]

Then the unbelievable occurred. On Saturday night, October 17, the following message was found outside the concert hall at Place des Arts, Montreal.

Faced with the arrogance of the federal Government and of its valet Bourassa, faced with their obvious bad faith, the FLQ has decided to take action.
Pierre Laporte, Minister of Unemployment and Assimilation, was executed at 6:18 tonight by the Dieppe Cell (Royal 22nd). You will find the body in trunk of a green Chevrolet (9J-2420) at the St. Hubert base.
We shall win. FLQ.

P.S. The exploiters of the Quebecois people had better watch out.[11]

Any credibility the radicals may have had, any sympathy that may have existed for their cause, any hesitation to crush their threat, disappeared. René Levesque, a man who was a passionate Quebec separatist but completely rejected the methods of the FLQ, summed up a prevailing opinion.

They have imported here, to a society that absolutely does not justify it, an icy fanaticism and methods from blackmail to assassination that are those of a jungle. . . .

One can only wish them the worst of punishments. To live long enough to see that they represent nothing and no one of worth, that their act was not only criminal but senseless.

If they really thought they had a cause, they killed it along with Pierre Laporte, and, by dishonoring themselves this way, they have more or less muddied everyone.[12]

And others reflected not only on the personal tragedy for Pierre Laporte but the tragedy for Canada.

Something has been lost to Canada and to all Canadians. There will be a sense of guilt left in the hearts of all of us who love our country that such a thing should have occurred. . .

John Diefenbaker.[13]

I can't help feeling as a Canadian a deep sense of shame that this cruel and senseless act should ever have been conceived in cold blood and executed in like matter.

Prime Minister Trudeau.[14]

I say to those individuals who assassinated him that they are forever unworthy to be Quebeckers and to be French Canadians.

This wretched murder of an innocent man testifies to the kind of society that these movements wish to establish.

But a few individuals, whatever their cruelty or the ignominy of their blackmail, cannot crush the will of entire people. Faith in the democratic regime is too deep and too authentic in Quebec to let itself be destroyed in this way.

I ask all Quebeckers to remain calm and to maintain confidence in their institutions. The blow dealt us today as a people is terrible, but it is a test of our sang-froid and of our firm determination to make justice and freedom triumph.

Premier Robert Bourassa.[15]

The unthinkable had happened, and there was fear that more was to come. Reporter Bill Trent described the atmosphere which prevailed in Montreal as rumours of more violence and possible insurrection drifted through the streets.

The soldier is grim and silent as he stands in the rain at this busy Montreal intersection. He wears battle dress and carries a fixed bayonet.

Some people don't like the idea of armed troops. But the group I'm with is happy to have them.

"Suppose there was an armed insurrection?"

The man who asks the question isn't kidding.

Revolution.

Incredibly, the violence of the word touches Canada's metropolis.

Suppose it *did* develop into a revolution?

Darkness will come early this rainy autumn day and people hurry to catch buses. Home is the safest place tonight.

A police car is parked across the road. It is empty. The cops are somewhere checking out a lead.

Everywhere you feel the sadness. It doesn't matter whether you are English or French-speaking.

Pierre Laporte, Quebec's minister of labor and immigration, is dead, strangled by terrorists who apparently used the medal chain around his neck to do the job.

British trade commissioner James Cross, kidnapped five days earlier than Laporte, is still being held by the Front de Liberation du Québec. And still alive at the time of writing, if you believe the FLQ.

I remember the words of Jeanne Schoeters, spoken seven years ago as I worked with her on the story of her life with her Belgian-born, revolutionary husband, Georges Schoeters. Georges, founder of the FLQ, was sentenced in Montreal in 1963 to 10 years in prison for his terrorist activities. Jeanne got a suspended sentence.

"They figure if they don't accomplish what they set out to do in 10 years, it will be too late," I recall Jeanne telling me.

Whatever it is they have in mind, 1972 is the deadline.

There is fear in the city tonight. It's in every conversation.

It's in the telephone call from home: "There was a bomb in the school today."

In the brief conversation between two girls in an office building lobby, "Don't take a cab. You could be kidnapped."

In the hurried warning from a security guard, "They've flushed out the sewers for explosives but don't get too close to them."

And in a nearly deserted cafe, a man wants to talk. He *has* to talk to somebody. Or else go mad.

He's a French-Canadian and a big man. But he's nearly in tears. He has called the police about some terrorist he knows. And now he wonders if the terrorists will come after him.

I don't know him or his friends. And I don't want to. But I listen. I owe him that much.

He uses a lot of words. But what he says, in effect, is that you can't condone murder.[16]

> *The revolution did not come. James Cross was released and his captors were allowed to fly to Cuba. The suspected kidnappers and murderers of Pierre Laporte were caught, jailed, and brought to trial. A sense of relief came to the country. In a calmer atmosphere it was possible to look back and consider the crisis from a fresh point of view. There were those who saw the gravest threat to Canada not in the actions of the FLQ, but in the methods used to combat the terrorists.*

The police came in the night. They broke down doors. They went into bedrooms. They broke windows and walls and made a litter of libraries. They put personal papers into green plastic garbage bags. They took men from their wives and children, off into the night, off to prison, and they would not say why. Except that there was a list of names given out in the night. . . .

Remember this: It was not a time when a President had been shot and killed in Dallas, it was not a time when a major black leader like Martin Luther King had been killed, it was not a time when another Kennedy had been shot, it was not a time when whole black ghetto populations were in riotous revolt sniping from the rooftops, it was not a time of the March on Washington or the Chicago Convention when angry thousands verged on the politicians, it was not a time of the Weathermen, an actual organized terrorist underground.

We had two cases of kidnapping.

Yet we, not they—the Americans we like to think of as ruthless in the rule of Cop law—suspended our civil rights, put aside our legal privileges, panicked and polarized, and gave symbolic significance to a smattering of thugs. It was called insurrection and now we are advised to acquiesce and see the political expediency of it all. And let the bleeding hearts bleed.

The fact is there were too few bleeding hearts. Let the intellectuals, the lawyers who still applaud, the politicians, the poets, the civil libertarians, the journalists, the professors, let them look within themselves, let us all look within ourselves, for we have entered into a new era and it is the ignorance of ourselves that we are entering into.

Barry Callaghan.[17]

The new era may have been entered, but it did not prevail. Our civil rights and legal privileges are once again with us. Canadian democracy did not collapse. The government did not use its power to become dictatorial. Some people suffered, and unjustly. But to the average Canadian the episode of 1970 was seen as an emergency, a threat to our way of life; therefore it must be crushed, even if a temporary suspension of liberties had to be endured. There was faith in our leaders that they would not abuse the power given them, nor extend it unnecessarily. That belief was described by Ron Haggart of the Toronto Telegram, a man who personally opposed the imposition of the War Measures Act.

This year, it happened quite by chance, an alumni group of McGill University chose October 5 to recall and discuss the events which began on that day a year before.

What they mostly remember, as we all do, is their own emotions from those terrible days. A bright young woman in her early 20s recalls her own satisfaction at the moment of the invocation of the War Measures Act. She felt better. The Government at last was doing something in this void of uncertainty.

The discussion, somewhat to my surprise, is almost an exact replay of one I had heard some time before in Toronto, at a meeting of the York County Law Society. Putting 400 people in jail, it was said at both places, may not be the most desirable thing in the world, but the sacrifice is small compared to the sacrifice exacted upon Mr. Laporte.

What, it was asked in both places, was the alternative? What else could have been done?

This is the real question, and the one which Canadians will forever ask themselves. The acceptable alternative, it has always seemed to me, was the alternative which was in fact eventually turned to when the first flurry of the pointless mass arrests had ended.

It was hard, tireless, boring, repetitive police work which found the house in Montreal north where Jasper Cross lay on his mattress, and it was the old-fashioned weapons in the arsenal of police procedures which led to the charges after Pierre Laporte's murder.

The War Measures Act was the great irrelevancy of our time. It put 497 citizens of Quebec behind bars, of whom 435 were released after imprisonment of one to three weeks without any charges being laid, not even any of the imprecise charges of membership in, or support of, the Front de Liberation du Québec. . . .

Yet there is no doubt that the War Measures Act had the effect which the young graduate of McGill claimed for it. A response which seemed to be the roar of authority from Ottawa did have the effect of calming and reassuring the people of Canada.

A lot of people went to jail, people who were not even guilty under the vague law that jailed them, but the memory most Canadians now wish to preserve is the memory of how good it felt to have their fears relaxed by something, anything, it didn't matter what.

Ron Haggart, 1971.[18]

Our Rebellious Heritage

The lessons to be learned from the events of 1970 are clear. We will not accept violent revolutionary activity; we will use prompt, and possibly excessive force against it; we will even give up temporarily some of our basic rights to fight the menace. But although we were startled by the October crisis, and despite our protestations, "It can't happen here," political violence and attempted revolutions have not been unknown in Canada; and our reactions to these earlier rebellions set the precedent for our behaviour in 1970.

1837 witnessed rebellions in the colonies of Upper and Lower Canada. In retrospect, some of the incidents associated with the rising in Upper Canada assume a farcical pose. But the men who engaged in the rebellion were deadly serious and had made a dramatic decision to risk their lives. What was the cause for which they were prepared to fight? Listen to the fiery, short, red-haired Scot, William Lyon Mackenzie.

CANADIANS! Do you love freedom? I know you do. Do you hate oppression? Who dare deny it? Do you wish perpetual peace, and a government founded upon the eternal heaven-born principle of the Lord Jesus Christ—a government bound to enforce the law to do to each other as you would be done by? Then buckle on your armour, and put down the villains who oppress and enslave our country. . . .

MARK MY WORDS, CANADIANS!

The struggle is begun—it might end in freedom—but timidity, cowardice, or tampering on our part will only delay its close. We cannot be reconciled to Britain—we have humbled ourselves to the Pharaoh of England, to the Ministers, and great people, and they will neither rule us justly nor let us go—we are determined never to rest until independence is ours—the prize is a splendid one. . . .

Up then, brave Canadians! Get ready your rifles, and make short work of it; . . .Our enemies in Toronto are in terror and dismay—they know their wickedness and dread our vengeance. . . .

William Lyon Mackenzie, 1837.[19]

And who were these oppressors who called forth such vituperative comment? They were a small band known as the Family Compact which controlled positions of power and influence in the colony. According to Reformers such as Mackenzie, the Compact used their power for their own advantages and thwarted the popular will. Years of frustration finally brought Mackenzie and his followers to the point of rebellion. And so on a December day in 1837, eight hundred men began the trek down Yonge Street to seize the city of Toronto; one of those was Thomas Sheppard.

Next day I said good-bye to my wife and the folks at home and went down to join the boys. There were seven or eight hundred of them at the tavern, I suppose; fine fellows, too, men who had families and farms to fight for. Some farmers drove in from up country, with their boys. They were brave enough, and if they'd all had muskets they would have beaten the Tories I believe. Lount and other blacksmiths who were reformers made a lot of pikes, but these were no weapons for real fighting.

But that Tuesday night we made a start. Mackenzie ordered us to march down Yonge street, and away we went. He led us. I was in the front rank, along with Thomas Anderson and his brother John. We stepped gently along until we were coming out of the woods at Jonathan Scott's corners. All at once some Tories who were in the brick house then with Sheriff Jarvis, fired on us; don't know but they fired another volley before they ran. They took the back track quick enough, and if our fellows had only been steady we would have taken the city that night. I don't know what started our men running, but most of them made off up Yonge street as fast as the other fellows did down to the town. For a while some of us at the front stood our ground, and I was firing away among the last of them. But after three or four minutes of this work, I said to myself, "Here, a handful of us can't go down and capture Toronto," so we took after the rebels who were making for Montgomery's again.[20]

A loyal Toronto newspaper, The Patriot, *dedicated a poem to the ignominious rout of the rebels.*

The next night came, December fifth,
(December fourth was first,)
When forward tramped the rabble rout,
Incendiaries accurst!!!

In darkness drear, they groped along,
Until they heard a pop!
When they all thought, as really 'twas,
A prudent thing to stop.

Most fiercely bent on fight were all,
Not then—some other day!
For which their courage they reserved;
Proof is, they ran away![21]

A more serious battle did however occur between the rebels and the militia at Montgomery's Tavern. The rebels were beaten, dispersed, and their leaders driven into exile or captured. For all practical purposes the rebellion in Upper Canada was over, for which The Patriot *rejoiced.*

Now good folks all, both great and small,
Your voices raise to Heaven,
With heart felt thanks for health and peace
At the end of thirty seven.

And pray, that on this new born day,
The first of thirty eight,
All wretched sneaking traitors may
Meet a deserved fate.

Now for the Queen give thrice three cheers,
On her be ever shed
Heaven's choicest gifts, and the same
For good Sir Francis Head.[22]

The rebellion in Lower Canada was a much more serious affair and involved vicious and prolonged fighting. The issue behind the rebellion was similar to Upper Canada—a small group, the Château Clique, which controlled the higher positions in government and business versus a reform element which controlled the elected parts of the government. A racial element, however, complicated the matter, for many in the Château Clique were English-speaking, whereas the bulk of the reformers were French. Joseph Papineau, the spiritual leader of the reformers, spoke out against a situation which was becoming intolerable.

The country is suffering under the worst possible evils, and grief and affliction prevail throughout the land. . . .Men ask "What is the meaning of representative government when its officials think they have the right to do and dare everything?". . .The English minority are untrue to their citizenship when they segregate themselves from their fellow-subjects in order to secure privileges for themselves only; and thenceforth they are no longer entitled to the protection of the laws, unless the people of this country are so far demoralized as to lie down submissively at the feet of the few, which I do not believe. But our opponents say to us: "Let us be brothers!" I am perfectly willing for my part, but you want all the power, all the places, and all the pay, and still you complain more than we do. This is something we cannot put up with.[23]

The reformers became rebels; they began to organize an army and drill in the outskirts of Montreal; revolutionary meetings were held and treasonous slogans were shouted. When the rebels formed their headquarters at St. Charles, the British army went into action. Sir George Bell described the attack on the rebel stronghold.

The town of St. Charles is prettily situated on the right bank of the river Richelieu, in a fertile champaign country. After receiving a few shots from some houses on the roadside, which we returned double quick, and fired the houses into the bargain, we advanced towards the town, the rebels keeping up a straggling fire from the opposite side of the river. At two o'clock we came in front of the town, where it was fortified by a breastwork. We halted in column, a short distance on the right of the road, out of the direction of their guns, and summoned the rebels to surrender. The reply was a volley of small-arms and a cheer. Then we opened a fire of round shot shrapnel amongst them; but they were well under cover, having the houses and barns loopholed....When I got up we brought our right shoulders forward, and with three cheers bore down upon the barns and breastworks, which were still lined with the rebels....Twenty-one of our men fell....On entering the town there was little quarter. Almost every man was put to death, in fact, · they fought too long before thinking of flight. Many were burned alive in the barns and houses, which were fired, as they would not surrender. Gun-barrels, and powder-flasks were exploded all night in the burning houses, and the picture that presented itself the following morning to my eyes was terrible. A number of swine got loose, and were eating the roasted bodies of the enemy who were burned in the barns and killed in the streets: those brutes were afterwards shot. The loss of the rebels was great. Their position was strong, and they defended it with desperation, but they were totally routed, and received a lesson that they are not likely ever to forget.

Major-General Sir George Bell, *Soldier's Glory*.[24]

St. Charles was only one of many clashes which took place, but the outcome was the same as it had been in Upper Canada. The rebellion was crushed. Punishment of course had to be meted out; treason cannot go without its penalty. In Upper Canada the unfortunate Lount and Matthews went to the gallows.

At eight o'clock today, thursday, the 12th, Lount & Matthews were executed. The gallows was erected just between the gaol & courthouse. Very few persons present, except the military & the ruff scruff of the city. The general feeling is in total opposition to the execution of these men. At their execution they manifested very good composure. Sheriff Jarvis burst into tears when he entered the room to prepare them for

The death of Lount and Matthews

execution. They said to him very calmly, *"Mr. Jarvis, do your duty. We are prepared to meet death & our judge."* They then, both of them, *put their arms around his neck & kissed him.* They were then prepared for the execution, they walked to the gallows with intire composure & firmness of step.

Egerton Ryerson, 1838.[25]

Twelve men were hanged in Lower Canada. On the scaffold the Patriot Delorimier spoke prophetically of the meaning of his and other patriots' sacrifice.

My friends and my children shall see better days; they shall be free...that is what fills me with joy when all about me is desolation and grief....The Canadian in peace shall see happiness and liberty reborn on the St. Lawrence...the blood and tears flowing today on the altar of liberty water the roots of the tree which shall fly the flag marked with the stars of the two Canadas.[26]

Although the executed men would have disagreed, considering the age and the seriousness of the crime of treason, the scope of the punishment was surprisingly small. Of 98 convicted rebels in Lower Canada, 12 were executed, 58 were deported to Australia, primarily to avoid the need of more severe punishment, and most of the others were set free on bail. There was no widespread blood-bath of revenge. A peculiarly Canadian approach was developing and was seen in the quick amnesty which was granted to the leaders of the rebels. In 1845 Papineau's exile came to an end; and in 1850 William Lyon Mackenzie returned to Toronto to live out his life in respectability. Official and public forgiveness was soon granted to the rebels.

The same was not true of that tragic and enigmatic figure, Louis Riel. Riel had the distinction of leading two rebellions; the first in the Red River settlement in 1869-70, and the second in Saskatchewan in 1884-1885. They were to lead not only to violence but to the bitterest racial strife this country has witnessed, and they left a legacy of distrust between French and English which has endured into modern times.

Both Riel Rebellions originated in legitimate protest and concern for the rights of the Métis as the tide of civilization moved west. Unfortunately the noble cause was muddied by indiscreet actions. When Riel and his fellow Métis at Red River rejected the authority of the Canadian government and set up a provisional government to bargain with the Canadians, there was much sympathy for him. But when the provisional government executed a nondescript troublemaker, Thomas Scott, the wrath of Ontario newspapers fell upon Riel. Thomas Scott, an English-speaking Orangeman from Ontario, had been murdered by Riel, a French-speaking, half-breed Roman Catholic. Riel, the murderer, must hang, cried Ontario newspapers and the Ontario public. Scott was hardly cast in the heroic mold, but the dramatic legend of his death and the mystery of his burial created an aura of martyrdom.

Some guards marched in and told Scott his hour was come. Not until then did the reality of his position flash upon poor Scott. He said "Goodbye" to the other prisoners, was led outside of the gate of the Fort with a white handkerchief covering his head; his coffin, having a piece of white cotton thrown over it, was carried out; his eyes were bandaged; he continued in prayer, in which he had been engaged on the way for a few minutes; he asked Mr. Young how he should place himself, whether standing or kneeling; he then knelt in the snow, said "Farewell," and immediately fell back pierced by three bullets, which passed through his body. The firing party consisted of six men, all of whom it is said were more or less intoxicated. It had been further stated

The death of Thomas Scott

that only three of the muskets were loaded with ball cartridge, and one man did not discharge his piece. Mr. Young turned aside when the first shots were fired, then went back to the body and again retired for a moment while a man discharged his revolver at the sufferer. The ball it is said entered the eye and passed round the head. The wounded man groaned between the time of receiving the musket shots and the discharge of the revolver.

Donald A. Smith's Report, 1870.[27]

It was supposed that the body of poor Scott was buried within the walls of Fort Garry, but this was disproved one morning before we had gone into barracks. I was present when an officer of the public works department with a fatigue party opened the grave which was situated between the officers' quarters and the south gate. An oblong, pine box was found, but there was no body in it; the box was empty, and had no doubt been buried in the fort to deceive people as to the true disposal of the remains of the murdered man. After this discovery there was a strong impression that his body had been taken away during the night after the murder, weighted with chains and forced through a hole in the ice of the Red River, but the mystery has never been cleared up.

Colonel S. B. Steele, *Forty Years in Canada*, 1915.[28]

Riel's first rebellion was quickly put down, and true to the Canadian technique, Riel was allowed to disappear without being hunted down. He was even elected to the House of Commons in 1873 and actually turned up in Ottawa, where warrants for his arrest were finally issued. In 1875 he was granted an amnesty conditional on five years' exile. He spent time in Quebec asylums, then went to the United States where he became an American citizen. His return to Canada in response to an appeal by the Métis of the North West Territories was to result in a new uprising. Not only the Métis were involved; for the first time in Canada, we witnessed what might be called an "Indian war".

The first we knew of the uprising was on the 2nd of April. At five o'clock in the morning, two of Big Bear's tribe came into our house, and told us our horses were stolen by the Half-breeds, and at the same time it was they themselves who had stolen the horses and hidden them. Soon after the arrival of these two Indians some thirty more—all armed, and most of them mounted—came to the house and forced their way in. They took all the arms and ammunition they could find, telling us they were short and wanted all. . . .We were not at all ill-treated so far, but there was every outward appearance of friendly feeling towards us. . . .During our last detention in our house Big Bear came in and told my husband that he was frightened some of his young braves intended shooting the whites, but that he, my husband, would be safe any-way. . . .they came to our house, and ordered us all up to the Indian camp. We departed, my husband and I, as well as all others, only taking with us what we had on our backs, not supposing we would be long away. At this time nothing of consequence had been taken from our house. It was not very cold. Before we had gone far from our house the Indians began to shoot down the whites. Mr. Quinn was shot first, though I did not see him shot. All who were killed were behind my husband and me, but I heard several shots fired, and, until otherwise informed, supposed the firing was into the air. At this time, however, Mr. Dill was killed, also Mr. Williscroft, Mr. Gouin, Mr. Gilchrist, and Mr. Gowanlock, the latter of whom I saw fall. Mrs. Gowanlock was beside her husband when he fell, and as he dropped she leaned down over him, putting her face to his, and as two shots had been fired at her husband some supposed she had fallen from the second shot. When I saw Mrs. Gowanlock fall, I saw also some hideous object, an Indian got up in frightful costume, take aim at my husband. Before I could speak, my husband staggered away, but came back and said to me "I am shot." He fell then, and I called the priest and told the latter what had happened. While he was praying with my husband the same hideous Indian fired again, and I thought this shot was meant for me, and I laid my head down upon my husband and waited. It seemed an age; but it was for my poor husband, and he never spoke afterwards. Almost immediately another Indian ran up, and ordered me away. I wanted to stay, but he dragged me off, pulling me along by the arms through the brush and briar and through the creek, where the water reached to my waist. I was put into an Indian tent, and left there until nightfall, without anything offered me to eat, though I could not have eaten anyway. I was not allowed outside of the tent, and so had no opportunity of returning to my dead husband, and have never seen him since. At night time, two Half-breeds, John Pritchard and Adolphus Nolan, came and purchased our release by giving horses to the Indians. . . .

Mrs. Delaney, 1885.[29]

Off went the troops again to fight the rebels and after some unsuccessful encounters they launched, at Batoche, a combined forces attack employing infantry, artillery, and the gunboat Northcote.

About five o'clock on the morning of the 9th inst. the entire force under the General left their camp of the previous night and moved on Batoche, about eight miles distant. . . .Major Boulton's scouts led the advance, and about eight o'clock the *Northcote's* whistle was heard and answered with volleys of blank cartridge from the Winnipeg Field Battery. In another minute the battle of Batoche was begun. No. 1 Company, Royal Grenadiers, was ordered to the front, followed by the remainder of the battalion, and the whole extended in skirmishing order under the fire rifle pits. While this was being done the guns and Gatling were ordered to the front, and the orders were obeyed at a gallop and with cheering. Howard, with his "pet," as cool as a right-down-easter, reached the open at the church and opened his rain-fall of lead upon the Indians with a "Take that, and that, you devils," as if he were sportingly firing into a covey of birds. With each turn of the crank he would repeat his set phrase, until the scene became humorous, and the Indians scattered before the hailstorm of bullets. The guns then came up and occupied a position upon the plateau overlooking the river and Batoche, and shelled the houses to the front. . . .

A soldier's account, 1885.[30]

Batoche broke the back of the rebellion and shortly afterward Riel surrendered. He was tried for high treason, found guilty, and sentenced to hang. But the issue was not settled yet. It was still within the power of the government at Ottawa to grant mercy to Riel. John A. Macdonald, Prime Minister and leader of the Conservative party, had to make not only the most difficult decision of his political career but also one of the most significant decisions in the history of Canada. The fate of Riel had ceased to be a legal question and had become a struggle for power between English and French-speaking Canada, between Quebec and Ontario. To the French, Riel was a hero, saint, defender of their rights. The newspaper L'Electeur left no doubt as to the significance of Louis Riel.

History will dedicate to you a glorious page, and your name will be engraved in the hearts of all true French-Canadians. . .Joan of Arc! Napoleon! Chenier! Riel! It is with the deepest respect that your sacred names are spoken. Chenier has his monument. Riel, you will have yours.[31]

Ontario and many English-speaking Canadians, especially those who belonged to the anti-Catholic, anti-French Orange Lodge, saw Riel as a traitor, rebel, and murderer of Thomas Scott. That young man's death continued to plague the nation. The Toronto Evening News *saw the issue of Riel's punishment in terms of a political and racial power struggle.*

The echoes of the gatling gun and the ringing cheers of our men in the assault of the rebel position at Batoche sounded the death-knell of French ascendancy. Behind the rebel rifle-pots were entrenched not merely the sharpshooters of Gabriel Dumont, but the long and warmly cherished aspirations of the entire French-Canadian race—the hope of building up on the prairies a second Quebec. The secret underlying motive of the half-breed uprising was to preserve intact for the French "their laws, their language, and their institutions", . . . Will our rulers throw away the results of Batoche . . . by concessions . . . which will inspire the Quebec visionaries with new hopes? . . . "[32]

Political pressure and racial tension mounted until Macdonald, in a moment of understandable frustration, uttered that most unfortunate phrase in Canadian history: "Riel shall hang though every dog in Quebec bark in his favour." Riel did hang and a deep breach was cut into French-English relations. The Conservative party was regarded by the French as the party which killed Riel, the party of English Canada; the political consequences of that conclusion still reverberate today. One has to possess a masochistic streak of impressive proportions to run as a Conservative in Quebec.

It was all a great tragedy and perhaps completely unnecessary. In 1886 the young politician Wilfrid Laurier looked back upon the Riel affair with thoughts which would, in time, replace the bitterness of the Riel Rebellions.

Sir, rebellion is always an evil, it is always an offence against the positive law of a nation; it is not always a moral crime. . . . Sir, what is hateful . . . is not rebellion, but is the despotism which induces that rebellion; what is hateful are not rebels, but the men who, having the enjoyment of power, do not discharge the duties of power; they are the men who, having the power to redress wrongs, refuse to listen to the petitions that are sent to them: . . . Where would be the half-breeds to-day if it had not been for this rebellion? Would they have obtained the rights which

The execution of Riel

they now enjoy? I say, Sir, that the Canadian Government stands convicted of having yielded their rights only to rebellion, and not to the just representation of the half-breeds and of having actually forced them into insurrection.... Though, Mr. Speaker, these men were in the wrong; though the rebellion had to be put down; though it was the duty of Canadian Government to assert its authority and vindicate the law, still, I ask any friend of liberty, if there is not a feeling rising in his heart, stronger than all reasoning to the contrary, that these men were excusable?"

Hansard, March 16, 1886.[32]

Respectable Rebels

All the rebels we have considered were suitably punished; the violence to which they resorted was rejected; order was maintained. Yet the causes for which they fought were quickly accepted as legitimate by the authorities. The Mackenzie and Papineau Rebellions resulted in the granting of responsible government to the colonies; Riel's Red River Rebellion brought Manitoba into Confederation as a full-fledged province with the rights of the Métis protected.

The rebels themselves were gradually seen in a different light so that today Canadians can look upon them with respect, affection, and sometimes, pride. Our historians have helped to give us a new perspective on men such as William Lyon Mackenzie.

William Lyon Mackenzie, ill-starred leader of an ill-starred revolt, may yet not be lightly be dismissed. Fanatic though he was, he was also something more. Although he cannot be hoisted into the position of the impeccable hero, on the plane of other rebels who have had better luck, it is also impossible to dissociate him from the cause of Canada. He stood for the plain man, for the many against the few, for democracy against privilege. He had the wit to discern what was wrong with his province and the courage to battle against it. Canada has had few men of rash courage and inflexible principle, and those few have each cut a wide swath. Mackenzie was one of these, a man whose many faults are lost in an essential integrity, a crusader for what he deemed the right and for what subsequent generations have approved as the right, and therefore a man to whom Canada owes much:...

Arthur Lower, *Colony to Nation*, 1946.[34]

ANTI IMPERIALIST DAY
1971
Join the march
TO COMMEMORATE THE 1837-1839 REVOLUTIONS IN UPPER AND LOWER CANADA AGAINST BRITISH IMPERIALISM AND FOR CANADIAN LIBERATION

ANTI-IMPERIALIST DAY, 1837 Patriots march down Yonge St. to liberate Toronto, December 1837

SATURDAY DECEMBER 4TH
DRESS ## 2:00 P.M. **WARMLY!**

MEET AT: *North-east corner of College and University Ave. at Subway exit.*

MARCH TO: *The Toronto Necropolis Cemetery (Sumach & Winchester)*
Bagpipes, fifes, drums, banners

AT THE CEMETERY: *Wreaths will be laid at the graves of William L.*
Mackenzie & revolutionary martyrs Samuel Lount and Peter Matthews

PARTY AFTERWARDS DONVALE COMMUNITY CENTRE 80 WINCHESTER ST.

SPONSORED BY: CANADIAN LIBERATION MOVEMENT, P.O. Box 41, Station 'E', Toronto 4.   Phone: 964-1174

And Toronto, "Tory" Toronto, "Loyal" Toronto, showed that it had forgiven Mackenzie his rebellious indiscretions when it officially declared Saturday December 2nd, 1972, the city's first annual Rebellion Day. One year earlier, a group of notables had participated in an interesting commemoration of the great Rebellion.

Prime Minister Pierre Trudeau this week congratulated a group of North York "rebels" on organizing an "armed rebellion" in Don Mills Dec. 4.

In a letter to R. W. Percy, Moatfield Farm Foundation chairman, Trudeau says:

"The re-enactment of the Battle between the Rebels from North York and the Queen's York Rangers will recreate an important and dramatic moment in the history of Canada.". . .

Dalton Bales, Ontario's minister of municipal affairs and MPP for York Mills, will play the role of a rebel ancestor and carry the vintage musket his ancestor carried in the original 1837 rebellion in Upper Canada. . . .

William Lyon Mackenzie is being played, also from horseback, by an officer of the Queen's York Rangers who had an ancestor on the loyalist side—in the Rangers—in 1837.

Lieut. John Murchison, who will don a red wig for the Mackenzie role, said this week: "I hope my loyalist ancestors will not resent my becoming a rebel for the day."[35]

Time too has softened the English-speaking Canadian attitude towards Riel. He has received a more understanding assessment by historians, has been granted the honour of a statue in Manitoba, and has been given the ultimate mark of respectability in Canada, a portrait on an official commemmorative stamp.

To present-day Canadians Riel appears, no longer as the wilful "rebel" or "murderer" of Thomas Scott, but as a sad, pathetic, unstable man, who led his followers in a suicidal crusade and whose brief glory rests upon a distortion of history. To the métis, the people whom he loved, he will always be, mad or sane, the voice of an inarticulate race and the prophet of a doomed cause.

George F. G. Stanley, *Louis Riel: Patriot or Rebel?*, 1954.[36]

"I know that through the grace of God, I am the founder of Manitoba."

These words, spoken by Louis Riel in July, 1885, have stirred a minor controversy in Manitoba since they were sandblasted into the concrete shell that now houses a statue of Riel on the south side of the provincial Legislature.

"Sacrilege," muttered the conservative establishment of Manitoba.

"Once a traitor, always a traitor," said one old-timer whose family were prisoners in the Riel rebellions. . . .

. . .The statue is a "humanoid" figure, a modernistic representation of Riel without ears and with empty sockets where there should be eyes. The posture of the figure suggests a man with his hands bound behind his back, straining against his bonds, head lifted as if in supplication to the heavens.

The similarity to both Riel's public hanging for treason in Regina in July 1885, and Christ's crucifixion, is too much to be coincdence. . . .[37]

> *Just though the cause may be, Canadians have consistently rejected the use of violence to achieve its goals. "There are other ways, better ways, than violence," seems to have been our attitude. And the understanding with which men such as Mackenzie, Papineau, and Riel are now regarded should not deceive anyone as to our basic repugnance towards revolutionary methods. At this point in our history for instance, it hardly seems likely that the men associated with the Cross kidnapping and the Laporte murder will ever gain any respectability or honour among Canadians. There is a sordidness about October 1970 unredeemed by nobility of character or the martyrdom of execution.*

Winning the West—Canadian Style

> *Canada can lay claim to the most famous police force in the world. Our Mounties have been glorified by legend, embarrassed by Hollywood movies, burlesqued in cartoons, and in recent times, subjected to criticism. Yet the role they played was to make the Canadian West a much different place from the wild west of the American experiences. In Canada the law preceded the rush of settlement. When the settler arrived in the West he found an orderly society with law and justice already established. And it was the Mounties who made this possible. Officially formed in 1873, the North West Mounted Police set forth in the summer of 1874 from Dufferin, Manitoba, on their long trek across the plains. It was a journey marked by hardship and adventure. The song, "Riders*

*of the Plains," reportedly written by a member of the force, commemorates
both that march and the challenge which faced the Mounties.*

The Riders of the Plains

So wake the prairie echoes with
    The ever welcome sound;
Ring out the "boot and saddle" till
    Its stirring notes resound.
Our chargers toss their bridled heads,
    And chafe against the reins.
Ring out! ring out the marching call
    For the Riders of the Plains.

O'er many a league of prairie wild
    Our trackless path must be,
And round it rove the fiercest tribes
    Of Blackfeet and of Cree.
But danger from their savage bands
    A dauntless heart disdains—
'Tis the heart that bears the helmet up,
    Of the Riders of the Plains....

Our mission is to plant the reign
    Of British freedom here,
Restrain the lawless savage,
    And protect the pioneer;
And 'tis a proud and daring trust
    To hold these vast domains
With but three hundred mounted men—
    The Riders of the Plains.

And though we win no praise or fame
    In the struggle here alone—
To carry out good British law
    And plant old England's throne;
Yet when our task has been performed,
    And law with order reigns,
The peaceful settler long will bless
    The Riders of the Plains.[38]

One of those riders was Samuel Benton Steele. His memories of that period in our history reveal the variety of tasks which the Mounties carried out. Throughout his recollections are two recurring themes: the law applies to everyone, and the law will be enforced.

1874—One of the principal posts of the traders in that region was Fort Hamilton, commonly known as "Whoop Up," situated at the forks of the Belly and St. Mary's rivers. . . .

The scenes which had been enacted round Whoop Up and other trading posts were just what might be expected when the wild redman obtained the "fire-water." The Indians who came to those posts to trade were soon maddened by drink, and settled old scores and family feuds by shooting or butchering one another in their camps or other places where they obtained the intoxicants. When the police arrived the victims of these orgies were to be seen lying dead in the vicinity.

The first raid on the persons engaged in this traffic was made during the same month in which the force established itself on the Oldman River. Three Bulls, a pominent Indian of the Blackfeet tribe, and later a chief, informed the assistant commissioner that a coloured man named Bond, who had a trading post at Pine Coulee, nearly 50 miles north of the police camp, had given him a couple of gallons of whisky in exchange for two of his horses. Potts obtained the necessary information, and arranged that Three Bulls should meet him next evening about dark on the trail to Pine Coulee. Inspector Crozier and a small party of well-mounted men, guided by Potts, left camp a little before dark with instructions to seize all robes and furs of any description which he suspected had been traded for whisky, and in addition a sufficient amount of goods and chattels to satisfy the fines which might be imposed.

Crozier executed his task, and two days later appeared in camp with Bond and four others in custody, all of whom had been captured about 45 miles distant. They had wagons laden with alcohol, 16 horses, 116 buffalo robes, and a Winchester Henry magazine rifle and a colt revolver each. The assistant commissioner confiscated the robes, destroyed the alcohol, fined the two principals and Bond, who was their guide and interpreter, 200 dollars each, and the other two, who were hired men, 50 dollars apiece. Next day a well-to-do trader of Fort Benton came to Lt.-Col. Macleod and paid the fines of all but Bond.

There were many raids to capture whisky outfits. These were very exciting and almost always successful, the traders being fined or imprisoned. Their furs and buffalo robes obtrained through the trade in whisky were confiscated and, as the force was in need of bedding, a sufficient number was issued for the purpose. . . .

1880—The large number of Indians now in the hills round the fort gave us a great deal of anxiety. Horse-stealing became prevalent amongst them, many of them coming over from the United States to run off the herds. Our own Indians were not free from the offence, and the Sarcees began the trouble by stealing from the Assiniboines. They came to the fort to lay a complaint, and one night, with a strong party and the interpreter, I went after them. The whole of the Sarcees were in the camp, and to take them by surprise we stole cautiously up a coulee. The scouts crept up the hill at the head of the coulee and reported all quiet.

The Indians seemed to be in deep slumber, and keeping a small reserve on the outside I threw a circle of men round the camp, which we then entered. The whole of the Indians by this time were out in the centre of the large ring of tents, the men with their rifles in their hands, but the chief and headmen, recognizing me, called out, "How, Manistotkos!" They shook hands and said that they were ready to obey my orders. I knew that the tribe were worth watching, and would do anything to permit the horse-thieves to escape, visits to the penitentiary near Winnipeg not being at all popular. I ordered all the tribe to assemble in the middle of the circle whilst some of our men searched the lodges and others watched every movement of the Indians from one lodge to another. We caught the thieves at last in the act of creeping back to lodges which had been searched from those that had not been inspected. Placing each thief between two men we galloped to the fort by another trail, arriving there about noon.

Some days later Major Crozier persuaded the Sarcees to leave for their reserves near Fort Calgary. An ample supply of provisions was served out to them before they left and we soon learned that they had taken with them a number of horses which they had stolen from the Assiniboines. I sent Staff-Sergeant Fraser and a party of six constables in pursuit. He overtook them near the Seven Persons Coulee, about 40 miles west, and, galloping to the front of the Sarcees where the horses were being driven ahead, cut out the "bunch" on the hill on the left. He was pursued by the majority of the Indians, who fired several rounds upon the party, but without effect, except to wound one of the stolen horses, and they were back in the fort within twenty-four hours, having covered 80 miles. . . .

1883—Fort Calgary—We had one brutal murder during the winter. The victim, a fine young fellow, had a store near us, and he was a regular attendant at the Presbyterian church east of the Elbow, and used to see to the lighting of the fires on Sunday and Wednesday evenings. On one of the latter a young man named Francie came to me in a great state of excitement, saying that he had been at the store and found the poor man lying near the desk with his throat cut from eat to ear and the whole place bespattered with blood. . . .

The murder caused a great deal of excitement, and when it was reported a large mob of citizens, headed by a very decent but excited individual, came to find out what I was going to do about it, and there were threats of lynching the perpetrator if captured. But I said to him, "You lads are all tenderfeet, and have visions before you of taking part in a Neck-tie Social. There never has been a lynching in Canada, nor will there be as long as our force has the police duties to perform, so go away like sensible men, and remember that any attempt at lynching will be bad for those who try it!" This settled the matter, and from that date he was one of the best friends of the force, always taking a leading part on our behalf.

Colonel Samuel Benton Steele, *Forty Years In Canada*, 1915.[39]

Gold Rush Justice

Canada has witnessed two great gold rushes, the Cariboo strike of the 1860s and the Klondike bonanza of the late 1890s. All of the elements of lawlessness were present in both, yet once again, law and order prevailed. For this we can thank the sound judges and stout constables who were determined that justice should prevail and lawlessness be punished. One of these men, Mathew Begbie, was to become a legend in his own time.

In the days of the Cariboo gold rush sixty thousand miners, adventurers and all the riff-raff that follow in the wake of a great mining excitement, filled the Cariboo country in Central British Columbia. . . . Yet with all this rabble of people, rough characters and law-abiding men drawn from every quarter of the globe, Cariboo maintained as an orderly, safe district through the efforts of one man, Sir Mathew Begbie, who was judge and various officials all in one. He administered justice with a ready and iron hand, and put fear into the hearts of those of lawless tendencies. On one occasion he had convicted and fined a malefactor $200.

"That's dead easy," flippantly said the culprit, "I've got it right here in my hip pocket."

"—and six months in jail. Have you got that in your hip pocket, too?", came the ready amendment to the sentence, thus vindicating the dignity of the court and proclaiming to all and sundry that a British court of justice, even though held under a pine tree, was not to be trifled with.

George Ham, *Reminiscences of a Raconteur*, 1921.[40]

Another imposing figure was constable John Kirchup, who presided over the gold boom town of Rossland in 1895.

But Rossland is a remarkable place. A year ago there were but two houses there—since then an American found a mine, tested the value of the ore (gold) with the result that it proved to be all that could be desired. Now there is a population of 2000, mostly from the other side of the line. These people, belonging as they do to a wild and lawless class, are accustomed to cut a gash and shoot at one another without any let or hindrance. But the moment they come into British territory they realize that "Aunt Peggy's laws" (this is their name for Her Majesty) are made to be obeyed—they drop their revolvers and are willing to be kept in order by one constable. This is actually the case at Rossland. There reigns one John Kirchup formerly of Revelstoke: a big burly man with the air of authority in every look and gesture. If a man gets drunk and begins to make a row the word whispered "John Kirkup's coming" is sufficient to make the miscreant look round in terror and bolt if possible. He has not even a lock-up wherewith to uphold his authority; but it seems that his method is simply to lay his hand on the guilty one's shoulder with a word warning—"you'll get into trouble"—should this not suffice he takes him by the collar and gives him a shake and removes him into the road—the worst penalty is a night on the sofa in his office....The remarkable thing is that he should be able thus to impose British law on people who fifty miles away utterly defy all restrictions.

Lady Aberdeen, *Journal of Lady Aberdeen*, 1895.[41]

Richard C. Anzer, an American who arrived in the Kondike in 1898, found that what was a normal precaution in American gold rush towns was neither allowed nor required in Canadian territory.

I was footsore and weary when I reached the end of the trail. A British flag was flapping from a flag pole in front of a large tent. Near the lake front was a tent with a sign, "Restaurant" in front and on the right of that was a smaller tent which Mr. Brackett told me was the one to which I was assigned. I pushed aside the flap and saw a double bunk on each side and one in the rear. Near the entrance was a three-foot Yukon sheet metal stove and some cooking utensils in a cupboard.

I deposited my satchel on the rear bunk and sat down to rest. After about a half-hour, I walked down to the water's edge where a small wharf had been built. The lake, I had been told, was about six miles long. It seemed to be about a quarter of a mile wide.

I was returning to the tent when a tall, smiling officer in a uniform with tight fitting striped pants confronted me.

"Where are you from?" he asked.

"Skagway," I answered.

"What have you got in your back pocket?"

"A revolver."

"Don't you know that's against Canadian law?"

"Almost everyone in Skagway carried one, so I thought I would too," I explained.

"It may be necessary in lawless Skagway, but not here in Canada," the officer said.

Richard C. Anzer, *Klondike Gold Rush*, 1959.[42]

An American reporter from Harper's Weekly *also had nothing but respect for the influence of officialdom in the Klondike.*

The mounted police, both officers and men, in their capacity as preservers of order and as individuals, commanded the respect of every miner. Captain Constantine, upon his departure from Dawson, received a testimonial in the form of two thousand dollars' worth of nuggets, which were subsequently made up in their natural form into a beautiful loving-cup, to show how the miners felt at a time when almost every branch of the public service had forfeited their confidence. It seems to be a well-ordered Canadian's belief that an "official," whether a policeman or a land-surveyor, is qualified, by reason of being an official, to fill any post under government. . . .

The police control of the country was as nearly perfect as one could expect. Thefts and misdemeanors were numerous, and effectively dealt with, and one or two murder cases were tried. The saloons were closed on Sunday, nor was any labor permitted on that day. A man sawing wood, for his own use, and another engaged in fishing were arrested. No city on the continent presented a more orderly appearance.

Tappan Adney, *The Klondike Stampede*, 1900.[43]

The Law is in our Blood

Canadians at the time took pride in their lawful condition, and began to develop a tradition that they were, by nature, a law-abiding people, and as such, much superior to their English-speaking cousins to the south.

From British Columbia to Cape Breton we, Canadians, can proudly point to one of the largest and finest countries in the world, with as well-behaved and law-abiding a population as can be found anywhere, while south of us, the lawlessness is wide-spread, and the crimes of violence almost without number.

George T. Denison, 1880.[44]

The law abiding condition of the Canadian Territories has been from first to last a familiar and highly creditable feature in their history. It is a fact that life and property are safer there than in any portion of the United States or the eastern Provinces of the Dominion. The isolated settlements in the North-West are scattered over an area almost equal to the whole continent of Europe, yet the most unprotected person of either sex can, and often does, travel alone in all directions with perfect safety. In the most unguarded settlements of the interior the door is seldom fastened by night, and theft and robbery is a rare occurrence everywhere. Crimes against the person are almost unknown, and in one, at least, of the Territories, murder has never been committed.

N. F. Davin, *Homes For The Millions*, 1891.[45]

In the Britisher is born respect for the law of the country, and the judiciary which administers the law. We like to think, and we believe that our judges are above reproach, and our courts free from the suspicion of corruption. . . . To tell the Britisher with his great, unshaken belief, that there is anything he can learn from the way law is administered is to arouse disbelief and protest. Yet from the viewpoint of judicial administration there is a great lesson we can learn from the Republic to the south of us, and that lesson is, "What not to do."

Regina Standard, 1904.[45]

A large number of immigrants from the U.S.A. are arriving, many of them originally Eastern Canadians, who have by no means realized their golden dreams of the Western States. It is to be hoped that they will leave all U.S.A. ideas behind them & realize that they have returned to a country where freedom & liberty exist for *all* & not for some, where law & order are respected, & where treaties with Indians are respected. A great number of these New immigrants are doing well & are heartily glad to be British citizens, but there is a remnant who would like to introduce American ideas as to what conduct in the West should be. These must be dealt with ruthlessly, & the magistrates & N.W. Mounted Police are determined that this shall be the case, if they can manage it. Our desire for the country to be filled up must not lead to any undue leniency towards these new comers.

Lady Aberdeen, 1895.[47]

Americans have been among the first to grant Canadians superiority in the law-abiding contest. One detects in their comments upon us not only respect, but a certain amount of awe.

Canadians are less impulsive than Americans and far less given to violence. The gun on the hip has never been part of the Canadian tradition, nor the cure of color blindness by auto-da-fe. Canada has hanged rebels but no "radicals." Nobody has ever tried to assassinate a Canadian Prime Minister, although the Fenians shot down a Canadian statesman of lesser rank in Thomas D'Arcy McGee. Gangsterism is only sporadic in Canada and organized racketeering unknown. No hooded figures have ever dominated the Canadian night scene. The law tolerates fewer technicalities and is far swifter. Relatively few Canadians murder each other and many are hanged when they do.

John MacCormac, *Canada—America's Problem,* 1940.[48]

I think everything goes easier in Canada, for the people are, by nature, law-abiding. There's an incontrovertible belief that if a law goes on the statute books, it is there to be observed, and not "got around." Said a Justice of Peace lately: "Let's have this law off the books—laws are not made to be broken. If we can't keep them, they're not reasonable, and we don't want them."

If you do not keep the law in Canada you pay the penalty. Authority is not equivocal about it.

Louisa and 'W. Peat, Canada: New World Power, 1945.[49]

> *The American attitude towards us was summed up neatly by Stephen Leacock.*

The Americans come up here and admire us for the way we hang criminals. They sit in our club and say, "You certainly do hang them, don't you!" My! they'd like to hang a few! The day may be coming when they will. Meantime, we like to hang people to make the Americans sit up.

Stephen Leacock, "I'll Stay in Canada".[50]

A Repressed People?

"We have for generation after generation been a repressed people, the repressed civility covering rage. A Canadian has been defined as someone who says "I'm so sorry" to a fellow who steps on his toe.

We like keeping people in prison, apparently—more per capita than any other Western liberal democracy. Though it has been less bloody by far and less noticeable than in most countries, we have had our recurrent violence in Canadian history, from the cruel repressions and hangings of 1838-39, to the two Riel rebellions, and the civic riots of which Winnipeg, 1919, and Halifax on VE Day are only perhaps the best known. It is not entirely surprising that our soldiers were the terror of the Hun on the Great War's Western Front.

Our self-disciplined souls give vent to sporadic outbursts of rage. Ours is a puritanism tempered by orgy.

William Kilbourn, 1970.[51]

> *The Winnipeg riot of 1919 began with a strike by the metal trade workers. Civic support for the unionists grew into a mass general strike. Although the workers maintained a peaceful posture, there were those who saw something ominous in the whole affair.*

It is to the general public of Winnipeg that we speak in stating without equivocation that this is not a strike in the ordinary sense of the term—it is revolution.

It is a serious attempt to overturn British institutions in this western country and to supplant them with the Russian Bolshevik system of soviet rule. . . .

Winnipeg Citizen.[52]

There is no longer any doubt about it. Bolshevism has for certain planted its tent at Winnipeg. There exists at present in that city a workers' news-sheet that claims the strikers aim to found a government of Soviets, as there is in Russia. The situation is so grave that the head of the military district where the crisis is taking place has appealed to all citizens of good will, inviting them to take up arms in order to preserve law and order. More than 5,000 citizens have already eagerly answered this call, and everything indicates that this little army will grow to considerable proportions.

La Presse.[53]

We are under the sway of Bolshevism in the city. Everything is quiet, but there are some ugly rumours floating around, and the Home Defence Guards are all ready for action at a given signal. . . .

Rev. Dr. John MacLean.[54]

The suspicions, rumours and fears set the stage for the confrontation which occurred with a mass parade planned by the strikers.

On Saturday about 2:30 P.M., just the time when the parade was scheduled to start, some fifty mounted men swinging baseball bats rode down Main Street. Half were red coated Royal North-West Mounted Police, the others wore khaki. They quickened their pace as they passed the Union Bank. The crowd opened, let them through and closed in behind them. They turned and charged through the crowd again greeted by hisses and boos, and some stones. There were two riderless horses with the squad when it emerged and galloped up Main Street. The men in khaki disappeared at this juncture, but the red-coats reined their horses and reformed opposite the old post-office.

Then, with revolvers drawn, they galloped down Main Street and charged into the crowd on Williams Avenue, firing as they charged. One man, standing on the sidewalk, thought the Mounties were firing blanks until a spectator beside him dropped with a bullet through his breast. Another standing nearby was shot through the head. . . .Lines of special police, swinging their big clubs were thrown across Main Street and the intersecting thoroughfares. Dismounted red-coats lined up across Portage and Main declaring the city under military control. Khaki-clad men with rifles were stationed on the street corners.

Western Labor News. [55]

As with the Winnipeg riot, the Regina disaster of 1935 grew out of troubled times. The Great Depression was in full swing; unemployed men who had been placed in relief camps by the thousands were resentful and frustrated. In June 1935, an On-to-Ottawa trek was organized by the relief camp men in Vancouver. Ronald Liversedge, a participant in that protest march, described the arrival in Regina.

Our entry into Regina was something of a triumph. We had been successful up to now, had built our forces up, and we were a proud little army.

. . .On the second day that we were in Regina we put on a demonstration in the heart of the city. . . .Our marches and demonstrations had been blown up out of all proportion by the papers and news broadcasts and our snake parade was made to appear a magic formula before which civic authorities capitulated quickly.

This was an exaggeration, of course; the snake parade had been devised by us in Vancouver as a defense measure. When we had seen, early in our struggles for relief, how easy it was for the police to barge into and by sheer force of weight and club, to disperse a crowd on the street, we decided that we would not be dispersed as easily as that.

We found that by linking arms, packing ourselves solidly together taking up the whole of the street by weaving from one side to the other we presented a more solid object. Add to this a loose revolving defence group on each side of the main body, these to engage the police and take the brunt of the first attacks, and it is true that we were hard to disperse, but always our best and sure defense were the masses of people that we could rally to the streets.

Ronald Liversedge, *Recollections of the On-to-Ottawa Trek, 1935.* [56]

Meetings with federal officials led to the trek being called off. But the tension in Regina had already risen too high; a meeting of the protesters resulted in tragedy.

Dominion Day, 1935, our country's birthday, and what a birthday celebration it turned out to be. . . .There were probably four or five hundred of us on Market Square. . . .The meeting wasn't long under way . . .when four large furniture vans backed up, one to each corner of the market square . . .and out poured the Mounties, each armed with a baseball bat. . . .In less than minutes the Market Square was a mass of writhing, groaning forms, like a battlefield.

The surprise was complete, and it was a victory for the Mounties, the only one they had that night. . . .We were not going to be allowed to get out of town. We were to be smashed up. How incredibly stupid. Immediately orders were given us to build barricades, and there was plenty of material to work with.

The street was lined with parked cars and we simply pushed them into the streets, turned them on their sides, and piled them two high. . . .It was then, before the first futile charge was made by the Mounties, that the miracle happened. The young boys, and even some girls, of Regina, organized our ammunition column. Without being asked, they came riding bicycles in from the side streets, their carrier baskets loaded with rocks, which they dumped behind the barricades, and then rode off for another load. . . .

It was a terrible night, downtown Regina a shambles. Not a store with a window left in, the streets piled with rocks and broken glass. . . .I was bewildered trying to weigh up the score. About a hundred of our members in jail, including Evans and some of our valuable comrades, forty of our comrades suffering from gunshot wounds, one man killed, scores of others casualties, of whom I think the Mounties could claim the majority. . . .

July 2, 1935, we arose from our straw to an . . .almost unbelievable sight. . . .The Exhibition Grounds at Regina were fenced in by that strong industrial fence . . .and at every entrance was a squad of Mounties with mounted Vickers machine guns. . . .It was the first Canadian concentration camp.

Ronald Liversedge, *Recollections of the On-to-Ottawa Trek, 1935.*[57]

In a strange epilogue to the story the marchers were freed and given transportation home. "Smash them first, and then be merciful," seems to be a Canadian technique in dealing with the rebellious.

In many ways the Halifax riots of 1945 do not deserve to stand alongside the disorders in Winnipeg and Regina which grew out of legitimate protests and causes. The Halifax orgy took place on VE-Day and simply served to release the pent-up frustrations of the war years. There was nothing constructive or purposeful about it. Its participants were revelling in disorder, destruction and debauchery. The Halifax riots were certainly an impressive example of what Canadians can do when they put their minds to it.

I have just walked, crawled and climbed through the ruins of Halifax business districts. There is devastation everywhere. The business area looks like London after a blitz. The streets are littered with broken plate glass, with paper, shoes, whiskey and beer bottles. The jails are jammed with civilians and service personnel—men and women alike. The hospitals are overflowing with injured, some of them dying. Three navy men are dead, one killed in the rioting and another, an 18-year-old Vancouver youth, who succumbed to over-intoxication. . . .

From the ocean terminals in the south-end to the colored settlement of Africville in the extreme north, from the waterfront to northwest Halifax, store after store lies in wreckage. Their stocks which were not carried away to caches by organized looters or "souvenir hunters," have been trampled into the street slimy with rain and debris. This is the final scene in Halifax's VE-Day riots which raged unchecked for hours on end and cost city merchants over $1,000,000.

Ambulance and police sirens, are shrieking in the streets this morning, as new casualities were being found in the morning clean-up. Police and services provost corps are still chasing soldiers, sailors, airmen and civilians over the streets, fences and rooftops.

Two downtown buildings stand charred in fire ruins. They were touched off by incendiarists early last evening as a last fling before a curfew was clamped on Halifax and all service personnel were ordered back to barracks. . . .

The rioting started when service men defied two policemen at a Sackville St. liquor store around midnight, Monday night, smashed through the window and pulled bottle after bottle, case after case of spirits and beer into the street. The store had been closed since Friday night.

Within seconds hundreds had joined them. Police were crushed in the rushes as they tried to stop them. "Come and get it," they shouted as they hurled the liquor out into the street.

Then everywhere in the business district further rioting flared. . . .

But this was only tame to what was coming. During yesterday morning and until about 3 o'clock in the afternoon there was a lull in the uncontrolled rampage as service personnel were called to attend a divine drumhead service in the garrison grounds.

With the ceremonies over the gangs raced down over the hill streets to the downtown area like a division of infantry in a bayonet attack, yelling and screaming. Their main target was Oland's brewery on Water St., where, word had quickly spread, thousands of gallons of beer lay.

At the gates and along the fences surrounding the brewery grounds the mobs found military police standing guard. They rushed the guards and smashed through into the building. The battle of the brewery was on. Within seconds the interior was a scene of utter destruction. Great vats of beer were overturned and flowed down the roadway into the gutters.

Almost simultaneously, another gang raced to the concrete warehouse of the Nova Scotia liquor commission almost 10 blocks further north. They hacked down the iron bars at the doors, pushed in the windows. Soon the tens of thousands of dollars' worth of spirits were coming out— —some carried, thrown, some flowing out in rivulets.

They went into the street, and up on to the slopes of Citadel Hill, passing out liquor to those they found without it. They drank, shouted, swore, kissed and kicked as they went. Everywhere glass came tumbling through the streets and looting was on in full force. People every-where—service men and women for the most part—collapsed every few feet from drunkenness. Many citizens were stopped by the mobsters and ordered to drink with them. . . .

The rioters burned a city police wagon, leaving only its chassis against a capstan on the waterfront wharf which stopped it from being pushed into the water.

They burned one street car almost to its wheels, wrecked another and broke 800 windows in 20 more.

They cut power lines and uncoupled hoselines as firemen tried to quell the flames.

"Parts of Halifax are more seriously damaged than they were by the 1917 explosion," said Chief Constable Judson Conrod. "We were powerless. The mob would have murdered anyone who got in their way."

Guns were taken from police to prevent an incident that might touch off pitched battles.

Toronto Daily Star. [58]

> *These orgies of violence aside, Canadians have maintained a peaceful and law-abiding posture. In the violent climate of the 1970s we have been able to preserve our society from the extreme political and social violence which has prevailed throughout the world, and especially in the United States. We are proud that our cities are still free from the street muggings and terrorism which plague the great American cities.*
>
> *There are prophets of doom who maintain that violence is lying beneath the surface ready to erupt. We hear rumblings from groups who predict violence unless social ills are quickly cured; we are told that our cities will naturally follow the American pattern as they grow in size; we have experienced violence at colleges, in union disputes, in the activities of the rumoured "organized crime."*
>
> *If there is an inevitability in these fears, it is hoped that the Canadian experience will be less extreme and less divisive than the American difficulties. We are, after all, basically a restrained and orderly people.*

The Queen: God Bless Her!

Canada is the only monarchy on the American continent. When the Fathers of Confederation established this nation there was no doubt but that it would remain under the authority of a monarch. John A. Macdonald even proposed that the new nation be named "The Kingdom of Canada", a title kindly rejected by the British government in favour of "The Dominion of Canada". The respect and affection which Canadians have felt for their monarch was never more evident than in the early years of our nation when Queen Victoria reigned.

Wherever I have gone, in the crowded cities, in the remote hamlet, the affection of the people for their sovereign has been blazoned forth against the summer sky by every device which art could fashion, or ingenuity invent. Even in the wilds and deserts of the land, the most secluded and untutored settler would hoist some rag or cloth above his

7 THOSE IN AUTHORITY OVER US

shanty, and startle the solitudes of the forest with a shot from his rusty firelock, and a lusty cheer from himself and his children in glad allegiance to his country's Queen. Even the Indian in his forest or on his reserve, would marshal forth his picturesque symbols of fidelity, in grateful recognition of a Government that never broke a treaty, or falsified its plighted word to the red man, or failed to evince for the ancient children of the soil a wise and conscientious solicitude.

Lord Dufferin, Governor-General of Canada, 1874.[1]

Victoria, our Queen

My heart throbs high at thought of thee!
    I hold thee in my hand,
And gaze upon thy loveliness—
    Queen of our Mother land.

Thy crown and lace, and fair round arms,
    And all thy rich array.
God bless the day thou cam'st to us—
    The twenty-fourth of May.

Dear art thou to the hearts of us,
    Thy subjects, great and small,
In bungalow, in wigwam wild,
    In castle, cot, and hall.

Never, since Time began his march,
    To this great Jubilee,
Was ever crowned woman loved,
    And honored like thee.

God bless and give thee length of days,—
    Thou of the noble mien—
Long may'st thou live, to hold the helm,
    Victoria, our Queen.

Clara Mountcastle, 1897.[2]

"The twenty-fourth of May
    Is the Queen's Birthday.
If we don't get a holiday,
    We'll all run away.

Traditional Chant of Canadian Children

Writers can talk of the constitutional and historical significance of the monarchy. But for children, the monarchy had a more practical impact on life.

Whatever sentiment of patriotism and loyalty we felt was embodied in The Queen's Birthday, May 24. For Toronto boys of my generation, and maybe for boys throughout Ontario, the three great days of the year were Christmas, the Twenty-Fourth and the birthday of the individual boy. Easter was nothing. New Year's was not much either except that with me for three or four years it marked the date on which I began a new diary which I would keep up for the best part of a month. It also marked the coming of another period of time in which I would have another birthday.

The twenty-fourth of May was the beginning of summer. On this date it was usual for us boys to shed our winter flannels, which in our family were called "flannens." Only in the winter did we have underwear. We had only the one kind, the thick, scratchy kind which were a torment when first put on. In the summer we went in our shirts, our pants, and shoes and stockings—no underwear. The thrill we received when we got rid of the underwear is suggested by the line of Rupert Brooke who describes a swimmer "into cleanness leaping"; and connected with it, somehow or other, was a feeling of gratitude to Queen Victoria. Perhaps subconsciously we felt that if it had not been for her we should have had to wear sweat-soaked "flannens" all the year round. "God bless the Queen", we cried with our elders.

We had a picture of the Queen in our living room, a highly coloured oleograph, which revealed a haughty, rather short-tempered lady with an imperious nose and a vast bosom covered with sashes and royal insignia. Nowadays we should not regard it as the picture of a wholly agreeable human being. But then we should no more have criticized it than a companion picture of Jesus on the Road to Emmaus. In truth, our boyhood imaginings suggested to us that God was a member of the Royal family. God and the Queen were equally remote, and as it seemed to us, of about approximate ages.

J. V. McAree, *Cabbagetown Store*, 1953.[3]

The strange, almost mystical hold which the monarchy had over many Canadians of British descent is evident in the following passage. It was printed in the Ontario Reader *of 1925, from which thousands of school children might learn the proper attitude to monarchy and the British heritage.*

Here in Canada, far away in the West, with the croon of the Pacific Ocean in my ears and the scents of a deep, cool pine forest stealing into the candles through the opening of a tent, I find my wonderment following the ancient trail of a far-away childhood. Does Edward the Seventh, I asked myself, ever reflect that in all the zones of the world, night after night, year in, year out, at the old familiar call "Gentlemen, the King!"—men of Shakespeare's blood and Alfred's lineage spring to their feet, as at the sound of a trumpet, and the local welkin rings with the anthem of the British. Is he conscious, wheresoever he be at this moment, of the low, strong, rumbling Amen of our anthem, which rolls through the tent as we set down our glasses and resume our chairs—"The King!—God bless him!" Every night, in every quarter of the globe, as constant as the stars, as strong as the mountains, this pledge of loyalty, this profession of faith by the clean-hearted British—"The King!—God bless him!"

Presently the chairman rises to propose another toast, but my thoughts cling to the ancient trail. I see a vision of Windsor Castle, with the Royal Standard streaming out against a sky of summer turquoise, exactly as it shone for my boyish eyes in a box of bricks. The fragrance of England's may-breathing hedgerows and the deep earthy scents of her glimmering woods of oak and elm, come to me from the fields of memory. All that makes England demi-paradise—her rose-hung hedges, her green woods, her creeping rivers, her April orchards, and her March-blown hills—all this gracious pageantry rises in a green and tender mirage to the eyes of my musing.

And as I feel the spell and magic of "this other Eden," I feel also the pomp and splendour of the British throne, I understand how it is that, whithersoever I go in Canada, men stand up like soldiers at the toast of the King, and, though but a moment before they were laughing over a story, sing with exaltation the anthem of the British: "The King!—God bless him!"[5]

"I feel the way most Canadians feel—indifferent." T.V. commentator Joyce Davidson made this statement regarding the Queen's visit in 1959. The ensuing uproar cost Miss Davidson her job, and showed that monarchists would still rise to defend the Crown. Their victory, however, may have been the last. Canada had changed since the days of Victoria. Immigrants had increased the non-British element; French Canada, seeking new freedom for itself, looked on the monarchy as a symbol of "foreign" rule; among many Canadians of British background, there was, indeed, a growing indifference. The monarchy was under attack.

The Royal Visit of 1964

Police, Soldiers Mass

For Safety of Queen

300 Montreal Students March

With "Liz Go Home", "La Reine, No"

QUEBEC POLICE CLUB SEPARATISTS

Redcoat Forces Charge Crowds

Quebec—The Queen left Quebec City last night after two days in which the pageantry of welcome from her loyal subjects went on inside strong walls while outside police nightsticks swung against separatist demonstrators and paddy-wagons rolled.

At one stage the Queen was booed by a few persons—perhaps 30—among a crowd estimated at about 1,000.

It was impossible to get an official count of how many demonstrators were locked up, almost all after being clubbed by municipal police in full view of crowds. Globe and Mail reporters alone witnessed 28 arrests, including two at gunpoint...

This police action came in all cases after young demonstrators, some in their teens and most in their early twenties, shouted separatist slogans while the Royal procession was passing or immediately after it passed. At the sound of such shouts, municipal police in fluorescent red raincoats would wade in and charge the demonstrators, running over anyone in their path.

Globe and Mail.[5]

The Monarchy Is Subjected to Critical Analysis

If you're asking what I think about the monarchy, I will tell you quite frankly I couldn't care less.

Pierre Elliott Trudeau, 1967.[6]

"What does Quebec think of the Queen?" I am asked during a seminar on Quebec's nationalism. Frankly I am embarrassed to answer, because I have not given much thought to this question. Does Quebec think of the Queen? Not often, almost never, except when Canada invites Her Majesty to visit the country. When the Queen's name is mentioned within my limited circle of friends our indifference is real—but there is no disrespect in our feelings. My son's entourage burst into laughter when I asked them what they thought of the question. *We do not think about Her Majesty. She has nothing to do with us. Prince Charles will never become King of Canada. He is not the type.* . . . I will venture this opinion towards the Queen; English Canada is sentimental, French Canada very emotional! But youth, French and English, is openly indifferent.

Solange Chaput-Rolland, 1969.[7]

   The monarchy exists in Canada for historical reasons and it exists in the sense that it's a benefit or it was considered to be a benefit to the country or to the nation. . . . If at any stage people feel that it has no further part to play then for goodness sake let's end the thing on amicable terms without having a row about it.

Prince Philip, 1969.[8]

   If the Quebec separatists knife Canada asunder, leaving all other provinces dripping with economic and spiritual blood, who will be most likely to hold together the riven halves of the English speaking mass, President Roland Michener, Prime Minister Pierre Trudeau or Her Most Gracious Majesty Queen Elizabeth II?
   A monarch is our strongest defence against a takeover by the United States during the weakness and confusion that might follow a clumsy breakaway by Quebec.
   A republic can swallow a top hat but not a crown. A republic can only smash up a crown by defeating the army that has sworn to protect it.
   A monarch is our strongest defence against a dictatorship that could spring up in other provinces during the general despair, disorder and regional jockeying for power that would follow the proclamation of a republic in Quebec.

McKenzie Porter, 1971.[9]

   . . .this is 1972, not 1872. The Empire has disappeared. The Orange parade in Toronto can't muster the vigor of an anti-war demonstration. The people here now are Canadians and of many cultures. The tie that binds them to a British crown is an anachronism.

The fiction that our elected representatives are legally subservient to a master on the other side of the world must be particularly puzzling to immigrants who came to Canada expecting a free country, in form as well as fact.

Our foreign figurehead is, to a growing number of Canadians, about as divisive symbol at a time when this country is gingerly trying to overcome such irritants.

Toronto Star editorial, 1972.[10]

The monarchy no longer divides most Canadians. If to some it seems anachronistic—irrelevant but harmless—to others it is a source of pride —and pleasure. We should let it be for that alone.

But that is not all that may be said in defence of modern monarchy. It helps distinguish ourselves from republican America. It cuts an incumbent prime minister down to size, stops him from hogging the ceremonial limelight as well as executive power.

The monarchy has unified before. In 1949, the Crown made possible India's staying, as a republic, a member of the Commonwalth. The King, by the sheer fact of his existence, was able to serve as a symbol of Commonwealth association.

Could it unify again? I think it's not fanciful at all to imagine a role for monarchy in devising some formula short of separation when the time comes, as it surely must, for a redefinition of Quebec's role *vis-à-vis* Confederation.

If monarchy did not exist, Canadians at this critical juncture of our history would find it useful to invent it.

James Eayrs, 1972.[11]

The majority of the members of the Committee would prefer a Canadian as Head of State who would no longer represent a Monarch beyond the seas but would assume office for an established period of years following an affirmative vote of Parliament. We therefore support the evolutionary process by which the Governor-General has been granted more functions as the Head of State for Canada.

However, in the present climate of Canadian opinion any sharp change would probably be an unduly divisitive step. As far as we are able to measure, Canadians are about equally divided between those who favour and those who oppose the Monarchy, with the proponents generally, being older, and the opponents generally younger.

In such circumstances, therefore, the Committee does not recommend any change in the Monarchy at the present time but eventually the question of retaining or abolishing it will have to be decided by way of a clear consultation with the Canadian peoplè.

Report of the Special Joint Committee of the Senate
and House of Commons, 1972.[12]

This Is Not an Easy Country to Govern

I think it is often not recognised what a great difficulty has to be contended within the government of this country through the necessity of every Administration having to be practically a coalition Ministry having a French speaking section and an English speaking section, and not only having to represent different races and creeds strongly antagonistic to one another, but also different Provinces each with different interests and with different Provincial laws.

Lady Aberdeen, 1895.[13]

The one calamity above all others which stands before this country is that political divisions should follow the division of race or the division of religion. The one danger which menaces the future of this country and the union of this country, now so happily being accomplished, is that men should stand arrayed against each other on the question of government, because they differ with regard to religion, because they differ with regard to race.

Sir John Thompson, 1892.[14]

Tensions in Canada are never merely two-way. Nothing so simple as north against south, English against Irish, French against German. In Canada the patterns of hostility are a kaleidoscope of regional and religious, personal and political, social and economic, cultural and linguistic prejudice in which no combination is reliably predictable. It is partly a cause, partly an effect of this condition that sovereignty itself is divided between two levels of authority, each supreme in its own sphere. Ten provincial governments, each a working model of Her Majesty's

Government in Westminster, are wholly independent of each other and partly independent of the central government in Ottawa that exercises its own kind of authority in all provinces.

In this situation it is hardly surprising that tension is chronic and crisis frequent. Canadians are used to it—so used to it that they may not even notice when the nation's normal malaise becomes suddenly acute.

Blair Fraser, *Search For Identity*, 1967.[15]

Macdonald: Holding the Nation Together

Sir John A. Macdonald was one prime minister who mastered the art of controlling the diverse pressures of this country.

When this man is gone, who will there be to take his place? What shepherd is there who knows the sheep or whose voice the sheep know? Who else could make Orangemen vote for Papists, and induce half the members for Ontario to help in levying on their own province the necessary blackmail for Quebec? Yet this is the work which will have to be done if a general break-up is to be averted.

Goldwin Smith, 1884.[16]

I think it can be asserted that for the supreme art of governing men Sir John Macdonald was gifted as few men in any land or in any age were gifted—gifted with the most high of all qualities—qualities which would have shone in any theatre, and which would have shone all the more conspicuously the larger the theatre. The fact that he could congregate together elements the most heterogeneous and blend them in one compact party, and to end of his life kept them steadily under his hand, is perhaps altogether unprecedented. The fact that during all these years he maintained unimpaired, not only the confidence, but the devotion—the ardent devotion—the affection of his party, is evidence that, besides these higher qualities of statesmanship to which we were the daily witnesses, he was also endowed with this inner, subtle, undefinable characteristic of soul that wins and keeps the hearts of men.

Sir Wilfrid Laurier, 1891.[17]

So divided a country is Canada that a Canadian prime minister must be continually walking a tight-rope. Macdonald performed his act superlatively well. Herein lay the real genius of the man: he was a perfect master of equilibrium: he could reconcile the irreconcilable. With steady rein year after year he drove his restless, ill-assorted six-horse team. Perhaps only he could have kept the Confederation structure going. And for that perhaps he considered easy political morality a cheap price.

Arthur Lower, *Colony To Nation*, 1946.[18]

Macdonald's opponents criticized his political and human failings; but with consummate skill Macdonald often turned his personal liabilities into political assets.

I know enough of the feeling of this meeting to know that you would rather have John A. drunk than George Brown sober.

Sir John A. Macdonald.[19]

Sir John Macdonald was the supreme student of human nature. That was the secret of his power. I doubt if any man of his century was his equal in the art of managing men. He could play on the strength and weakness of each and all his followers at his will. . . .Perhaps his chief disservice was to make his countrymen feel that politics was not only a game but a game without rules. He was our greatest Canadian, but he did more than any other man to lower the level of Canadian public life.

Sir Wilfrid Laurier.[20]

"Ah, John A., John A., how I love you! How I wish I could trust you!"

Liberal politician, 1867.[21]

"I guess you come from Canada?"
"Yes, Ma'am."
"You've got a very smart man over there, the Honorable John A. Macdonald."
"Yes, Ma'am, he is."
"But they say he's a regular rascal."
"Yes, Ma'am, he's a perfect rascal."
"But why do they keep such a man in power?"
"Well, you see, they cannot get along without him."

A 'RIEL UGLY POSITION.

"But how is that? They say he's a real skalawag, and . . ."
Just then her husband, the Senator, stopped us and said:
"My dear, let me introduce the Honorable John A. Macdonald."
The lady's feelings can be imagined, but Sir John put her at her ease,
saying: "Now, don't apologize! All you've said is perfectly true, and
it is well known at home."

Anecdote concerning an incident in Washington, 1871.[22]

*Macdonald's technique of delaying difficult decisions gained him the title
"Old To-morrow". The following poem was printed in* Punch *magazine
on Macdonald's death.*

Punch sympathizes with Canadian sorrow
For him known lovingly as "Old To-morrow."
Hail to "the Chieftain"! He lies mute to-day,
But fame still speaks for him and shall for aye,
"To-morrow——and to-morrow" Shakespeare sighs.
So runs the round of time; man lives and dies.
But death comes not with mere surcease of breath
To such as him. "The road to dusty death."
Not "all his yesterdays" have lighted, Nay,
Canada's "Old To-morrow" lives to-day
In unforgetting hearts, and nothing fears
The long to-morrow of the coming years.[23]

Laurier: The Middle Path

I pledge my honour that I will give the whole of my life to the cause
of conciliation, harmony, and concord among the different elements of
this country of ours.

Sir Wilfrid Laurier, 1864.[24]

I have had before me as a pillar of fire by night and a pillar of cloud
by day a policy of true Canadianism, of moderation, of conciliation.

Sir Wilfrid Laurier, 1911.[25]

*Such was Laurier's policy as he saw it. His task was doubly difficult.
First of all, he led Canada when English Canadians demanding fuller*

participation in the foreign and military affairs of the British Empire clashed with French Canadians who saw such commitments as unnecessary and dangerous; secondly, as a French Canadian, he was exposed to the suspicions of both English and French.

And so, he sought the middle road between two extremes, hopefully appealing to the broad mass of Canadians.

There is a school abroad, there is a school in England and in Canada, a school which is perhaps represented on the floor of this parliament, a school which wants to bring Canada into the vortex of militarism which is the curse and the blight of Europe. I am not prepared to endorse any such policy.[26]

If Britain is ever in danger—nay, I will not say that—if Britain is ever on trial, I, a Canadian of French origin, will be the first to go to the people and call upon them to assist with all our might.[27]

I do not pretend to be an imperialist. Neither do I pretend to be an anti-imperialist. I am a Canadian first, last and all the time.[28]

If England is at war we are at war and liable to attack. I do not say that we shall always be attacked, neither do I say that we would take part in all the wars of England. That is a matter that must be guided by circumstances, upon which the Canadian parliament will have to pronounce, and will have to decide in its own best judgement.[29]

I am branded in Quebec as a traitor to the French, and in Ontario as a traitor to the English. In Quebec I am branded as a Jingo, and in Ontario as a Separatist. In Quebec I am attacked as an Imperialist, and in Ontario as an anti-Imperialist. I am neither, I am a Canadian.[30]

To the racial rivalries dividing the nation, Laurier brought an approach which stressed harmony and unity.

I do not want French Canadians to domineer over anyone, nor anyone to domineer over them. Equal justice; equal rights. . . .Cannot we believe that in the supreme battle on the Plains of Abraham, when the fate of arms turned against us, cannot we believe that it entered into the designs of Providence that the two races, enemies up to that time, should henceforth live in peace and harmony? Such was the inspiring cause of Confederation.[31]

We may not assimilate, we may not blend, but for all that we are the component parts of the same country. We may be French in our origin—and I do not deny my origin—I admit that I pride myself on it. We may be English, or Scotch, or whatever it may be, but we are Canadians; one in aim and purpose; and not only Canadians, but we are also members of the same British Empire. This fact, that we are all Canadians, one in our objects, members of the British Empire, proud of being British subjects and Canadian, is evidence that we can keep pride of race without any detriment to the nation.[32]

...As long as I live, as long as I have the power to labour in the service of my country, I shall repel the idea of changing the nature of its different elements....I want the sturdy Scotsman to remain the Scotsman; I want the brainy Englishman to remain the Englishman; I want the warm-hearted Irishman to remain the Irishman; I want to take all these elements and build a nation that will be foremost amongst the great powers of the world.[33]

King, the Enigma

Judged by his length of term as prime minister, William Lyon Mackenzie King was our most successful leader, and probably the master compromiser. He left no doubts regarding his political strategy.

In politics one has to do as one at sea with a sailing ship, not try to go straight ahead but reach one's course having regard to prevailing winds.[34]

I would just give you one bit of advice, to remember that in the course of human history far more has been accomplished for the welfare and the progress of mankind in preventing bad actions than in doing good ones.[35]

I really believe my greatest service is in the many unwise steps I prevent.[26]

If there is anything to which I have devoted my political life, it is to try to promote unity, harmony and amity between the diverse elements of this country. My friends can desert me, they can remove their confidence from me, they can withdraw the trust they have placed in my hands, but never shall I deviate from that line of policy. Whatever may be the consequences, whether loss of prestige, loss of popularity, or loss of power, I feel that I am in the right, and I know that a time will come when every man will render me full justice on that score.[37]

During the Second World War, when Canada's unity was threatened by divisions between French Canadians who opposed conscription and English Canadians who demanded conscription, King announced the following policy.

Not necessarily conscription, but conscription if necessary.

King, 1942.[38]

A firm believer in the occult and a frequenter of mediums, King felt that his life was guided by a supernatural power.

I could see a Divine Providence guiding me most lovingly. This will determine my course largely thro' life. I am determined to make it the beginning of an honourable career. I intend to go on now ever upward if God so wills.[39]

In 1907 King thought seriously of entering politics.

Lastly there is the purpose of God in all, the realization of the dream of my life, the page unfolds as by the hand of Destiny. From a child I have looked forward to this hour as that which should lead me into my life's work. I have believed my life's work lies there, and now I am lead to the threshold by the Invisible Hand.[40]

Many years later, King was to attribute his triumphs in Parliament to the same "Invisible Hand".

To have a majority of 73, I could think only in terms of manifestation of spiritual powers that were making all things work together in accordance with the will of God and in answer to prayer, and the law of God with respect to the power of faith. The result was really a miracle.[41]

If ever a man in this world was guided from beginning to close in

shaping the whole course of a session, I am that person. It has been
the clearest evidence to me of guidance from Beyond that anyone could
possibly have. What had seemed impossible, God has made not only
possible but actually joyous and triumphant. Now it may come to be
the same with the election itself.[42]

...the whole course of events have now so shaped themselves that
once again I may become the instrument to make clear to the country
that God's will and purpose have been behind what my life has stood
for in these times in the accomplishment of things which could only
be accounted for by His purpose working out its aim. . . .I believe the
present government will yet carry through to the end of the war and
I may yet be the one chosen to at least make the beginning in the winning
of the peace in relation to world organization for the preservation of
the peace.[43]

The Judgment of King

Alone among the outstanding British Canadian leaders today, Mr. Mackenzie King trusts, and consequently is trusted by, the French Canadian.
He views national unity, not as a means but as an end. He will delay,
he will compromise, he will travel only part of the road he would follow
if he can travel with French and British Canadians pulling in double
harness. For this he is often bitterly blamed by the Imperialists in Canada,
but their criticism does not deflect him. He has seen the mistakes of
the past, and what is rare, he has learned from them. . . ."

American Minister to Ottawa, 1940.[44]

However the current riddle of Canada may be dissected in the future,
at the core will be found the enigma of King, who was its authentic
expression. As Canada is the least understood nation, so King is the
least understood statesman of our era. Outwardly the dullest, he was
inwardly the most vivid, fascinating, and improbable issue of the Canadian
race. The mystery grows, the fascination deepens, and the enigma retreats
farther from our clutch when the private man emerges and suddenly
is overtopped by the public shadow. . . .

To the end he kept his secret. The caricature already becomes a legend
to mislead all future Canadians. A King who never existed is erected
as a statue. The man is as unrecognizable in death as in life, precisely
as he desired. Through spiritualistic mediums he sought the other world
but in this temporary abode he took infinite pains, and even built his

own stone ruins at Kingsmere to be remembered for something he was not. The disguise deceived its own creator. He came to believe utterly in a fairy-tale hero of his own imagining.

If the Canadian people also believed in a fictitious King, they never liked him. At times they hated him and often laughed at his diminutive figure in the newsreels. But they came to respect him as they respected no other leader, they relied on him as on the seasons, and when he died they missed him as a comfortable piece of furniture which had long served in every Canadian home.

Bruce Hutchison, *The Incredible Canadian*, 1953.[45]

W.L.M.K.

How shall we speak of Canada,
Mackenzie King dead?
The Mother's boy in the lonely room
With his dog, his medium and his ruins?

He blunted us.

We had no shape
Because he never took sides,
And no sides
Because he never allowed them to take shape.

He skilfully avoided what was wrong
Without saying what was right,
And never let his on the one hand
Know what his on the other hand was doing.

The height of his ambition
Was to pile a Parliamentary Committee on a Royal Commis-
    sion,
To have "conscription if necessary
But not necessarily conscription",
To let Parliament decide—
Later.

Postpone, postpone, abstain.

Only one thread was certain:
After World War I
Business as usual,
After World War II
Orderly Decontrol.
Always he led us back to where we were before.

He seemed to be in the centre
Because we had no centre,
No vision
To pierce the smoke-screen of his politics.

Truly he will be remembered
Wherever men honour ingenuity,
Ambiguity, inactivity, and political longevity.

Let us raise up a temple
To the cult of mediocrity,
Do nothing by halves
Which can be done by quarters.

F. R. Scott.[46]

Aberhart: Prophet of the Plains

The success of King led many to consider him not only typical of our politicians, but of Canadians generally—cautious, prosaic, dull. Nothing could be further from the truth. We have not been without our dullards in politics, but we have had our share of colourful personalities, silver-tongued orators, and charismatic leaders. Any country which has seen the likes of John A. Macdonald, Aberhart, Diefenbaker, Smallwood and Trudeau, has not lacked colour at the top.

In Alberta, they called him "Bible Bill" Aberhart. And they had reason. "Oh Lord," he used to pray at campaign meetings. "Do Thou grant us a foretaste of Thy millennial reign. Organization is not enough, Lord. Our help must come from above." On Thursday, August 22, 1935, organization turned out to be a pretty good thing to have around, too; because of it, the world's first Social Credit government was returned with fifty-six out of sixty-three seats in the Alberta legislature.

It was organization and Aberhart that did it, though Aberhart was never loath to share the credit with God. As for God's millennial reign, it has been somewhat deferred; but the government elected that day is still in power in Alberta, and the mark of Bible Bill Aberhart is still upon it.

There were many who hated him—and with a bitter hatred that few Canadian leaders have ever been able to attract. An editor in Calgary concluded a series of attacks with this final broadside: "Aberhart is a dishonest, dishonourable, lying, blaspheming charlatan, who insinuated himself into power by deception and misrepresentation and is morally unfit to hold the office of Premier." And there were many more who loved him with an equal intensity, although not all as fanatically as the zealot in Drumheller who screamed out at a Social Credit meeting: "Arise and worship Aberhart, the Son of God!" When it came to invective Aberhart himself was no slouch; he would call his opponents "these rats, sons of Satan, liars, fornicators."

Alan Anderson, 1964.[47]

Opponents of Aberhart found his power too much to overcome by sheer reason or argument.

...just as soon as it became apparent that I was going to discuss Aberhart's theories in a critical way, down went the people's heads. The men would scowl fiercely at me. They didn't want to hear Aberhart criticized. If the Apostle Paul had been loose in Alberta for six months, he couldn't have stopped Social Credit.[48]

Aberhart used radio more effectively than any other Canadian politician; and his devoted followers found that his magic over the airways was just as effective as his presence on the platform.

Mr. Aberhart won my complete loyalty because of his sympathy with the poor and unemployed. I've seen him cry. I've seen tears rolling down his cheeks when he was describing the suffering caused among the poor by the depression—through no fault of their own, as he made clear to us....He had a voice that made the pilot lights on your radio jump. You simply had to believe him. Sometimes when I heard him, I used to say to my wife: "This man seems to be in direct contact with the Supreme Being."[49]

John Diefenbaker: The Chief

The prairies, which had seen the power of Aberhart, gave rise to another imposing figure. From Prince Albert, Saskatchewan, came John Diefenbaker, lawyer, Conservative politician, and legend in his own time. His rise to power was definitely not meteoric; he suffered defeats and rejection at the hands of his own party. But when he rose to speak in Winnipeg on the night of February 12, 1958, the years of political frustration and disappointment were behind him. In the coming decade he would dominate the Canadian political scene, in or out of office. On that night he challenged the Canadian voter with a new vision.

Sir John A. Macdonald gave his life to this party. He opened the West. He saw Canada from East to West. I see a new Canada—a Canada of the North. . . .

As far as the Arctic is concerned, how many of you here knew the pioneers in Western Canada. I saw the early days here. Here in Winnipeg in 1903, when the vast movement was taking place into the Western plains, they had imagination. There is a new imagination now. The Arctic. We intend to carry out the legislative programme of Arctic research, to develop Arctic routes, to develop those vast hidden resources the last few years have revealed. . . .

This party has become the party of national destiny. I hope it will be the party of vision and courage. The party of one Canada, with equal opportunities to all. The only party that can give to youth an Elizabethan sense of grand design—that's my challenge.

The faith to venture with enthusiasm to the frontiers of a nation; that faith, that assurance that will be provided with a government strong enough to implement plans for development.

To the young men and women of this nation I say, Canada is within your hands. Adventure. Adventure to the nation's utmost bounds, to strive, to seek, to find, and not to yield. The policies that will be placed before the people of Canada in this campaign will be ones that will ensure that today and this century will belong to Canada. The destination is one Canada. To that end I dedicate this party.

John Diefenbaker, 1958.[50]

The people of Canada caught the vision and give Diefenbaker the largest majority in the House of Commons ever granted a prime minister.

But the fates were cruel, and by 1963, Diefenbaker was out of office. And yet John Diefenbaker as Leader of the Opposition was in some ways even more imposing and devastating than he had been as Prime Minister.

When the Chief let fly in the House in one of his Wagnerian performances, complete with the rumble of off-stage artillery, Government Ministers would wince, noticeably drawing away from the one among their number who happened to be the target. Those who escaped, or having been through the baptism of fire, congratulated themselves for having survived, seemed to derive as much pleasure from the Chief's salvos as the press and his own members behind him.

When the Chief was in full flight it was fatal to interrupt. His expression would turn to horrified astonishment, the pointing finger would flick like a rapier, and the member, pinked with a phrase, would fall back gasping. Interrupted by Paul Martin, he quoted Scripture: "Paul, Paul, thou art beside thyself." He loved interruptions and interjections and had a number of "spontaneous" ripostes ready for such occasion. He counted as lost any Hansard report of one of his speeches not plentifully sprinkled with interruptions. "Shows I was getting to them," he would say with satisfaction. When a brilliant young Newfoundland member thought he would try foils with the Chief, the Chief shot out without breaking stride, "When a hunter is after big game, he does not stop for rabbit tracks." The member subsided rather breathlessly. . . .

Watching the Chief get up to speak was like watching Babe Ruth at bat. There was the same sense of occasion. One expected him to point to a corner of the Chamber and knock one out over the Speaker's head. Most Speakers went out of their way to cater to the Chief's foibles. He didn't abuse the privilege except for questions which, coming from any other member, would instantly have been ruled out on grounds of prolixity and controversy. He seldom had recourse to the rule book and sometimes gave the impression of writing the rules as he went along. Yet one had the conviction that in Beauchesne or Erskine May there was certain to be a rule substantiating his position to the letter.

He would catalogue with outraged gusto the failings of Government policy or Government Ministers, sweep back a drooping lock with his hand and pause, overwhelmed at the enormity of it all. "I ask you," he would say in a voice dripping with scorn. . . .

Some wrote that Mr. Diefenbaker rambled, that his thoughts were not organized, or that he introduced into his remarks sordid and nonconstructive references to Hal C. Banks, organized crime, or unjustified government expenditures, and that in general his performance was not such as is recommended in political science courses. This was a bit like complaining that Mount Vesuvius in full eruption was contravening the forest fire regulations. As a national institution, like Mount Eisenhower or Niagara Falls, the Chief went his own sweet way, regardless of the barbs of pundits.

Thomas Van Dusen, *The Chief*, 1968.[51]

"He cared enough to come." The sign greeted Diefenbaker as he rolled across the prairies on his whistle-stop crusade. It was 1965, and he was fighting his last political campaign as the Leader of the Conservative party.

John Diefenbaker moved like a legend over the land. Everywhere his train stopped, clusters of people would seek the sight of him under the cool Prairie sun. The men with hands hooked into the front of their broad belts gazed at the former prime minister, seeing him in a warm glow of recognition, as someone with whom they'd shared the experience of hard times. The wind fluttered the hair of the women as they shyly shook his hand to extend a mute blessing.

It was the presence of John Diefenbaker more than his words that excited the people. Here was a communion of instinct that no other politician could fully understand, much less duplicate. John Diefenbaker was the political poet who in his very being could evoke the pioneer virtues and the glories of a simpler past when the Red River carts still creaked along the Battleford Trail and buffalo bones littered the horizonless prairie. At Melville, Saskatchewan, he spoke to several old timers at the rear of the station platform, demanding: "When did you come here?" The oldest of them said, proudly, that he'd arrived in 1903. "But *when?*" Diefenbaker insisted. "In September," was the reply. A gleeful Diefenbaker shot back: "We came in August!"

The journey was illuminated with moments of lucid pathos. At Fort Macleod, 78-year-old Norman Grier confided to the Chief: "Heck, I wouldn't vote for that Pearson. He wants to give away Crowsnest Mountain to Quebec." At Settler, two raggedy kids were holding up a huge, hand-lettered cardboard sign with the letters: DEIF FOR CHEIF. At Morse, local musicians serenaded him with a wavering version of *The Thunderer* and reporters couldn't file their copy because the telegrapher was playing the drums. As the train pulled out, the brave little aggregation struck up *God Be with You till We Meet Again* and John Diefenbaker cried. At Swift Current, twenty-one blue-gowned ladies on the back of a truck broke into *Land of Hope and Glory* and sang *Mademoiselle from Armentières* for an encore. At Taber, Diefenbaker told an audience of hushed school children: "I only wish that I could come back when you're my age to see the kind of Canada that you'll see. So dream your dreams, keep them and pursue them." Somewhere along the route, an old man sat by the tracks in the twilight, holding up a sign that read: JOHN, YOU'LL NEVER DIE.

Peter C. Newman, *The Distemper of Our Times*, 1968.[52]

Joey Smallwood

Almighty God said, "I think I'll raise him up to persuade Newfoundland to join Canada. If he persuades them, Newfoundland is going to need a Premier.

Joey Smallwood.[53]

I love this job. I love it to death. I love every waking minute of it, from the time I get up to the time I go to bed.

Joey Smallwood.[54]

A diminutive figure crouched over the wheel of a vast, custom-built Cadillac or Chrysler Imperial, Smallwood can commonly be sighted hurtling through fog at seventy miles an hour, two wheels across the centre line, or smartly overtaking round a corner. According to St. John's legend, he was once spotted doing this by an RCMP control car, which gave chase and finally overtook him. As the officer approached, notebook in hand, a familiar face peered out the window. "My God," the officer said. "Yes," replied the Premier, "and don't you forget it." With cars, as with cameras, tape-recorders, intercoms, and hi-fi sets, all of which he delights in but quickly demolishes, Smallwood is a mechanical illiterate. Only quick reflexes have saved him from worse accidents than a moose decapitated on a New Brunswick highway, a carload of provincial cabinet ministers overturned on a back road, and a night spent in reading official documents in the back of his car, in the midst of a snow-covered field, after a skid off the highway.

At home, Smallwood answered his own telephone, whether the caller was a plumber or the Prime Minister of Canada. Anyone could see him at any hour of the day or night. An interview with the Premier was a happening. Visitors crowded into the corridor outside his ground-floor office at Canada House. If the wait happened to be too long, as it usually was, they were welcome to drop into the kitchen and brew a pot of tea. Once inside, knee-booted fishermen and double-breasted corporate presidents picked their way around untidy mountains of papers, books, and documents in search of the Premier. Often they found him crouched on the floor, excitedly examining a set of blueprints spread out in front of him. Or he might be behind his desk holding a telephone receiver to each ear. As the visitor stated his business, he would call a brief halt to the telephone conversations and then ask what the newcomer thought about the matter under discussion. Federal civil servants, in particular were astounded to find themselves giving advice on local and not necessarily democratic politics. . . .

Whatever interested him at the moment absorbed him totally, and had to be acted upon immediately. Unaware that the metabolisms of others responded to different time clocks, Smallwood telephoned ministers and civil servants at all hours of the night to demand their instant appearances. Dishevelled and bleary-eyed, the wretched men would stumble into Canada House to be confronted with an inhumanly wide-awake Smallwood excitedly expounding some complex and costly project. To argue with him at any time was next to impossible; at four in the morning, sheer exhaustion muffled the mildest pleas for caution.

Richard Gwyn, *Smallwood, the unlikely revolutionary, 1968.*[55]

Smallwood's great passion has been Newfoundland. Even before he entered politics, as a journalist and broadcaster he dedicated his energies to Newfoundland.

. . .my Barrelman broadcasts were a considerable achievement. For six years, six nights a week, there has never been anything like them, before or since. They christened me the blind patriot. I was like Ziegfeld with the American girl. I glorified Newfoundland. I became known as a fellow who would stand up for Newfoundland. Stories, anecdotes, countless stories of the strength, prowess, ingenuity, resourcefulness, courage, daring, unconventionality, a glorification of Newfoundlanders, I had an enormous correspondence, tens of thousands of letters. There has never been anything like it. I always carried a torch for Newfoundland.[56]

As Premier he continued to fight for Newfoundland and New-foundlanders.

I set out to convince our people that Newfoundland had a great future, that this was an exciting place to stay. I think I went a long way toward making it that.[57]

This is *our* land, this is *our* river, this is *our* waterfall. Newfoundland first, Quebec second. The rest of the world last.[58]

I would, however, have you remember one important point that is frequently lost, that perhaps never has been understood by the people of what I sometimes call "Continental Canada". Canada did not take over Newfoundland. Canada did not absorb Newfoundland. It would be historically and constitutionally as correct to say that Newfoundland absorbed Canada or took her over as that Canada absorbed Newfoundland. It was not the absorption of one country by another.[59]

I have never been in the least bothered when somebody says to me that something I did today completely contradicts something I did before. I haven't had time—in trying to build Newfoundland—to think about such things.[60]

At the end of his political career, Smallwood received the affection and adulation of Newfoundlanders who would never forget him.

"You fed the hungry and clothed the naked. God bless you for it, Mr. Premier."[61]

"There'll never be another like you."[62]

There was a man sent from God whose name was not John, but Joey.[63]

Everything I did, I wish I had done better. I wasn't big enough, smart enough to do better.

Joey Smallwood, 1972.[64]

It is typical of Smallwood that one of his most recent statements of intent has been issued from Communist China where he announced his plans to join a commune.

"FRANK, MY BOY, WHATEVER GAVE YOU THE IDEA THAT I'M CLINGING TO OFFICE?"

The indomitable Smallwood reasons with his political opponent.

I'll work with my hands in the fields. I'll do any of the jobs required of me as a full-fledged member of a commune.

I'll be able to attend all the commune meetings, to listen—and talk, too.

If I were 10 years younger, I would like to settle down for two or three years in China to help them build the society they are building.

They sent college professors out to clear the latrines—they got the dirtiest of jobs until they understand that everyone was the same.

I'm excited about China—they are working like Trojans with incredible devotion, love and affection.

Joey Smallwood, 1973.[64]

Trudeau: Charisma and Mania

Something happens to people's faces when they see Trudeau. You can manufacture noise and screaming kids, but you cannot manufacture that excitement in the eyes, that glistening look of rapturous excitement which is on the faces Trudeau now sees when he makes his little speeches, saying nothing, in the hotel ballrooms where the delegates gather to see him. It is not madness, not in these excited matrons and lawyers. It is belief. It is belief, perhaps at this stage only shallow belief in one man's shy appeal, but it is belief, too, that an interesting and uniquely intermingled Canadian society produced this man.

Ron Haggart, 1968.[66]

TEEN-SCREAM WELCOME GREETS HIS ARRIVAL[67]

He is the man who can solve our country's problems and keep our party in power.

Convention delegate, 1968.[68]

What if I faint when he comes by?

Delegate's wife, 1968.[69]

Pierre is better than medicare—the lame have only to touch his garments to walk again.

Joey Smallwood, 1968.[70]

I feel happy leaving the country and the Government of Canada in his hands. . . .

This man is a truly outstanding person. He is a man for all seasons but especially for the season of tomorrow.

Lester Pearson, 1968.[71]

But who was this man? His personal history was gradually revealed and only added to the charismatic image.

Trudeau left school, theoretically to gather material for a Ph.D. that never got written, and went on a world tour that was to lead to many of the stories and many of the legends that later sprang up around his name. He went alone, travelling with a knapsack, shorts and an untidy beard. He wandered through Germany, using papers he had faked himself, and flew to Belgrade, in an attempt to get into Yugoslavia without a visa. He was jailed, then deported to Bulgaria, where he joined a group of Spanish-speaking Jewish refugees, with whom he rambled through Greece and Turkey. By later accounts he also swam the Bosphorus, which he remembers as cold, with "a bloody strong current". He wandered into Palestine and was arrested as an Israeli spy; he was released and began wandering again, only to be picked up by desert bandits, whom he frightened off by feigning madness. He wandered further, to India, where he was attacked by pirates while travelling in a sampan, and escaped in a providential fog. He visited the Khyber Pass during the India-Pakistan conflict, crossed Burma during a civil war, and, after visiting Vietnam, managed to get into China during the final throes of civil war there.

Walter Stewart, *Shrug: Trudeau in Power*, 1971.[72]

This exotic background was merely a prelude to the new style which Trudeau brought to politics; driving a Mercedes with flair while clothed in ascot and sandals; leaping hedges on Parliament Hill to avoid the press; kissing pretty teenagers; wise-cracking with press and bystanders; performing diving exhibitions in motel pools. But could this man with a playboy image be taken seriously as a potential prime minister? In Montreal, during the evening of St. Jean Baptiste Day, Trudeau gave an impressive display of physical courage.

By the light of a burning police car, amid the screams and curses of the wounded, the thud of exploding Molotov cocktails, the clatter of police horses and the crunch of clubs breaking heads, the parade went on. The band of the St. Jean Baptiste society in their medieval costumes, plumes shining in the firelight, halted briefly before the reviewing stand while police threw demonstrators into a paddy-wagon, then blasted forth a happy tune. Go-go girls squirmed on floats, ignoring the carnage around them. A golden palomino police horse was felled by a crowbar and the rider's legs broken. A demonstrator was dragged backwards, spurting blood, across a carpet of broken glass. Rocks and pop-bottles flew as the police charged.

While hairy students howled "Trudeau to the gallows!" the Prime Minister leaned forward in his front seat on the reviewing stand, waving at the parade and winking at the girls. It was election eve, 1968. Montreal was winding up St. Jean Baptiste Day with its traditional night-time parade and several thousand separatists had turned it into a scene from the Inferno, carried live on television.

Beside Pierre Elliott Trudeau sat his bitterest political enemy, Premier Daniel Johnson of Quebec.

As the cameras watched, a pop bottle whizzed across Sherbrooke Street and into the center of the reviewing stand. Missing Trudeau's head by six feet, it shattered on the marble front of the Montreal public library.

The VIPs, including Premier Johnson, scattered and ran. Pierre Trudeau sat on, alone but for his two Mountie bodyguards. When they tried to shield him with a plastic raincoat he angrily brushed them aside.

At that moment the next day's election was decided. Trudeau's personal triumph was complete. Reporters on their stand across the street burst into spontaneous cheers. Even policemen turned from their savage battle to shout "Bravo". The Prime Minister stood up and waved both arms limply in a sort of shrug.

It was his style. He had sidled his way into power with an air of cool detachment, discovering that there was more magic in that shrug than in all the pounding and roaring of his competitors.

Gordon Donaldson, *Fifteen Men*, 1969.[73]

Enlightened Despot or Machiavellian Dictator?

Like every Messianic elitist, Trudeau sees himself as a shepherd chosen by destiny to steer a dumb herd into paradise he alone perceives.

A dictator endowed with this type of mind and vision simply breaks and smothers all resistance. The glorious end result he is sure to accomplish justifies the use of every coercive means at his disposal.

Trudeau does not have complete dictatorial powers. Not yet.

That's annoying to a man of his mental makeup, for it necessitates compromises, delays and even postponements of some of the structural changes that are indispensable for implementation of his grand design.

Hence Trudeau's distaste for the parliamentary process, his disdain of the "nobodies" in the Commons who have not yet accepted the purely ornamental role assigned to them in his concept of "participatory democracy" that boils down to participation in bowing to his will.

Lubor J. Zink, 1971.[74]

We have often heard this man speak of efficiency in the terms of the technocrat, cold and distant. He has used the power of his office to confuse rather than to clarify, to manipulate rather than to evoke participation, even to distort when he thought it necessary. We have heard him dismiss the tragedy of unemployment as a mere annoyance. We have seen him mouth unpleasant words even in this House of Commons and insult workers who could not strike back. He treated all Canada as his stage to act out his moods as if the nation's business was little more than a game.

David Lewis, Leader of the NDP, 1972.[75]

In Pierre Elliott Trudeau, Canada has at last produced a political leader worthy of assassination.

Irving Layton, 1969.[76]

And it came about, in the Third Year of his Reign and in the Fifty-Second year of his Youth, that the King did choose to leave his capital on the Hill and to pass among certain of his people.

And they hailed his coming and strewed his path with Placards, for, in all that time, they had heard little from him and had seen him in his own person not at all, although from time to time, when he deemed it to his advantage to do so, he had permitted himself to be portrayed at the controls of an airplane, or upon the ski slopes, or astride a camel.

And he said unto them: "Beware false prophets, for I alone am the Truth. And when there is some Thing that should be made known to you, and upon the knowing of which you will re-elect me and mine, then I shall come among you and proclaim it. . . .

'Which dictator are you guarding?'

Tito of Yugoslavia visits Trudeau of Canada.

Do not trouble yourselves with the events of your time, for they are in Good Hands, for, are they not in Mine and those of the persons who inhabit the Privy Council Office, in which all wisdom reposes? Put from your minds all efforts to comprehend wars and famines and layoffs of persons from their work and troubles of all sorts, for they are beyond you and can only serve to disturb your sleep."

And he told them What Was Not Possible, and What They Could Not Expect, and What They Should Not Ask, and What They Should Not Worry Themselves About, and, further to reassure them, he told them nothing of what his Government had done, was doing, or might do, for it would only Burden Them and possibly make them Restive. . . .

George Bain, 1971.[77]

And in 1972 the People chastised the King, and granted him no majority in the elections, and gave his enemies, the Conservatives, almost as many seats as Him in the House of Commons. And to his followers and the People, the King made new pronouncements.

The important thing now is that if there is a low profile, let it be mine and not you people out there. We don't want a low profile for the Liberal party. I've got enough humility for the rest of you.[78]

I don't think I've changed in demeanor. In attire? I think I was perhaps not guided enough by the principle of behaving properly in the proper place. You go to the opening night of a concert. Black tie is called for. If you really want to shock the people, you don't wear black tie. You go in sandals and an ascot.

I just think if you want to concentrate your energies and emotions on the proper things, you shouldn't be expending them on unimportant things like that. If you want to show up as an original thinker, you don't have to rely on turtlenecks or on sandals.[79]

Pierre, Pierre. Why hast thou forsaken us?

Political Variety: A Canadian Tradition

I find Canadian politics more interesting, more fruitful, and more creative than the politics of almost any country I have studied, because it is so wonderfully varied, because it is plural. . . . Canada allows provincial governments to go off into the most extraordinary heresies, heresies it of course forbids in the federal parliament as far as possible. I therefore find federal government a bit boring, but provincial government is absolutely fascinating. One travels across Canada through different kinds of government, different kinds of people expressing themselves in different ways and allowed to do so and encouraged to do so, having ideas which, expressed locally in this way, impinge on the nation so that the nation can draw from local experiments for its central planning. It is a wonderful richness and a wonderful variety.

Richard Crossman, an English political observer, 1964.[80]

Social Credit: "Heresy" or Salvation?

The economic theory of Social Credit was developed by Major C.H. Douglas. To many observers, it was a complicated, impractical, and possibly fraudulent political doctrine. But during the desperate years of the Great Depression it was seized upon with great enthusiasm as a possible solution to unemployment and economic crisis. And what was the meaning of Social Credit?

There are 731,000 in Alberta and it's our duty to look after them. It's funny in this province of ours there is a law that prevents you starving or illtreating a dog, cow, or any other animal, and yet they allow people to go hungry, illclothed and suffer. Social Credit with its basic dividend to every man and woman of $25.00 per month starts out with the corrective measures at once. It places purchasing power in the hands of the consumer. We have found a scientific way out of our troubles, and if we don't do it, then nobody else will. We have the best brains in the province at our disposal, let us use them and put Social Credit into force. Where does all the money come from? We don't use money. Then where does all the credit come from? Why out of the end of a fountain pen. Social Credit is a scientific principle that can be adopted and can easily be understood.

William Aberhart, 1935.[81]

"You don't have to know all about Social Credit before you vote for it; you don't have to understand electricity to use it. . .all you have to do is push the button and you get the light.

William Aberhart, 1934.[82]

I have all the damn fools on my side and all the clever men against me.

Major Douglas, founder of Social Credit,
after meeting Aberhart.[83]

I had lost my job as the result of the depression and was down and out, feeling pretty sorry for myself. I used to feel so tired out that I would fall asleep over the newspaper after supper. Then I heard Mr. Aberhart expound Social Credit at the Bible Institute. He made me see why we had a depression. He told us we could end it if we all pulled together. So I decided to take up Social Credit and work for Mr. Aberhart. An amazing change took place. After Social Credit came into my life, I had plenty of pep and energy. It was amazing.

A follower.[84]

"Wacky" Bennett and Social Credit in British Columbia

It is not known if there is necessarily an connection between Social Credit beliefs and unusual behaviour. It is possible that Premier Bennett of British Columbia owes the title "Wacky" more to the combination of his initials, W.A.C., and personal behaviour, than to his politics.

Several years ago, after a campaign promise to make the province debt-free, he called in about $200 million worth of long-outstanding bonds, on which as little as 3 per cent interest was being paid. Ceremoniously he had them piled onto a floating raft, and, with press photographers present, fired a flaming arrow into the bundle. Then, to finance new projects, he blandly borrowed new money at 5.5 per cent interest.

Gerald Clark, *Canada: The Uneasy Neighbors*, 1965.[85]

Bennett has been called a puritan and an anti-intellectual. He did once choose between politics and the priesthood, and certainly many of his actions support the image.

On his first visit to Japan, in 1965, he sat uncomfortably on the floor of one of Tokyo's leading restaurants, attended by the pick of that city's Geisha girls. The bill for each: around $20 an hour. Their sole function: to help him innocently unwind and enjoy himself.

TRUDEAU: "You know, why doesn't he (Real Caouette) go to British Columbia where there's a Social Credit government and make a speech about the bigot who happens to run the government there. You know, this great Canadian who thinks there are too many French people in Ottawa...who talks about the Quebec Mafia and the great power we have here."(Quoted in *Time*, Feb. 28, 1972)

BENNETT'S SPOKESMAN: "If the Prime Minister has nothing better to contribute to public life in this country than profanity, the fuddle-duddle, the shrug of his shoulders, the smirk on his face, it is time he resigned." (Quoted in the *Globe*, Feb. 19, 1972)

But across the low-slung table, loaded with such delicacies as carp soup, quail's eggs and bamboo shoots, was a television set showing a Japanese baseball game, which he watched as the meal progressed. A thousand nuances of what was for him a new and exotic culture waited in vain for his study. The sake flask turned cold, stayed full; the rice beer bubbled untouched; the principal geisha gained his favor by bringing in ginger ale. . . .

The more-or-less Puritan, however, has a weak spot. He loves to gamble. At a football game, he will bet not only on who will win the game and by what score, but on who will carry the ball next, how many yards he will carry it and who will stop him.

With his small group of friends he will play gin rummy for hours, for small stakes. For hours each day on a holiday he will play bridge, often with Gunderson. His bridge is like his politics. He plays a good game, his opponents say, but he is a gambler on his bidding.

An Admiral's wife who played with him in the early days summed it up; "I would bid one spade, then he would respond with six spades." I asked her; "Did you make it?" She replied; "Sometimes." At cards, cabinet or conference, Bennett tends to play his game the same way.

Paddy Sherman, *Bennett*, 1966.[86]

I sat near the premier at a dinner not long ago. We had steaks that must have been two inches thick. The premier finished his before anyone else, and never stopped smiling.[86]

They see in me what Social Credit stands for—it gets things done.

W.A.C. Bennett, 1965.[88]

The Socialist Vision

Canada has had a long flirtation with socialism. For twenty years the CCF held power in Saskatchewan, and the New Democratic Party, the title which replaced the old Co-operative Commonwealth Federation, is at present in office in Manitoba, Saskatchewan and British Columbia. In 1933 the CCF issued its program in the Regina Manifesto.

We aim to replace the present capitalist system, with its inherent injustice and inhumanity, by a social order from which the domination and exploitation of one class by another will be eliminated, in which economic planning will supersede unregulated private enterprise and competition, and in which genuine democratic self-government, based upon economic equality will be possible. The present order is marked by glaring inequalities of wealth and opportunity, by chaotic waste and instability; and in an age of plenty it condemns the great mass of the people to poverty and insecurity. . . . We believe that these evils can be removed only in a planned and socialized economy in which our natural resources and the principal means of production and distribution are owned, controlled and operated by the people.

The new social order at which we aim is not one in which individuality will be crushed out by a system of regimentation. Nor shall we interfere with cultural rights of racial or religious minorities. What we seek is a proper collective organization of our economic resources such as will make possible a much greater degree of leisure and a much richer individual life for every citizen. . . .

We do not believe in change by violence. We consider that both the old parties in Canada are the instruments of capitalist interests and cannot serve as agents of social reconstruction, and that whatever the superficial differences between them, they are bound to carry on government in accordance with the dictates of the big business interests who finance them. The CCF aims at political power in order to put an end to this capitalist domination of our political life.[89]

Arise, Ye Prisoners of Starvation

> In 1921, a group of people huddled in a barn near Guelph, Ontario, created the Communist Party of Canada. The party and its members have suffered periodic repressions; in 1931 during the depression when leaders were seized and imprisoned on conspiracy charges; and in 1940 when the party was banned for opposing the war. Since that time, the party has become perfectly legal and almost respectable. At the party's fiftieth birthday celebration came reflections on its past and future.

Our Party has been here for 50 years and it is here to stay! . . .

Capitalism is sick and becoming sicker day by day . . . Socialism is growing and winning in its contests with capitalism all down the line. . . .

Yes, after 50 years we should have been bigger. But the advance of a revolutionary movement doesn't always go in a straight line. . . .

. . .there is the conception that if the Communist Party came to power everything would be taken from them. We just advocate ending the exploitation of man by man—we're not against people having their own house and car, and we're not against small businesses. We would simply nationalize strategic areas like banking, transportation and communications. . . .

It's hard to estimate when people will make the leap. There are so many imponderables. . . .But it's safe to say profound changes will envelop the world within the next 25 years and Canada will not be immune to those changes. Come back in 25 years and check over what I've said.

William Kashtan, National Leader, 1972.[90]

Oh, 50 years ago, I thought I'd see something. Now, maybe, another 50 years.

John Boychuck, one of the original founders, 1972.[91]

The Day of the Strong Man

The range of political doctrine and personality which Canadians have tolerated is wide enough to include what might tentatively be called dictatorship. In Maurice Duplessis, the man who dominated Quebec politics for almost a quarter of a century, and was premier of that province from 1933 to 1939 and from 1944 until his death in 1959, we found a Canadian representative of that political breed which is so widespread in the twentieth century, the despot who controls massive popular support.

Some day I'll run this province and make Ottawa listen.

Duplessis, while a student at University of Lavel.[92]

To some, Duplessis "ran" the province of Quebec far too well.

. . .his gay, bantering exterior was a mask for one of the most ruthless, despotic personalities Canada has ever produced. Behind the jaunty platform postures and the cheap puns lay a tough, uncompromising will and a 19th Century mind in which the capacity for vindictiveness was vivid. . . .

Duplessis operated on a simple principle: Father Knows Best. His Padlock Law—declared ultra vires in 1957—was introduced into the statutes in 1937 and permitted the Attorney-General (M. Duplessis) to close premises "suspected" of fomenting subversive ideas or propaganda. Those accused were compelled to prove themselves innocent, a remarkable switch on the ancient Commonwealth traditions.

Civil liberties accepted as commonplace in other Canadian provinces got short shrift at the hands of Quebec's Prime Minister. Censorship was tightened—on 16 mm. movies, "ham" radio operators and even bingo and two-piece bathing suits.

Reporters witnessed with dismay the attacks of club-swinging provincial police on labour pickets at Valleyfield, Lachute, Asbestos and Murdochville. The range of the Prime Minister's influence became vividly apparent after the Asbestos siege when Archbishop Charbonneau—the popular Montreal prelate who had ordered a collection taken up in his churches for the families of strikers—was banished to Victoria, where he served out his life as a humble hospital chaplain.

Pierre Laporte, *The True Face of Duplessis*, 1961.[93]

Though his opponents might call him "despot", "dictator", "fascist", Duplessis held the loyal support of the voters. His election campaign in 1948 was typical of the style which maintained him in power.

On the appointed day, before the Premier's motorcade drove into town, bands would be playing and down at the hotel there would be hard liquor in abundance for the thirsty. Local henchmen would move among the people, discussing with this one and that his personal troubles, asking, "What can we do for you? Trust us, Maurice will fix it." The day would end with a great rally in the park or public square for this was mid-summer and the Québecois likes his rallies out of doors. In the evening, the crowds would gather around a bandstand or platform mounted on trucks joined together. On it would be the local Member or party candidate, the mayor, the local dignitaries, the parish priest, a Cabinet Minister or two and the Great Man himself. For an hour orators would work the crowd into a frenzy by extolling the leader and the cause, leading up to the grand climax, the long-awaited speech of Duplessis.

He would begin almost casually with ironic quips and shafts aimed at his enemies, and digs at the expense of local Liberals, the men his audience knew, not some distant "enemy of the people" whom his auditors would never hear or see in person. Almost gently he would work his way into his theme—the saving of Quebec from the hated outsider, of the country man from the fiendish ways of the city slicker, of the family and the Church from the invasions of the foreign, corrupt influences of the exploiter and the Communist. Soon the plumpish man with the beak-nose would be mopping his brow with a handkerchief; the hawk-nose would glisten under the arc-lights. Proudly he would point to the fleur-de-lis flag of Quebec, the flag "I, Maurice Duplessis, have given you, as the standard of our rights and our freedom from all oppressors!" By any yardstick of political measurement these were classic performances. There may have been truth in the wry remarks of a Liberal adversary, "These occasions were the only times Maurice was ever known to take physical exercise"; but it was effective exercise, leading as it invariably did to highly practical exhortations on local issues. "You want the road leading out to the highway at St. Pacome paved? Then vote for my man and you shall have it!" "You want a bridge over the river to replace the old ferry? Tell me so with your votes!" "The treasury of your town is depleted? Then send my man to Quebec and he will arrange about your bonds!

Leslie Roberts, *Duplessis—The Chief*, 1963.[94]

I have no family. My only responsibility is the welfare of Quebec. I belong to the province.

Maurice Duplessis.[95]

The Urge to Serve

There is in the Canadian a mad desire to serve others, a strong inclination to answer the call for service and sacrifice whenever it comes and whatever the circumstances with a resounding "Ready, Aye Ready!" Throughout our history we have been involved in four wars, and in each of them, no matter how the specific circumstances or the calls to battle differed, we went to war because we felt we "ought to do something." Not once have we gone to war because of any deep-seated lust for blood, or desire for national expansion, or messianic fervour to spread an ideology. We went to help others and because it was the right thing to do. War has not been the only activity which has appealed to our penchant to serve; international service for peaceful and humanitarian purposes has been one of our roles during the last twenty-five years. But war has been the most dramatic evidence of our zeal.

The Boer War was the first of the conflicts to illustrate this facet of the Canadian character, for it was a war which did not really threaten

READY, AYE READY

Canada at all. It did, however, involve duty, honour, loyalty—the virtues celebrated in a poem which was printed in Songs of the Great Dominion, *a patriotic anthology published in 1889.*

The Veteran

The call "To arms!" resounded through the city broad and fair,
And volunteers in masses came, prepared to do and date;
Young lads, whose cheeks scarce showed the down, men bearded, stout and strong,

Assembled at the first alarm, in bold undaunted throng.
"I'll volunteer!" an old man cried, "I've served the Queen before;
I fought the Russ at Inkerman, the Sepoy at Cawnpore;"
And as he stood erect and tall, with proud and flashing eye,
What though ,his hair were white as snow,—he could but do or die!
"You are too old," the answer was; "too old to serve her now."
Then o'er his face a wonder flashed, a scowl came on his brow,
And then a tear stole down his cheek, a sob his strong voice shook,—
"Sir, put me in a uniform, and see how old I'll look!"

J. A. Fraser.[1]

To Canadians of British descent the resistance of the Boers in South Africa was a challenge to the British Empire, the motherland, the Queen, and they responded to the crisis with the enthusiastic loyalty of "The Veteran". The reaction of the citizens of Toronto on receiving news of Canada's decision to send troops to South Africa provides an interesting contrast to modern attitudes towards war.

The patriotic spirit of Torontonians was manifested in a most emphatic manner at the armouries last night, where an immense crowd had gathered to witness the parade of the 48th Highlanders. Shortly after the "fall in" the companies left the building to practise company drill on the surrounding grounds, the brass, bugle, and pipe bands remaining inside. . . . There was a wait of some minutes, and then word went round that the Cabinet had definitely decided to send a contingent of 1,000 men to the Transvaal, and that Lieut-Col. Otter had been summoned to Ottawa to assist in arranging the details. While this news was being discussed the brass band struck up "The Soldiers of the Queen". A tremendous cheer greeted the opening bars of the stirring martial air. When the chorus was reached the bandsmen sang it, and sang it well. Round after round of applause greeted this, and the verse and chorus was repeated, the crowds joining in the latter. "Rule Britannia" and "The Maple Leaf" followed, and again the most hearty enthusiasm was displayed by the crowds, who also liberally applauded marches played by the bugle and pipe bands.[2]

Off went the volunteers (which illustrates another Canadian characteristic—we have always adhered to the policy that only volunteers should go off to battle; any exceptions to this rule have occurred only under extreme duress and in moments of panic) with the songs and tributes of a grateful public ringing in their ears.

Soldiers of the Queen

It's the soldiers of the Queen, my lads, who's been, my lads, who've seen, my lads,
In the fight for England's glory, lads, when we have to show them what we mean,
And when we say we've always won, and when they ask us how it's done,
We'll proudly point to every one of England's soldiers of the Queen.[3]

To The First Contingent

We send you forth, oh brave, devoted band,
With deafening cheer and high uplifted hand,
And tears that mingle with a nation's pride,
That gives her best to fight at England's side.

We send you forth to keep what England won
For all who wear the title of a son,
What now she battles for beyond the sea,
The Briton's right and broad humanity.

We send you forth beneath the Triune Cross,
The Victor's sign of triumph won through loss.
In loyal fealty you bravely stand
To live or die for Queen & Motherland.

We send you forth with joy and fervent prayer.
In danger's hour God keep you everywhere,
Your guerdon be, though Life, though Death ye find,
The Laurel with the Maple Leaf to bind.

Margaret G. Yarker, *Echoes of Empire*, 1899.[4]

It was a strange war for Canadians to be involved with, taking place as it did in a continent thousands of miles away and against a foe we knew nothing of and who certainly did not threaten us. Still, it had to be done, for England and Queen Victoria. In a retrospective and rather detached editorial, the Canadian Magazine *commented on the significance of the struggle.*

The Boer War is over, and Canada is thankful. This is our first Imperial war—the first for the generations now living—and for that reason it was interesting while it lasted. Since the Boers rode across the borders of the two Republics and invaded British territory on October 12th, 1899, Canadians have watched the progress of the struggle with mixed emotions. They shuddered when the news of Maagersfontein flashed across the cable, because it was a battle which came home to them. It was more real to them than any battle since the heavy engagements in Egypt. They trembled with fear and joy when the name of Paardeberg burned in red letters upon the record, for their brothers and their sons were there. Paardeberg will always be a holy name. They did not rejoice because Cronje was defeated, but because their sons had become men in the eyes of the world. It was not a question of whether the Boers were in the wrong or in the right, whether Lord Roberts was a greater general than Piet Cronje, but "How do we look in the eyes of the world?".

So their sons went to fight for the Empire, for the old flag, and for Canada. The first Contingent, the Second Contingent, the Canadian Quota to the South African Constabulary, the Third Contingent and the Fourth. The last instalment of our Imperial contribution had scarce cleared the dock at Halifax when the word came, "It is enough. The war is ended." The whistles blew, the bells rang, the rectors led in thanksgivings, the unthinking youngsters lighted their firecrackers, and the rest of us heaved a sigh of relief. Canada was glad. Because of the triumph over the Boers? No, for there was no hate. The Boer is and was a colonial—a man who went out into the edges of the world to lead the way for following civilization. He fought as Canadians would have fought—perhaps not so honourably, but just as sturdily. This feeling of brotherhood removed our hate, and yet we were glad he was beaten, very glad. He had to learn that ignorance and prejudice are not virtues and that the Empire is something too big for him to dismember.

Canada sent seven thousand of her sons. Two hundred and fifty of them will never come back, for they have been laid away in the sandy veldt. Nearly four thousand are still there, struggling against disease, accident and fate, and some of them may not return. These are part of the price we pay for our nationhood. Canada gave them willingly and will keep their memory green.[5]

The Great War: Civilization On Trial

The torrent of patriotic fervour for the Boer War was by no means unanimous throughout Canada. The enthusiasm of the newspapers would lead one to have expected more than seven thousand volunteers who actually went off to battle. There were many French Canadians who had severe doubts about Canada's involvement in a foreign war for causes which were not particularly Canadian. The cries of "Queen, Empire, and Motherland" hardly touched them in the same way they would impress English Canadians. There were many native-born Canadians of English-speaking descent who also lacked the dedication of the more recent arrivals from the British Isles. This reluctance and uncertainty caused another rift in French-English relations already weakened by the Riel crisis.

There was no such reluctance when it came to Canada's participation in the Great War, World War I. Throughout Canada there was a unanimity of dedication. Legally, since Canada was not yet an independent nation, when Britain was at war, Canada was at war. But the bonds between English-speaking Canadians and the motherland would have ensured our participation, legality or no. Once again the voice of English Canada was raised in loyalty and devotion to the motherland and its cause.

Canada's Voice

Oh, we know your cause was a just one if ever cause were just;
But did we pause for a moment when we heard your trumpet peal?
When we saw you fling down the gauntlet, O Mother, was it lust
For pomp and fighting and conquest that swept our souls in a gust,
And made us shoulder our rifles and grasp the pointed steel?
Nay, love and duty called us; the duty of free-born men
To quit ourselves with honour in the work men have to do,
Whether to build up an Empire or tear one down again!

The lion he lives in his lair and the cub he dwells in his den,
But the Brood shall go fight together; for the pact of their love is
true!

Envoi:

God speed you, sons and brothers, in this mighty last crusade;
Far better were death than shirking: take ye your appointed
place.
In the roll-call of the nations Canada hath her answer made:
Trusting and faithful, Mother, stalwart and unafraid,
We'll march with thee to the uttermost for the glory of God
and our race!

L.S.[6]

The growl of the Canadian whelp of the old lion has become a roar.
Canada is in it to the end. She will not stop until "Rule Britannia" and
"The Maple Leaf" sound on the streets of Berlin. One contingent has
gone, another is in the course of preparation, and I am given to understand
now that if the necessity arises they will be followed by another and
another and another. And they will all go gladly with the same spirit
of patriotic determination. It is Britain's war, and it is Canada's war.

Premier Hearst of Ontario, 1914.[7]

Answer to the Motherland's Call

We sons have answered the Motherland's call,
True to the old flag, whatever befall,
To conquer her foes united we'll stand,
Fighting for Empire and dear Motherland.

Our cause is a just one; we cannot fail;
The strife may be long, but right will prevail.
On battlefield we our duty will do,
Aye trusting in God to carry us through.

If honor and justice our watchwords be,
We'll conquer our foes by land or by sea;
We'll vanquish oppression, liberty bring,
Then through our Empire will Victory's song
ring.

We must haste away, loud the trumpets call;
We'll guard the old flag whatever befall.
For God and for King united we'll stand,
Fighting for Empire and dear Motherland.

Isabella Watson, *War Time Poems and Heart Songs*, 1918.[8]

This time the French Canadian could also find a cause to raise his ardour. The spectacle of German militarism ravaging France was employed by Wilfrid Laurier as a rallying point for his fellow Canadiens.

England is at war because she wishes to defend the independence of Belgium and the integrity of the soil of France. Never has a nation drawn sword for a cause so sacred. We of French origin have a double duty to perform. It is true that it is not our land that is being ravaged, and it is not our farms that are being fired by the Germans, but it is the lands and the farms of France. It is not our cathedrals, it is not our churches, that the German shells demolish, but it is the monuments and treasures of France, and they are French women who are outraged and massacred. French-Canadians who listen to me, is there among you one who can remain unmoved before these acts?[9]

Other French Canadians added their support for Canada's participation in a war which could not be considered a colonial struggle in the sense of the Boer War.

England being at war, Canada, like all parts of the British Empire, is at war. Our destinies are bound to those of England, our duty and our interest command us to aid her to triumph, to protect ourselves and to protect France. Loyalty, patriotism, our most sacred interests make it a duty for us to contribute in the measure of our strength to the triumph of their arms. The defeat of England and France would be a disaster for the world, for Canada, for the province of Quebec especially, for the French Canadians. It would be a mortal blow to our political and national destinies, to our dearest and most sacred interests and sentiments.

L. O. David, 1914.[10]

England is engaged in a terrible war, which she sought to avoid at all costs. Loyal subjects, recognizing in her the protectress of our liberties, we owe her our most generous co-operation. Indifference at the present hour would be on our part a fault, and also the gravest error. Is it not evident that our fate is bound to the fate of her armies?

Monseigneur Bruchési, The Archbishop of Montreal, 1914.[11]

There are no longer French Canadians and English Canadians. Only one race now exists, united by the closest bonds in a common cause.

La Patrie, 1914.[12]

And for anyone who could not be aroused by appeals to the ancient ties with his European homeland, there was the vision of the rampaging Hun, invader of tiny Belgium, murderer of civilians. War against such an enemy was a crusade to which all civilized men must dedicate themselves.

England to-day is not engaged in an ordinary contest. The war in which she is engaged will in all probability—nay, in absolute certainty—stagger the world with its magnitude and its horror. But that war is for as noble a cause as ever impelled a nation to risk her all upon the arbitrament of the sword. That question is no longer at issue; the judgement of the world has already pronounced upon it. I speak not only of these nations which are engaged in this war, but of the neutral nations. The testimony of the ablest men of those nations, without dissenting voice, is that to-day the allied nations are fighting for freedom against oppression, for democracy against autocracy, for civilization against reversion to that state of barbarism in which the supreme law is the law of might.

Sir Wilfrid Laurier.[13]

And so the young men volunteered to go overseas to fight for England, Empire, Queen, France, civilization. Yet these were still distant causes, no matter how strongly they might touch the heart and mind. The sense of being a Canadian, fighting as a Canadian for a Canadian cause, was still to be developed. We found that spirit in the valour and sacrifice of our fighting men.

Ferocious Warriors

Whenever the Germans found the Canadian Corps coming into the line, they prepared for the worst.

Lloyd George, *War Memoirs*.[14]

Regarding them as storm troops, the enemy tended to greet their appearance as an omen of a coming attack.

Liddell Hart, *The Real War 1914-1918*.[15]

These men in physical fitness and strength excelled all the troops of any of the European armies. In their ruthless self-confidence, their individual initiative, their impatience of form, ceremony and tradition, they bore upon themselves the unmistakable mark of the new nations.

C.R.M.F. Cruttwell, *A History of the Great War 1914-1918*.[16]

The Canadians are known to be good troops, well suited for assaulting.

German Officer, 1916.[17]

If anybody can do it, the Canadians can.

Lord Byng, 1917.[18]

In the Great War Canadians discovered a side of their character which they had hitherto only suspected. They were soon revealed as formidable fighters and quickly gained a reputation, among friend and foe alike, for being stubborn, aggressive, and competent warriors. One European observer attributed these qualities to the sturdy agrarian and peasant-like background of the Canadian troops, but a Canadian historian has offered another explanation for our men's ferocity.

One of the more exasperating absurdities of dress was the kilt, and no fewer than eight Canadian battalions wore it with a fierce pride that made nonsense out of reality. Heavily pleated, the kilt was a happy haven for vermin. Made of coarse, unyielding wool, it could not be cleaned properly under battlefield conditions. On the march, when the kilted columns hunkered down for the ten-minute break that was decreed each hour, the garment picked up gobs of wet mud, which, when it dried, lacerated the calves of the marching legs. All men smelt in the line, but none gave off so basic an odour as a kilted Highlander.

The Canadians who wore this costume of a vanished peasantry did so with all the ferocity they observed in their counterparts of the British armies. Before the end of the war, tradition and prejudice gave way to the pressure of outraged medical opinion, and trews or trousers made an appearance. But at Vimy the kilt still lacerated its wearers while reaping a reward in terrified Germans who feared Highlanders more than their own officers. The Ladies from Hades took few prisoners and seemed harder to kill than other men, and, revelling in their role, they were difficult to withstand. How much of this was due to the discomfort of their costume cannot be assessed.

Herbert Fairlie Wood, *Vimy!* [19]

Canadians, it may be observed, also acquired a reputation for being nasty fighters. Lance-Corporal McWade recalled how this spirit was inculcated in himself.

His officer had said to them, before they began the march forward, "Remember, no prisoners. They will just eat your rations." That *did* impress McWade, who thought the food bad enough as it was. "The next day," he said, "any bugger who stood up in front of me, I shot at him." [20]

As the accomplishments of the Canadian Corps grew in number, the legend of invincibility became part of the Canadian mystique. On April 22, 1915, at Ypres, the Canadians faced the challenge which first established their reputations as first-class soldiers.

Suddenly we saw the gas rolling up in a brownish-yellowish bank. It was between four and 12 feet high and it wouldn't rise higher unless it was pulled up by the wind.

We saw the French-Africans running away choked with gas, not as a body, but as individuals. We paid no attention to them. We were sorry for them.

I went over to where the line had been broken and where there was confusion. No Canadian troops were running.

The gas was dreadful and suffering was immediate. The only thing we could do was soak our handerchiefs in urine and hold them over our noses.

Thousands were lying around gasping and crying. They were being drowned by the gas. They didn't know how to protect themselves.

But we held our position.

Major-General Victor W. Odlum.[21]

When that gas came along we knew the *Boches* were springing a new one on us. You know how it is if a man is hit in the face by a cloud of smoke when he is going into a burning building to get somebody out. He draws back—and then he goes in. We went in. We charged—well, it was the way we felt about it. We wanted to get at them and we were boiling mad over such a dastardly kind of attack.

Canadian infantryman.[22]

The Canadians had many casualties but their gallantry and determination undoubtedly saved the situation.

British War Office communiqué.[23]

Out of that battle came the self-confidence and pride which were to grow during the bloody days ahead. "We held where others failed", became the boast of the Canadians. Even today, when war is unfashionable, and bravery and patriotic sacrifice are considered naive if not evil, the memory of Ypres can still tug at the Canadian soul.

Ypres—1915

That old man on television last night,
a farmer or fisherman by the sound of him,
revisiting Vimy Ridge, and they asked him
what it was like, and he said,
There was water up to our middles, yes,
and there was rats, and yes,
there was water up to our middles
and rats, all right enough
and to tell you the truth
after the first three or four days
I started to get a little disgusted.

Oh, I know they were mercenaries
in a war that hardly concerned us.
I know all that.
Sometimes I'm not even sure that I have a country.
But I know they stood there at Ypres
the first time the Germans used gas,
that they were almost the only troops
in that section of the front
who did not break and run,
who held the line.

Perhaps they were too scared to run.
Perhaps they didn't know any better
—that is possible, they were so innocent,
those farmboys and mechanics, you have only to look
at old pictures and see how they smiled.
Perhaps they were too shy
to walk out on anybody, even Death.
Perhaps their only motivation
was a stubborn disinclination.

Private MacNally thinking:
You squareheaded sons of bitches,
you want this God damn trench
you're going to have to take it away
from Billy MacNally
of the South End of Saint John, New Brunswick.
And that's ridiculous, too, and nothing
on which to found a country.
                    Still
it makes me feel good, knowing
that in some obscure, conclusive way
they were connected with me
and me with them.

Alden Nowlan, 1969.[24]

The battle at Ypres also inspired the best-known poem of World War I, written by Captain John McCrae of the Canadian Medical Corps.

In Flanders Fields

In Flanders fields the poppies blow
Between the crosses, row on row,
    That mark our place; and in the sky
    The larks, still bravely singing, fly
Scarce heard amid the guns below.

We are the Dead. Short days ago
We lived, felt dawn, saw sunset glow,
    Loved and were loved, and now we lie,
    In Flanders fields.

Take up our quarrel with the foe:
To you from failing hands we throw
    The torch; be yours to hold it high.
    If ye break faith with us who die
We shall not sleep, though poppies grow
    In Flanders fields.[25]

Ypres was impressive, but the achievement there paled by comparison with the great victory at Vimy Ridge on Easter Monday, 1917. Today two great white pylons dominate the heights from which the Germans looked down upon the British and Canadians during the first two and a half years of war. The monument stands on Canadian soil, on ground given to Canada by a grateful France to commemorate that day when Canadian troops surged up Vimy Ridge and drove back their desperate foe. To the men who were at Vimy, Canada gained more than just a military victory.

But while other great days seem to be forgotten the memory of Vimy still lives, and I like to think that this was because on that day Canada grew up and became a nation in fact. It was on that day that the whole might of Canada's ground forces, as one unit of all arms, working as a united force, struck a mighty blow against enemy strength.

On that particular day I was in command of the 28th North West Battalion of the Sixth Infantry Brigade of the Second Canadian Division. . . .It was a cold grey morning but the visibility was good and I could see far over the waste of desolation which was our battlefield. Shells were still falling up front, but the rear areas seemed deserted, save for some batches of prisoners hastening to the cages, and some walking wounded.

But at zero hour all this was changed. The barren earth erupted humanity. From dugouts, shell holes and trenches men sprang into action, fell into artillery formations, and advanced to the ridge—every division of the Corps moved forward together. It was Canada from the Atlantic to the Pacific on parade. I thought then, and I think today, that in those few minutes I witnessed the birth of a nation.

Brigadier General Alex Ross.[26]

Before April 1917 we were content to be Colonials with one thought in common—that of going "home" to fight for the mother country. But Vimy Ridge was the first battle in which Canadian divisions fought as a whole, and it was a purely Canadian effort, planned and fought our own way.

The resounding victory, the first in Britain's two and a half years of war, gave every man a feeling of pride, the more so because the long battle line to our right had failed. A national spirit was born, and now to be British was not enough; we were Canadian and could do a good job of paddling our own canoe. . . .

I never felt like a Canadian until Vimy. After that I was Canadian all the way. We had a feeling that we could not lose, and if the other Allies packed it up we could do the whole job ourselves.

Major-General F. F. Worthington.[27]

On July 26, 1936, the monument on Vimy was officially unveiled by King George V, who spoke of the significance of Vimy Ridge.

For this glorious monument crowning the hill of Vimy is now and for all time part of Canada. Though the mortal remains of Canada's sons lie far from home, yet here where we now stand in ancient Artois their immortal memory is hallowed upon soil that is as surely Canada's as any acre within her nine provinces.

By a gesture which all can understand, but soldiers especially, the laws of France have decreed that here Canada shall stand forever.

We raise this memorial to Canadian warriors. It is an inspired expression in stone, chiselled by a skillful Canadian hand, of Canada's salute to her fallen sons. It marks the scene of feats of arms which history will long remember, and Canada can never forget. And the ground it covers is the gift of France to Canada.[28]

The war also brought us our first Canadian military heroes as distinct from the traditional figures such as Wolfe and Brock, who had really been Britishers fighting in Canada through chance circumstances. The Canadian knights of the air were the figures who most clearly emerged from the carnage of the war as great heroes: Billy Bishop, our outstanding air ace with seventy-two German aircraft to his credit; Roy Brown, conqueror of the Red Baron, von Richthofen; Billy Barker, whose incredible one-man dogfight against sixty enemy aircraft in 1918 won him the Victoria Cross and the following citation.

On the morning of October 27th, 1918, this officer observed an enemy two-seater over the Forêt de Mormal. He attacked this machine, and after a short burst it broke up in the air. At the same time a Fokker biplane attacked him, and he was wounded in the right thigh, but managed, despite this, to shoot down the enemy aeroplane in flames. He then found himself in the middle of a large formation of Fokkers, who attacked him from all directions, and was again severely wounded in the left thigh, but succeeded in driving down two of the enemy in a spin. He lost consciousness after this, and his machine fell out of control. On recovery he found himself being again attacked heavily by a large formation and, singling out one machine, he deliberately charged and drove it down in flames. During this fight his left elbow was shattered and he again fainted, and on regaining consciousness he found himself still being attacked, but, notwithstanding that he was now severely wounded in both legs and his left arm shattered, he dived on the nearest machine and shot it down in flames. Being greatly exhausted, he dived out of the fight to regain our lines, but was met by another formation which attacked and endeavored to cut him off, but after a hard fight he succeeded in breaking up this formation and reached our lines where he crashed on landing.[29]

General McNaughton, in 1918 a young officer in the Canadian Corps, recalled how the sight of that combat impressed the infantry in their muddy trenches.

The spectacle of this attack was the most magnificent encounter of any sort which I have ever witnessed. The ancient performances of the gladiators in the Roman arenas were far outclassed in the epic character of the successive engagements in which enemy machines, one after the other, were taken on and eliminated. The spectators, in place of being restricted to the stone walls of a Roman arena, had the horizon as their bounds and the sky as their stage. The hoarse shout, or rather the prolonged roar, which greeted the triumph of the British fighter, and which echoed across the battlefront, was never matched in Rome, nor do I think anywhere else or on any other occasion.[30]

> *The legend of the Canadian warrior was firmly established. When the last and decisive Allied offensive began in August 1918, Canadian troops were in the spearhead. "Canada's Hundred Days" we have called that period from August to November 11 when the Canadian Corps achieved uninterrupted and total victory over its enemy. At the end of one of the battles which took place during that surge, Sir Arthur Currie paid his tribute to the Canadian troops under his command.*

You have taken in this battle over seven thousand prisoners and two hundred Field and Heavy guns, thus bringing the total captures of the Canadian Corps since the 8th August of this year to twenty-eight thousand prisoners, five hundred guns, over three thousand machine guns, and a large amount of stores of all kinds.

Even of greater importance than these captures stands the fact that you have wrested sixty-nine towns and villages, and over one hundred and seventy-five square miles of French soil from the defiling Hun.

In the short period of two months the Canadian Corps...has encountered and defeated decisively forty-seven German Divisions—that is nearly a quarter of the total German forces on the Western front....

The victories you have achieved are the fruit of the iron discipline you accepted freely and of the high standard you have reached in the technical knowledge of your arms and the combined tactical employment of all your resources.

You must therefore with relentless energy maintain and perfect the high standard of training you have reached, and guard with jealous pride your stern discipline.

Under the lasting protection of Divine Providence, united in a burning desire for the victory of right over might, unselfish in your aims, you are and shall remain a mighty force admired by all, feared and respected by foes.

I am proud of your deeds and I want to record here my heartfelt thanks for your generous efforts and my unbounded confidence in your ability to fight victoriously and crush the enemy wherever and whenever you meet him.

Special Order by Lieutenant-General Sir A. Currie, 1918.[31]

The First World War made Canada a nation. There were, of course, the political consequences of our participation; official recognition as a nation which had contributed to the final victory, a seat at the peace conference, membership in the League of Nations. These were all important landmarks in a transitition from our status as a colony of Britain to an independent nation. But it was the emotional impact of the Great War which really moulded us into a nation. That war touched us in our hearts and guts. "We fought as Canadians and by God we were good at it," was our boast and our pride. Looking back on the war, an old soldier voiced an opinion which would become official Canadian doctrine.

I've always thought that the Canadian nation was, in fact, born on the battlefields of Europe. I'm sure that that's true, that the fierce pride developed in the Canadians in their own identity, in their own nationhood, was a very real thing, and it survived over into the peace. Whenever they give the Canadians a chance to show their identity or to be proud of their identity, they are, and they always rise to the occasion.[32]

World War II: A Restatement of Traditional Canadian Virtues

The idea that every twenty years this country should automatically and as a matter of course take part in a war overseas for democracy or self-determination of other small nations, that a country which has all it can do to run itself should feel called upon to save, periodically, a continent that cannot run itself, and to these ends risk the lives of its people, risk bankruptcy and political disunion, seems to many a nightmare and sheer madness.[33]

If this outburst by Prime Minister Mackenzie King in March 1939 has a rather petulant ring to it, there is a reasonable explanation. By 1939 it was clear that the Great Powers in Europe were on a collision course which might involve Britain in a struggle against Germany. Since 1918 Canada had gradually won full status as an independent nation, and King was jealous of that new independence which he had done much to achieve. His statement was intended to make it clear that Britain, and others, should not expect Canada to support her automatically in every foreign adventure, and to demonstrate that we would make our own decision based on the merits of the case and not on blind devotion to the motherland. It was a reflection, too, of Canada's disillusionment with international affairs and an urge to retreat into isolationism.

This cautious approach was reflected in the fact that when Britain and France declared war on Germany on September 3, 1939, the Canadian government waited one full week before it officially entered the fray, and then only after a long and soul-searching debate in the House of Commons. There was, however, no real doubt that we would go to war; but our attitude was not the lusty "Ready, Aye Ready" of 1914; it was a more mature and restrained statement by a nation conscious of its duty to mankind.

I never dreamed that the day would come when, after spending a lifetime in a continuous effort to promote and to preserve peace and good-will, in international as well as in industrial relations, it should fall to my lot to be the one to lead this Dominion of Canada into a great war. But that responsibility I assume with a sense of being true to the very blood that is in my veins. I assume it in the defence of freedom—the freedom of my fellow-countrymen, the freedom of those whose lives are unprotected in other countries, the freedom of mankind itself. Hitler has said: "Whoever lights the torch of war in Europe can wish for nothing but chaos." "Nothing but chaos"; that is what the leader of the Nazi party in Germany is seeking to bring upon the world to-day. And it is to prevent chaos becoming the fate of this and other lands that it becomes our duty, as citizens of Canada, to stand to a man in the defence of our country and at the side of Great Britain in the defence of freedom.

Prime Minister King, September, 1939.[34]

The time has come when, to save our Christian civilization, we must be prepared to lay down our lives for its preservation. The young men who are enlisting in our forces to-day, to serve on land, on the sea and in the air, are first and foremost defenders of the Faith. Like others who have gone forth to battle in the past, they are placing their lives at the service of King and Country, but theirs is an even greater mission. It is the preservation, for our own and future generations, of the freedom begotten of persecutions, martyrdoms, and centuries of struggle. It is the preservation not alone of national and of personal freedom but of freedom also of the mind and of the soul.

Prime Minister King, October 27, 1939.[35]

We took up arms with great reluctance. We shall bear them with even greater firmness. We shall not lay them down until honor walks the earth again, until we and the rest of the democratic world are safe from the menace of Nazi attack and the threat of Nazi thraldom.

Angus L. Macdonald, 1941.[36]

The Canadian experience in the Second World War differed in many ways from the Great War. Our men fought in a greater variety of theatres—Sicily, Italy, France and northern Europe—and, unlike the First World War, our first contact with the enemy resulted in disaster and defeat. The tragic surrender of inexperienced Canadian soldiers at Hong Kong and the bloody catastrophe of Dieppe shocked and angered the Canadian public. Our airmen once again distinguished themselves, but in an anonymous fashion unlike the days of Billy Bishop. They did, however, receive from Joseph Goebbels a tribute for their effective bombing raids on Germany.

The damage is colossal and indeed ghastly....Nobody can tell how Krupps is to go on....It drives one mad to think that some Canadian boor, who probably can't even find Europe on the globe, flies here from a country glutted with natural resources which his people don't know how to exploit, to bombard a continent with a crowded population.[37]

It was refreshing also to see that Canadian troops maintained the qualities which had made them the terror of the German soldier on the Western Front in 1918. There was much of the same valour displayed, and also, unfortunately, there emerged a new ruthlessness possibly engendered by a war in which barbaric behaviour became widespread. During the ill-fated raid on Dieppe, Canadian troops handled awkward situations with a cool ferocity.

Private Sam Block was one of a section that cleaned out the main street, taking prisoners two or three at a time. "On seeing how this situation was depriving us of manpower for fighting, we started to dispose of the prisoners in the usual way," he reported laconically. "A good German is a dead one."

Corporal Rainville agreed. "There were a lot of Germans in civilian clothes who were obviously pointing out our positions to snipers. Whenever we came across them we shot them out of hand. The German tactics seemed to be that they would keep giving themselves up, thus weakening our fighting power. So we killed them on the spot, thus keeping our fighting power."

Private E. H. Shock, made angry in the first few minutes of the street fighting when an impertinent machine gun in a large hotel split his rifle butt, rushed into the hotel, tossed grenades about indiscriminately, and finally wiped out the machine-gun nest, taking four prisoners. "Somehow they got killed accidentally later," he reported briefly.

Terence Robertson, *The Shame And The Glory—Dieppe*, 1962.[38]

In 1944, during the bitter battles in Normandy against the elite and fanatical S.S. divisions, the Canadians demonstrated their own brand of ruthless fighting.

I witnessed a real carnage of infantry troops (Germans) in a field close to Carpiquet. The Germans had succeeded in infiltrating the advance post of the Régiment de la Chaudière, tough, rugged French-Canadians who brawl on weekends for divertissment, at home. We were very close by when the alarm sounded at around 0400 hours. The Régiment de la Chaudière scurried in the semi-darkness and actually slit the throats of most soldiers they found, wounded as well as dead. This horrible carnage I actually saw from the turret of my tank at first light. These boys were actually crazed by some frenzy at being caught napping; the officers of the Regiment had to draw their pistols against their own men to make them come back to reason. This was shortly before the so-called "massacre" of some Canadian prisoners by the S.S. Are you surprised?

Canadian tank commander.[39]

The Germans weren't too eager to surrender. We Canadians never took any S.S. prisoners now, and sometimes dealt with Wehrmacht formations in the same way. One German came in covered all over in Red Crosses, to make quite sure we wouldn't shoot him.

Private in South Saskatchewan Regiment.[40]

When the Jerries come in with their hands up, shouting, "Kamerad", we just bowl them over with bursts of Sten fire.

Canadian infantryman.[41]

A German historian commented unfavourably on the behaviour of a Canadian tank detachment near Caen.

For no obvious reason this Canadian detachment had behaved in the most brutal fashion. The violence and fanatical ferocity of the invasion battle, which led to excesses on both sides, had culminated here in a particularly ugly incident. During the general beating-up of the German prisoners Zeissler had slipped away into the undergrowth and had later made his way back to the German lines. His account was borne out in a horrible and deplorable fashion the following day.

The one-armed Colonel Luxenburger was found severely injured on top of a Canadian tank which had been knocked out by a German anti-tank gun. He had been tied to the turret. Three days later he died in a German field hospital.

Paul Carell, *Invasion—They're Coming!*[42]

It is no wonder the German troops believe Nazi propaganda about Canadian soldiers being savages with scalping knives. Many of the captured enemy are quite surprised to find that these Canadian who have fought like wild dervishes are really quiet, civilized, calm and well-disciplined when one meets them after the battle.

Special Correspondent for *Daily Telegraph*.[43]

These incidents are not feats for Canadians to be proud of. They are not mentioned here to discredit the Canadian soldier, but to illustrate that although we are a "quiet, civilized, calm" folk and slow to anger, once our ire is deeply aroused, we can react savagely. It does not pay to stimulate those barbaric impulses which lie within us.

In the Service of the International Community

The Second World War was the last occasion when it was at all possible to call upon Canadians to serve by using loyalty, responsibility, affection for Britain as a rallying cry. The old cries of Queen and Empire which had aroused us in 1900 and 1914 were, of course, completely out of date, and would bring absolutely no reaction at all today. But the issue of serving mankind in general which had emerged in the Second World War began to play the strongest role in our policy and attitude towards international affairs. Since 1945, Canada has devoted herself to serving the international community, especially through her commitment to the goals of the United Nations Organization.

This is not the first time that Canadians have dedicated themselves to an international cause. During the 1930s Spain became the battleground of opposing political viewpoints and the military testing area of the rising totalitarian nations. Some Canadians, living themselves in a nation confused and disturbed by the crisis of the depression, saw in Spain a struggle between good and evil, and went there to fight against Fascism and Nazism. In a small pamphlet published in 1937, a tribute was paid to their sacrifice.

I cannot but feel that the noblest thing in Canadian history is that, some five hundred Canadians have gone to Spain to help the Spanish patriots in their desperate struggle for liberty and democracy.

There was between Canadians and the people of Spain no ancient friendship. Canadians knew, perhaps, less about them than about any of the major peoples of Europe, and what they did know was mostly of savage hostilities in a far past.

It was enough for these Canadians that here were people who were trying to shake off old tyrannies that were now, with the help of merciless fascist powers, trying to stamp them back into the earth. There will be a time, maybe, in the history of liberty and democracy, when no Canadian will have a more honoured place than these Canadians who have gone to the help of strange but brave people most unjustly and savagely assailed.

In their consciousness of their fellowship with the patriots of '37, these Canadians have called themselves the Mackenzie-Papineau Battalion of the International Brigade. . . .

Hello Canada! Canada's Mackenzie-Papineau Battalion. [44]

The Spanish Civil War also called to a man who might be described as the unknown Canadian hero, Dr. Norman Bethune. In 1937, Bethune was one of the most outstanding and respected surgeons in Canada.

He was Chief of Thoracic Surgery at Sacré Coeur Hospital in Montreal; his reputation had brought him world-wide renown; he was successful and wealthy. Yet there was in the back of his mind a persistent concern which was leading him to make a tremendous personal decision.

Go to Spain? Last week I had to decide whether to operate on my child. Now I have to decide whether I go to Spain. I am surprised, honored—and perplexed. Am I the right person? Am I ready? Yesterday's answers seem to prepare new questions for today. And tomorrow—what? The times impose cruel and irreversible decisions on us![45]

Bethune's dilemma arose from a request for him to head a Canadian medical unit which would assist the Spanish Republic in its struggle against the Fascists. The evil menace of Nazism and Fascism was becoming more and more of deep concern to Bethune, and he concluded that unless the madness was confronted and stopped in Spain, it would engulf the entire world. One night he sat down, wrote out letters of resignation and arranged his personal and financial affairs in case of death. On that evening when he made the irrevocable decision to go to Spain he wrote the following poem.

And this same pallid moon tonight,
Which rides so quiet—clear and high—
The mirror of our pale and troubled gaze,
Raised to a cool, Canadian sky,
Above the shattered Spanish mountain tops
Last night rose low and wild and red,
Reflecting back from her illumined shield
The blood-bespattered faces of the dead.
To that pale moon I raise my angry fist,
And to those nameless dead my vows renew:
Comrades who fall in angry loneliness,
Who die for us—I will remember you.[46]

Bethune's work in Spain resulted in great advances in battlefield medicine, including the development of the first combat blood transfusion unit. When the Spanish conflict ended in defeat for Bethune's chosen allies, he left Spain, and after a short stay in Canada, went to China to serve the cause of humanity in that war-torn nation. His efforts won him a place in Chinese hearts and made him a national hero of the modern Republic of China. The following tribute to Bethune by Madame Sun Yat-Sen is representative of the honour paid to a hero who has only recently been recognized in his own homeland.

The hero in any age is one who carries out with a surpassing degree of devotion, determination, courage, and skill the main tasks with which his times challenge *every* man. Today these tasks are worldwide, and the contemporary hero—whether he works at home or in a foreign land——is a world hero, not only in historical retrospect but now.

Norman Bethune was such a hero. He lived, worked and fought in three countries—in Canada, which was his native land; in Spain, where forward-looking men of nations flocked to fight in the first great people's resistance to the darkness of Nazism and fascism; and in China, where he helped our guerrilla armies to capture and build new bases of national freedom and democracy in territory which the military fascists of Japan fondly hoped they had conquered, and where he helped us forge the mighty people's army which finally liberated all China. In a special sense he belongs to the peoples of these three countries. In a larger sense he belongs to all who fight against oppression of nations and of peoples.

Norman Bethune was a doctor, and he fought with and within his profession with weapons he knew best. He was an expert and a pioneer in his own science—he kept his weapons sharp and fresh. And he devoted his great skill, consciously and consistently, to the vanguards of the struggle against fascism and imperialism. To him fascism was the disease holding a greater evil for mankind than any other, a plague that destroys minds and bodies by tens of millions, and by denying the value of man also denies the value of all the sciences which have arisen to minister to man's health, vigor and growth. . . .

The new China will never forget Dr. Bethune. He was one of those who helped us become free. His work and his memory will remain with us forever.

Madame Sun Yat-Sen, 1952.[47]

Bethune's service, and that of his comrades in Spain, were individual acts without official recognition or great public support. The years following World War Two saw both official and public acceptance of Canada's policy of international involvement. Many Canadians felt that we had come of age during the war as a significant member of the world com-

munity and would have to take on the responsibilities of that role. And when the entire western world seemed threatened by an aggressive Soviet communism, Canada's Prime Minister St. Laurent made a statement of Canadian intent and policy which was to lead to the formation of the North Atlantic Treaty Organization.

It is now, I believe, an accepted fact that practically everything of importance that happens in the international sphere is of interest to Canada—often of direct and immediate interest. For us there is no escape, even if we wish to seek one, in isolation or indifference. Recent events have brought home to all of us the increasing threat to our democratic national existence of the rising title of totalitarian communism. . . .

It may be that the free states, or some of them, will soon find it necessary to consult together on how best to establish a collective security league. . . . The formation of such a defensive group of free states would not be a counsel of despair but a message of hope. It would not mean that we regarded a third world war as inevitable, but that the free democracies had decided that to prevent such a war they would organize so as to confront the forces of communist expansionism with an overwhelming preponderance of moral, economic and military force and with sufficient degree of unity to ensure that this preponderance of force is so used that the free nations cannot be defeated one by one. . . .

Our foreign policy today must, therefore, I suggest, be based on a recognition of the fact that totalitarian communist aggression, endangers the freedom and peace of every democratic country, including Canada. On this basis and pending the strengthening of the United Nations, we should be willing to associate ourselves with other free states in any appropriate collective security arrangements. . . .

Prime Minister St. Laurent, 1948.[48]

Canada entered wholeheartedly into NATO, stationing Canadian army and air forces in Europe, undertaking naval manoeuvres with NATO fleets, training NATO forces in Canada. But NATO membership was only part of our growing responsibilities. We had declared ourselves in support of the United Nations; but how would we react when the United Nations was faced with a crisis which tested its ability to keep peace? In 1950, when the communist forces of North Korea invaded South Korea, Canadian leaders and public opinion showed that they supported United Nations condemnation of the invasion, and were prepared to contribute to a United Nations police force which would confront the aggressor.

You don't get peace by talking about it or by talking the language of the Kremlin. You've got to do something about it, and we have been trying to do something about it. Specifically, we have been trying to do something about it in South Korea. . . .

Korea perhaps isn't very big or very important. But what is important is that the people of Asia wouldn't feel that the Communist forces were free to override their agreements and that no one dared to stand up against them. . . .

I truly believe that this stand will succeed. It will succeed in Korea and bring a great assurance of peace not only in Korea, but in the rest of the world.

Prime Minister St. Laurent.[49]

Canadians seek a neighborly world and the good of all nations. If, at this moment, they are disposed to lend themselves to the aims of the United Nations in the Far East, it is because they desire for Koreans and Russians, as well as for themselves and all other peoples, that security and happiness that can come only from the rule of law.

Newspaper editorial.[50]

And what is Canada's position in all this? It is, I suggest, dictated by the necessity of supporting United Nations action. That is our only obligation. . . .We have accepted that obligation as a government, as a parliament and as a people, and we are discharging it."

Lester B. Pearson.[51]

Toronto recruiting stations are being flooded with inquiries today as the Korean War continues unchecked.

Officers of the navy, army, and air force said queries concerning enlistments are greater than at any time since the close of the last conflict. And the consensus of military observers is that many men, particularly ex-servicemen, are ready to get back into uniform immediately if Canada orders general mobilization.

Progress Report.[52]

Korea was followed by other crises which saw Canada's participation flow into new directions. There was the traumatic shock of 1956 when Britain and France attacked Egypt over the Suez Canal. This was a turning point for Canada. It was the first time when Canadian leaders and the Canadian public chastized the British harshly. The action was condemned and at the United Nations, Lester B. Pearson not only supported a resolution which called for a ceasefire in the trouble spot, but made a recommendation which established a new role for Canadians.

I therefore would have like to see a provision in this resolution—this has been mentioned by previous speakers—authorizing the Secretary-General to begin to make arrangements with member governments for a United Nations force large enough to keep these borders at peace while a political settlement is being worked out. . . .My own government would be glad to recommend Canadian participation in such a United Nations force, a truly international peace and police force.

We have a duty here.[53]

"We have a duty here." It was the old battle cry, but in a new context and with a different rationale. It not only sent a Canadian peacekeeping force to Suez, but in the next seventeen years would send Canadian soldiers to Cyprus, Kashmir, Indo-China, the Congo, as part of United Nations peacekeeping and truce observation teams.

Ready? Ah . . .Perhaps

Following his fourth ballot Liberal leadership victory Saturday, Mr. Trudeau set out some of the policies and programs he hopes to develop in the future:

• Withdrawal of Canadian forces stationed with NATO in Europe.
• A reduction in the costly peace-keeping role Canada has undertaken.
• An entirely new concept of foreign affairs based on Canada's position as a minor power.

Ottawa Citizen, April 8, 1968.

The Trudeau statement was an official recognition of a trend which was emerging by the end of the 'sixties. The roles which had been so clearly defined earlier, the zeal with which we pursued them, and the reasons for which we had undertaken responsibilities, were all being seriously questioned. Communism was no longer regarded as a serious menace; there was disenchantment with the effectiveness of our peacekeeping teams; the maintenance of strong and effective armed forces was

294 THE CANADIAN STYLE

unfashionable. And so the government proceeded with its plan. Our NATO forces were reduced, and eventual withdrawal completely from Europe, although denied, seemed to be clearly indicated. "Defence of our sovereignty" became the primary role of our armed forces. Defence against whom was not clearly defined, but one suspects it was against the United States and its "invasion of the Arctic". Equipment which would allow us to fight a serious war was to be replaced by equipment which would permit us to carry out reconnaissance. The new trend and its effect on the military was deplored by some observers.

Canadian soldiers have never been emotional, or agressively patriotic. That doesn't mean they don't—or didn't— have strong feelings. The Canadian corps, man for man, was perhaps the best in World War I. In that most frightful of wars, Canadians became the specialists in night raids; they covered the March Retreat; and they spearheaded the last 100 days. They were the allies' "élite". It was World War I that spiritually melded Canada into a nation.

In World War II Canadians held up their end everywhere. They fought well, efficiently, professionally. In Korea, too, the only other major conflict Canadian troops have indulged in recently, the "volunteers" did not join to defend democracy against Communism, as was the theme of the '50's. They went to Korea for a variety of reasons, including nostalgia—they were bored, unemployed, or sought adventure. Hardly any hated Communism or Communists *per se*. Hardly any knew anything about Communism or Communists. That didn't make them any the worse soldiers. In fact they were better, by far, than the more anti-Communist-indoctrinated American forces.

The pity of Canada today is that our military is virtually finished. It has been emasculated by the Government, has no definable role, is rudderless and redundant. We soon will have no tanks left, no navy, nor air force. The "anti-war" agitators (many of whom support the CIC) will cheer, for they don't understand or appreciate the military, and insist on viewing it as they do the Pentagon war machine. This is simply wrong.

Peter Worthington, 1972.[54]

By 1973 Canadians seemed to have become unsure of what their role and responsibility were. The achievement of a truce in Vietnam placed us once again in a position where we would have to make a decision. Who were the obvious people to participate in a truce team? Canadians, of course. Who had the most experience? Canadians. Who could be trusted to fulfil their duties properly as members of a truce team? Canadians. The pressures for us to serve mounted despite a statement made by External Affairs Minister Mitchell Sharp in 1972 which reflected Canadian disillusionment with peacekeeping generally.

We do not intend again if we can avoid it to take on a responsibility for peacekeeping without the terms being better understood by both sides and without a very clear mandate.[55]

But could we refuse? The views pro and con reveal the quandary of Canada in 1973.

As one of the world's richest countries, whose prosperity depends more on international stability than does that of most other countries, we must fulfil our responsibilities. We can't sit back and leave it to Liberia and Luxembourg. If the world boils over, what difference does the auto pact make?

This is not to say that we should without canny scrutiny of the terms, get heedlessly involved in pulling other people's chestnuts out of the fire. Lending a hand at getting American troops out of Indo-China is, in any case, serving not just an American national interest but a Canadian one also. We have long wanted the Americans to get out of Viet Nam. We can't reject hastily a part in achieving that end....

Unlike the Americans, our besetting sin has been avoiding rather than exaggerating our international responsibilities. If we want to replace a Pax Americana with something more multi-lateral, we have to take on some unpleasant assignments ourselves—but only of course when we are sure that we are acting on behalf of the international community.

Former diplomat John Holmes.[56]

...we ought to make a contribution to a truce if we can....It's very much in our interests and the interests of the whole world that it succeed.

External Affairs Minister Mitchell Sharp.[57]

In 1972 we've had all the time in the world to think it over. And the more time there is to think of rushing once more unto the South-east Asian breach, the more evident become the reasons for letting someone else take a turn—the likelihood of continued fighting, the elusiveness of political settlement, the eagerness of the Americans to have us as their agents, our previous deviations from a peacekeeper's proper role. When the signal comes from Washington, we should answer loud and clear: "Hell, no! We won't go!"

James Eayrs.[58]

...we are trapped by our image in the world as objective and efficient peackeepers.

We are also compromised by the decision to stay on in the ICC long after it was clearly defunct.

And finally, we are hostage to the fact that even though Canadians are disillusioned with peacekeeping, it's apparently a lesser evil than other defence responsibilities.

So, whether peacekeeping in Viet Nam turns out to be a relatively simple matter of supervising elections, or getting involved in some hard, frustrating and thankless policing operation, there seems to be no respectable way out of the obligation.

Trudeau's "no guns or other war-like equipment" stipulation may cause many Canadians and the rest of the world to shake their heads in wonderment. But if we're finally included on the team, hopefully his prohibition will not exclude what may then become a vital necessity for every Canadian soldier, i.e., a good pair of running shoes.

Robert Cameron.[59]

You are going as men of peace and you will be highly respected. You will be welcomed because in the past several years—as a result of Kashmir, Cyprus, the Congo—Canadians have come to assure that war will be followed by diplomacy and peace.

Prime Minister Trudeau.[60]

We went to Viet Nam of course, because it was the thing to do and because everyone expected it of us. We are, after all, the mediators par excellence, the peacekeepers and the violations-of-peace observers. The decision to go was hesitant, and accompanied by warnings of disaster and hints of withdrawl. It was hardly a unanimous commitment and there was no groundswell of public opinion in its favour.

Has something gone out of the Canadian character, or have we become less naive and more cynical about duty, honour, service? Perhaps, after seventy-three years of rushing into foreign adventures, we are finally

'We're ready to go,' say commandos
who may police Viet truce

Canadians on truce force
won't be armed, Sharp says

Is Canada the U.S. patsy in Vietnam?

Sharp's Saigon party a smashing success

Don't pull Canada
out of truce role,
Sharp being urged

—even Viet Cong turned up

Viet Nam peace
or we'll get out
in 90 days: Sharp

Viet pullout

by Canada

looks sure

Japanese plead with Canada
to stay on Viet peace team

If 'war' kills our men
we leave, Sharp says·

CANADA TRUCE DEATH

Whole truce effort
in doubt: Sharp

Time to pull out
of Viet Nam

Killing of Canadian
makes team ponder
reduced truce role

Our frustrated truce force pulls
out of Viet Nam

calling it quits and retreating into a continental isolation which will see us concentrate on defending our sovereignty. Vietnam may well have been the last service we perform for anyone for a long, long time — our last "Ready, Aye Ready."

Living next to you is in some ways like sleeping with an elephant. No matter how friendly or even-tempered is the beast, if I can call it that, one is affected by every twitch and grunt.

Pierre Elliot Trudeau, 1969.[1]

Canada Confronts the Twitching and Grunting American Beast

Canada tells the U.S. . . .
CAN'T PUSH US

9

IN BED WITH AN ELEPHANT

Don't dump your filth in Canada, Greene tells U.S.

Canada-U.S. relations at low point and it's our fault, N.Y. Times says

U.S. drug rings use Canada addresses

Benson warning: U.S. could start a great depression

U.S. plans to take action against Canada's exports

Who's in charge here – U.S. or us?

Eric Kierans links top civil servants to foreign companies

GALLUP POLL OF CANADA
67% believe there is enough U.S. investment in Canada

Foreign control hurts research in Canada

Science Council says

NADER CLAIMS CANADA LOST CONTROL OF DESTINY
Foreign-owned firms show fastest growth in Canada: Survey

U.S. company buys out six Canadian credit bureaus

U.S. firms move in on baggage-handling, skycapping services

A multi-national giant controls 58 companies across our country

Head Office U.S.A.

CBC bowed to wish of giant U.S. firm

50 companies own 40% of industry in Canada: report

Regan says some foreign firms are 'parasites'

End U.S. control, Toronto guild urges

Stephen Lewis, in U.S., assaults domination of Canada

Foreign investment threat to independence labor congress declares

U.S. firms in Canada warned
Consider our needs: Sharp

No wealth for Canadians to share if U.S. isn't checked, Otto says

Independence a fragile state: Gray's refrain

American investment makes it hard to be 'Canadian', report says

Walter Gordon's warning:

Five years to stop takeover of Canada 'or kiss it goodby'

Americans made up largest group of immigrants to Canada in 1971

U.S. man named police chief controversy rages in Calgary

He blames 'intense nationalistic feelings'

Toronto artists demand a meeting to protest hiring of a U.S. curator

American police chief quits as Calgary votes to oust him

THEY'VE CHEATED US . . . .

U.S. professors accused

Professor says Canada 'mad' to hire from U.S.

Faculties urged to hire Canadians

Universities given 14 days to submit foreign-teacher list

American named chief of GM Canada

Canadians only should get top art jobs, artists say

Top jobs in government-supported art institutions — like art galleries and colleges or art — should be given only to Canadian citizens, an artists' group told government yesterday.

The Canadian Artists Representation, representing 500 artists, said this is vital if Canada is to develop its own culture rather than have international tastes, trends and standards imposed on it.

The group appeared before Ontario's Select Committee on Economic and Cultural Nationalism.

It said Canada's major fine arts institutions are "staffed by Americans, Englishmen and other aliens" who advise, guide and control Canadians on all facets of their culture.

This hinders Canadians' ability to develop their own culture and cultural viewpoints it said.

The group also urged the Province to devote 1 per cent of the money it spends on new buildings each year on visual art, as an encouragement to painters, to make sure all books or films it commissions are by Canadians and to permit only 15 per cent foreign teachers in art colleges.

Mavor Moore wants Canadians hired even if foreigners better

CANADA'S SURVIVAL KIT.

COUNTER CHEQUE	DATE_____
NAME OF BANK _____	
BRANCH_____	
PAY TO THE ORDER OF **COMMITTEE FOR AN INDEPENDENT CANADA** $_____	
_____ DOLLARS	
ACCOUNT NUMBER [_____] _____	

(SEND IN THIS CHEQUE AND HELP SAVE A COUNTRY. OURS.)

Artists want grants for Canadians only

Quebec an ally against Americans – Bourassa

College staffs may be only 51% Canadian – Carleton professor

Government may restrict U.S. artists

Calgary (CP) — The Canadian Government may soon place restrictions on the entry of U.S. entertainers, says Secretary of State Gerard Pelletier.

20 artists protest hiring of American for gallery

Munro threats end plan to expand CFL with American teams

Foreign publishers called parasites at book hearing

STOP THE U.S. TAKEOVER

CANADIAN LIBERATION MOVEMENT - P.O. BOX 41 - STATION "E" - TORONTO

Foreign ownership: Concern mounts ove

17% of cottage lots sold to U.S. *recreational land*

U.S. cottagers own
Erie beaches: judges

Ottawa, provinces to investigate
issue of foreign land ownership

Higher taxes could control foreign cottagers,
MPPs told

Canada must have total control
of Arctic pipeline, Gordon says

Professor warns U.S. capable
of taking our water by force

Barrett claims B.C. 'skinned by Yankees'
on Columbia treaty

CANADIAN LIBERATION MOVEMENT
P.O. Box 41, Station 'E', Toronto 4, Ontario

'Ammunition for Canada's claim to Machias Seal Island'

Canada is losing the energy game
to U.S., says brief

Alberta land
curbs to halt
foreign sales

The tiny island America
wants to take from us

Drive
U.S. Imperialism
out of Canada

JOIN THE
Canadian
Liberation
Movement

BOX 41, STATION 'E', TORONTO 4, ONTARIO

printed by union labour

Fortunately, war was not declared.

The preceding display of concern, frustration, and anger burst forth in the 1970s as crises in our relations with the United States appeared to escalate. One wonders how we were able to survive it all.

The truth is, of course, that this sort of thing has been going on for a long time. Canadians have had periodic bouts of anti-American sentiments for almost two hundred years. Second to hockey, hitting out at the Yankees is our great national sport. At times we play the game with greater vigour than usual, but it remains a constant pastime.

Occasionally, as occurred between 1971 and 1973, there emerges in the minds of Canadians what might be called the Great American Conspiracy theory. This pictures some American master plan of great cunning directed, probably, by some central agency in the United States. The directors of this conspiracy secretly encourage American businessmen to invest in Canadian enterprises and to "take over" any Canadian businesses which become available; they deliberately recruit and send American professors to Canadian universities to corrupt our youth with American social and political ideologies; they craftily organize American publishers to flood the Canadian market with American books, not for profit, but to brainwash the Canadian public; they plan, and provide cash for, the purchase of Canadian recreational areas; they plant in the minds of Canadian businessmen and politicians the deceptively attractive possibilities of a continental energy policy; and, in moments of mischievousness, they pollute our water and air.

The purpose of the Conspiracy is a complete takeover of Canada, culturally, economically, physically. The Americans are out to get us any way they can. To those who believe in the Conspiracy Theory, this has been, is now, and will always be the policy of the United States. It is not difficult to detect a touch of paranoia in this line of thought. If the condition is paranoid, it is an ailment well justified by the evidence of the past.

That Canadians should be suspicious of the United States is not surprising considering our historical experience with that nation. It should be remembered that two of our provinces were founded by men and women fleeing from the American Revolution, people who were hostile to its principles and victims of its persecution. These were the United Empire Loyalists, whose story became a legend to inspire Canadians,

to strengthen the bond of empire, and to lay a firm foundation of suspicion
towards the United States.

The war was over. Seven red years of blood
Had scourged the land from mountain-top to sea:
(So long it took to rend the mighty frame
Of England's empire in the western world).
With help of foreign arms and foreign gold,
Base faction and the Bourbon's mad revenge,
Rebellion won at last; and they who loved
The cause that had been lost, and kept their faith
To England's crown, and scorned an alien name,
Passed into exile; leaving all behind
Except their honour and the conscious pride
Of duty done to country and to king.

Not drooping like poor fugitives, they came
In exodus to our Canadian wilds;
But full of heart and hope, with heads erect
And fearless eyes, victorious in defeat.
With thousand toils they forced their devious way
Through the great wilderness of silent woods
That gloomed o'er lake and stream; till higher rose
The northern star above the broad domain
Of half a continent, still theirs to hold,
Defend, and keep forever as their own;
Their own and England's, to the end of time.

To keep the empire one in unity
And brotherhood of its imperial race,—
For that they nobly fought and bravely lost,
Where losing was to win a higher fame!
In building up our northern land to be
A vast dominion stretched from sea to sea,—
A land of labour, but of sure reward,—
A land of corn to feed the world withal,—
A land of life's rich treasures, plenty, peace;

Content and freedom, both to speak and do,
A land of men to rule with sober law
This part of Britain's empire, next the heart
Loyal as were their fathers, and as free!

William Kirby, *Canadian Idylls*, 1894.[2]

These were the men and the sentiments which created New Brunswick, the "Loyalist Province", and Ontario, which maintains as its official motto, Ut Incepit Fidelis, Sic Permanet, "Loyal she began, loyal she remains". The Loyalist story, and the distrust of the United States with which it is associated, forms part of a deep tribal memory of Canadians.

But there is more than the prejudice of these exiles and losers to alert us to the dangers of our neighbour; we have the words of Americans—presidents, statesmen, writers—which periodically have rung out timely warnings to verify the wicked intentions of the United States. Listen to their maddeningly confident and malevolent tone.

The unanimous voice of the continent is that Canada must be ours.

John Adams, 1776.[3]

I trust I shall not be presumptuous when I state that I verily believe that the militia of Kentucky are alone competent to place Montreal and Upper Canada at your feet.

Henry Clay, 1810.[4]

The annexation of Canda this year as far as the neighbourhood of Quebec, will only be a mere matter of marching, and this will give us experience for the attack on Halifax next, and the final expulsion of England from the American continent.

Thomas Jefferson, 1812.[5]

Let us hear no more of Canadian liberty. The provinces are still tied to their mother's apron strings, and whatever way she may jump or kick up her heels they imitate her example. But as they have not yet attained to the stature or the good sense of manhood, we must excuse their childish course. When they are annexed to the Republic, which is only a question of time—a present year—we will show them the way to act an independent part, and to assert the dignity and freedom of the Anglo-Saxon race.

New York Herald, July 1861

And, from time to time, reports of American intentions filtered back to keep us vigilant.

Mr. Seward, who is no doubt, as ignorant of the feeling in the British North American Provinces, as he has proved to be of that feeling in the Southern parts of this Country, very probably supposed that there is a strong American feeling in Canada. He publickly advocated, during the Presidential Canvass, the annexation of Canada as a compensation for any loss, which might be occasioned by the disaffection of the South.

British Ambassador to Washington, 1861.[6]

I visited a member of Congress with whom I am on terms of intimacy . . .he stands well with the present executive of the U.S. . . .He gave me to understand . . .that it is accepted as a settled conviction that annexation will follow as a matter of course and at no distant day. The policy of the American government will be that of just watching events and moulding them as they occur.

›   Canadian "Secret Service" Report, 1865.[7]

"If we don't get you one way, we'll get you another" seemed to be the feelings of an editorial in a Chicago paper in 1905.

There has been more or less talk for many years about the annexation of Canada to the United States, and, while the prospect for a union of the two countries have been growing less favourable of recent years, the conquest of Western Canada, which was begun five years ago, is going on at a *rapid* rate through the occupation of that country by enterprising American farmers.

. . . Conservative leaders have foolishly opposed the American invasion and have accused Sir Wilfrid Laurier and the Liberal party of an intention to "Americanize" Canada, to sink British interests and individuality under a flood of immigration; and it has even been charged that this invasion is the first step toward the annexation of Northwestern Canada to the United States.[8]

The most blatant statements were uttered by Champ Clark, Speaker of the American House of Representatives, in 1911.

We are preparing to annex Canada....I hope to see the day when the American flag will float on every square foot of the British North American possessions clear to the North Pole.[9]

You let me run for President on a platform for the annexation of Canada, in so far as this country can accomplish it, and let President Taft run against me opposing annexation—and —well, I'd carry every State in the nation.[10]

This century has witnessed few repeats of such talk, although occasionally we hear rumours of strange statements made by American congressmen which are not so much ominous as ludicrous. Still, Canadians can be pardoned if they look for deeper and possibly sinister meanings even in the well-intentioned words of John F. Kennedy when he spoke to the Canadian Parliament in 1962.

Geography has made us neighbors. History has made us partners. And necessity has made us allies. Those whom nature hath so joined together let no man put asunder.[11]

The threatening words of Americans have been backed by action; in the nineteenth century our soil was invaded more than once by Yankees bent on conquest. In 1812 an American army crossed over from Detroit and Canadians had to endure the following proclamation by General Hull.

Inhabitants of Canada

...The army under my command has invaded your country. The standard of the Union now waves over the territory of Canada. To the peaceable, unoffending inhabitants it brings neither danger nor difficulty.

I come to find enemies, not to make them; I come to protect, not to injure you.

Separated by an immense ocean and an extensive wilderness from Great Britain, you have no participation in her councils, nor interest in her conduct. You have felt her tyranny; you have seen her injustice; but I do not ask you to avenge the one, or to redress the other. The United States are sufficiently powerful to afford every security consistent with their and your expectations. I tender you the invaluable blessings of civil, religious, and political liberty, and their necessary result—individual and general prosperity; . . .

. . .Many of your fathers fought for the freedom and independence we now enjoy. Being children, therefore, of the same family with us, and heirs of the same heritage, the arrival of any army of friends must be hailed by you with a cordial welcome. You will be emancipated from tyranny and oppression, and restored to the dignified status of freemen. . . .

I doubt not your courage and firmness. I will not doubt your attachment to liberty. If you tender your services voluntarily, they will be accepted reaily. The United States offer you peace, liberty, and security. Your chance lies between these and war, slavery and destruction. . . .[12]

> *Canadians disrespectfully rejected Hull's offer, and had the satisfaction of seeing him driven out of Canada and his career brought to an end by his ignominious surrender of Fort Detroit to the wily and energetic Isaac Brock. General Brock became our great national hero and today his statue, atop a lofty column at Queenston Heights, stands with one hand raised defiantly towards the United States across the Niagara River. As the war continued, it was marked by "atrocities" which are not forgotten and form part of our anti-American mythology. There was the day the Yankees descended upon the town of York to perpetrate all kinds of barbarous deeds.*

. . .At the peep of the day on the 27th, I descried from the Bedroom Window the whole Yankie Fleet 13 in number off the Light House. I called Donald and we armed ourselves with Muskets provided the evening before, went to the Garrison where we found the Grenadiers of the 8th Regt. 110 Strong, a few of the Newfoundland Regt. and some Militia already on the Parade. The fleet came gradually to anchor off the old French Fort & prepared to Land, we opposed but could not prevent, 70 of ye Grenadiers were killed & wounded besides others, the Indians took fright ran away and never stopt 'till they got to Matchedash neither

Donald nor me were hurt—finding it idle to remain near the old Fort any longer we retreated to the Batteries, which we were shortly afterwards obliged to abandon, the Enemy coming up in such Force, having Landed 4000 men, our whole strength did not amount to more than 450...at length General Sheaffe ordered the Powder Magazine to be blown up, His Majesty's Colours to be struck, and the Bugle to sound a general retreat—the enemy advanced and were wofully cut up by the Explosion, 250 killed upon the spot the numbers wounded not known....The Town captitulated & His Majesty's Troops retreated to Kingston....The moment they [the Americans] got in they began to plunder and burn the public Buildings which they continued for four days....The public Buildings burnt on this occasion were—The Governt. House, The Block House at the Garrison, The Naval Store, the Brick Buildings at the East end of the Town and Mr. Russell's Block House. They plundered all my poultry & some few things from the House which we considered as triffling being glad to get off so.

John Beikie, 1813.[13]

Even worse were the villainous acts carried out in the little town of Newark under the orders of the American General George McClure in December 1813.

...The ill-fated town of Newark was burnt, under his orders the night of the 10th of December, 1813. Here was exhibited a scene of distress which language would be inadequate to describe. Women and children were turned out of doors in a cold and stormy night; the cries of infants, the decrepitude of age, the debility of sickness, had no impression on this monster in human shape....In the destruction of this town he was aided by the most active exertions of Joseph Wilcox, who had for a number of years resided in this pleasant village...he, like a cowardly sycophant deserted the cause of his country and actually led a banditti through the town, setting fire to his neighbors' dwellings...and applying the epithet of "tory" to everyone who disapproved of this act of barbarity.[14]

We "won" that war. Our history books and historical sites commemorate the victories of British soldiers and Canadian militiamen over the invader at Queenston Heights, Crysler's Farm, Chateauguay. The Americans, however, seemingly were not convinced that we were determined to pursue a separate destiny. During the American Civil

*War our relations with the United States deteriorated to such an extent
that one Canadian politician foresaw a definite threat of invasion.*

The Americans are, now a warlike people. They have large armies,
a powerful navy, an unlimited supply of warlike munitions, and the carnage
of war has to them been stript of its horrors. The American side of
our lines already bristles with works of defence, and unless we are willing
to live at the mercy of our neighbors, we, too, must put our country
in a state of efficient preparation. War or no war—the necessity of placing
these provinces in a thorough state of defence can no longer be postponed.
Our country is coming to be regarded as undefended and indefensible. . . .

George Brown, 1865.[15]

*Invasion did come, not from the United States army, but from the
fanatic band of Irish malcontents known as Fenians.*

We are a Fenian Brotherhood, skilled in the arts of war,
And we're going to fight for Ireland, the land that we adore.
Many battles we have won, along with the boys in blue,
And we'll go and capture Canada, for we've nothing else to
   do.[16]

FENIAN RAID

Our readers were prepared by the intelligence published in THE GLOBE
yesterday morning for the stirring news laid before them to-day. The
Fenians have actually entered the Province on the Niagara Frontier with
arms in their hands. Their numbers at that point do not probably exceed
1,500—and it will be seen that measures have been taken promptly and
vigorously to crush them where they landed.

We confess our utter astonishment at the placid manner in which the
American Government continue to look on while our Province is being
invaded, openly, defiantly of their authority, by American citizens from
American soil . . .

The *Globe*, June 2, 1866.

When I was a little boy, I knew an old gentleman who as an 18-year-old
had gone with the Queen's Own Rifles to fight the Fenians. Being an
avid reader of Chums and the Boys' Own Paper, I used to pester him

for details. In this I was unsuccessful, for he did not care to talk about what I imagined had been a great adventure. He had been brought up in an age when unpleasant incidents were not discussed in front of women and children. There was another reason for his reticence, which I found out for myself years later on a hill in Italy. He did, however, show me the medal the Government had given to him and his comrades in recognition of their service. It was silver with a scarlet and white ribbon. The medal bore a bust of Queen Victoria and the legend Victoria Regina et Imperatrix. Engraved on the reverse side was the Canadian Ensign within a wreath of maple leaves. On a bar were the words "Fenian Raid 1866." I was full of admiration. Only once did my old friend lift the curtain on the past. "It was a hot day," he said, "and I was thirsty." Just one sentence.

Frank Jones, 1956.[17]

Tramp, tramp, tramp our boys are marching,
Cheer up, let the Fenians come!
For beneath the Union Jack we'll drive the rabble back,
And we'll fight for our belov'd Canadian home.

Canadian Militia Song, 1866.[18]

The Fenians were quickly crushed and driven out of Canada; their raids were the last time American troops have entered Canadian soil on unfriendly terms, although during the Alaska Boundary dispute at the turn of the century, a blustering Teddy Roosevelt gestured with his "big stick" and threatened force unless the United States had its own way with the boundary settlement. It is little wonder that Canadians during the latter part of the nineteenth century and early twentieth were wary of American intentions.

A brilliant future would await us were it not for those wretched Yankees, who hunger and thirst for Naboth's field. War will come some day between England and the United States, and India can do us yeoman service by sending an army of Sikhs, Gurkhas, Beloochis, etc. across the Pacific to San Francisco and holding that beautiful and unusual city as security for Montreal and Canada.

John A. Macdonald, 1867.[19]

I have always preached it to our people, that the Yankees are our greatest if not only enemies and that we should never trust them.

George T. Denison, 1909.[20]

Most Canadians believe today that the United States has shown a steady, deliberate dislike of their country and has pursued a policy more or less injurious to their interests.

Castell Hopkins, 1893.[21]

...Does any sane, sober-thinking Canadian doubt for a moment that it is only the British flag that prevents the aggressive and greedy nation to the south of us from stripping us to the bone of all desirable territory?

Ottawa Citizen, 1903.[22]

I have often regretted, and never more than on the present occasion, that we are living beside a great neighbor who, I believe I can say without being unfriendly to them, are very grasping in their national actions and who are determined on every occasion to get the best in any agreement which they make.

Sir Wilfrid Laurier, 1903.[23]

Uncle Sam, the Seducer

Forcible violations of our sovereignty by the United States have always been rejected, vigorously and successfully. We have not been so successful in recognizing or resisting more subtle lures with which Uncle Sam has tempted us to desert our Candian identity. We have always found seduction infinitely preferable and much more satisfying than rape. Let the American rake dangle before our eyes promises of wealth, fame, opportunity, and more than once we have gladly made fools of ourselves and clutched at the offerings, surrendering both innocence and pride. In 1849, for instance, business men in Montreal, miffed by British economic policies which had hurt the economy, proposed the following course of action.

Of all the remedies that have been suggested for the acknowledged and insufferable ills with which our country is afflicted, there remains but one to be considered. It propounds a sweeping and important change in our political and social condition involving considerations which demand our most serious examination. THIS REMEDY CONSISTS IN A FRIENDLY AND PEACEFUL SEPARATION FROM BRITISH CONNECTION AND A UNION UPON EQUITABLE TERMS WITH THE GREAT NORTH AMERICAN CONFEDERACY OF SOVEREIGN STATES.

The Annexation Manifesto, 1849.[24]

The virtue of loyalty sacrificed for economic security! It was almost unthinkable that Canadians would desert their ties and heritage, but in song and speech many proclaimed that they would do just that.

On Loyalty we cannot live,
One ounce of Bread it will not give,
Clear the way for Annexation,
Or we shall meet with starvation.

Annexation Ballad, 1849.[25]

A union with the United States will give Canada a place among nations; the accumulated wisdom of their legislators will become our own; we shall share in the triumph of their unparalleled progress; we shall reap the fruits of that political skill which has thus far shielded their institutions from harm; our interests will be watched over, and our industry protected and encouraged, by their wise commercial policy: ...

Alexander Galt, 1849.[26]

But I very well remember that on my return to Canada in 1856, after several years' absence, I spent some considerable time in travelling over Western Ontario, and I was both astonished and disgusted to find how strong and widespread at that period was the sentiment in favour of a union with the United States. Even those who disliked the idea *per se* appeared to look upon it as a foregone conclusion. ...

Sir Richard Cartwright.[27]

And in 1891, that great proponent of union with the United States, Goldwin Smith, set forth his reasons for considering such a move.

That a union of Canada with the American Commonwealth, like that into which Scotland entered with England, would in itself be attended

UNCLE SAM GOES A-WOOING.

U.S.—" Mr. Bull, I want to open negotiations with you for the hand of your beautiful darter."

J.B.—" Mr. Samuel, I don't control either her 'and or her 'art ; she's over twenty-one, and will 'ave to speak for 'erself ! "

Grip, Sept. 1, 1888

THE TRUE STATE OF HER FEELINGS.

BROTHER JONATHAN (*soliloquizing*)—" Ah, she loves me ; I know it ; I feel it in my very bones. She wants to jine me in the holy bands of political union."

MISS CANADA (*overhearing the whisper*)—" Mr. Jonathan, pray don't deceive yourself on that point. My heart is perfectly whole I assure you. I simply want to trade freely with you, that's all."

Grip, Jan. 19, 1889

with great advantages cannot be questioned. . . . Canadians almost with one voice say that it would...bring with it a great increase of prosperity. The writer has seldom heard this seriously disputed, while he has heard it admitted in the plainest terms by men who were strongly opposed to Union on political or sentimental grounds. . . . Canadians who live on the border, and who from the shape of the country form a large proportion of the population, have always before their eyes the fields and cities of a kindred people, whose immense prosperity they are prevented from sharing only by a political line, while socially, and in every other respect, the identity and even the fusion is complete.[28]

> *The great lure of the nineteenth century which Uncle Sam held out to us was free trade, or reciprocity, that marvellous word which has baffled history students for generations. The implications of free trade between Canada and the United States were ominous. It would lead inevitably, said its opponents, to annexation, political union with the Republic. It was the hint of reciprocity which led John A. Macdonald to utter one of his most moving pronouncements.*

A British subject I was born, a British subject I will die. With my latest effort, with my utmost breath, will I defy the "veiled treason" that with sordid means and mercenary proffers would win our people from their allegiance.[29]

> *Whenever the issue arose, whenever an agreement between the two countries for free trade seemed imminent, the forces of opposition could always raise the spectre of U.S. political domination. In 1911, when Wilfrid Laurier and his Liberal party negotiated a Reciprocity Treaty with the United States, all the anti-American and pro-British forces, led by the Conservative party, rose to the challenge. By preying upon the fear of political absorption in song and cartoon, they defeated Laurier, the Liberals, and reciprocity.*

> President Taft he made a pact
> With Laurier and Fielding
> And in the trade that Tafty made
> He found them very yielding.

Yankee Doodle Laurier,
Crafty Taft's a dandy,
Fielding bust the Farmers' Bank,
Railroad Hill's the candy.

We'll take our stand throughout the land
And preach to you this story
That ancient rag, the British flag,
Must float below Old Glory.[30]

It was not easy to resist the attractive economic temptations; there was, for example, the obviously sincere affection of Americans for Canada and Canadians. Even today many Canadians may experience a point during conversations with Americans when, almost wistfully, they will talk of "us getting together". They are not being grasping or devious or machiavellian. They simply cannot understand the illogic of two peoples so obviously alike and with so much in common living apart. So if Americans have seemed overly eager to bed or wed us, their enthusiasm was founded in a legitimate belief that we were destined by God or fate to be one.

We are one people,—in laws, religion, sympathy, and pursuits, and descended from a common origin, and our trade and intercourse are constantly growing in importance.

S. J. Ritchie, *Commercial Union in North America*, 1885.[31]

Regarding the apparent future of the Dominion but few words will suffice. This is but one Continent from the "Pole to Panama," then why should not interests be mutual, and the inhabitants brothers, let their residence be above the Lake of the Woods or below the table lands of Mexico. Whether Canada annexes the United States, or in time becomes a part and parcel of the country where so many Canadians have found a welcome and a home, would make but little difference to the people at large, and the amalgamation of interests would but be opposed by the politicians, who are, all over the Continent, each year losing more

DIGNIFIED ATTITUDE OF THE "LIBERALS."
BLAINE, IF THESE FELLERS GIT INTO OFFICE, CANADY IS OURS!
ANNEXATION
PLEASE ACCEPT OUR COUNTRY
GIVE US RECIPROCITY

and more of the feeble hold and sway they have over the minds of the people; . . .

Captain Mac, *Canada from the Lakes to the Gulf,* 1881.[32]

Our task and that of the Canadians is the same. We are both engaged in the work of converting a great continent to civilization, freedom, and Christian faith. They are the only co-workers with us with whom we can feel the closest sympathy, for our neighbors southward are separated from us by barriers higher and more impassable than those of political division. If for a time Canada seemed to be drawn by attraction to an un-American ideal of her position, and to cherish political and industrial dependence upon Europe, that time has passed away. Every recent movement in her history has brought us in to more intimate agreement as to the goal of our common endeavor, and the means by which it is to be attained. The time seems to have come for removing the last barrier to the closest fellowship in the administration of our common heritage of resources and capacities.

Wharton Barker, *Commercial Union in North America,* 1886.[33]

The issue is not yet decided. Lurking within some American hearts is still the belief that we will, eventually, surrender our independence to share in the good life. In 1968, George Ball, former Undersecretary of State to presidents Kennedy and Johnson, wrote the following words.

Canada, I have long believed, is fighting a rearguard action against the inevitable . . .

I wonder, for example, if the Canadian people will be prepared indefinitely to accept, for the psychic satisfaction of maintaining a separate national and political identity, a per capita income less than three-fourths of ours. The struggle is bound to be a difficult one—and I suspect over the years, a losing one. . . .

Sooner or later, commercial imperatives will bring about free movement of all goods back and forth across our long border; and when that occurs, or even before it does, it will become unmistakably clear that countries with economies so inextricably intertwined must also have free movement of the other vital factors of production—capital, services and labor.

The result will inevitably be substantial economic integration, which will require for its full realization a progressively expanding area of common political decision.[34]

Reluctant (?) Exiles

Anyone who has heard Bagshaw knows what an impressive speaker he is, and on this night when he spoke with the quiet dignity of a man old in years and anxious only to serve his country, he almost surpassed himself. . . .

"I am an old man now, gentlemen," Bagshaw said, "and the time must soon come when I must take my way towards that goal from which no traveller returns."

There was a deep hush when Bagshaw said this. It was understood to imply that he thought of going to the United States.[35]

> *In this passage from* Sunshine Sketches of a Little Town *Stephen Leacock pinpointed a traditional Canadian quandary; for the truth is that the United States has been the place of no return for many of our countrymen. Although there are some who would disagree, Walter Gordon and the Committee for an Independent Canada in particular, it can be said that as a nation we have not surrendered ourselves to the Americans. However, the case is completely different when we consider individuals. Our history is replete with examples of Canadians who have forsaken our land for the bright lights of the U.S.A.; immigrants who came to Canada only because they could not enter the United States, and left as soon as possible for the south; artists and performers who felt the need to prove themselves in a more challenging setting; businessmen seeking to play in the big leagues. Thousands of our most talented and ambitious people have made the move which usually becomes irrevocable. Although he was not a Canadian, Wyndham Lewis made a cynical comment which reflects a view commonly held by Canadians, especially with regard to their creative compatriots.*

As one naturalized Canadian explained to me "No one would be *here* who could be anywhere else." He admitted he would much rather be in Europe, or the U.S.A. but said he was very stupid and bad at his job so he couldn't help himself.

Wyndham Lewis, *Letters of Wyndham Lewis*[36]

Lewis was depressed at the time, and may be excused for his harshness. Unfortunately, there is more than a grain of truth in his comment. There has been a "brain drain" to the United States for almost a century. Looking back on the Canada of the nineteenth century, Sir Richard Cartwright made the following observations.

...it was still more evident that a tremendous drain of the best elements of our population had set in towards the United States. The latter factor in the situation had become very alarming indeed, and it so continued with very little cessation up to 1896 or 1897. The class of people who left Canada, moreover, were the very ones of all others we could least spare. They consisted for the most part of the most vigorous and enterprising of our young men and women. I think I have already mentioned that it was computed, after careful examination, that by 1896 at least every third able-bodied man in Canada between the ages of twenty and forty had emigrated to the United States.

Sir Richard Cartwright, *Reminiscences*, 1912.[37]

And Goldwin Smith, up to his old tricks of pushing for union with the United States, described how Canadians were freely mingling with Americans in the 1880s and 1890s.

The continent was one. Social fusion was rapidly advancing. The commercial union of the continent dictated by nature only awaited the repeal of unnatural and iniquitous laws. Drawn to American centres of employment, Canadians were mingling with the people of the United States at the rate of twenty thousand in a year. The churches interchanged pastors. A Canadian clergyman, just after reviling continental union and its supporters, accepted an American cure. Societies such as that of the Free Masons crossed the line. The Canadian Pacific Railroad, Canada's great line of communication, the administration of which, it was proclaimed, was to be purely Canadian, soon had an American President. The Canadian currency was not pounds and shillings, but dollars and cents. Intermarriage was frequent. Circumstance of every sort, besides race and language, foretold ultimate union. The attempts of United Empire Loyalism in Canada to keep alive international antipathy were fruitless.[38]

Why have Canadians deserted this nation? The comments of contemporary exiles reveal the range of opportunities offered by the States. Dr. Samuel Hayakawa, formerly president of San Francisco State College, gave his reasons.

After I'd got my Ph.D. in '36 I'd have given anything, right then, to come back to Canada. But there were no jobs. There weren't a lot of jobs here for that matter.

I would have given anything if I could have gone to the University of Toronto or New Brunswick or, even more, British Columbia, but I didn't have a chance. I must say I wrote a lot of Canadian universities at that time.[39]

A physicist who departed in the 1960s explains.

I had to come if I wanted to grow as a scientist. The leading people in my field are here, and the kind of vigorous, exciting research no Canadian firm can offer is going on in the labs of the U.S.A. I naively thought I could come back when the scientific scene at home had improved, but I doubt now that it will—certainly not until I'm an old, old man.[40]

As for the mavericks of the business world ...

Opportunities; that's why so many come. Now Jack Cooke; he had the ball club in Toronto and I'm sure he wanted very much at that time to get a major league franchise but he was never able to get one. He came down here and now he's got the Lakers and the Kings. There is no question: the opportunities are here, which they are not in Canada.

John B. Parkin, 1971.[41]

Of all the exiles, none seem to have been so numerous or vociferous as the show business types. Their tales of woe have a long and familiar ring to them—lack of opportunity in Canada; sparse recognition or appreciation of talent; little financial reward.

Why do some of the most talented people this country has to offer leave Canada to go and work in American entertainment? It's the money partially, of course, but there are other reasons. The story of Chris Beard's departure is a classic.

In Toronto, he was one of the main forces behind the CBC's one and only foray into the kind of late night programming that would woo watchers away from Johnny Carson. The program was called *Nightcap*.

Chris remembers that show this way:

"We did the most heavy satire ever put on Canadian television. When we were taken off the air, we had pickets outside the CBC. We had Judy LaMarsh stand up in the House of Commons and say 'Why did they take the show off the air? That's the kind of stuff we need.'"

The cancellation of *Nightcap* to Chris was symbolic. Symbolic of many other "cancellations" in his own seven-year stint with the CBC. It had reached the point where the final "no" had tipped the scales in favor of the expanded thinking (and audiences) in the United States.

In the television production centre of Los Angeles these days there is a new minority group known as "snowbacks". In excess of 600,000 Canadians live and work in Los Angeles. They've left an impression.

Brian Brenn and Harold Walters, 1971.[42]

You know, the country should be proud of us; there are a lot of us down here doing well. People keep thinking that Canada's greatest export to the United States is hockey players. It's not true. It's us.

Why hasn't Canada taken advantage of what we have to offer? We've offered our talent.

At Lorne Green's home there was the cream of Canadian talent down her and everybody said: "Ya, I'd love to go back." And nobody said: "Pay me." Nobody brought up the big dollars.

We'd love to go back. Maybe do a special up in Canada. Why not? It'd be fun.

Writer-producer Saul Ilson.[43]

The people back home consider you as someone who went away and deserted them.

We are just as Canadian even though we are not living at home. Canadian in feeling. . . . You've got to face facts. . . . There is a tendency to small thinking back in Canada.

Are U.S. war books brainwashing Toronto pupils?

Let's have Canadian textbooks

See U.S. texts glorify war
See Canadians using them!

VICTORIA, B.C. (UPI) — American textbooks being used in a reading program in two north Vancouver elementary schools were attacked by Education Minister Donald Brothers yesterday for glorification of militarism.

"I'm distressed to find the glorification of war that appears in these books and the continual allusion to American philosophy and ideals," he said.

One of the books shows a picture

of men by tanks with the cutline: "Dave was a brave man. He lost his life in the last world war." A second picture on the page shows a gravestone with the cutline: "This is Dave's grave, a brave man rests in his grave."

Other war references include such statements as: "The men went to war with guns and tanks," "It's fun to fly a jet," "Jets can win a war," and a picture of soldiers hiding behind a bunker with the cutline: "We duck while shots whiz by."

Ontario plans laws to encourage higher sales of Canadian books

Beware of trends seeping from U.S. educators warned

OISE favors U.S. studies, teacher says

U.S. publications swamping ours on the newsstands

Canadian book firms get $2 million in survival grants

Pelletier unveils aid worth $1.7 million for book publishers

Publishers urge Davis to act on foreign ownership

Canadian professors called keys to nation's tradition

Foreigners hurt OISE, says Reid

Sociologist sees U.S. bogeyman as the chief menace to French culture

Professor would compel teachers to be citizens

Third of university staffs foreign

Ontario report: Force all theatres to show Canadian films

PSST!... WANNA READ A CANADIAN BOOK?

great Canadian 5 PACKS
They last longer, and you can keep the empties!

Ottawa tells CTV to raise Canadian content -- or else

Canadian control of advertising can protect culture: Report

The strongest criticism I have ever received, the strongest, harshest criticism I have ever received in the press, has been in Toronto, one of my home towns.

Monty Hall.[44]

...First—I think it interesting to note that no major American network has ever landed a top CBC executive—just the CBC writers, directors, actors, singers and musicians. I don't believe this speaks too highly for CBC brass (especially the ones who have come here job hunting at the taxpayers' expense). Second (and most important) Mr. Davidson (Mr. CBC) says CBC-TV must remain Canadian. Mr. Davidson, if you had ever tried to do that, most of us would still be in Canada. A glance at the TV listings instantly reveals more American shows in prime time in Canada than Canadian shows.

Actor Larry Mann.[45]

And so it goes.

The Great Culture Crisis

No country but a country of alienated madmen would hire 75 per cent of its professors in one year from outside the country.

Canadian professor, 1972.[46]

You are aware, I know, of the growing concern within Ontario about the degree of influence that seems to be asserted on Canadian society by a proximity to, and close association with, the United States.

Of particular concern in some quarters is the relatively high proportion of American professors who have been appointed to positions in our universities and colleges...

I am very conscious of the fact a university must give full consideration to a candidate's record of scholarship and achievement, as well as nationality, when considering him for an appointment. I am also aware of the shortage of qualified Canadians that has existed in many areas, particularly social sciences, during recent years.

Nevertheless, I feel that most citizens of Ontario would be reassured if they could feel that academic openings in our province were being offered, wherever possible, to qualified Canadian candidates and that the overall balance in faculty members was becoming more markedly Canadian.

Letter to University Presidents from Premier
Davis of Ontario, 1971.[47]

> *In the '70s we suddenly discovered a new dimension to the American threat to our identity. Having failed to annex us physically or woo us successfully, the Americans, it seemed, had developed a far more subtle and potentially more dangerous tactic; they would dominate our brains, mould our culture in their style, and achieve a bloodless victory. Through American professors, American books, American films, American art curators, they would completely and eternally subjugate us.*
>
> *As with so many of our concerns about Americanization, this too has had a long and distinguished history. More than one hundred years ago outraged observers viewed with alarm the growing American control of our culture, beginning with the brainwashing of tender and innocent Canadian school children.*

In many parts of the province the teachers are Americans. . . . These men are utterly ignorant of everything English and could not if they tried instruct their pupils in any of the duties which the connnection of the province with England casts upon them. The books they use are all American, filled with inflated accounts of American independence and the glorious wars with England. The exploits of General Jackson and the heroes of '76 fill the youthful mind to the exclusion of everything glorious or interesting in English history. The young man grows up without a single prepossession in favor of his country; he looks upon a British soldier as a person whom it would be honorable and glorious to oppose with the rifle; the British government in his mind is a chimerical monster 4000 miles off, . . . The boy gains a smattering of geography out of an American compilation in which the state of Rhode Island occupies as much detail as the eastern hemisphere and in which England appears a pitiful little island filled with tyrannical landlords and very fat clergymen, and a great number of squalid tenants and labourers. Ireland is a joyless land of bogs, pigs and Catholics, and Scotland an out of the way place in which the mountains and the men have a national and barbarious prejudice against decent covering.

R. B. Sullivan, 1839.[48]

I went into the school room, where I saw American schoolbooks in which Great Britain was not spoken of in the most respectful terms. I also saw American maps in which we were altogether excluded from the shores of the Pacific, the American and Russian territory joining in the northwest; also the boundary of the northeast brought up to the St. Lawrence.

J. E. Alexander, 1833.[49]

It is really melancholy to traverse the Province and go into any of the Common Schools; you find a herd of children instructed by some anti-British adventurer instilling into the young and tender mind sentiments hostile to the present State; false accounts of the late war—geography setting forth New York, Philadelphia and Boston as the largest and finest cities in the world; historical reading books describing the American population as the most free and enlightened under heaven; insisting on the superiority of the laws and institutions to those of all the world; American spelling books, dictionary and grammar, teaching them an anti-British idiom and dialect.

Thomas Rolph, 1832.[50]

The exodus of many Americans to Canada explains the presence of those people in our classrooms; but why were American books being used? The answer given then has many interesting parallels with the modern situation.

The traffic in books from the United States employs a great many young men, who travel through the country, selling and taking up subscriptions for new works. . . .

Of books published in the Colony, we have very few indeed; and those which have been issued from a Canadian press have generally been got out, either by subscription, or at the expense of the author. It is almost impossible for any work published in Canada to remunerate the bookseller, while the United States can produce reprints of the works of the first writers in the world, at a quarter the expense. The same may be said of the different magazines which have been published in the Colony.

Susanna Moodie, 1853.[51]

The inevitable result of all this American influence was clear for anyone who cared to analyse the situation.

The proximity of these provinces to the United States is one cause of our agitation and discontent. Without this fatal proximity, we might long have continued prosperous and happy as British Colonists. We suffer neither taxation nor oppression; and we abound in the necessaries and comforts of life. Consequently, we *feel* no grievances. But, presenting an extensive frontier to the United States, new opinions about politics have been introduced from that great manufactory of such commodities; and many native Americans, settling among us, have doubtless imported with them a prejudice against G. Britain which, among the lower classes of the United States' citizens, has, ever since the revolution, descended from father to son. . . .

Thomas Carr, Justice of the Peace, 1836.[52]

The Canadians are neither British nor American: the local circumstances and situation of the country tend towards the latter; and the tendency is increased by the vicinity of, and intercourse with the States. . . .I think they are more American than they believe themselves to be, or would like to be considered; and in the ordinary course of things, as the emigrants cease to be so large a proportion as they do now to those born in the province, they must become more so.

John R. Godley, *Letters From America*, 1844.[53]

The twentieth century saw the problem magnified by the development of mass media which presented even more insidious techniques of persuasion. Radio was the first of the new devices, and, naturally, a Royal Commission was appointed to report on its role in our society.

In our survey of conditions in Canada, we have heard the present radio stituation discussed from many angles with considerable diversity of opinion. There has, however, been unanimity on one fundamental question—Canadian radio listeners want Canadian broadcasting. . . .

At present the majority of programmes heard are from sources outside of Canada. It has been emphasized to us that the continued reception of these has a tendency to mould the minds of the young people in the home to ideals and opinions that are not Canadian. In a country of the vast geographical dimensions of Canada, broadcasting will undoubtedly become a great force in fostering a national spirit and interpreting national citizenship.

Report of Royal Commission on Radio Broadcasting, 1929.[54]

It was quite obvious who those "sources outside of Canada" were. It is to this concern that we owe the development of the publicly owned Canadian Broadcasting Corporation, that guardian of our culture, accent, pronunciation, which today strives to defend the concept of "Canadian content" in radio and TV.

In 1947 another Royal Commission made what was, and still is, a definitive statement on the influence of the United States on our way of life. In its impressive presentation it gave full credit to the Americans for their contribution to our intellectual and cultural life, pointing out that we have gained much from American books, newspapers, universities, teachers, radio. This cultural debt was, however, a two-edged sword.

We have gained much. In this preliminary stock-taking of Canadian cultural life it may be fair to inquire whether we have gained too much....

...Teachers from English-speaking Canada who wish to improve their talents or raise their professional status almost automatically make their pilgrimage to Teachers' College at Columbia University or to one of half a dozen similar institutions. They return to occupy senior positions in elementary and high schools and to staff our normal schools and colleges of education. How many Canadians realize that over a large part of Canada the schools are accepting tacit direction from New York that they would not think of taking from Ottawa?...But for American hospitality we might, in Canada, have been led to develop educational ideas and practices more in keeping with our own way of life.

It may be added that we should also have been forced to produce our own educational materials—books, maps, pictures and so forth. As it is, the dependence of English-speaking Canada on the United States for these publications is excessive. In the elementary schools and high schools the actual texts may be produced in Canada, but teachers complain that far too much of the supplementary material is American with an emphasis and direction appropriate for American children but unsuitable for Canadian. As an illustration of the unsuitability of even the best American material, the statement was made in one of our briefs that out of thirty-four children in a Grade VIII class in a Canadian school, nineteen knew all about the significance of July 4 and only seven could explain that of July 1.

In our universities the situation is very much more serious. The comparative smallness of the Canadian university population, and the accessibility of American publishing houses with their huge markets has resulted in an almost universal dependence on the American product. It is interesting that a vigorous complaint of American text books should come from a scientist:

> "Where personalities and priorities are in question, American writings are very much biased in favour of the American. This is not to suggest that the facts will be distorted, but by mentioning the American names and industries and omitting mention of any others, a very unbalanced picture can be given. To subject Canadian students year in and year out to these influences is not particularly good for the growth of a wholesome Canadianism."...

The American invasion by film, radio and periodical is formidable. Much of what comes to us is good and of this we shall be speaking presently. It has, however, been represented to us that many of the radio programmes of the "crime" and "horror" type, are positively harmful. News commentaries too, and even live broadcasts from American sources, are designed for American ears and are almost certain to have an American slant and emphasis by reason of what they include or omit, as well as because of the opinions expressed....

American influences on Canadian life to say the least are impressive. There should be no thought of interfering with the liberty of all Canadians to enjoy them. Cultural exchanges are excellent in themselves. They widen the choice of the consumer and provide stimulating competition for the producer. It cannot be denied, however, that a vast and disproportionate amount of material coming from a single alien source may stifle rather than stimulate our own creative effort; and, passively accepted without any standard of comparison, this may weaken critical faculties. We are now spending millions to maintain a national independence which would be nothing but an empty shell without a vigorous and distinctive cultural life. We have seen that we have its elements in our traditions and in our history; we have made important progress, often aided by American generosity. We must not be blind, however, to the very present danger of permanent dependence.

Royal Commission on Arts, Letters and Sciences, 1951.[55]

The true extent of American cultural domination was forcefully put forward by F. R. Scott in a poem written in 1963.

The Canadian Centenary Council
Meeting in Le Reine Elizabeth
To seek those symbols
Which will explain ourselves to ourselves
Evoke bi-cultural responses
And prove that something called Canada
Really exists in the hearts of all
Handed out to every delegate
At the start of the proceedings
A portfolio of documents
On the cover of which appeared
In gold letters

not

A Mari Usque Ad Mare

not

Dieu Et Mon Droit

not

Je Me Souviens

not

E Pluribus Unum

but

COURTESY OF COCA-COLA LIMITED[56]

Thank God I Am a Canadian

One might gather that we experience nothing but the emotions of fear, resentment, anger towards the United States. Not so. There is another feeling which runs very deep in our attitudes towards Americans; self-satisfaction. For, despite all the inadequacies we feel in comparing ourselves with our big neighbour, we have one redeeming quality. We are morally superior! No true Canadian doubts the truth of that statement. Observe how righteous Canadians compared themselves to Americans in the last century.

For my own part, I admire the great Republic with its noble work for humanity and freedom, and I like the American people. But as a nation, they have their dangers. They have still unsolved their negro problem, the Mormon scandal, the Socialistic conspiracy, which steadily becomes more dangerous, and lynch law, which continues to prevail over a large part of the Union. The Continental Sunday, too, with its open theatres, concert halls and baseball matches, is becoming alarmingly common.

James Young, *The National Future of Canada*, 1887.[57]

In the United States—as in every purely democratic community—where there is nothing to differentiate one man from another, but wealth, nothing therefore to aim at but wealth, character becomes materialized, and love of personal well being usurps a disproportionate and unhealthy place in the mind....

N. F. Davin, 1873.[58]

We are free from many of the social cancers which are empoisoning the national life of our neighbours. We have no polygamous Mormondon; no Ku-Klux terrorism; no Oneida communism; no Illinois divorce system; no cruel Indian massacres.

Canadian Methodist Magazine, 1880.[59]

...For myself, my antipathy to the essential spirit of the American people, their customs, their everything grows every time I come into contact with them, and my thankfulness that there is still such an essential difference between them and the Canadians—how any Canadian with a grain of common-sense or self-respect can even consider the possibility of his country throwing in its lot with the United States is as much a mystery to me as the craze young Englishmen seem to have for marrying American girls.

Lady Aberdeen, 1895.[60]

Behold also how Canadian cartoonists criticized the American Indian policy and contrasted with it our just and fair attitude toward the Red Man.

The Dominion Illustrated, 1891

SITTING BULL ON DOMINION TERRITORY.

U. S. SOLDIER — Send him over to our side of the line and we'll take care of him.

N. W. MOUNTED POLICE OFFICER — So long as he behaves himself, the British right of asylum is as sacred for this poor Indian as for any royal refugee.

*In more recent times there have been many incidents and causes which
have allowed Canadians to look askance at the United States. We have
looked with disapproval and some smugness at urban violence in American
cities; we have demonstrated in favour of the Civil Rights movement
in the United States; we have protested against American involvement
in Vietnam. At times, U.S. consulate buildings in Canadian cities
have become the most popular rallying places for those of us who have
been displeased with anything.*

*One of the more interesting episodes occurred in connection with the
U.S. nuclear test on Amchitka Island in 1971. This provided a field
day for thousands of Canadians and the furious protest which was whipped
up was most impressive.*

Niagara Falls—An estimated 10,000 students sealed off Canada's border
crossings to the United States at three points in Ontario yesterday in
a massive protest against the U.S. nuclear explosion on Amchitka Island
Saturday.

The Rainbow Bridge crossing at Niagara was closed for an hour as
more than 2,000 singing, chanting students marched in a "funeral procession" to deposit a coffin and an effigy of a melted man before New
York state troopers guarding the U.S. customs office.

About 5,000 students who swarmed across the Ambassador Bridge,
linking Windsor and Detroit, came face to face with steel-helmeted Detroit
police. The mass of students blocked the normally busy bridge for more
than two hours and traffic was backed up for miles.

Another 3,000 Canadian students sealed off the Bluewater Bridge border
crossing connecting Sarnia and Port Huron, Mich. At the centre span,
an effigy of President Richard Nixon was burned and thrown into the
water.[61]

Winnipeg—Police reinforcements were called in to protect the U.S.
consulate yesterday after demonstrators protesting the Amchitka nuclear
blast threatened to storm the building.

About 2,500 demonstrators surrounded the consulate in downtown
Winnipeg and one window was broken when a demonstrator hurled a
piece of ice.

Consul-General W. B. Kelly met with several spokesmen for the group,
but did not allow reporters to attend. As the U.S. official spoke to the
delegation, his office was showered with snowballs.[62]

Stop Amchitka!

A lifeless planet rotates ceaselessly around an undying sun. On it prevails the deafening silence of death. The air and water lie stagnant, engulfed by a sea of radioactivity. No wind, no sound, no flowers, only a barren expanse of dust, the final remnant of a long forgotten life. Is this fantasy or is it reality?

On Nov. 4, President Nixon will play russian roulette with the fate of our lives and our environment. Planned to be detonated is a five megaton nuclear warhead on Amchitka Island, a warhead whose destructive capacities could annihilate metropolitan Toronto in a matter of minutes. The detonation of this warhead could result in tidal waves throughout the Pacific, submerging the coastal regions of the North American Pacific coast. It can also contaminate the north Pacific Ocean, upon which Canada depends heavily for its annual fish catch.

Will Canadians sit passively by while President Nixon conspires to destroy our environment?

On November 3, the city of Vancouver will shut down. Tens of thousands of high school students will be leaving their classes in Vancouver, and other cities in western Canada. As time runs out, the urgent need to demonstrate grows. Amchitka can be stopped, but only if people take the initiative to stop it.

On November 3, there will be a rally of high school students at Nathan Phillips Square at 3:00 o'clock, with speakers, rock bands, etc. We urge all students and staff to suspend all normal activites at 2:00 p.m. and come and join the rally at Nathan Phillips Square. At 4:30 p.m. there will be a march to the United States consulate on University Avenue, where we will be joined by thousands of university students who are against Amchitka.

Wasn't one Hiroshima enough?

Leave classes 2:00 pm   Join rally 3:00 pm

Nathan Phillips Square   Wed., Nov. 3

Among the Sponsors of the rally: League for Student Democracy
Ontario New Democratic Youth
Volunteers
Toronto Alternate Press Service
Riverdale High School Association
Young Socialists
Students Against the War in Vietnam
Toronto Free Music Committee
High School Teachers Against Amchitka

"WHO IS GOING TO STOP ME?"

About 4,000 shouting, placard-waving students swept through downtown Toronto streets during rush hour last night after demonstrating in front of the United States consulate on University Ave. against the Amchitka underground nuclear blast planned for Saturday.

More than 200 police on foot, horses, motorcycles, or in cars and a sound truck kept demonstrators to the sidewalks on Yonge St. from Queen St. north to College St. as they ran shouting "Stop Amchitka. Stop the Bomb".[63]

Vancouver—Gangs of chanting youths stood in front of the U.S. consulate yesterday afternoon in a driving rain, blocking traffic in what a spokesman said was a protest against the Amchitka nuclear test expected Saturday.

They then broke away and began surging down city streets toward a federal Government building six blocks away in what another spokesman said was a protest march against the Canadian Government for its lack of effective action in halting the U.S. nuclear test.[64]

Secret report: Amchitka could set off string of quakes.[64]

> *Much to the disappointment of the protestors, the test did proceed. Even more disillusioning for some of them was the fact that the world did not end in an American-planned holocaust.*

But on the Other Hand

May the Stars and Stripes wave briskly forever;
may it wave from the highest mountain peak,
the breeze bringing to tyrants and terrorists everywhere
a fatal, bone-chilling pneumonia
but to Canadian socialists & nationalists & academic creeps
only the common cold for with us parochialism and stupidity
                              are geopolitical
fate for the same reason that moralic syrup is the favourite
                              beverage of all
little peoples condemned to crawl between the feet of towering
                              historic giants.
Without its warming taste how could they endure themselves
                              or one another

as croaking in their barren frogponds their round, empty eyes
blink across
the surrounding gloom: cowardice is wisdom; mediocrity,
sanity, philistinism.
olympian serenity; and the spitefulness of the weak, moral
indignation.

I'm sorry for you, America.
You deserve grander neighbours
than assholes covered with ten-gallon hats!

Shine on, glorious republic, shine forever.

Irving Layton.[66]

We ought to get back to sanity and recognize that living next door
to the United States, we are always going to be a small fellow living
next door to a big fellow. And a small fellow pushing for all he is worth,
cannot exert as much pressure as a big fellow can with just a little push
with one arm. That is just one of the facts of life, and we have got
to take it for granted. We have got to learn to take the Americans for
granted and not to think it is immoral of them to puruse what they
understand is their own interest. The Americans, of course, have to learn
not to take us for granted, and it is going to be just as hard for one
side as for the other to learn those necessary things.

We have been building up a Canadian nation here for a century since
1867. We came into this world of nation-states very late. We are worrying
about this question just at this moment when nationalism is becoming
obsolete. Maybe one of the prices we will have to pay in the future
for being Canadian is the willingness to give up a very considerable part
of our Candian sovereignty—to give it up for the purpose of preserving
a free prosperous world.

Frank Underhill, *The Price of Being Canadian*, 1961.[67]

I am an avowed Yankee-lover and so quite out of tune with a current
fashion in our land, which regards Americans as thick-skinned, selfish
meddlers in Canadian affairs.

I like and respect the United States of America, and am glad it has
involved itself so heavily in Canadian development, which has proceeded

faster in the 25 years of U.S. involvement than it had when we had the help of others, or were going it alone. . . .

The United States does not deserve the anger of Canadians for what it has done in Canada, or to Canada.

It may well deserve the anger of Cubans for what it did in and to Cuba, or of Southeast Asians for what it did in and to Southeast Asia. The Chinese may have a big anti-Yankee beef, and so may the Arabs, and assorted East Europeans, Africans and Latin Americans.

We do not. No nation, no people have helped more than the U.S. to make Canada what it is today—one of the most desirable places to live in the world. . . .

Charles Lynch, Chief of Southam News Services, 1972.[68]

A comment on the attempts to protect Canadian culture from the dangerous influences of American books, magazines, professors, writers, artists.

Can we, who deplore the Reader's Digest, and never looked to the Saturday Evening Post or lending library novels, for intellectual sustenance, accept Maclean's as one of our cultural bastions or feel spiritually diminished by the passing of Ryerson Press?

Can those of us who are old enough to remember the late Senator Joe McCarthy and the Un-American Activities Committee, recalling them with a chill, clap hands for Robin Matthews and his ad hoc Un-Canadian Activities Committee?

Isn't it time the nationalists stopped declaring all things Canadian-made or owned intrinsically good, even inviolate, and started to go in for tougher distinctions, say—for openers—putting excellence in a professor before country of origin?

Playing the Canadian campus circuit, mindful of nationalist zealotry, I have warned students again and again, that if 20 years ago Canadian writers suffered from neglect, what we must guard against now is overpraise. The largest insult. The dirty double-standard. One test for Canadian writers, another, more exacting litmus applied to foreigners. Good Canadian writers, I told them, stand in no need of a nationalist's dog license, and the rest are simply not worth sheltering. . . .

And so to all of you I say let's not be diverted into chauvinism, a stagnant stream, and accept or burnish cultural wooden nickels, even if they are stamped with the Maple Leaf. Literature is more than a local address, or familiar street names, or good intentions. It's what, hopefully, makes our short passage here more endurable. And to my fellow artists I say eschew the cultural policy of the closed door, reject the proffered nationalist crutch: Instead, seize the day.

Mordecai Richler, 1973.[69]

...Canada ranks 4th in the world in terms of per capita GNP and yet is not a highly developed, economically mature country. Our relationship with the United States might have something to do with that high standard of living. . . .

What would be folly is to embark on adventures in economic nationalism that, while they would clearly reduce American investment in Canada, are less certain to generate viable Canadian substitutes.

The golden egg of the American goose may be tarnished, but let's not get rid of it until we have as productive a Canadian hen.

Seymour Friedland, 1971.[70]

Let's not look down our noses at foreign capital. It's been good for Canada.

G. Arnold Hart, Chairman of the Bank of Montreal.[71]

It is our destiny and good fortune to share the North American continent with the richest nation on the earth's surface. It makes good sense to exploit that advantage for all it is worth. It makes good sense to work with the United States for our mutual benefit. . . .

The central problem for Canada is how to live in harmony with, but distinct from, the most powerful and dynamic society on earth. . . .

Every Canadian should pray every morning and evening that the U.S. economy will continue to prosper. . . .

What is possible and desirable, and what we are doing is to avoid drifting into total dependency upon the United States by suitable domestic policies and by developing closer and more effective relationships with other countries. Some of them among our oldest friends, others with whom we can co-operate despite deep differences in policy and philosophy. . . .

We are a far stronger and independent nation today than we were at the end of the Second World War because we took advantage of our proximity to the United States to become a modern industrial state.

Now as the power centres of the world become more diversified, we can, without diminishing our friendship with the United States, extend our contacts east, west and north and thus reinforce our independence and our national unity.

External Affairs Minister Mitchell Sharp.[72]

These are not the voices of men who have sold out to the Americans. Their views represent the feelings of a larger segment of the Canadian population than might be suspected. There is even the possibility that we see here the voice of the "great silent majority". For, by and large, we could have done much worse in our choice of a neighbour. In its relations with Canada the United States has not rivalled the behaviour of great European powers who regularly devastated and carved up smaller neighbours. The "great undefended border" between the United States and Canada may be a cliché, but it is a fact.

We are not foolish enough to ignore the possibility that if Canadian independence and policy ever conflicted seriously with United States' needs, desires or existence, the Americans would use their power to right the situation. Canadian nationalists can talk, for instance, of preserving our natural resources of oil and water against the insatiable demands of the United States; but if the existence of the American way of life depends upon those resources, we are not going to be able to resist the pressures for a continental resources policy for long. The Americans might be willing to pay or deal for vital products, but they will have them.

This is nothing new in world history, nor is it a condemnation of the United States. The weak and meek have never inherited the earth, nor are they likely to. Our problem is that we are destined to live beside a big voracious neighbour; our advantage is that our neighbour, despite periodic blusterings and bullyings, has been the most charitable that any small nation could have asked for. To which a fervent Canadian nationalist might retort, "That's because the Americans can get it all anyway."

In analysing Canadian-American relations, Northrop Frye made the following statement.

If the Canadian faces south, he becomes either hypnotized or repelled by the United States: either he tries to think up unconvincing reasons for being different and somehow superior to Americans, or he accepts being "swallowed up by" the United States as inevitable. What is resented in Canada about annexation to the United·States is not annexation itself, but the feeling that Canada would disappear into a larger entity without having anything of any real distinctiveness to contribute to that entity: that, in short, if the United States did annex Canada it would notice nothing except an increase in natural resources.

Northrop Frye, *The Bush Garden*, 1971.[73]

Frye's prediction is wrong. Putting aside the desirability or undesirability of joining the United States, there is more than a strong possibility that any union would see Canadians become a great new American minority which would dominate in a way no other minority has ever done. Think of our men in public life and the opportunities for them. Compare Trudeau, cool intellectual, fashionable dresser, brown belt judo practitioner, with drab, middle-class Nixon; is there any doubt who the next president would be? Picture Diefenbaker in the American Senate, stunning his colleagues with oratory which has not been heard in that chamber since pre-Civil War days. Envision Joey Smallwood, ending his retirement and leading a new States' Rights movement. And picture Drapeau as the new super-mayor, besides whom Lindsay of New York appears as a small-thinking hick. And off in the wings are waiting a new generation of actors, singers, National Film Board film-makers, not to mention a score of new Arthur Haileys, waiting to make the big time with their talents. We would not be absorbed quietly and painlessly. We might very well end up dominating the American way of life. Ask Lorne Greene.

The Birth of a Nation

Canada is a nation in search of a destiny. The search has not been a frenzied or loudly proclaimed pursuit, but a quiet, hesitant, and at times, reluctant quest.

Our nation was not born out of an enthusiastic crusade for some noble ideal. It did not come forth out of some dramatic struggle for independence against a foreign tyrant. Its creation was not an event to inspire magnificent statements such as "conceived in liberty" or "forged by blood and iron". The birth of Canada in 1867 came about because the Confederation of British North American colonies seemed to be the best practical solution to serious problems.

Certainly, there were some men who had uttered prophetic statements concerning the future of this land. The immigrant D'Arcy McGee was one who spoke with typical Irish eloquence about his adopted land.

I have spoken...with a sole single desire for the increase, prosperity, freedom and honor of this incipient Northern Nation. I call it a Northern

10   IN SEARCH OF A DESTINY

Nation—for such it must become, if all of us do our duty to the last....I look to the future of my adopted country with hope, though not without anxiety. I see in the not remote distance one great nationality, bound, like the shield of Achilles, by the blue rim of Ocean. I see it quartered into many communities, each disposing of its internal affairs, but all bound together by free insitutions, free intercourse and free commerce. I see within the round of that shield the peaks of the Western Mountains and the crests of the Eastern waves, the winding Assiniboine, the five-fold lakes, the St. Lawrence, the Ottawa, the Saguenay, the St. John, and the basin of Minas. By all these flowing waters in all the valleys they fertilize, in all the cities they visit in their courses, I see a generation of industrious, contented, moral men, free in name and in fact—men capable of maintaining, in peace and in war, a constitution worthy of such a country!

Thomas D'Arcy McGee, 1860.[1]

McGee may not have been alone in his dream of some future great Northern Nation, but one does not encounter many expressions of such a vision in the words of the Fathers of Confederation. The men who sat down to hammer out the plans for Confederation at Charlottetown and Quebec were sound, sensible, practical men. Their discussions reek with the realities of life—trade, railways, tariff barriers, economic problems, the threat of the United States. They were seeking hard-headed solutions to a host of difficulties, not searching for dreams. Only occasionally does a glimmer of imagination and the vision of nation-building flash forth. As might have been expected, it was John A. Macdonald who rose to the occasion and offered to the people of British North America something more than a businesslike political deal.

. . .if we wish to be a great people; if we wish to form a great nationality, commanding the respect of the world, able to hold our own against all opponents, and to defend those institutions we prize:. . .this can only be obtained by a union of some kind between the scattered and weak boundaries composing the British North American Provinces. . . .

We find ourselves with a population approaching four million souls. Such a population in Europe would make a second, or at least, a third rate power. And with a rapidly increasing population — for I am satisfied that under this union our population will increase in a still greater ratio than ever before — with increased credit — with a higher position in the eyes of Europe — with the increased security we can offer to immigrants, who would naturally prefer to seek a new home in what is known to them as a great country, than in any one little colony or another — with all this I am satisifed that, great as has been our increase in the last twenty-five years since the union between Upper and Lower Canada, our future progress, during the next quarter of a century, will be vastly greater. And when, by means of this rapid increase, we become a nation of eight or nine millions of inhabitants, our alliance will be worthy of being sought by the great nations of the earth. . . .

In conclusion, I would again implore the House not to let this opportunity pass. It is an opportunity that may never recur. At the risk of repeating myself I would say, it was only by a happy concurrence of circumstances, that we were able to bring this great question to its present position. If we do not take advantage of the time, if we show ourselves unequal to the occasion, it may never return, and we shall hereafter bitterly and unavailingly regret having failed to embrace the happy opportunity now offered of founding a great nation under the fostering care of Great Britain, and our Sovereign Lady, Queen Victoria.

Sir John A. Macdonald, Quebec, 1865.[2]

That other great architect of Confederation, George Etienne Cartier, the man who persuaded the French that their future lay in Confederation, also caught the vision of an expanding nation.

When I think of the nation we would compose if all our provinces were organized under a single government, I seem to see the rise of a great British American power. The provinces of New Brunswick and Nova Scotia are like the arms of the national body able to embrace Atlantic trade....And Canada will be the very trunk of this vast creation. The two Canadas, stretching far out towards the West, will bring to Confederation a huge part of the western territories.[3]

And so, on July 1, 1867, the Dominion of Canada officially came into existence. At that time it only contained four provinces, Quebec, Ontario, New Brunswick, and Nova Scotia; but before the end of the century British Columbia and Prince Edward Island joined the new nation, and the prairies and mountains of the west and north were added to its domain. A transcontinental railway was built also and there was a beginning of a tide of immigration to the west. It was a time of expansion and a time for confidence, even though the optimism might be diminished by the racial crises, the intermittent economic depressions, the loss of population to the United States. There were some Canadians who felt that the expansion which had occurred might be just a small portent of greater things to come. Was it possible that Canada might not only rival the United States in development, but maybe, just maybe, even surpass the great republic? From Confederation in 1867 to the early years of this century Canadians voiced their confidence in the destiny of their land.

We can then look forward to the future with hope and confidence....In one hundred years the United States have passed through all the phases of national life that took a thousand to mould Europe, and they are fast hastening to a premature old age. . . . Already they show signs of dissolution. The evils of the old civilization amid which they were begotten, and the corruption engendered by the civil war, are doing their work. . . . As power steps from the disorganized grasp of the United States, it will fall to Canada as her natural right, making her the first nation on this continent, as she is now the second. United closely, as we shall be from the Atlantic to the Pacific by a common nationality, our country will go on, increasing from age to age in wealth, in power and in glory; and it may not be too much of a stretch of the imagination to think, that as it is the latest developed portion of a new world — as it was the first, by millions of years, to nurse and cradle in her bosom the first spark of animal life in the eozoon, — it may be the country where a last great, and fully developed humanity may find its fitting habitation and abode.

William Norris, 1880.[4]

It requires no such faith as Abraham's to look forward to a time when Canada will be a great nation. . . . We already count ourselves by millions; we live in historical times; we are the heirs in possession of the moral and intellectual wealth of centuries; we carry in our veins the blood of races which have been prolific in martyrs and heroes, poets and statesmen; in beauty, which gives sweetness to strength, and in art, which renders that beauty immortal.

N. F. Davin, *The Irishman in Canada*, 1877.[5]

Looking into the future, I perceive my country spanning this broad continent, her bosom throbbing with life and great plenty. Upon the pages of her history I can read the record of her achievements, it is worthy of a land with so rich an inheritance. I see her artists kneel for inspiration before her majestic and lovely landscapes, while able pens are moulding the traditions and legends with which the land is so richly strewn into an imperishable literature, encompassing history, romance and song.

Later on I imagine that I see a people—intelligent, thrifty and well-ordered—who, with roll of drum and the joyous waving of flags, celebrates the centennial anniversary of the birth of Canada; and I hear statesmen alluding to this nineteenth year of the Confederation, as the one which saw unworthy men strive to sever the ties of the sisterhood. Later on still, it seems as if I heard them relate with pride that in spite of these men's treason, the loyalty and faith of the people remained unshaken; that they went on adding and building, striving and achieving, until they crowned their work with a nationhood that in the eyes of civilized mankind stood second to none in prosperity, intelligence and general contentment.

Edmund Collins, 1887.[6]

Canada

O Child of Nations, giant-limbed,
Who stand'st among the nations now
Unheeded, unadored, unhymned,
With unanointed brow, —

How long the ignoble sloth, how long
The trust in greatness not thine own?
Surely the lion's brood is strong
To front the world alone?

How long the indolence, ere thou dare
Achieve thy destiny, seize thy fame? —
Ere our proud eyes behold thee bear
A nation's franchise, nation's name?

The Saxon force, the Celtic fire,
These are thy manhood's heritage!
Why rest with babes and slaves? Seek higher
The place of race and age.

I see to every wind unfurled
The flag that bears the Maple Wreath;
Thy swift keels furrow round the world
Its blood-red folds beneath;

. . .

But thou, my country, dream not thou!
Wake, and behold how night is done, —
How on thy breast, and o'er thy brown
Bursts the uprising sun!

Sir Charles G. D. Roberts, 1884.[7]

The people, not the resources of the country, will make Canada great. Concerning the variety, abundance and value of the resources which lie north of the 49th parallel, between the Atlantic and Pacific oceans, there is no longer any doubt and there will soon be little ignorance. Our material heritage is sufficient. How this shall be used is now the problem.

The Canadian people are a worthy people. They have strong bodies, eager and capable minds, and a traditional devotion to high moral and religious standards. Their fathers have done much for them. The pure air and free, clean life of our Canadian summers and winters have helped them towards strength and clearness of vision. Their teachers have led them wisely and vigorously. This is why the Canadian name is an honourable name to-day on the battlefields of South Africa, in the council chambers of Great Britain, and in the great universities of the United States and Europe. The strong grip of our great business men, the clear vision of our statesmen, the ability of our students and the heroism of our soldiers, are not the product of a day or a week. In quietness and obscurity our people have been "climbing upward," and now are showing themselves fit for their day of great duty and great opportunity.

Chancellor Wallace, McMaster University, 1902.[8]

Forward, Canada!

Northland of our birth and rearing,
Bound to us by ties endearing, —
Forward ever, nothing fearing!
    Forward, Canada!

Hear thy children's acclamations!
Vanquish trials and vexations!
Higher rise among the nations!
    Forward, Canada!

Not by battles fierce and gory,
Not by conquest's hollow glory,
Need'st thou live in deathless story:
    Forward, Canada!

Not by might and not by power, —
Truth shall be thy fortress tower;
Arts of peace shall be thy flower:
    Forward, Canada!

Yet if tyrant foe should ever
'Gainst thee come with base endeavor,
Strike, and yield thy freedom never:
    Forward, Canada!

W. M. Mackeracher, *Canada, My Land*, 1908.[9]

As the nineteenth century was that of the United States, so I think that the twentieth century shall be filled by Canada.

Sir Wilfrid Laurier.[10]

On the Threshold of Greatness—or— Delusions of Grandeur

By 1950 Canadians sensed that this nation was about to meet its appointment with destiny. It had taken almost half a century since Laurier's prediction, but it seemed that we had finally arrived after an unseemly long period of preparation. The adolescent had come of age. From 1900 to 1931 Canada had gradually slipped the official ties of the Imperial connection with Britain. The story of this movement, "Colony to Nation", was the major preoccupation of historians of the 1940's and 1950's, and Canadian students learned by heart the dramatic events which marked our progress to full independence—the Halibut Fisheries Act, the Chanak crisis, the Statute of Westminster. What has been called the "Liberal tradition of history" portrayed Britain's control over our foreign affairs as the great impediment to our independence and achievement of true destiny.

Then came the forties, World War II, and the preparation for the great decade of the fifties. The "Fabulous Fifties" they were called, and for Canada they were years of optimism, fulfillment, and tremendous confidence.

To many nations, the next fifty years will present problems of survival and of unity, of needed changes in institutions or traditions: but to Canada the next half-century presents a happier prospect, of a people greatly blessed with goods and resources, as yet unspoiled by power or riches, with a record of representative government remarkably free from corruption, and with habits of honesty and decency of inestimable value. If it is not given to us to map the future, we can at least get a running start into it by discovering where we are and by what stages we have come thus far, and by gaining a sense of direction and an awareness of possible dangers.

We are not yet a reading people in the best sense, a thoughtful people who have contributed richly to the world's philosophy, theology and political theories. But we are a people mature enough to indulge in self-examination; we are more self-conscious as a nation that we would have thought possible in 1903, and other people no longer take us for granted. . . .

We are envied, yet we do not appear dreadful to anyone. It is an unprecedented combination, the more so because the envy is without sting as yet. Other people look on us with friendly rather than malicious eyes as a most favoured nation whose history, circumstances and temperament are still without hint of aggression or dangerous design. They seem to be actually pleased that things are at last going well with us, and to hope that we will not spoil our future or worsen theirs by repeating the mistakes of older nations or misusing our heritage. We are no powderkeg that men eye askance lest it touch off a world explosion. We sing of ourselves as "the true north strong and free", and no man is offended or afraid.

G. P. Gilmour, *Canada's Tomorrow*, 1954.[11]

At the beginning of the nineteenth century Canada had a population of only a quarter of a million—today her population is over fourteen million. At the beginning of the nineteeth century her population hovered about the St. Lawrence. Today it is scattered from coast to coast and north to the Arctic Ocean, over an area twice as large as Europe and as extensive as the United States.

Forty years ago when I entered politics one was afraid to risk a prophecy that Canada could ever have more than an agricultural, fishing, lumbering, and, in a limited way, mining population. Today one does not hesitate to claim that we have the greatest nickel deposits, the greatest iron deposits, and the greatest uranium deposits in the world. We do not hesitate to claim that our power development, our coal supplies, our oil possibilities and our aluminum production is comparable with that of any country. We say without any hesitation Canada can become one of the greatest industrial countries in the world.

James G. Gardiner, Minister of Agriculture, 1951.[12]

Our achievement, our wealth, our opportunities were recognized not only by Canadians but by others as well.

The Canadian giant is stirring; this northern nation is beginning to bring into use the huge reserves of natural resources which will make it one of the most important of nations in the latter half of the twentieth century.

Anne Merriman Peck, *The Pageant of Canadian History*, 1963.[13]

Canadians believe that this is Canada's century. Since the war their economy has expanded at an astonishing rate, and they have an infective confidence in the future. They share in the technical progress and immense wealth of the North American economy: but they are to some extent free of the burden of world leadership which has fallen heavily, and univited on the shoulders of their neighbour to the south. At international conferences Canadian opinions are increasingly respected because of the great and growing power of the country; on international commissions Canadians are welcome because they are free of the so-called stigma of ever having owned an empire. Canadians must be about the friendliest people in the modern world; by and large I think they are probably the happiest.

Gordon & Elspeth Winter, *Ourselves in Canada*, 1960.[14]

A delegate to a conference held to examine Canada's Tomorrow offered an interesting and pleasing analysis of our situation.

It is half a century since a great Canadian, Sir Wilfrid Laurier, announced that this was to be the Canadian century....

Today, after a Second World War, the spirit if not the letter of Laurier's prophecy is coming true. It is so evident that even the most deliberately pessimistic, the most determined touchers of wood in the panel of the Conference have not been able, like Dr. Johnson's would-be philosophic friend, to keep from letting cheerfulness come creeping in. But there is, all the same, in most of the papers an uneasiness that is perhaps natural. On the whole Canada has, from the days of Champlain, had it hard. Everything has had to be fought for and worked for. Compared to the United States, even to Australia, there have been, till recent times, no windfalls in Canada. You have thus escaped the temptations (which affect nations as well as individuals) of behaving like "Coal Oil Johnny", to quote a representative figure from United States mythology. You have not been tempted like Dr. Johnson's young man to "show the spirit of an heir". And even if there had been fewer people of Norman and Caledonian origin in the Canadian population, this would have been true. Even the Irish-Canadians submit, I am told, to the genius of the country and display a moderation that would strike oddly in Dublin—or in Belfast.

But this long training in thrift, in industry, in prudence has, in recent years, been threatened by the sudden good fortune that has made what used to be considered the great, useless, empty northern space of Canada, one of the treasure-houses of Canada and of the world. You seem to me to be rather like a family that has come into a fortune and doubts the truth of the lawyer's letter or, to use an analogy more true to modern British life, like one of those winners of a hundred thousand pounds in a football pool who announces that he's going to work as usual next morning and won't let his good fortune change the tenor of his life. After a few months, when he discovers that it *is* true, he *does* change the tenor of his life. So I think, and hope, will you. Some of the pessimistic things said about culture, the fine arts, the state of basic scientific research, the general conditions of education in Canada will change for the better when the reality, the permanence of your good fortune, really soaks into your minds.

Denis William Brogan, 1954.[15]

> *The reality was beginning to soak into our heads. The optimism of the fifties was infectious and increased with the news of each fresh development—oil strikes, uranium finds, seaway construction, industrial expansion, and northern development. Some of the excitement of the era was captured by an English author.*

Down North! they say in Edmonton and Winnipeg and Prince Albert, where the cargo planes which are to-day's bullock carts waddle down the runways or splash across a lake, then soar off toward the Land of the Midnight Sun. Perhaps they're bound for some remote lake, to set down a pair of prospectors or trappers who will spend a season at their jobs before they're picked up again. Perhaps they carry men or materials for the mines which are boring out the North's frozen mineral wealth. They carry fantastic loads of machinery, somtimes livestock for some ambitious settler. Sometimes they wear skis instead of wheels or pontoons, to bring them down safely on frozen lakes or snow-packed runways.

Just as likely these days they carry engineers, workmen—and service personnel—to build and man radar posts of the Distant Early Warning Line, the Arctic outposts that would give North America its first warning of any attack across the top of the world (which is the direction from which an attack is believed to be most likely to come).

Down North! You hear the same refrain in brokers' offices in Toronto and Montreal. The men with calculating eyes who know where money is to be made look at their maps and listen to the reports of their "spies"—the weather-browned men with big shoulders who forage in lonely, far places, tapping with their hammers at this bit of rock, squinting through a magnifying glass at that fragment. The city men scan analysts' reports and weigh the findings. Perhaps a pen scratches figures and a signature on a cheque—and like a snowball growing in size with mounting speed a new town comes into being.

Planes drone low over the trees of a distant lake, shacks spring up, machinery gnaws at the rock. A mill is built; a village wins a name. Men develop *camaraderie* and enmity. They eat, work, sleep, laugh and fight. Some head back to the big cities with swaggering rolls of money in their pockets. Some go back sick and penniless. Some die of disease or underground beneath a fall of rock. Except for a few months in summer the cold bites with deadly fangs.

Down North! It is Canada's New Land. It is her treasure box, frozen by ice and geography. It holds incalculable wealth in minerals—uranium, gold, silver, iron, coal, the list is endless. It is where a few men win fortunes and where more men cast away everything they possess. It will never support a large settled population, but men will dare its vastness and its harshess as long as it promises them a key to comforts in the big cities. It is a man's land, but some of its happiest, most successful residents are women.

John Dauphinee, *Opportunity in Canada*, 1958.[16]

Wherever they went, Canadians found that they and their nation were receiving a recognition previously accorded only to the great powers of the world. It was an exhilarating sensation.

Of great interest to me, of course, was the attitude toward Canada, that I found on every hand. The prestige of this country was never higher abroad, than it is today. At the political level the part that Canada played in the last war is not forgotten, but, perhaps, even more than this, the diplomatic skills of our Prime Minister, Mr. St. Laurent, and our Secretary of State for External Affairs, Mr. Pearson, in the difficult postwar world of the past ten years, are greatly admired and greatly respected.

At the level of the man in the street, Canada is regarded as a land where dreams come true, a treasure trove of the Western world where work and bread are found in plenty and where the people are truly free and friendly.

In the minds of Europeans, Canada stands as a strong and united nation. Our representatives abroad in the diplomatic service are men of high calibre and certainly the voice of Canada in the councils of the world is listened to with respect. It must, therefore, be a source of tremendous pride and gratification to every Canadian that our country ranks in this high position.

Talking to the Prime Minister of Belgium, Achille Van Acker, he said to me, "I wonder if you Canadians realize what a wonderful country you have and what wonderful opportunities lie at your hands."

John Bassett, Jr., 1955.[17]

It was becoming increasingly clear that the approbation we were receiving from the outside world was due not just to our impressive resources and economic development, but to the role we were playing in world affairs. A new concept of our destiny emerged during the fifties. We were, it seemed, well-suited, perhaps better qualified than any other nation, to perform a vital role in the world as a middle power, a mediator between great nations, a force for peace. The origins of that mission were traced to our contributions to the victory in World War II, and to our part in establishing an effective United Nations Organization.

In the course of the present war we have seen Canada emerge from nationhood into a position generally recognized as that of a world power.

Prime Minister Mackenzie King, 1943.[18]

And as a world power, Canada played an effective role in the San Francisco Conference from which emerged the United Nations Organization.

Conscious of her magnificent war effort, her new industrial prowess, her great stock of foodstuffs, her vastly augmented activities as a world trader, and her strategic position as an air power, her delegates and advisers were able to speak with such confidence, conviction and competence that Canada seemed often to be automatically regarded at the conference table as occupying a position only less important than the three great powers. That the matter of her full national status and indeed her position as a world power of middle rank seemed never in question proved a pleasant surprise to many Canadian participants and observers.

C. C. Lingard and R. G. Trotter, *Canada in World Affairs: September 1941 to May 1944*, 1950.[19]

At the great San Francisco conference the work of the Canadian delegation again won them a high place in the consideration of the representatives of the nations great and small. The Canadian proposal that certain of the smaller powers which, like Canada had made vital contributions of men and supplies to the war should be considered middle powers and should have special consideration among the nations to be elected to the security council was adopted. . . .

This is the contribution which Canada's experience and the ability of her representatives, has enabled her to make to the world organization. It is for Canadians a matter of legitimate pride. It also gives ground for the hope that Canada may find herself more and more able to serve the great cause of maintaining peace in the world. In the conflict which will still rage between the forces of nationalism and internationalism Canada has placed herself squarely on the side of internationalism, by voting unanimously to approve the charter of UN, and thus accepting her obligation to share in providing the required armed forces whenever the Security Council decides that only by the use of military power can the peace of the world be maintained.

. . .Canada finds herself possessed of unique advantages. Perhaps the greatest of these is that no other nation has quite the same qualifications. No one in the world is afraid of her. She has no enemies. She covets no territory. The only axe she wishes to grind is that of securing a peaceful world and so security and prosperity for Canada among the other nations. . . .Her views, therefore, are likely to be received without suspicion. . . .

No small country has in modern times such an opportunity to forward the growth of international co-operation or so great a degree of influence with which to attempt the realization of this opportunity. Canadians can, through enlightened self interest make Canada a better and better country for all its citizens to live in, while at the same time it can give great service to the forces seeking to heal the world of its grievous wounds.

Margaret McWilliams, *This New Canada*, 1948.[20]

Does not, indeed, the world's future and hope of peace depend upon Canada, in her young and growing strength, taking upon herself, and a small but determined people, the role in this New World of the Western Hemisphere which, for centuries, the Mother Country assumed and discharged, to the undoubted good balance of peace and civilization, in the continent of Europe?

That is, the role of maintaining the balance of power.

May it not be Canada's destiny to show no hesitation in maintaining that balance, if necessary, between the U.S.S.R. and the United States of America, the two great powers whose boundaries we alone touch and share, and whose clashing destinies can meet in our skies? . . .

That, then, surely is Canada's greatest, truest, destiny, the assumption of the balance of power in the new world, as Great Britain has historically assumed and discharged it through centuries in the Old.

Charlotte Whitton, 1951.[21]

The world is suffering from many kinds of frustrations and will continue to do so. In such a world there is a particular role for Canada. What that role is depends on what sort of an image you have of a heroic Canadian. For myself, I think of Mike Pearson at the United Nations at the time of Suez, producing a resolution that set up the United Nations Emergency Force and that got the world by a very awkward corner. Or I think of those Signallers of the Royal Canadian Corps of Signals, being mauled and man-handled in the Congo and under orders not to retaliate in any way. This is a role, a national purpose, that we can be proud of. If we think that we have a chance of filling that kind of a role in the world today, we will be more prepared to live with our own frustrations as well as with the frustrations that are to be found everywhere in the world, and will try to strengthen ourselves, invigorate ourselves, to live with them in this kind of world.

Frank Underhill, *The Price of Being Canadian*, 1961.[22]

The view that Canada has some special sort of mission which she is peculiarly suited to carry out has remained a persistent carry-over from the fifties. Even as late as 1969, one writer could make the following plea.

Today the civilized western nations are looking for a saviour. Europe cannot lead. Without North America, it would have fallen long since into the barbarism, darkness and starvation that the European national warlords of the 20th century seemed to want: Yet in the United States today and among intellectuals abroad, American or not, the almost universal opinion is that the United States of America has also failed. Having come to this conclusion, the intellectuals think that western man is at the end of his life. The long course that began in Thebes, Athens, Jerusalem, that went on through Rome, Italy, Spain, France, England, America and finally touched the moon, has now in napalm and assassination, in national wars and genocide, gone to bloody death.

Perhaps. But we in Canada can say no to this thesis. The failure of Europe and America has been that men have turned politics into war. The success of Canada has been that we turned war into politics. The wars of the French and English, or the Americans and Canadians, of the Indians and the whites, have all been converted into issues, elections, debates and solutions.

The refugees are pouring in from the USA already. Soon the world will look to us and wonder. We must be ready.

We must get ready.

Now.

James Bacque, 1969.[23]

It was the best of times; we had a serious and respectable mission to fulfill in the world; we had a recognized status as an influential middle power; we were experiencing unchecked economic expansion; we were a free people in a happy and contented land. All that we could ask would have been more of the same.

Return to Reality

Something happened. Even as we entered the sixties and approached the one hundredth anniversary of Confederation there was a vague feeling of unease, a sense that we were beginning to drift and had passed the peak of our success. It is difficult even now to pin down precisely how and why the change in attitude occurred. But one event which symbolized the change was the cancellation of the Avro Arrow production program. The Arrow aircraft was the pride of the Canadian aeronautic industry and was to have been our entry into the lucrative fighter market provided by NATO. When our allies rejected what we knew was a superior aircraft, it was signal that we were no longer as important, influential or significant as we had thought.

The sixties were the beginning of the age of protest when existing values were subjected to critical examination. The roles we had created for ourselves—staunch defender of our NATO allies against militant communism, partner with the U.S. in NORAD which would defend our skies against Russian attack, peacemaker in the United Nations—lost some of their glitter when the premises upon which they were based were attacked.

The new decade also ushered in the crisis of separatism. All of the frustrations of Quebec and French Canada which most English-speaking Canadians thought had long ago been laid to rest suddenly exploded. It became very clear that this was not the contented land we had believed it to be.

I no longer want to be considered a second-class citizen in my own country.

I no longer want to think of my compatriots living outside Quebec struggling heroically for a right to speak and pray in French.

I no longer want to think of the unjust sacrifices to which parents in an English area are forced to agree in order to give their children a French education, when, in fact, their numbers justify the construction of French and Catholic schools. I am particulary concerned with the question of the separate schools in all the provinces of Canada (except Quebec) which sets French and English Canadians in opposition to one another.

I can no longer accept the fact that my son, for example, should occupy a lesser position in the service of his country simply because his companion in the civil service or the armed forces possesses, over him, the sole advantage of being unable to speak one word of French.

I no longer want to believe that in 1967 there will still be places where it will be unacceptable to speak French.

I no longer want to have to prove in a book, an argument, a conversation, or a newspaper article that Quebec is not still living, in the words of Goldwin Smith, "like an antediluvian animal preserved in Siberian ice".

I refuse to look forward to a future time when one of my children will come home hurt—devastated—because he in his turn has been ordered to 'speak white'.

I will no longer accept bad service anywhere in Canada because I am French-speaking. I do not ask to be understood, but I shall not tolerate contempt, bad manners, or sarcasm if I am overheard expressing myself in my own language by your compatriots.

Solange Chaput-Rolland in Dear Enemies, 1965.[24]

. . .What does Quebec want to be?

The answer: a homeland for a people; "patrie"; a nation in the fullest (English) sense of the word.

It's an old dream. A very powerful and no less normal dream, but so long repressed that it's often relegated deep down in the recesses of the French-Canadian mind. Some of us have given up on it. Others are scared of the changes it would require: so they hide it and caress it secretly, when nobody is looking, and since for them it's like an illicit love affair, they'll be the last to admit it.

But they will eventually. For the first time in a couple of hundred years, the dream is now clearly feasible. That was all it needed. As this becomes more evident, the latent majority that was always there will reveal itself and grow and pretty soon fulfil the dream.

René Lévesque, 1968.[25]

Q. Mr. Lévesque, is a separate Quebec a real possibility in the foreseeable future?

A. If you look at "separate" in the sense that, politically, it's going to be a different country, I think it's not just a possibility—it's inevitable. We feel a growing need—modestly akin to the Jewish one—for our own "homeland."

Q. How soon could that happen?

A. The way things are moving, it should take between one and three elections inside the Province of Quebec—about five or six years at the most, perhaps less—to bring to power a majority government in Quebec with a mandate to make Quebec a sovereign state. . . .

Q. Is there anything that English-speaking Canada could do to take the steam out of the Quebec-sovereignty drive?

A. I don't think so. It is something which is like a vital force. You have a population which was sort of patient, rather undereducated for too long, shielded by ignorance from any pressures for change, and living in a setup which was like being a colony inside a country. Now this is changing through education, and you can't go on.

Canada was based on two cultures, French and English. If we had become assimilated as French Canadians in a melting-pot setup, the kind that made the U.S. grow and last and keep on growing, there would be no problem. But Quebec, instead of assimilating, is developing in its own way.

You might stop it in a crazy way with guns and things like that. But this is a political situation that must run its course. And the course is, as in all maturing societies that have the tools for it, to have your own self-government.

So I don't see anything that the rest of Canada could do. If they try to block it, the effect will be just to accelerate it. If they try to buy it off by saying: "All right, what does Quebec want! We'll do this, we'll do that," the answer will be: "Quebec wants more."[26]

REVOLUTION BY THE PEOPLE FOR THE PEOPLE

ANNOUNCEMENT TO THE POPULATION OF THE

STATE OF QUEBEC

The QUEBEC LIBERATION FRONT (F.L.Q.) is a REVOLUTIONARY MOVEMENT made up of volunteers who are ready to die for the POLITICAL AND ECONOMIC INDEPENDENCE OF QUEBEC.

The SUICIDE-COMMANDOS of the QUEBEC LIBERATION FRONT (F.L.Q.) have as their principal mission to DESTROY COMPLETELY, by SYSTEMATIC SABOTAGE.

a. all colonial (federal) symbols and institutions, especially the R.C.M.P. (Royal Canadian Mounted Police) and the ARMED FORCES,

b. all the media of information in the colonial (English) language which hold us in contempt,

c. all the commercial enterprises and establishments which practice discrimination against the Québécois, which do not use French as their principal language and which put our signs in the colonial language (English),

d. all the factories which discriminate against French-speaking workers.

THE QUEBEC LIBERATION FRONT will proceed to the progressive elimination of all persons collaborating with the powers of occupation.

THE QUEBEC LIBERATION FRONT will also attack all commercial and cultural interests of American colonialism, the natural ally of English colonialism.

All the volunteers of the F.L.Q. have in their possession at the moment of committing their actions of sabotage papers of identification from the REPUBLIC OF QUEBEC. We demand that our wounded and our prisoners be treated according to the statute provided for POLITICAL PRISONERS and according to the GENEVA CONVENTION, in accordance with the laws of war.

INDEPENDENCE OR DEATH

THE INDEPENDENCE OF QUEBEC IS ONLY POSSIBLE THROUGH SOCIAL REVOLUTION. SOCIAL REVOLUTION MEANS A "FREE QUEBEC."

STUDENTS, WORKERS, PEASANTS FORM YOUR SECRET GROUPS AGAINST ANGLO-AMERICAN COLONIALISM.

F.L.Q. Manifesto, 1963.

These people were serious! And as the Québécois poured out their pent-up grievances, as the chain-smoking René Lévesque so reasonably explained the inevitability of Quebec's separation, as the bombs of the terrorist began to go off, the rest of Canada realized that there was more than a possibility that the Canadian experiment in nationhood might end in chaos. The glitter of our centennial celebrations, and especially Expo 67, pushed such unpleasant thoughts temporarily into the background, and allowed Canadian leaders to make optimistic statements.

This day, the 100th anniversary of the beginning of our Confederation; this day, our Centennial birthday, belongs to every Canadian. . . .

Every one of you, and every Canadian before you, has had some part, however humble and unsung, in building the magnificient national structure of Confederation that we honour and salute today.

As the world, to survive the nuclear future, must become a community of peace for all mankind, so must our country be a true homeland for all Canadians as it moves into its second century.

The Fathers of Confederation, and those who followed them, have built a strong foundation for this Canadian home.

As we begin our second hundred years, we must continue the work of furnishing it so that it will fulfil the hopes and aspirations of all our people for a good life.

This is a memorable day for Canada.

Ours is a good land. Our Centennial resolve must be to make it better for our children and our children's children.

God bless our country.

Prime Minister Lester Pearson, July 1, 1967.[27]

No nation on the threshold of its second century has had the assurance of the same promise as has Canada.

Ours is a mighty destiny of freedom, prosperity and expansion, of equality among races and colors and unstinted aid to lands not equally blessed.

John Diefenbaker, July 1, 1967.[28]

Unfortunately, centennial year ended, and we were to witness the escalation of separatism culminating in the disastrous events of 1970. Separatism, however, was not the only threat to our destiny. We had also discovered the menace of "foreign takeover". "Foreign" in Canada, of course, means American. The danger of American economic control in Canada had been pointed out as early as 1950 by the voice of Canada, John Fisher.

It is so easy to be cautious now. On this oil and iron ore development the thing that bothers me is this, that the Canadian does his best to entice American investment capital to come into this country. We say that is fine...it flatters us to think the Yanks are so impressed with the stability and potential of Canada that they will send billions into this country. Then when they get their money in we sit back and nip at them and you say we will soon be owned by the United States.

Well, now this is true. Instead of being owners ourselves of our resources we will wake up some day to find we are owers...the "n" is gone. Owners...Owers..note the difference.

Today I think sixty per cent of every dividend is passing out of the country. That is why in Alberta, despite the predictions it is going to be another Texas, you do not see the direct result of the boom as in Oklahoma and Texas. That is good to a point. You don't see the apartment buildings, the garages, the little factories, the office buildings that should be thrown up on the Alberta landscape today. You do not see it because the cream, the gravy is not left there, because Canadians in this great tremendous thing called Toronto, Montreal, and big fat, middle-aged London, will not get off their seat and take a chance in oil to the same extent the Yanks do. Play if safe! As long as you have a nice bank deposit, you will hold on to it, or a slice of Brazilian Traction, which is outside the country. That is true. There is very little Canadian money coming in to Alberta oil.

In Edmonton they had a banquet to honour the retirement of a President of an oil company. There were six hundred at the banquet and I don't suppose there were enough local Albertans or Canadians, except four, with enough money in Alberta oil to provide axle grease for their own cars to drive there and home from that meeting.

Why? You can't tell me there isn't money in Toronto or Montreal. Sure there is money. Canadians are Ottawa conscious...they play safe every time. We are going to wake up with an awful jolt if we don't have a little faith in our own country.[29]

Other voices too were raised in warning.

Is Canada growing too fast? Far too fast for it to be an all-Canadian financial effort. And many Canadians, reading of the high percentage of foreign ownership in many segments of the Canadian economy, are genuinely worried.

Star Weekly, 1956.[30]

At the root of Canadian concern about foreign investment is undoubtedly a basic, traditional sense of insecurity *vis-à-vis* our friendly, albeit our much larger and more powerful neighbour, the United States. There is concern that as the position of American capital in the dynamic resource and manufacturing sectors becomes ever more dominant, our economy will inevitably become more and more integrated with that of the United States. Behind this is the fear that continuing integration might lead to economic domination by the United States and eventually to the loss of our political independence. This fear of domination by the United States affects to some extent the political climate of life in Canada today.

Royal Commission Report, 1957.[31]

By the late 1960s the prophets of doom were loudly trumpeting the takeover of our economy and warning that we had little time in which to act. One Canadian had earlier come to the conclusion that it was too late, that we had already succumbed to the economic, social, and political influence of the United States. In his book Lament for a

> Nation, *published in 1965, George Grant presented a most gloomy analysis of our destiny.*

All the preceding arguments point to the conclusion that Canada cannot survive as a sovereign nation. In the language of the new bureaucrats, our nation was not a viable entity. . . .

Canada has ceased to be a nation, but its formal political existence will not end quickly. Our social and economic blending into the empire will continue apace, but political union will probably be delayed. Some international catastrophe or great shift of power might speed up this process. Its slowness does not depend only on the fact that large numbers of Canadians do not want it, but also on sheer lethargy. Changes require decisions, and it is much easier for practising politicians to continue with traditional structures. The dominant forces in the Republic do not need to incorporate us. A branch-plant satellite, which has shown in the past that it will not insist on any difficulties in foreign or defence policy, is a pleasant arrangement for one's northern frontier. The pin-pricks of disagreement are a small price to pay. If the negotiations for union include Quebec, there will be strong elements in the United States that will dislike their admission. The kindest of all God's dispensations is that individuals cannot predict the future in detail. Nevertheless, the formal end of Canada may be prefaced by a period during which the government of the United States has to resist the strong desire of English-speaking Canadians to be annexed.[32]

> The day is going to come when people are going to say, "Why were you so stupid? Why did you give it all away?"
>
> Eric Kierans, 1973.[33]

> *The optimism is gone. We no longer view with heady enthusiasm a horizon full of opportunities as we did twenty years ago. It would not be fair to say that we are pessimistic about our destiny, but we have far more doubts and questions about where we are going. Newspaper editorials on July 1, 1972 reflected this hesitancy.*

How long ago it sometimes seems, that heady year of 1967 and its July 1 celebrations! That year of color and spectacle, music and laughter, when we dazzled the world with Expo—never mind the cost—and dazzled ourselves with dreaming of dreams become real. The old question of what is a Canadian had miraculously been answered, or at least we could almost put our finger on it. Even the cruel little newfie jokes were a sign (to some) that Canada had unearthed its own raucous vein of humor.

The dream began to dissolve in 1968, but then there was the new wonder boy of politics, a glass-of-water reintoxification of a champagne hangover. Pierre Elliott Trudeau, Canada's own distinctive revolution in democratic political style; the swinger, the all-round athlete; Trudeaumania as overture to the Just Society.

The awakening to dull, grey reality came soon enough; the old doubts and problems crowded back. The Centennial magic had not changed them much, and Mr. Trudeau in the trappings of a prime minister looked more and more like just another Liberal (though brighter than most) trying somewhat waspishly to cope.

And here we are in 1972, at the beginning of the sixth year of Canada's second century. The times seem very ordinary. Inflation is coming back, and unemployment is still with us. There are strikes and lockouts. Everything is taxed to distraction, and not even the best things in life are free. There will probably be a federal election sometime in the next few months, but the electoral choice so far fails to excite. . . .

The dreamers are gone with the dreams and perhaps that is a good thing when dreaming has been an escape from reality. . . .[34]

Canada's 105th birthday is, regrettably, no occasion to sound a note of satisfied and confident patriotism. That wouldn't be honest. Centennial euphoria is far behind us, and it is hard to see 1972 as one of Canada's triumphant years. The nation's birthday should be a day of questioning: How far have we come as a nation? How far are we likely to go?

The truth is that, after 105 years, we're still preoccupied—even, our critics say, obsessed—with the need to survive. The nation's endangered. Its unity is threatened from within. In the face of these challenges, we have done little more than mark time.[35]

The same uncertainty was expressed by other Canadians.

The fact of the matter is that social values are changing rapidly in Canada and the United States. Economic fluctuations have been so great, changes so great. Many people have been hit with so many uncertainities that everybody is worried.

There is a sort of fear syndrome going across the country.

John Munro, 1971.[36]

I do not feel proud to be a Canadian. I feel lucky. I enjoy the political and social freedoms, the living space, the opportunity and the affluence, and there's no place I'd rather be. But I fear that we are living in a Canadian golden age which will not last long: A small population occupying a vast territory in an overcrowded world, and digging wealth from the ground which in many countries won't even grow enough food....

So, while we are lucky to be Canadian, we have no great cause for national chest-thumping. The century does not belong to us and we do not have an appointment with destiny.

Anthony Westell, 1972.[37]

Where Do We Go from Here?

We remain now where we were one hundred and six years ago, a nation still in search of destiny. Granted that we are presently passing through a stage of disillusion, but surely we could begin again with fresh vigour and seek some remarkable achievement. Unfortunately, we have run short of models that we would want to, or could, imitate. In 1867 we had the United States and its exuberant nationalism as a model. Considering the crises the Americans are passing through these days, no Canadian would seriously suggest that we attempt to go their route. At any rate, nationalism is out of style in the modern world, or so we are told.

Perhaps we could gird ourselves for militaristic adventures and national expansion. This, too, seems out of the question. Our military preparedness would hardly allow such folly; there are very few people left to conquer; and we can do without additional ethnic groups in our multicultural domain.

We have wearied of the roles as World Saviour and Mediator which so excited us at mid-century.

It is quite possible that we are not really interested in the type of destiny made popular in the nineteenth and twentieth centuries. We may well be prepared to continue on with no spectacular achievement of greatness. Greatness certainly has eluded us so far and it is, after all, an embarrassing role, requiring more sacrifice than we are prepared to give. We may be satisfied to exist, to endure, to survive. This may be our unique destiny.

Already there are signs that we have survived the worst threats of *separatism, although it is possible that the movement has gone underground. In 1971 Pierre Vallières, author of* White Niggers of America *and prophet of the FLQ, publicly renounced the use of force in political movements and took a job in a government agency. Recent polls in Quebec suggest that separatism is not gaining ground. And in July 1972, a St. Jean Baptiste Day protest rally was dominated by a young woman stripped down to blue panties who made speeches in favour of women's rights. Even the shrill outcries against American takeover have begun to fade away, possibly as a result of overkill. In each case we may be experiencing the lull before a new storm, but the worst seems either to have passed or to have been pushed into the background.*

In October 1972, Prime Minister Trudeau offered his analysis of the Canadian mood.

The more I talk with Canadians, the more I am confirmed in my feeling that the great majority of them do indeed care about the land as a whole. They care not just about their own future but about the direction our whole society is moving.

Moreover I sense that their concern is not a gloomy, pessimistic one. They care about Canada's future, but they reveal an optimistic confidence that this country is heading for great things and that they are happy to be part of it.

We retain in this country the same sense of excitement and initiative that was so evident in frontier days. This is to me ample proof that Canadians share with me a great confidence in the future of Canada and a desire to participate in the same disciplined, yet hospitable and compassionate way as did their forebears on the frontiers of Canada in centuries past.[38]

Prime ministers are expected to make statements of this nature. Trudeau, however, found support in the cooly analytical British journal, The Economist.

This should be a time for optimism in Canada. Mistakes will occur; intricate balances between federal and provincial power will go wrong; the struggle in French Canada will continue; envy and mistrust of the American powerhouse will always be there. The difficulties in Canada certainly speak for themselves. But economic advance, more civilised living and cultural progress have been there to see over the years, and they will gather heightened pace in the future.[39]

> *"Mistakes will occur." The problems will continue. There will be no final solution to the difficulties which plague us, but we can outlast them. We are a stubborn people who can keep on going. Survival is our forte and our destiny.*

REFERENCES

References to Chapter One

1. Cited by Leslie F. Hannon in *Forts of Canada* (Toronto: McClelland & Stewart, Ltd., 1969), pp. 154-155.
2. *The United States and Canada as Seen by Two Brothers in 1858 and 1861* (London, 1862).
3. J.J. Rowan, *The Emigrant and Sportsman in Canada* (London: Edward Stanford, 1876), pp. 428-429.
4. Hector W. Charlesworth, "The Canadian Girl", in *The Canadian* Magazine Vol 1, (Ontario Publishing Co., 1893), pp. 186-193.
5. W.W. Mackerachen, "My Own Canadian Girl", in *Canada My Land* (Wm. Briggs, 1908), pp. 25, 26.
6. Cora Murciano from the Philippines, quoted in "As Immigrants See Us", in *The Toronto Star*, January 8, 1972.
7. Marta Lopez from Mexico, quoted in "As Immigrants See Us", in *The Toronto Star*, February 12, 1972.
8. Richard J. Needham, "I am looking for Mr. Right", in *The Globe and Mail*, November 24, 1971.
9. Michelle Bedard, *Canada in Bed* (Toronto: Pagurian Press Ltd., 1969) pp. 65, 66, 136, and 137.
10. Madeleine de Verchères, from Francis Parkman, *Count Frontenac and New France under Louis XIV* (Boston: Little, Brown & Co., 1903), pp. 318-323.
11. Mari-Lou MacDonald, "The Perils of Mari-Lou", by Peter Moon, in *The Canadian Magazine*, August 8, 1970, p. 8.
12. Bob Pennington, "Physical fitness study shows women stronger than men", in *The Toronto Star*, April 15, 1972.
13. Werner Hirschmann from Germany, quoted in "As Immigrants See Us", in *The Toronto Star*, April 1, 1972.
14. Ernest Watkins, *Prospects of Canada* (London: Secker & Warburg, 1954), pp. 223, 224.
15. *Sawney's Letters*, 1866, (Toronto Public Library), p. 11-12.
16. E.L. Chicanot, "Woman Hunger", *Homestead Rhymes*, (North York Public Library), p. 36, 37, 38.
17. Raymond Souster, "Summer's Girls", in *Uncollected Poems* (Toronto: Clarke, Irwin Ltd., 1968), p. 12.
18. Irving Layton, "Plea For My Lady" in *Nail Polish* (Toronto: McClelland & Stewart Ltd., 1971), pp. 42, 43.
19. Susanna Moodie, *Roughing It in the Bush* (Toronto: Hunter, Rose & Co. 1871.
20. Catharine Parr Traill, *The Backwoods of Canada* (London: M.A. Nattali, 1846).
21. Anthony Trollope, *North America*, Vol. 1, (Leipzig, 1862), pp. 112-113.
22. George Tuthill Barrett, *Out West*, (1866), pp. 23, 45 and 46.
23. Alexander McLachlan, *The Poetical Works of Alexander McLachlan*, (Toronto: William Briggs, 1900), pp. 208-209.
24. Leslie F. Hannon, *Canada At War*, (Toronto: McClelland & Stewart Ltd., 1968), p. 31.
25. LaVerne Barnes, *The Plastic Orgasm*, (Toronto: McClelland & Stewart Ltd., 1971), pp. 17, 79.
26. *The Sun* (Toronto), October 5, 1972.
27. *The Globe and Mail*, May 1, 1972.
28. "What, Me Work?", by Alan Edmonds, in *The Canadian Magazine*, March 3, 1973, p. 8.

29.   Prime Minister Trudeau, quoted in *The Toronto Star*, March 13, 1972, and March 14, 1972.
30.   W. Kilbourn, *A Guide to The Peaceable Kingdom*, (Toronto: Macmillan Co. of Canada, 1970), p. xv.
31.   James Dixon, *Personal Narrative of a Tour Through a Part of the U.S. and Canada* (1849), pp. 166-167.
32.   Anthony Trollope, *North America*, pp. 69, 71, 72.
33.   J. MacCormac, *Canada—America's Problem* (New York: Viking Press, 1940), pp. 153-154.
34.   Cited in "What Americans Really Think of Us", by Shirley Moir, in *Macleans Magazine*, April 20, 1963, pp. 51, 53.
35.   Anne Merriman Peck, *The Pageant of Canadian History*, (David McKay, 1963), p. 361.
36.   K. Naegele, in *Canadian Society*, first edition (Toronto: Macmillan Co. of Canada, 1961), p. 27.
37.   *Canadian Sport Monthly*, Volume XL, June 1952, p. 7.
38.   *The Globe and Mail*, February 10, 1972.
39.   Prime Minister Trudeau, *The Toronto Star*, October 14, 1972.
40.   *The Toronto Star*, February 12, 1972.
41.   Hugh MacLennan, *Two Solitudes*, (Collins, 1945), pp. 90, 91 and 92.
42.   "I sacrificed pleasure in order to make what I have", by Dr. Daniel Cappon, in *The Toronto Star*, November 10, 1971.
43.   N. K. Dhalla, *These Canadians*, (Toronto: McGraw-Hill, 1966), pp. 166-167.
44.   Robert Fulford, *Crisis at the Victory Burlesk*, (Toronto: Oxford University Press, 1968), pp. 176, 177, 178, and 179.
45.   B. R. Myers, *North of the Border*, (Vantage Press, 1963), p. 49.
46.   Bruce Hutchison, "The Canadian Personality", in *Our Sense of Identity*, ed. Malcolm Ross (Toronto: Ryerson Press, 1954), pp. 42, 43.
47.   B. Richardson, *Canada and Mr. Diefenbaker*, (Toronto: McClelland & Stewart Ltd., 1962), p. 110.
48.   F. Alexander, *Canadians and Foreign Policy* (Toronto: University of Toronto Press, 1960), p. 121.
49.   Robertson Davies, *Marchbank's Almanack*, (Toronto: McClelland & Stewart Ltd., 1967), p. 172.

References to Chapter Two

1.   "Brock" by Charles Sangster, from *Hesperus, and Other Poems and Lyrics*, (1860), found in *Songs of the Great Dominion*, selected and edited by William D. Lighthall, (London: Walter Scott, 1889), p. 254.
2.   George T. Denison, in *The Struggle for Imperioal Unity*, 1909, quoted in Frank Underhill *The Image of Confederation*, (Toronto: CBC Publication, 1963), p. 15.
3.   An address by William Foster, published in 1871; quoted in W. A. Foster, *Canada First*, (Toronto: Hunter Rose, 1890), p. 25.
4.   Robert Haliburton, from his speech on "The Young Men of the New Dominion", reprinted in the *Ottawa Citizen*, January 27, 1870.
5.   W. A. Foster, *Canada First*, pp. 48, 49, 50 and 52.
6.   Address by Rev. W. D. Reid, Montreal, "The Non-Anglo-Saxons in Canada—Their Christianization and Nationalization", *Pre-Assembly Congress of the Presbyterian Church*

in Canada (Toronto, 1913), pp. 119-126.

7. Rupert Brooke, *Letter From America*, (Toronto: McClelland, Goodchild, and Stewart Ltd., 1916), pp. 111, 112.

8. Andrew Macphail, "The Immigrant", *Canadian Club Year Book, 1919-1920*, (Ottawa, 1920), p. 171.

9. *Dominion Illustrated: A Canadian Pictorial Weekly*, (April 11, 1891), p. 338.

10. "Canadianizing the Newcomer", in *The Canadian Courier*, February, 1914.

11. Emily P. Weaver, *Canada and the British Immigrant*, (London: The Religious Tract Society, 1914), p. 245, 246.

12. C. J. Cameron, *Foreigners or Canadians*, (Standard Publishing Co., 1913), p. 25.

13. Howard Angus Kennedy, *New Canada and New Canadians* (Horace Marshall & Sons, 1907), pp. 108, 109, 110.

14. W. L. Mackenzie King; report in *Sessional Paper No. 36a*, 1908, pp. 7, 8.

15. K. A. Foster, *Our Canadian Mosaic*, (Dominion Council, Y.W.C.A., 1926), p. 18.

16. Titles from *Maclean's* Magazine articles. In order of listings: October 1921; May 1922; May 1933; June 1930; February 1930.

17. *Lord Durham's Report*, ed. Gerald M. Craig (Toronto: McClelland & Stewart Ltd. 1963), pp. 146-151.

18. H. Langevin, *Confederation Debates*, February 21, 1865, pp. 362-92.

19. George Cartier, *Confederation Debates*, February 7, 1865, pp. 53-62.

20. Abbé Groulx, *Soirées de l'Action française*, (Montreal, 1926), pp. 7-9; quoted in Mason Wade, *The French Canadians 1860-1967*, Vol. II, (Toronto: Macmillan Co. of Canada, 1968), pp. 869-870.

21. Henri Bourassa, *le 5e Anniversaire du Devoir* (Montreal (1916), pp. 58-59.

22. J. O. Pelland, ed., *Biographie, discours, conferences, etc., de l'Honorable Honoré Mercier* (Montreal, 1890), pp. 689-691; translation in K. A. MacKirdy, J. S. Moir, and Y. F. Zoltvany, *Changing Perspectives in Canadian History* (Don Mills: J. M. Dent & Sons, 1967), p. 243.

23. J. P. Tardivel, in *La Vérité*, May 15, 1904; translation in *Changing Perspectives in Canadian History*, p. 239.

24. Henri Bourassa, *Pour La Justice* (Montreal, 1912), p. 30; quoted in Mason Wade, *The French Canadians 1860-1967*, Vol. II, pp. 618-619.

25. Abbé Groulx, *L'Action Française VI*, December 1921, p. 706; quoted in Mason Wade, *The French Canadians 1860-1967*, Vol. II, p. 879.

26. *La Presse*, February 20, 1918.

27. Henri Bourassa, during his debate with J. P. Tardivel, from *Le Nationaliste*, April 3, 1904; quoted in Mason Wade, *The French Canadians 1860-1967*, Vol. II, pp. 524-525.

28. J. O. Pelland, ed., *Biographie, discours, conferences, etc., de l'Honorable Honoré Mercier*, (Montreal, 1890), pp. 689-91; translation in *Changing Perspectives in Canadian History*, p. 243.

29. Henri Bourassa, *le 5th Anniversaire du Devoir* (Montreal, 1915), pp. 67, 68.

30. Israel Tarte to Willison, November 28, 1900, in *Willison Papers*, quoted in R. C. Brown and M. E. Prang, eds., *Confederation to 1949*, (Toronto: Prentice-Hall, 1966), p. 121.

31. Oliver Mowat, February 18, 1891, in G. T. Denison, *The Struggle For Imperial Unity* (Toronto: Macmillan Co. of Canada, 1909), pp. 186, 187.

32. André Siegfried, *Canada* (London: Jonathan Cape, 1937), pp. 231, 232, 233.

33. "The Canadian", poem by J. E. Middleton, in *The Ontario Readers Third Book*. (Facsimile edition reprinted by Coles Pub. Co., Toronto, 1971), p. 169.

34. "Canada Speaks of Britain", poem by Charles G. D. Roberts, in *Voices of Victory* (Toronto: The Ryerson Press) p. xi.
35. *Canada—America's Problem,* by John MacCormac (New York: The Viking Press, 1940), p. 127.
36. Vincent Massey, *Speaking of Canada* (Toronto: Macmillan Co. of Canada, 1959), p. 35.
37. Sidney Smith, in Joseph Kirschbaum, *Slovaks in Canada* (Canadian Ethnic Press Association of Ontario, 1967), p. 315.
38. W. L. Morton, *The Canadian Identity,* (Toronto: University of Toronto Press, 1961), p. 85.
39. Hugh Hood, "Moral Imagination: Canadian Thing", in *The Toronto Daily Star,* December 9, 1967.
40. A. R. M. Lower, *Canadians in the Making* (Toronto: Longmans, 1958) p. 377.
41. "The Maple Leaf Forever", by Alexander Muir, 1867; quoted in Robert M. Hamilton, *Canadian Quotations and Phrases* (Toronto: McClelland & Stewart Ltd., 1952), p. 132.
42. Arthur Hawkes, *The Birthright* (Toronto: J. M. Dent & Sons, 1914), pp. 185, 186.
43. Jean-C. Farlardeau, *Roots and Values in Canadian Lives,* Alan B. Plaunt Memorial Lectures (University of Toronto, 1961), pp. 19, 20, 21.
44. E. G. Nelson, from G. T. Denison, *The Struggle For Imperial Unity,* p. 157.
45. Poem by Lesperance, in G. T. Denison, *The Struggle For Imperial Unity,* p. 151.
46. "The Colours of the Flag", by Frederick George Scott, in *Ontario Teachers' Manual, History* (Toronto: Copp, Clark, 1915), p. 74.
47. "The Union Jack", in *Ontario Teachers' Manual, History,* p. 74, 75.
48. T. S. Ewart, *A Flag for Canada* (Ottawa, 1947), pp. 2, 3.
49. Eric Nicol, *Shall We Join The Ladies* (Toronto: The Ryerson Press, 1955), pp. 86, 87, 88.
50. Bruce Hutchison, *Canada: Tomorrow's Giant* (Toronto: Longmans, Green & Co., 1957), pp. 3, 4, 5.
51. Lester B. Pearson, *Words and Occasions* (Toronto: University of Toronto Press, 1970), pp. 229, 230, 232.
52. Cited in Peter C. Newman, *The Distemper of Our Times* (Toronto: McClelland & Stewart, Ltd., 1968), p. 238.
53. *Ibid.,* p. 239.
54. Lester B. Pearson, *Words And Occasions,* p. 244.
55. Richard Gwyn, *Smallwood, the unlikely revolutionary* (Toronto: McClelland & Stewart Ltd. 1968), p. 228.
56. *A Preliminary Report of the Royal Commission on Bilingualism and Biculturalism* (Ottawa: Queen's Printer, 1965), p. 133.
57. *Report of the Royal Commission on Bilingualism and Biculturalism* (Ottawa: Queen's Printer, 1968), p. 7.
58. *A Preliminary Report of the Royal Commission on Bilingualism and Biculturalism,* pp. 138, 139.
59. *Report of Royal Commission on Bilingualism and Biculturalism,* Book I, pp. 147, 148.
60. Joseph R. Smallwood, *Peril and Glory* (Keswick, Ontario: High Hill Publishing House, 1966), p. 35.
61. Prime Minister Trudeau, in *The Globe and Mail,* Toronto, July 20, 1972.
62. A civil servant's letter to Douglas Fisher, in "B and B isn't working but is it bigotry?", in *The Sun* (Toronto), April 12, 1972.
63. Prime Minister Trudeau, quoted in *The Toronto Star,* October 23, 1972.

378 THE CANADIAN STYLE

64. *A Preliminary Report of the Royal Commission on Bilingualism and Biculturalism*, p. 51; (Presentation at a preliminary hearing in Ottawa).
65. *Ibid.*, p. 46. (An English-speaking participant's rejection of concept of "equal partnership").
66. *Ibid.*, p. 51.
67. William Boleslaus Makowski, *History and Integration of Poles in Canada* (The Canadian Polish Congress, Niagara Peninsula, 1967), p. 229.
68. *A Preliminary Report of the Royal Commission on Bilingualism and Biculturalism*, p. 49, 50; (Indian chief's comments to Indian Advisory Committee of the Ontario Department of Public Welfare).
69. Walter Currie, *The Toronto Star*, January 4, 1972.
70. Chief John Albany, in *The Way of The Indian* (Toronto, CBC Publications) p. 58.
71. Alex Jamieson, *The Globe and Mail*, Toronto, January 13, 1971.
72. Federal Government's Response to Book IV of the Report of the Royal Commission on Bilingualism and Biculturalism, found in *House of Commons Debates*, October 8, 1971, p. 8580.

References to Chapter Three

1.   Henri Bourassa (Canadian Club, Toronto, January 22, 1907).
2.   Rupert Brooke, *Letters From America* (Toronto: McClelland & Stewart, Ltd., 1916), pp. 102, 103.
3.   Wyndham Lewis, *The Letters of Wyndham Lewis*, ed. W. K. Rose (London: Methuen, 1941), p. 288.
4.   Robert Fulford, in "As a People, We Don't Like Each Other Much", in *Saturday Night*, July, 1971, p. 7.
5.   Jack Davis, "What do Western Liberals Want?" in *The Globe and Mail*, Toronto, December 21, 1971.
6.   Harold Fishleigh, MP, Toronto, reported in *The Toronto Star*, November 25, 1955.
7.   *The Toronto Star*, November 24, 1956.
8.   *The Toronto Star*, November 25, 1952.
9.   Stephen Leacock, *My Discovery of the West* (Thomas Allen, 1957), pp. 55, 56.
10. Owen Anderson in *The Unfinished Revolt*, edited by John Barr and Owen Anderson (Toronto: McClelland & Stewart Ltd., 1971), p. 59.
11. Peter Desbarats, "The West's shocking hate for the East", in *The Toronto Star*, November 23, 1971.
12. John J. Barr, "Beyond Bitterness", in *The Unfinished Revolt*, pp. 16, 17.
13. Peter Desbarats, "Western Canada says: "Let Quebec Go", in *The Toronto Star*, Nobember 30, 1971.
14. Peter Desbarats, in "Prairie separatism is alive but faltering", *The Toronto Star*, November 9, 1971.
15. Solange Chaput-Rolland, *My Country, Canada or Quebec?* (Toronto: Macmillan Co. of Canada, 1966), pp. 86, 87.
16. *The Globe and Mail*, Toronto, November 24, 1971.
17. Letter to the editor, in *Saturday Night*, March, 1972.
18. A brief from the Winnipeg Producers Association Branch of the CBC, in *The Globe and Mail*, Toronto, February 21, 1973.
19. Don Williams, alternate director of the Winnipeg Producers Association, of the CBC, in *The Toronto Star*, February 21, 1973.

20.   *The Toronto Star*, January 25, 1973.
21.   *The Globe and Mail*, Toronto, January 20, 1973.
22.   *The Toronto Star*, February 5, 1973.
23.   *The Toronto Star*, February 24, 1973.
24.   Prime Minister Trudeau, *The Toronto Star*, February 17, 1973.
25.   John Sebastian Helmcken, March 9, 1870, quoted in *British Columbia: A Centennial Anthology*, edited by Reginald Eyre Watters (Toronto: McClelland & Stewart Ltd., 1958), p. 17.
26.   Joseph D. Pemberton, Letter to the *British Colonist*, Victoria, B.C. 1870.
27.   James Cappon, *Queen's Quarterly*, Vol. XIX, 1911.
28.   Douglas Sladen, *On the Cars and Off* (London: Ward, Lock, Borden Ltd., 1895), p. 395.
29.   Solange Chaput-Rolland, *My Country, Canada or Quebec?*, pp. 56, 57.
30.   Bruce Hutchison, in *The Unknown Country* (Toronto: Longmans, Green & Co., 1948), pp. 264, 265.
31.   *The Sun* (Toronto), November 5, 1972.
32.   The Toronto *Globe*, December 27, 1861.
33.   Editorial in Toronto *Evening News*, April 20, 1885.
34.   *The Week*, July 16, 1885; cited in A.R.M. Lower, *Canadians in the Making*, (Toronto: Longman's Co., 1958), p. 300.
35.   Israel Tarte, cited in *The Apprenticeship*, by Laurier LaPierre, (CBC, 1967), p. 40.
36.   Marcel Chaput, *Why I Am A Separatist* (Toronto: Ryerson Press, 1962), pp. 28, 29.
37.   Ann Charney, "Many Quebeckers say vote was anti-French", in *The Toronto Star*, November 4, 1972.
38.   Maurice Lamontagne, cited in *The Toronto Star*, November 4, 1972.
39.   Jim Proudfoot, "Thanks, Montreal but no thanks", in *The Toronto Star*, February 6, 1973.
40.   Joseph Howe, speech in Nova Scotia, cited in J. M. Grant, *Joseph Howe* (Halifax, 1906), p. 2.
41.   E. Wilson, *O Canada*, (New York: Farrar, Straus, Giroux, 1964), pp. 42, 43.
42.   George Rawlyk, "Nova Scotia Regional Protest, 1867-1967", *Queen's Quarterly*, LXXV, No. 1, (Spring, 1968).
43.   Isabella Moore, cited in Luella Creighton, *The Elegant Canadians*, (Toronto: McClelland & Stewart Ltd., 1967).
44.   The Chatham *Gleaner*, New Brunswick, September 3, 1864.
45.   The Charlottetown *Islander*, January 6, 1865.
46.   *Eastern Chronicle*, New Glasgow, July 3, 1867.
47.   *Eastern Chronicle*, New Glasgow, April 26, 1866.
48.   Andrew R. Wetmore, N.B. election speech, March, 1865; quoted in *Genesis of a Nation*, ed. Laurier LaPierre (Toronto: CBC Publications 1967), p. 117.
49.   Joseph Howe, in *The Novascotian*, Halifax, August 13, 1866.
50.   Dr. E. L. Brown, Nova Scotia, in *Debates and Proceedings of the House of Assembly* (Halifax, 1871), pp. 162, 163.
51.   Halifax *Morning Chronicle*, 1886, cited in Donald Creighton, *Dominion of the North* (Boston: Houghton Mifflin, 1944), pp. 356, 357.
52.   W. S. Fielding, Liberal premier of Nova Scotia, in "Repeal Resolution", reported in Nova Scotia Assembly *Journal, 1886* (May 8, 1886) pp. 47, 49.
53.   H. W. Corning, reported in *Halifax Herald*, April 23, 1923.

54.   Premier Louis Robichaud of New Brunswick, from the *Constitutional Conference Proceedings*, Second Meeting, Ottawa, February 10-12, 1969.
55.   Premier Smallwood, from the *Constitutional Conference Proceedings*, Second Meeting, Ottawa, February 10-12, 1969.
56.   *House of Commons Debates*, February 25, 1972, p. 294.
57.   *The Toronto Star*, June 14, 1972.
58.   A Brief presented by the Atlantic Provinces Economic Council, cited in *The Toronto Star*, June 14, 1972.
59.   Gerald Stanley Doyle, cited in Edith Fowke, Alan Mills, and Helmut Blume, *Canada's Story in Song* (Toronto, 1960), pp. 106, 107.
60.   Laurier LaPierre, *The Apprenticeship*, p. 3.
61.   Newfoundland House of Assemblies, 1870, cited in Toronto *Weekly Globe*, February 25, 1870.
62.   Ballad composed by Responsible Government League, 1948.
63.   Poem by Albert Perlin, April 1, 1949, cited by Richard Gwyn in *Smallwood, the unlikely revolutionary* (Toronto: McClelland & Stewart Ltd., 1968), pp. 120, 121.
64.   Dorothy Henderson, *The Heart of Newfoundland* (Harvest House Press), pp. 62, 63.
65.   Solange Chaput-Rolland, in *My Country, Canada or Quebec?*, p. 95.
66.   "Bound for Canada" in *The Book of Newfoundland*, material collected and edited by Joseph Smallwood, 1936.
67.   E. J. Pratt, "Memories of Newfoundland", in *The Book of Newfoundland*.
68.   Songs by Roy Payne and Judy Krytuik, from "Goofy Newfies" (Toronto: Crown-Vetch Music Ltd.).

References to Chapter Four

1.   Bruce Hutchison, in *Canada Tomorrow's Giant* (Toronto: Longmans, Green & Co., 1957), p. 59.
2.   Arthur R. M. Lower, in *Colony to Nation* (Toronto: Longmans, Green & Co. 1946).
3.   Dick Diespecker, *Between Two Furious Oceans* (Toronto: Oxford University Press).
4.   overnor General Dufferin, quoted in *History of the Administration of the Earl of Dufferin in Canada* (Toronto: William Leggo, 1878), p. 599.
5.   Charles Mair, quoted in *Homes for the Millions: The Great Canadian North-West*, edited by N. F. Davin (Ottawa, 1891), p. 11.
6.   Dr. William Osler, "Anglo-Canadian and American Relations", *Addresses delivered before the Canadian Club of Toronto Season 1904-1905* (Toronto), p. 65.
7.   John J. Rowan, *The Emigrant and Sportsman in Canada* (London: Edward Stanford, 1876), p. 49.
8.   R. G. Haliburton, *The Men of the North and Their Place in History: A Lecture delivered before the Montreal Literary Club, March 31st, 1869* (Montreal, 1869).
9.   John C. Parkin, "Blueprint for the nation: build for a Canadian image", in *The Globe and Mail*, Toronto, May 3, 1971.
10.   Prime Minister Trudeau, excerpts from a speech delivered at the National Newspaper Awards Dinner in Toronto; quoted in *The Globe and Mail*, Toronto, April 10, 1972.
11.   Lawren Harris, "The Group of Seven in Canadian History", Canadian Historical Association *Report*, 1948, pp. 30 and 32.
12.   Emily Carr, *Hundreds and Thousands, Journal of Emily Carr* (Toronto: Clarke, Irwin, 1966), pp. 6 and 7.

13. *Ibid.*, p. 31.

15. Robert Fulford, "The Authentic voice of Canada", in *Crisis at the Victory Burlesk* (Toronto: Oxford University Press, 1968), pp. 190, 191, 192 and 193.

15. André Siegfried, quoted in *Time*, August 29, 1969.

16. Comock, *The Story of Comock the Eskimo*, as told to Robert Flaherty, edited by Edmund Carpenter (New York: Simon & Schuster, Inc., 1968), pp. 22, 24 and 25.

17. Nuligak, in *I. Nuligak*, edited and translated by Maurice Metayer (Toronto: Peter Martin Associates Limited, 1966), pp. 16, 17 and 20.

18. Robert W. Service, "The Law Of The Yukon", in *Songs of a Sourdough* (Toronto: The Ryerson Press, 1907), p. 11.

19. J.C. Critchell-Bullock, quoted in George Whalley, *The Legend of John Hornby* (Toronto: Macmillan of Canada, 1962), pp. 210, 211.

20. Farley Mowat, *Canada North* (Toronto: McClelland & Stewart Ltd., 1967), p. 6 and 7.

21. Al Purdy, "Eskimo Hunter (New Style)", *North of Summer* (Toronto: McClelland & Stewart Ltd., 1967), p. 57.

22. A. J. M. Smith, "The Lonely Land", *News of the Phoenix and Other Poems* (Toronto: The Ryerson Press, 1943).

23. Herbert T. Schwarz, *Windigo and Other Tales of the Ojibways* (Toronto: McClelland & Stewart Ltd., 1969), p. 11.

24. Fathers Drusilletes and Dablon, in *Jesuit Relations*, Volume 46, editor R. G. Thwaites (Cleveland: Burrows Bros., 1897), pp. 263, 265.

25. Ruth Landes, *The Ojibway Woman* (New York: W. W. Norton & Co., Inc. 1971), p. 221.

26. P.F.X. de Charlevoix, *Journal of a Voyage to North America* (London, 1761), Volume 1, pp. 111-114.

27. Marquis de Denonville to the Minister, 13 November 1685, *Public Archives of Canada*, *Archives des Colonies, Serie*, C11 A, M.G. 1/3, Vol. 7, pp. 44-45, (translation).

28. Alexander Ross, *The Fur Hunters of the Far West* (London, 1855), Vol. 11, pp. 236, 237.

29. B. K. Sandwell, *The Privacity Agent* (Toronto: J. M. Dent & Sons).

30. Hugh Lorren, in *Weekend Magazine*, May 6, 1971.

31. Sir Francis Butler, *The Wild North Land* (Musson Peade Co., 1924, orginally published 1873), p. 50.

32. Gabriel Franchère, *Narrative of a Voyage to the Northwest Coast of America in the Years 1811, 1812, 1813, and 1814*, or, *The First American Settlement on the Pacific*, translated and edited by J. V. Huntington (New York, 1854), pp. 321, 324.

33. John Kerr, quoted by Constance Kerr Sissons in *Kerr's Journal*, in *A Book of Canada*, edited by William Toye (Toronto: Collins Sons and Co. Ltd., 1962), pp. 288, 289.

34. John McDougall, *Pathfinding on Plain and Prairie*, (Toronto: Wm. Briggs 1898), pp. 17, 18.

35. Frank Roberts, quoted by Sarah Ellen Roberts, in *Of Us and the Oxen* (Saskatoon: Modern Press, 1968), pp. 192, 193 and 196.

36. Thomas Wilby, *A Motor Tour Through Canada* (Toronto: Bell and Cockburn, 1914), p. 157.

37. James H. Gray, *The Winter Years* (Toronto: Macmillan Co. of Canada, 1966), pp. 106, 107, 108.

38. *Ibid.*, pp. 110, 111.

39. A farmer near Hann, Alberta, quoted in *Next-Year Country, A Study of Rural Social Organization in Alberta* (Toronto: University of Toronto Press, 1951), pp. 6 and 7.

40. Anne Marriott, *The Wind Our Enemy* (Toronto: The Ryerson Press, 1939), pp. 2 and 3.

41. Pierre Charlevoix, *Journal of a Voyage to North America*, found in *A Book of Canada*, edited by William Toye, p. 269.

42. Lathrop Roberts, quoted in *Of Us and the Oxen*, pp. 97, 98.

43. Pierre Trottier, cited "Return to Winter", from *Mon Babel* (Montreal: Editions HMH, 1963), in *Canada: A Guide To The Peaceable Kingdom*, ed. William Kilbourn (Toronto: Macmillan Co. of Canada, 1970), pp. 82, 83.

44. Reverend D. V. Lucas, *All About Canada* (Montreal: Witness Printing House, 1882), p. 18.

45. Sara Jeanette Duncan, "Saunterings (Montreal in Carnival)", in *The Week*, Volume IV, 1887.

46. G. M. Fairchild, *My Quebec Scrap-Book* (Frank Carrel, 1907), p. 79, 80.

47. J. Peat Young, *A Newcomer In Canada* (Cecil Palmer Pub., 1924), pp. 133, 135.

48. Thomas Conant, *Life In Canada* (Toronto: Wm. Briggs, 1903), pp. 266, 267.

49. Scott Young, "Galoshes!" in *The Globe and Mail*, March 24, 1972.

50. Alden A. Nowlan, *Under the Ice* (Toronto: Ryerson Press, 1961).

51. Dorothy Livesay, "Winter" cited in *A Pocketful of Canada*, ed. John D. Robins (Toronto: Collins Sons & Co., (1948), p. 121.

52. Marjorie Pickthall, "Snow in April", from *The Complete Poems of Marjorie Pickthall* (Toronto: McClelland & Stewart Ltd., 1925).

53. Mordecai Richler, *Son of a Smaller Hero* (New York: Paperback Library, Inc. 1965), pp. 145-147.

References to Chapter Five

1. *The Toronto Star*, December 18, 1971.

2. Charles Durand, in *Reminiscences of Charles Durand* (Toronto: Hunter, Rose, & Co., 1897), p. 118, 119.

3. Baron Lahontan, in *Lahontan's Voyages*, ed. S. Leacock (Ottawa: Graphic Publishers, 1932), p. 34.

4. G. F. Hayter, *History of Methodism in Canada* (Toronto, 1862), p. 50.

5. *The Pioneers of Old Ontario*, ed. W. L. Smith (Toronto: G. N. Morang, 1923), p. 313.

6. W. J. Rattray, *The Scot in British North America* (Toronto: Maclean & Co., 1880-1883).

7. Ernest Watkins, *Prospect of Canada* (London: Secker & Warburg, 1954), p. 222.

8. Edmund Wilson, *O Canada* (New York; Farrar, Straus, Giroux, 1964), p. 107.

9. John Charlton, *Speeches and Addresses* (Moran & Co., 1905), p. 259.

10. Cited in Nish and Harvey, *The Social Structures of New France* (Toronto: Copp Clark, 1968).

11. W. L. Mackenzie, *Ordinances of the City of Toronto, 1834* (North York Public Library).

12. *Regina Standard*, September 24, 1903.

13. James H. Gray, *Red Lights on the Prairies* (Toronto: Macmillan Co. of Canada, 1971), p. 5.

14. John Charlton, *Speeches and Addresses*, p. 268.

15. Rev. W. A. Mackay, in *Zorra Boys at Home or How to Succeed* (Toronto: Wm. Briggs 1900), pp. 12, 13.

16. Lister Sinclair, quoted in W. R. T. Allen, *A Treasury of Canadian Humour* (Toronto: McClelland & Stewart Ltd.) p. 82.

17. Bruce West, *The Globe and Mail*, Toronto, June 1, 1971.

18. *The Toronto Star*, April 22, 1972.

19. H. C. Cox, *Oh, Canada* (Ilfracombe, Devon: H. Stockwell, Ltd. 1966) pp. 14, 15.

20. Thomas Conant, *Life In Canada* (Toronto: Wm. Briggs, 1903), p. 83.

21. John Kenneth Galbraith, *The Scotch* (Toronto: Macmillan Co. of Can., 1964), pp. 119, 120.

22. W. L. Smith, ed., *The Pioneers of Old Ontario* (Toronto: G. N. Morang, 1923), pp. 291, 292 and 293).

23. Goldwin Smith, *Canada And The Canadian Question*, (Toronto: Hunter, Rose & Co. 1891), p. 26.

24. Peter O'Leary, *Travels and Experiences in Canada, in the Red River Territory and the United States* (London: John B. Day, 1897).

25. Edward Roper, *By Track and Trail* (London: W. H. Allen & Co., 1891), p. 256.

26. L. A. MacKay, quoted in *The Blasted Pine*, ed. F. R. Scott and A. J. M. Smith (Toronto: Macmillan Co. of Canada, 1957), pp. 22, 23.

27. Edmund Wilson, *O Canada*, p. 39.

28. Robert Fulford, *The Toronto Star*, December 4, 1971.

29. John Kenneth Galbraith, *The Scotch*, pp. 24, 25, 26.

30. Roch Carrier, *La Guerre, Yes Sir!* (Toronto: The House of Anansi, 1970), pp. 31, 32.

31. T. Raddall, *Halifax, Warden of the North* (New York: Doubleday and Co., 1965), pp. 150, 151.

32. James H. Gray, *Red Lights on the Prairies*, pp. 11, 12, 50, 51.

33. *The Toronto Star*, November 26, 1948.

34. Bob Hesketh, *Saturday Night*, November 22, 1958.

35. *The Toronto Star*, November 29, 1954.

36. *The Toronto Star*, November 23, 1956.

37. *The Globe and Mail*, Toronto, November 30, 1959.

38. *The Toronto Star*, November 26, 1965.

39. *The Globe and Mail*, Toronto, November 30, 1970.

40. *The Toronto Star*, November 26, 1971.

41. *The Globe and Mail*, Toronto, November 27, 1971.

42. Lady Aberdeen in *The Journal of Lady Aberdeen, 1893-8*, ed. Saywell, (Toronto: Champlain Society, 1960), pp. 60, 61.

43. Remark attributed to Conn Smythe.

44. Stan Obodiac, Publicity Director, Maple Leaf Gardens, *The Toronto Telegram*, June 7, 1970.

45. Henry Roxborough, *The Stanley Cup Story* (Toronto: Ryerson Press, 1965), p. 109.

46. Andy O'Brien, *Fire-Wagon Hockey* (Toronto: Ryerson Press, 1967), pp. 64, 65.

47. Foster Hewitt, *Hockey Night in Canada* (Toronto: Ryerson Press, 1961).

48. *The Globe Magazine*, September 21, 1968.

49. *Canadian Magazine*, April 19, 1969.

50. *The Globe and Mail*, Toronto, January 8, 1972.

51. *House of Commons Debates*, April 21, 1972, p. 1518.

52.   *The Toronto Star*, September 2, 1972.
53.   *The Globe and Mail*, Toronto, October 2, 1972.
54.   *The Toronto Star*, October 2, 1972.
55.   *Ibid.*
56.   *The Globe and Mail*, October 2, 1972.

References to Chapter Six

1.   ·Frank Underhill, *In Search of Canadian Liberalism* (Toronto: Macmillan Co. of Canada, 1960), p. 12.
2.   Claude Bissell, (from an address delivered at the Canadian Studies Seminar, University of Rochester, March 16, 1962), cited in *Canadian Society*, eds. Blishen, Jones, Naegele, Porter (Toronto: Macmillan Co. of Canada, 1962), p. 479.
3.   James Cross, reported in *The Globe and Mail*, Thursday, December 10, 1970, from a CBC tape transcript.
4.   FLQ Communique, October 6, 1970, in John Saywell, *Quebec 70* (Toronto: University of Toronto Press, 1971), p. 37, 38.
5.   FLQ Chenier Cell Communique, Sunday, October 11, 1970, cited in *Quebec 70*, p. 58.
6.   CBC Special News Report, Tuesday, October 13, 1970.
7.   Prime Minister Trudeau's message to the nation, Friday, October 16, 1970, reported in *The Toronto Telegram*, October 17, 1970.
8.   Hon. T. C. Douglas, *House of Commons Debates*, October 16, 1970.
9.   Hon. John Diefenbaker, *ibid.*
10.   Hon. David Lewis, *ibid.*
11.   Hand written message found outside the concert hall at Place des Arts, Saturday night in downtown Montreal, October 17, cited in *The Globe and Mail*, October 19, 1970.
12.   Réné Levesque, Sunday, October 18, 1970, in *The Globe and Mail*, October 19, 1970.
13.   John Diefenbaker, Sunday, October 18, 1970, in *The Globe and Mail*, October 19, 1970.
14.   Prime Minister Trudeau, Sunday October 18, 1970, in *The Globe and Mail*, October 19, 1970.
15.   Premier Robert Bourassa, Sunday, October 18, 1970, text of broadcast reported in *The Globe and Mail*, Monday, October 19, 1970.
16.   Bill Trent, *Weekend Magazine*, November 21, 1970.
17.   Barry Callaghan, *The Toronto Telegram*, March 27, 1971.
18.   Ron Haggart, *The Toronto Telegram*, October 8, 1971.
19.   William Lyon Mackenzie, Broadside delivered November 27, 1837, (Toronto Public Library).
20.   Thomas Sheppård, a rebel, cited in *Old Toronto*, ed. E. C. Kyte (Toronto: Macmillan Co. of Canada, 1954), pp. 115-117.
21.   *The Patriot*, Toronto, January 2, 1838.
22.   *Ibid.*
23.   Joseph Papineau's speech during the debates of 1835, cited in *Genesis of a Nation*, Laurier LaPierre, (Toronto: CBC Publications, 1967), p. 53.
24.   Major-General Sir George Bell, *Soldier's Glory, Being Rough Notes of an Old Soldier* (London: G. Bell & Sons Ltd., 1956), p. 160-162.

25. John Ryerson, 1838, in C. B. Sissons, *Egerton Ryerson, His Life and Times* (Toronto, 2 vols., 1937, 1947), Volume I, pp. 445-448.
26. *Les Patriotes de 1837-1838*, L-O David (Montreal: Eusebe Senecal et Fils), p. 201.
27. Donald A. Smith, "Report on The Mission to Red River", *Toronto Daily Leader*, April 29, 1870.
28. Colonel Samuel Benton Steele, *Forty Years in Canada* (Toronto: McClelland & Stewart Ltd. 1915), p. 35.
29. Mrs. Delaney, survivor of Frog Lake Massacre, cited in C. P. Mulvaney, *The North-West Rebellion of 1885* (A. H. Hovey & Co., 1885), p. 401-404.
30. Eyewitness account of the Battle of Batoche, cited in *The North-West Rebellion of 1885*, p. 217-218.
31. *L'Electeur*, June 25, 1885.
32. *Toronto Evening News*, April 20, 1885.
33. Wilfrid Laurier, *House of Commons Debates*, March 16, 1886.
34. Arthur R. M. Lower, *Colony to Nation* (Toronto: Longmans, 1946), p. 243.
35. *The Mirror*, Toronto, November 24, 1971.
36. George F. G. Stanley, *Louis Riel: Patriot or Rebel?* (Ottawa: CHA Booklet No. 2, 1954), p. 24.
37. *The Globe and Mail*, December 25, 1971.
38. "The Riders of the Plains", by a member of the North-West Mounted Police, cited in *The North-West Rebellion of 1885*.
39. Colonel Samuel Benton Steele, *Forty Years In Canada*, pp. 55, 77-78, 152-153, 177-179.
40. George Ham, *Reminiscences of a Raconteur*, (Toronto: Musson Co., 1921), p. 198.
41. *Journal of Lady Aberdeen, 1893-8*, ed. J. Saywell (Toronto: Champlain Society, 1960), pp. 288-290.
42. Richard C. Anzer, *Klondike Gold Rush* (New York: Pageant Press Inc. 1959), pp. 60-61.
43. Tappan Adney, *The Kondike Stampede* (New York: Harper & Brothers, 1900), pp. 432-434.
44. George T. Denison, *Centennial of the Settlement of Upper Canada by the United Empire Loyalists* (Toronto, 1880), Vol. 1, p. iii.
45. *Homes For The Millions, The Great Canadian North-West*, edited by N. F. Davin (Ottawa, 1891), p. 18, 19.
46. *Regina Standard*, August 31, 1904.
47. Lady Aberdeen, August, 1895, (Journal of Lady Aberdeen, MSS in the Public Archives of Canada; cited in S. F. Wise and R. C. Brown, *Canada Views the United States* (Toronto: Macmillan Co. of Canada, 1967).
48. John MacCormac, *Canada—America's Problem* (New York: Viking Press, 1940), p. 154.
49. Louisa & W. Peat, *Canada: New World Power* (New York: Robt. McBride & Co., 1945), pp. 130-131.
50. Stephen Leacock, "I'll Stay in Canada", in *Canadian Anthology*, by C. F. Klinck and R. E. Watters (Toronto: W. J. Gage, Ltd., 1955), p. 211.
51. William Kilbourn, *The Globe and Mail*, December 12, 1970.
52. Winnipeg *Citizen*, May 21, 1919.
53. *La Presse*, May 21, 1919.
54. Rev. Dr. John MacLean, May 20, 1919, cited in K. McNaught, *A Prophet In Politics* (Toronto: University of Toronto Press), p. 111.
55. Strike Bulletin, *Western Labor News*, June 23, 1919.

56. Ronald Liversedge, *Recollections of the On-to-Ottawa Trek, 1935.*
57. *Ibid.*
58. *Toronto Daily Star,* May 8, 1945.

References to Chapter Seven

1. *Canada, The Place for the Emigrant,* Speeches by Lord Dufferin, (1874), p. 30, 31.
2. "Victoria, Our Queen", from Clara Mountcastle, *Canada to England* (Toronto: Imrie, Graham, & Co., Printers, 1899), p. 63.
3. J. V. McAree, *Cabbagetown Store* (Toronto: The Ryerson Press, 1953), pp. 43, 44.
4. Harold Begbie, "Gentlemen, The King!", in *The Ontario Readers Fourth Book* (Toronto: Coles Publishing Co., 1970), pp. 107, 108.
5. *The Globe and Mail,* Toronto, October 10 and 12, 1964.
6. Pierre Elliott Trudeau, cited by Dalton Camp, in "Trudeau our disappearing symbols", in *The Toronto Star,* March 6, 1972.
7. Solange Chaput-Rolland, *The Second Conquest* (Montreal: Chateau Ltd. 1970), p. 50, 51.
8. Prince Philip, cited by Charles Lynch, in "Crown not dead", in *The Gazette,* Montreal, March 17, 1972.
9. McKenzie Porter, "Separatists more than anti-Crown", in *The Toronto Telegram,* May 3, 1971.
10. Editorial in *The Toronto Star,* April 3, 1972.
11. James Eayrs, "Federalism, not monarchy, is divisive now", in *The Toronto Star,* February 14, 1972.
12. Report of the Special Joint Committee of the Senate and House of Commons, 1972 (Votes and Proceedings of the House of Commons, March 16, 1972).
13. *Journal of Lady Aberdeen, 1893-8,* ed. J. Saywell (Toronto: The Champlain Society, 1960), p. 234.
14. Sir John Thompson, *The House of Commons Debates,* September 7, 1892.
15. Blair Fraser, *Search for Idenity,* (Toronto: Doubleday Pub., 1967), p. 248.
16. Goldwin Smith, *The Week,* February 28, 1884, p. 194.
17. Sir Wilfrid Laurier, in O. D. Skelton, *Life and Letters of Sir Wilfrid Laurier,* Vol I (Toronto: S. B. Gundy, Oxford University Press, 1921), p. 426.
18. Arthur R. M. Lower, *Colony to Nation* (Toronto: Longmans, Green & Co., 1946), p. 370.
19. Sir John A. Macdonald, cited in E. B. Biggar, *Anecdotal Life of Sir John A. Macdonald* (U.S. Book Co., 1891).
20. Sir Wilfrid Laurier in O. D. Skelton, *Life and Letters of Sir Wilfrid Laurier,* Vol. I, p. 425.
21. Liberal member of the Legislature, 1863, cited in Richard Cartwright, *Reminiscences* (Toronto: Wm. Briggs, 1912), p. 47.
22. Edwin C. Guillet, *You'll Never Die, John A!* (Toronto: Macmillan Co. of Canada, 1967), p. 52.
23. *Punch,* June 20, 1891.
24. Wilfrid Laurier, cited in Peter McArthur, *Sir Wilfrid Laurier* (Toronto: J.M. Dent & Sons, 1919).
25. Wilfrid Laurier in O. D. Skelton, *Life and Letters of Sir Wilfrid Laurier,* Vol. II, p. 380.
26. *Ibid.,* p. 293.

27. Sir Wilfrid Laurier, speech in Cobalt, Ontario, September 18, 1912.

28. Sir Wilfrid Laurier, in O. D. Skelton, *Life and Letters of Sir Wilfrid Laurier*, Vol. II, p. 327.

29. *Ibid.*, pp. 327, 328.

30. *Ibid.*, p. 380.

31. Wilfrid Laurier, cited in Barthe, Turcotte, and Merand, *Wilfrid Laurier on the Platform* (Quebec, 1890), pp. 527, 528.

32. Laurier speaking at Toronto in 1886, from *Wilfrid Laurier on the Platform*.

33. Wilfrid Laurier, from a speech at Arichat, Nova Scotia, August 15th, 1900.

34. W. L. M. King, cited in Peter C. Newman, *The Distemper of Our Times* (Toronto: McClelland & Stewart Ltd., 1968), p. 56.

35. *Ibid.*, p. 57.

36. W. L. M. King, *ibid.*, p. 56.

37. W. L. M. King, *House of Commons Debates*, November 27, 1944.

38. W. L. M. King, *House of Commons Debates*, June 10, 1942.

39. King *Diary*, July 12, 1897, quoted in R. MacGregor Dawson, *William Lyon Mackenzie King*, Vol. I (Toronto: University of Toronto Press), p. 65.

40. King *Diary*, July 25, 1907, quoted in *ibid.*, p. 186.

41. W. L. M. King, in J. W. Pickersgill and D. F. Forster, *The Mackenzie King Record*, Vol. II (Toronto: University of Toronto Press 1968), pp. 270, 271.

42. W. L. M. King, cited in *ibid.*, p. 364.

43. W. L. M. King, cited in *ibid.*, pp. 317, 318.

44. J. Pierrepont Moffatt, from *The Moffatt Papers*, ed. Nancy Hooker (Cambridge: The Harvard University Press, 1956), pp. 339, 340.

45. Bruce Hutchison, *The Incredible Canadian* (Toronto: Longmans, Green & Company, 1953), pp. 2 and 5.

46. F. R. Scott "W.L.M.K." from *Selected Poems of F. R. Scott*, (Oxford University Press, 1966), pp. 60, 61.

47. Alan Anderson, "A Passion on the Prairies", in *The Flamboyant Canadians*, ed. Ellen Stafford (Baxter Publishing Co., 1964), pp. 259, 260.

48. J. A. Irving, *The Social Credit Movement in Alberta* (Toronto: University of Toronto Press, 1959), p. 317.

49. *Ibid.*, p. 265.

50. John Diefenbaker, in J. M. Bliss, ed., *Canadian History in Documents 1763-1966* (Toronto: The Ryerson Press, 1966), pp. 332, 334 and 335.

51. Thomas Van Dusen, *The Chief* (Toronto: McGraw-Hill Company of Canada Ltd., 1968), p. 57, 89, 90.

52. Peter C. Newman, *The Distemper of Our Times*, pp. 319, 320.

53. Joey Smallwood, in *Time*, November 8, 1971, p. 6.

54. Cited in Richard Gwyn, *Smallwood, the unlikely revolutionary* (Toronto: McClelland & Stewart Ltd., 1968), p. 138.

55. *Ibid.*, pp. 136, 137, 138.

56. Joey Smallwood, in *The Last Post*, February, March issue, 1972, p. 23 (The Canadian Journalism Foundation, Montreal).

57. *Time.* February 14, 1972, p. 15.

58. Richard Gwyn, *Smallwood, the unlikely revolutionary*, p. xiv.

59. Joey Smallwood, Premier of Newfoundland, November 19, 1959, *The Empire Club of Canada—Addresses 1959-1960* (Don Mills: T. H. Best Printing Co. Ltd., 1960). p. 105.

60. Richard Gwyn, *Smallwood, the unlikely revolutionary*, p. 136.

61.   *The Toronto Star*, March 24, 1972.
62.   *The Globe and Mail*, Toronto, January 29, 1972.
63.   *The Toronto Star*, March 24, 1972.
64.   *The Toronto Star*, January 14, 1972.
65.   *The Sun* (Toronto), April 26, 1973.
66.   Ron Haggart, in *The Toronto Daily Star*, cited in Peter C. Newman, *The Distemper of Our Times*, p. 416.
67.   *Ottawa Citizen*, April 4, 1968.
68.   *Ottawa Citizen*, April 2, 1968.
69.   Cited in Peter C. Newman, *The Distemper of Our Times*, p. 417.
70.   *Ibid.*, p. 416.
71.   *The Globe and Mail*, Toronto, June 20, 1968.
72.   Walter Stewart, *Shrug: Trudeau in Power* (Toronto: New Press, 1971), pp. 9 and 10.
73.   Gordon Donaldson, *Fifteen Men* (Toronto: Doubleday Canada Ltd., 1969) pp. 237, 238.
74.   Lubor J. Zink, *The Sun* (Toronto), November 22, 1971.
75.   *House of Commons Debates*, February 18, 1972.
76.   Irving Layton, *The Whole Bloody Bird* (Toronto: McClelland & Stewart Ltd., 1969), p. 55.
77.   George Bain, *The Globe and Mail*, Toronto, September 14, 1971.
78.   Prime Minister Trudeau, *The Toronto Star*, April 16, 1973.
79.   Prime Minister Trudeau, *The Globe and Mail*, Toronto, May 7, 1973.
80.   Richard Crossman, cited in G. Hawkins, ed., *Order and Good Government*, 33rd Couchiching Conference, Canadian Institute of Public Affairs, p. 56.
81.   J. A. Irving, *The Social Credit Movement in Alberta*, p. 114.
82.   C. B. Macpherson, *Democracy in Alberta* (Toronto: University of Toronto Press, 1962), p. 152.
83.   Alan Anderson in *Flamboyant Canadians*, "A Passion on the Prairies", p. 271.
84.   J. A. Irving, *The Social Credit Movement in Alberta*.
85.   Gerald Clark, *Canada: The Uneasy Neighbors* (Toronto: McClelland & Stewart Ltd., 1965), pp. 250, 251.
86.   Paddy Sherman, *Bennett* (Toronto: McClelland & Stewart Ltd., 1966), pp. ix and 125.
87.   Cited in *Maclean's* Magazine, May 10, 1958.
88.   Cited in Gerald Clark, *Canada: The Uneasy Neighbors*, p. 260.
89.   "The Regina Manifesto", 1933; full text in K. McNaught, *A Prophet in Politics: A Biography of J. S. Woodsworth* (Toronto: University of Toronto Press, 1959).
90.   The Canadian Magazine, Toronto, January 22, 1972, pp. 24, 25.
91.   *Ibid.*, p. 25.
92.   Leslie Roberts, *Duplessis—The Chief* (Toronto: Clarke, Irwin, Ltd., 1963), p. 19.
93.   Stuart Keate, quoted in Pierre Laporte, *The True Face of Duplessis* (Harvest House, 1961), pp. 10, 11 and 12.
94.   Leslie Roberts, *Duplessis—The Chief*, pp. 121, 122.
95.   Pierre Laporte, *The True Face of Duplessis*, p. 33.

References to Chapter Eight

1.   Poem by J. A. Fraser, in *Songs of The Great Dominion*, edited by William Douw Lighthall (London: Walter Scott, 1889), p. 269.

2.   The *Globe*, October 14, 1899.

3.   "Soldiers of the Queen", cited in Lower, *Canadians in the Making* (Toronto: Longmans, 1958).

4.   'To The First Contingent", poem written in Toronto, October 30, 1899, quoted in Margaret G. Yarker, *Echoes of Empire* (Toronto: William Briggs, 1900).

5.   Norman Patterson, "The War and Canada", in *The Canadian Magazine*, July, 1902, pp. 204, 205.

6.   "Canada's Voice", cited by Simpkin Marshall in *Oh, Canada!* (London: Kent and Co., 1916), p. 92.

7.   Premier Hearst of Ontario, in The *Globe*, Toronto, October 17, 1914.

8.   Isabella Watson, *War Time Poems and Heart Songs*, (Toronto: Wm. Briggs, 1918), p. 9.

9.   Sir Wilfrid Laurier (his speech at St. Lin, his birthplace, at a meeting in his honour, in 1915) in O. D. Skelton, *Life and Letters of Sir Wilfrid Laurier*, Vol. II (Toronto: S. B. Gundy, Oxford University Press, 1921), p. 447.

10.   L. O. David, *Le Canada*, August, 1914.

11.   The Archbishop of Montreal, Monseigneur Bruchesi, cited in Ralph Allan, *Ordeal By Fire* (Doubleday, 1961), p. 129.

12.   *La Patrie*, September 1914.

13.   Sir Wilfrid Laurier's Speech in House of Commons on August 18, 1914, quoted in O. D. Skelton, *Life and Letters of Sir Wilfrid Laurier*, Vol II, p. 433.

14.   Lloyd George, *War Memoirs*, Vol VI (London: Ivor Nicholson and Watson Ltd., 1933-36), p. 3367.

15.   Liddell Hart, *The Real War 1914-1918* (Boston: Little Brown and Co., 1930), p. 434.

16.   C. R. M. F. Cruttwell, *A History of the Great War 1914-1918* (Oxford: Clarendon Press, 1940), p. 138.

17.   German officer's assessment, cited in Herbert Fairlie Wood, *Vimy!* (Toronto: Macmillan Co. of Canada, 1967), p. 29.

18.   Lord Byng, cited in John Swettenham, *To Seize the Victory* (Toronto: Ryerson Press, 1965), p. 222.

19.   Herbert Fairlie Wood, *Vimy!*, p. 48.

20.   *Ibid.*, p. 130.

21.   Major-General Victor W. Odlum, *The Winnipeg Tribune*, March 9, 1967.

22.   Frederick Palmer, *The Maple Leaf Folk* (Toronto: McClelland, Goodchild and Stewart, 1915), p. 353.

23.   Cited in Larry Worthington, *Amid the Guns Below* (Toronto: McClelland & Stewart Ltd., 1965), p. 29.

24.   Alden Nowlan "Ypres—1915", in *Notes For A Native Land*, ed. Andy Wainwright (Ottawa: Oberon Press, 1969), pp. 101, 102.

25.   Cited in *The Penguin Book of Canadian Verse*, ed. Ralph Gustafson (Harmsworth: Penguin Books Ltd. 1958), p. 109.

26.   Brigadier General Alex Ross, quoted by Lieut. Col. D. E. Macintrye, in *Canada At Vimy*, pp. 192, 193. (Toronto: Peter Martin Associates Limited, 1967), Preface.

27.   Major-General F. F. Worthington, quoted by Herbert Fairlie Wood, in *Vimy!*, p. 5 and 164.

28.   Cited by Lieutenant-Colonel D. E. Macintrye, in *Canada At Vimy*, pp. 192, 193.

29.   Official citation for Billy Barker for his Victoria Cross, cited in Ralph Allen, *Ordeal By Fire* (Doubleday, 1961), p. 171.

30.   General McNaughton (to Army Historical Section, February 20, 1962), cited in John Swettenham, *To Seize the Victory*.

31.   Special Order by Lieutenant-General Sir Arthur W. Currie, October 3, 1918, *Public Archives of Canada*.

32.   "In Flanders Fields", a CBC production on the 50th anniversary of World War I, cited in D. C. Masters, *The Coming of Age* (CBC Publications, 1967), p. 11.

33.   *Debates of the House of Commons*, March 30, 1939, p. 2419.

34.   Prime Minister King in *Debates of the House of Commons*, September 8, 1939.

35.   Prime Minister King's broadcast to the nation, October 27, 1939, cited in W. L. M. King, *Canada at Britain's Side* (Toronto: Macmillan Co. of Canada, 1941), p. 40.

36.   Angus L. Macdonald, Minister of Defence for the Navy, *Canada Fights*, ed. J. W. Dafoe (Farrar & Rinehart, 1941).

37.   Joseph Goebbels, *Diary*, February-March 1943, cited in Ralph Allen, *Ordeal By Fire*, p. 421.

38.   Terence Robertson, *The Shame and the Glory—Dieppe* (Toronto: McClelland & Stewart Ltd., 1962), p. 282.

39.   Recollections by Sergeant Gariepy, cited in Alexander McKee, *Caen: Anvil of Victory* (London: Souvenir Press, 1964), p. 199.

40.   Private of the South Saskatchewan Regiment, cited in *ibid.*, p. 201.

41.   Canadian soldier, cited in *ibid.*

42.   Paul Carell, *Invasion—They're Coming!* (translated from the German by E. Osers), (Bantam Books Inc., 1964), p. 163.

43.   *Daily Telegraph*'s Special Correspondent, cited in Alexander McKee, *Caen: Anvil of Victory*, p. 198.

44.   *Hello Canada! Canada's Mackenzie-Papineau Battalion* (privately published, 1937), pp. 3, 4.

45.   Cited in Ted Allan and Sydney Gordon, *The Scalpel, The Sword* (Toronto: McClelland & Stewart, Ltd. 1952), p. 106.

46.   *Ibid.*, p. 107.

47.   *Ibid.*, Preface, pp. ix, x, xii.

48.   *Debates of the House of Commons*, April 29, 1948, pp. 3438, 3443, 3449 and 3450.

49.   Prime Minister St. Laurent, *Toronto Daily Star*, July 8, 1950.

50.   Editorial, *Toronto Daily Star*, June 30, 1950.

51.   Lester B. Pearson, *Toronto Daily Star*, July 14, 1950.

52.   *Toronto Daily Star*, June 29, 1950.

53.   Lester B. Pearson, *Words and Occasions* (Toronto: University of Toronto Press, 1970), p. 150.

54.   Peter Worthington, "Jingoism vs. Patriotism", in *The Sun* (Toronto), July 27, 1972.

55.   *The Globe and Mail*, January 3, 1972.

56.   John Holmes, director-general of the Canadian Institute of International Affairs in Toronto, "Former diplomat says Canada has a duty to supervise truce", in *The Toronto Star*, January 24, 1973.

57. External Affairs Minister Mitchell Sharp cited in *The Toronto Star*, January 24, 1973.
58. James Eayrs, "Canada must tell U.S. we're staying out of Viet Nam", *The Toronto Star*, December 6, 1972.
59. Robert Cameron, "Canada is obligated to a Viet Nam peacekeeping force", *The Toronto Star*, January 16, 1973.
60. Prime Minister Trudeau, cited in *The Toronto Star*, January 27, 1973.

References to Chapter Nine

1. Pierre Elliott Trudeau, *Time*, April 4, 1969, p. 27.
2. William Kirby, "The Hungry Year", in *Canadian Idylls*, 1894, pp. 135, 136.
3. John Adams, cited in Joseph Barber, *Good Fences Make Good Neighbors* (Toronto: McClelland & Stewart Ltd., 1958), p. 31.
4. Henry Clay, cited in Fred Landon, *Western Ontario and the American Frontier* (Toronto: McClelland & Stewart Ltd., 1967), p. 22.
5. Thomas Jefferson, cited in Joseph Barber, *Good Fences Make Good Neighbors*, p. 31.
6. Lord Lyons, British Ambassador to Washington, 1861, in J. H. Stewart Reid, Kenneth McNaught, and Harry S. Crowe, *A Sourcebook of Canadian History* (Toronto: Longmans Canada Limited, 1959), p. 195.
7. Gilbert McMicken, Director of Macdonald's Secret Service, 1865, in *ibid.*, p. 194.
8. William E. Curtis, *Chicago Record-Herald*, October 7, 1905.
9. Champ Clark, Speaker of the House of Representatives, cited in O. D. Skelton, *Life and Letters of Sir Wilfrid Laurier*, Vol. II (Toronto: S. B. Gundy, Oxford University Press, 1921), p. 375.
10. Champ Clark, Speaker of the American House of Representatives, 1911, *Canadian Annual Review*, 1911, p. 270.
11. John F. Kennedy, in *Debates in the House of Commons*, May 17, 1962.
12. Proclamation of the American General Hull, 1812, in *A Sourcebook of Canadian History*, p. 67.
13. John Beikie, 1813, in *Selkirk Papers, Public Archives of Canada*.
14. E. A. Cruikshank, ed., *Documentary History of Campaigns Upon the Niagara Frontier in 1812-1814* (Lundy's Lane Historical Society Publications, Vol. IX).
15. George Brown, 1865, *The Confederation Debates*, p. 73.
16. Song of the Fenian Brotherhood, 1866, cited in John Murray Gibbon, *Canadian Mosaic* (Toronto: McClelland & Stewart Ltd., 1938).
17. Frank Jones, *The Globe and Mail*, Toronto, November 10, 1956.
18. Cited in John Murray Gibbon, *Canadian Mosaic*.
19. John A. Macdonald, 1867, cited in *Macleans* Magazine, July 1, 1949.
20. George T. Denison, *The Struggle For Imperial Unity* (Toronto: Macmillan Co. of Canada, 1909).
21. Castell Hopkins, "Canadian Hostility to Annexation", *Forum XVI*, November, 1893, p. 326.
22. *Ottawa Citizen*, October 27, 1903.
23. Sir Wilfrid Laurier, cited in J. MacCormac, *Canada—America's Problem* (New York: Viking Press, 1940), p. 136.
24. *The Annexation Manifesto*, Montreal, 1849 (D. English & Co., Printers, Toronto News Company, 1881).
25. Saint John *Morning News*, February 15, 1849.
26. Alexander Tilloch Galt, 1849, cited in *A Sourcebook in Canadian History*, p. 135.
27. Richard Cartwright, *Reminiscences* (Toronto: William Briggs, 1912), p. 26.

28.   Goldwin Smith, *Canada and the Canadian Question*, (Toronto: Hunter Rose, 1891), p. 268, 269.

29.   John A. Macdonald, 1891, February 7, in "To the electors of Canada".

30.   Tories campaign song, cited in Ralph Allen, *Ordeal By Fire* (Toronto: Doubleday, Canada, 1961), p. 31.

31.   S. J. Ritchie, 1885 letter, *Commercial Union in North America* (Toronto News Co., 1886).

32.   Captain Mac, *Canada From The Lakes To The Gulf*, 1881, p. 196.

33.   Wharton Barker, 1886 letter, *Commercial Union in North America* (Toronto News Co., 1886).

34.   George Ball, Undersecretary of State to Presidents Kennedy and Johnson, in his book, *The Discipline of Power* (Boston: Little Brown & Co., 1968), p. 113.

35.   Stephen Leacock, *Sunshine Sketches of a Little Town* (London: Bodley Head, 1912), p. 137.

36.   Letters of Wyndham Lewis, ed. W. K. Rose (London: Methuen & Co., 1941). p. 297.

37.   Richard Cartwright, *Reminiscences*, p. 239.

38.   Goldwin Smith, cited in Arnold Haultain, ed., *Reminiscences* (Toronto: Macmillan Co. of Canada 1911), p. 441.

39.   Dr. Samuel Hayakawa, cited by Terrance Wills, in "Scholars who had to go south for opportunities", in *The Globe and Mail*, Toronto, August 11, 1971.

40.   William A. Tiller, Canadian physicist, cited by Christina McCall Newman, in "The Canadian American", in *Macleans* Magazine, July 27, 1963, p. 12.

41.   John B. Parkin, Canadian architect, cited by Terrance Wills, in "New Careers for Successful Men", in *The Globe and Mail*, Toronto, August 12, 1971.

42.   Brian Brenn and Harold Walters, "Well, They Left", in *Weekend Magazine*, August 14, 1971, p. 14.

43.   Saul Ilson, writer-producer, cited by Terrance Wills, in "Canadian exiles lament rejection", in *The Globe and Mail*, July 27, 1971.

44.   Monty Hall, cited in *ibid*.

45.   Larry D. Mann, (Toronto actor now living in Hollywood), in a letter to *The Weekend Magazine*, August 14, 1971, p. 16.

46.   Professor Robin Mathews, cited in *The Toronto Star*, July 10, 1972.

47.   Letter by William Davis, cited by Al Sokol, in "This anti-Americanism is illegal", in *The Toronto Telegram*, July 12, 1971.

48.   R. B. Sullivan, 1839, cited in *A Sourcebook of Canadian History*.

49.   J. E. Alexander, *Transatlantic Sketches or Visits to the Most Interesting Scenes in North And South America and the West Indies*, Vol. II (London, 1833), p. 164.

50.   Thomas Rolph, 1832, cited by J. E. Middleton and F. Landon, in *The Province of Ontario*, Vol. I (Toronto: Dominion Publishing Co. Ltd.) p. 570.

51.   Susanna Moodie, *The Introduction on Mark Hurdlestone, the Gold Worshipper* (London: Bentley, 1853), cited in *Canadian Anthology*, C. F. Klinck and R. E. Watters (Toronto: W. J. Gage Ltd., 1955), p. 58.

52.   Thomas Carr, Justice of the Peace, 1836, letter to Sir Francis Bond Head, June 24, 1836, Upper Canada Sundries (*Public Archives of Canada*).

53.   John R. Godley, *Letters From America* (London, 1844).

54.   *Report of Royal Commission on Radio Broadcasting* (Ottawa: King's Printer, 1929), p. 6.

55.   *Royal Commission on Arts, Letters and Sciences* (Ottawa: Queen's Printer, 1951).
56.   F. R. Scott, in *Macleans* Magazine, June 1, 1963.
57.   James Young, *The National Future of Canada*, (1887).
58.   N. F. Davin, *British versus American Civilization, A lecture delivered in Shaftesbury Hall, Toronto, April 19, 1873.*
59.   *Canadian Methodist Magazine*, XI, February 1880, p. 188.
60.   *Journal of Lady Aberdeen, 1893-8,* ed. Saywell (Toronto: Champlain Society, 1960).
61.   *The Toronto Daily Star*, November 4, 1971.
62.   *The Toronto Daily Star*, November 3, 1971.
63.   *The Toronto Daily Star*, November 4, 1971.
64.   *The Globe and Mail*, Toronto, November 4, 1971.
65.   Headline from *The Toronto Daily Star*, November 4, 1971.
66.   Irving Layton, "Pomes", in *The Whole Bloody Bird* (Toronto: McClelland & Stewart Ltd., 1969), p. 146.
67.   Frank Underhill, *The Price of Being Canadian* (Canadian Institute of Public Affairs, University of Toronto Press, 1961), p. 49.
68.   Charles Lynch, "We Really Love Uncle Sam. We *Have* to Love Him", in *The Canadian Magazine*, Toronto, January 15, 1972, p. 2.
69.   Mordecai Richler, cited in "An Author warns art isn't good just because it's Canadian", in *The Toronto Star*, March 26, 1973.
70.   Seymour Friedland, "Let's get our own hen before we kill the American goose", in *The Toronto Star*, December 11, 1971.
71.   G. Arnold Hart, Chairman of the Bank of Montreal, cited by Frank Jones, in " 'Buy back Canada', is an unwise policy says Molson Boss", in *The Toronto Star*, December 1, 1972.
72.   External Minister Mitchell Sharp: first extract, *The Toronto Star*, November 8, 1971; second extract, cited in *The Globe and Mail*, Toronto, January 18, 1972.
73.   Northrop Frye, *The Bush Garden* (Toronto: The House of Anansi, 1971), p. iv.

References to Chapter Ten

1.   Thomas D'Arcy McGee, speech in the Legislative Assembly, May 2, 1860, cited by Fennings Taylor, in *The Hon, Thos. D'Arcy McGee: A Sketch of His Life and Death* (Montreal: John Lovell, 1868), p. 24.
2.   Sir John A. Macdonald, *Confederation Debates*, Quebec 1865.
3.   George-Etienne Cartier, Joseph Tasse, ed. *Discours de Sir George Cartier* (Montreal: Senecal & Fils, 1893), p. 395.
4.   William Norris, (Rose-Belford's *Canadian Monthly*, Vol. 4), February 1880.
5.   N. F. Davin, *The Irishman In Canada* (Toronto: Maclean & Co., 1877), p. 1.
6.   Edmund Collins, "New Papers on Canadian History" in G. M. Fairchild, ed. *Canadian Leaves* (Napoleon Thompson & Co., 1887), p. 17.
7.   "Canada", in *Selected Poems of Sir Charles G. D. Roberts, 1860-1943* (Toronto: Ryerson Press, 1955).
8.   Chancellor Wallace, McMaster University, "Canada and the Empire", *The Canadian Magazine*, Toronto, August, 1902, p. 310.
9.   W. M. Mackeracher, *Canada, My Land* (Toronto: Wm. Briggs, 1908), p. 7.
10.   Sir Wilfrid Laurier, cited by G. M. Craig, in *United States and Canada* (Cambridge: Harvard University Press, 1968), p. 165.

11. George Peel Gilmour, *Canada's Tomorrow* (Toronto: Macmillan Co. of Canada, 1954), pp. 3, 4, 5, 6.

12. Rt. Hon. James G. Gardiner, Minister of Agriculture, November 15, 1951, *The Empire Club of Canada, Addresses, 1951-52* (Toronto: T. H. Best Printing Co., 1952), p. 98.

13. Anne Merriman Peck, *The Pageant of Canadian History* (David McKay Co. Ltd. 1963), p. 325.

14. Gordon and Elspeth Winter, *Ourselves In Canada* (London: Seeley, Service & Co. Ltd., 1960), p. 15.

15. Denis William Brogan, in *Canada's Tomorrow*, pp. 259, 260, 261.

16. John Dauphinee, *Opportunity in Canada* (London: Charles Birchall & Sons Ltd., 1958), pp. 113, 114

17. John Bassett, Jr., Publisher of the *Toronto Telegram*, *The Empire Club of Canada, Addresses 1955-56*, June 16, 1955, p. 11.

18. Prime Minister Mackenzie King, *Debates in the House of Commons*, July 1, 1943, p. 4317.

19. C. C. Lingard and R. G. Trotter, *Canada in World Affairs: September 1941 to May 1944*, Canadian Institute of International Affairs (Toronto: Oxford University Press, 1950), pp. 268, 269.

20. Margaret McWilliams, *This New Canada* (Toronto: J. M. Dent & Sons, 1948), pp. 42, 43, 44.

21. Charlotte Whitton, March 1, 1951, *The Empire Club of Canada, Addresses 1950-51*, pp. 278, 279.

22. Frank Underhill, *The Price of Being Canadian* (Toronto: Canadian Institute of Public Affairs, University of Toronto Press, 1961), p. 46.

23. James Bacque, A. Wainwright, ed., in *Notes on a Native Land* (Ottawa: Oberon Press, 1969), pp. 38, 39.

24. Solange Chaput-Rolland, in Gwethalyn Graham and Solange Chaput-Rolland, *Dear Enemies* (Toronto: The Macmillan Co. of Canada, 1965), pp. 105, 106.

25. Réné Levesque, "Why I Believe a Free Quebec is the Best Thing for You Too", in *The Toronto Daily Star*, January 20, 1968.

26. "The Case for a 'Free Quebec': Interview with a Leader in the Separatist Movement", *U.S. News and World Report*, January 15, 1968, p. 44-46.

27. Lester Pearson, *The Globe and Mail*, Toronto, July 1, 1967.

28. John Diefenbaker, *The Globe and Mail*, Toronto, July 1, 1967.

29. John Fisher, November 2, 1950, *The Empire Club of Canada, Addresses 1950-51*, pp. 65, 66.

30. Robert Taylor, *Star Weekly*, Toronto, May 26, 1956.

31. *Report of the Royal Commission on Canada's Economic Prospects* (Ottawa: Queen's Printer, 1957), pp. 389, 390.

32. George Grant, *Lament for a Nation* (Toronto: McClelland & Stewart Ltd., 1965), pp. 86, 87.

33. Eric Kierans, cited by John Doig, in "Eric Kierans widens his fight to save Canada from the U.S.", in *The Toronto Star*, March 10, 1973.

34. Editorial in *The Globe and Mail*, Toronto, July 1, 1972.

35. Editorial in *The Toronto Star*, July 1, 1972.

36. Health and Welfare Minister John Munro, cited by David Allen, in "A mood of fear in the country", in *The Toronto Star*, December 15, 1971.

37. Anthony Westell, "Canada can't go it alone in an interdependent world", *The Toronto Star*, April 20, 1972.
38. Prime Minister Pierre Trudeau, *The Globe and Mail*, Toronto, October 26, 1972.
39. "Towards the new Canada", in *The Economist*, February 12, 1972, p. 46.

ACKNOWLEDGEMENTS

For permission to use copyrighted material grateful acknowledgement is made to the following authors and publishers:

House of Anansi Press Limited for excerpt from *The Bush Garden* by Northrop Frye, ©1971; and *La Guerre, Yes Sir!* by Roch Carrier, © 1970.

Thomas Allen & Son Limited for excerpt from *My Discovery of the West* by Stephen Leacock,©1957.

Barrie & Jenkins Limited for excerpt from *Opportunity in Canada* by John Dauphinee, published by Rockliff Corporation Limited. Reprinted by permission.

James Bacque for excerpt from *Notes for a Native Land*, ed. A. Wainwright, Oberon Press 1969. Reprinted by permission.

Sid Barron for permission to reproduce three cartoons originally published in *Maclean's* Magazine.

Baxter Publishing Company for excerpt from "A Passion on the Prairies" by Alan Anderson in *The Flamboyant Canadians*, ed. Ellen Stafford, ©1964.

G. Bell & Sons, Ltd., for excerpt from *Soldier's Glory* by Sir George Bell, © 1956.

Claude Bissell for quotation from an address delivered at the University of Rochester, Canadian Studies Seminar, March 16, 1962.

Brian Brenn and Harold Walters for excerpt from "Well, They Left," reprinted from *Weekend Magazine*.

Barry Callaghan for excerpt from the *Toronto Telegram*, March 27, 1971.

Canadian Broadcasting Corporation Publications Branch for excerpts from "The Way of the Indian," legend told by Chief John Albany.

Jonathan Cape Ltd. for excerpt from *Canada* by André Siegfried ©1937.

Dr. Daniel Cappon for excerpt from "I Sacrificed Pleasure in Order to Make What I Have," published in the *Toronto Star*.

Roch Carrier for excerpt from *La Guerre, Yes Sir!*

Mme. Solange Chaput-Rolland for excerpts from *The Second Conquest* published by Chateau Books Ltd., also from *My Country, Canada or Quebec?*, and *Dear Enemies* published by Macmillan of Canada.

Ann Charney for excerpt from "Many Quebeckers Say Vote was Anti-French," published in *The Toronto Star*, November 4, 1972.

Clarke, Irwin & Company Limited for "Summer's Girls" from *Lost and Found* by Raymond Souster, ©1968; also for excerpts from *Hundreds and Thousands, Journal of Emily Carr* ©1966; for excerpt from *Egerton Ryerson, His Life and Letters* by C. B. Sissons ©1937; also for excerpt from *Duplessis—The Chief* by Leslie Roberts ©1963.

Coles Publishing Company Limited for "The Canadian" by J. E. Middleton, an excerpt from the *Third Book, Ontario Readers* and for excerpt from "Gentlemen, The King!" by Harold Begbie, in the *Ontario Readers Fourth Book*.

Columbia University Press for excerpt from *The Ojibwa Woman* by Ruth Landes ©1938 reprinted by permission of the publisher.

Copp Clark Publishing Company for excerpt from *The Social Structures of New France* by Cameron Nish and Pierre Harvey.

H. C. Cox for excerpts from *Oh, Canada*, published by Arthur H. Stockwell Ltd., 1966.

Crown-Vetch Music Ltd. for excerpt from "Goofy Newfies," song by composers Roy Payne and Jury Krytiuk.

J. M. Dent & Sons (Canada) Limited for excerpts from *Changing Perspectives in Canadian History* by K. A. MacKirdy, J. S. Moir, Y. F. Zoltvany, ©1967; also for excerpt from *This New Canada* by Margaret McWilliams, ©1948; and for excerpt from *The Privacity Agent* by B. K. Sandwell.

N. K. Dhalla for excerpt from *These Canadians*.

The Rt. Hon. John G. Diefenbaker for excerpts published in *Canadian History in Documents 1763-1966*, edited by J. M. Bliss.

Doubleday & Company, Inc. for excerpt from *Fifteen Men* by Gordon Donaldson, copyright ©1969; *Search for Identity* by Blair Fraser copyright ©1967; *Halifax, Warden of the North* by T. Raddall, copyright ©1965.

Milt Dunnell and the *Toronto Star* for excerpt from "Whole Soviet Team Depressed" from his column of March 7, 1955. Reprinted by permission.

E. P. Dutton & Co. Inc. and George G. Harrap & Co. Ltd. for excerpt from *Invasion—They're Coming* by Paul Carell, translated from German by E. Osers. Copyright ©1963.

James Eayrs for excerpt from "Canada Must Tell U.S. We're Staying Out of Vietnam," in the *Toronto Star*, December 1, 1972; also for excerpt from "Federalism, not Monarchy, is Divisive Now," in the *Toronto Star*, February 14, 1972.

The Empire Club Foundation for excerpt by John Bassett Jr. from *Empire Club Addresses 1955;* The Rt. Hon. James G. Gardiner and Charlotte Whitton from *Empire Club Addresses 1951-2;* John Fisher from *Empire Club Addresses 1950-1.*

Farrar, Straus & Giroux, Inc. Publishers, for excerpts from *O Canada* by Edmund Wilson, copyright ©1964.

Seymour Friedland for excerpt from "Let's Get Our Own Hen Before We Kill the American Goose," published in the *Toronto Star.*

The Globe & Mail, Toronto, for excerpts from a series of articles by Terrance Wills, 1971; also for excerpts from columns by George Bain, Richard Needham, Bruce West and Scott Young.

Ron Haggart for an excerpt from the *Toronto Star*, 1968, and the *Toronto Telegram*, October 8, 1971. Reprinted by permission.

The *Halifax Chronicle-Herald* for permission to reprint two cartoons.

Hamish Hamilton Ltd. and Houghton Mifflin Company for excerpts from *The Scotch* by John Kenneth Galbraith.

Lawren P. Harris for an excerpt from "The Group of Seven in Canadian History", published in *The Canadian Historical Association Annual Report,1948.*

Harvard University Press for excerpt from *The Moffat Papers* ed. by Nancy Hooker.

Harvest House Limited Publishers for excerpts from *The True Face of Duplessis* by Pierre Laporte; also for excerpt from *The Heart of Newfoundland* by Dorothy Henderson.

Foster Hewitt and McGraw-Hill Ryerson Limited for excerpt from *Hockey Night in Canada.*

Bob Hesketh for excerpt from "That Grey Cup; Canada's Annual Touch of Madness" published in the November 22, 1958 issue of *Saturday Night.*

John Holmes, Director-General of the Canadian Institute of International Affairs, for excerpt from an article in the *Toronto Star*, January 24, 1973.

Hugh Hood for an excerpt from "Moral Imagination: Canadian Thing," first published in the *Toronto Star.*

Bruce Hutchison for excerpt from "The Canadian Personality," talk delivered over the CBC network September 1, 1948.

Frank Jones for excerpt from an article in the *Globe & Mail*, November 10, 1956.

William M. Kilbourn for excerpt in the *Globe & Mail*, December 12, 1970.

La Presse, Ltée for cartoons by Jean-Pierre Girerd and P. Vennat. Reproduced by permission.

The Legislative Library of Ontario, Queen's Park, for the reproduction of the print of the Hanging of Lount and Matthews, in the *Caroline Almanack and American Freeman's Chronicle.*

Little, Brown and Company (Atlantic) for excerpt from *The Discipline of Power* by George Ball.

Ronald Liversedge for excerpt from *Recollection of the On-to-Ottawa Trek.*

Dorothy Livesay for her poem "Winter."

Longmans Canada Limited for excerpts from *Colony to Nation* and *Canadians in the Making* by A.R.M. Lower. Also for excerpts from *Canada: Tomorrow's Giant* and *The Incredible Canadian* by Bruce Hutchison.

McClelland and Stewart Limited for excerpts from: *The Unfinished Revolt* by John Barr and Owen Anderson; *The Plastic Orgasm* by La Verne Barnes; *Canada: The Uneasy Neighbour* by Gerald Clark; *The Elegant Canadians* by Louella Creighton; *Marchbank's Almanack* by Robertson Davies; *Lament for a Nation* by George Grant; *Smallwood: the Unlikely Revolutionary* by Richard Gwyn; *Canada at War* and *Forts of Canada* by Leslie Hannon; the poems "Plea for My Lady" from *Nail Polish* and "Pomes" from *The Whole Bloody Bird* by Irving Layton and a short prose excerpt from the latter book; *Canada North* by Farley Mowat; *The Distemper of Our Times* by Peter Newman; for the poem "Eskimo Hunter (New Style)" from *North of Summer* by Al Purdy; *Canada and Mr.Diefenbaker* by B. T. Richardson, *Son of a Smaller Hero* by Mordecai Richler; *The Shame and the Glory* by Terence Robertson; *Bennett* by Paddy Sherman; and *Windigo and Other Tales of the Ojibways* by Herbert T. Schwarz; all these reprinted by permission of McClelland and Stewart Limited, the Canadian Publishers.

McGraw-Hill Ryerson Limited for excerpt from *Why I am a Separatist* by Marcel Chaput; also an excerpt and a cartoon from *Shall We Join the Ladies* by Eric Nicol; and excerpts from *Les Canadiens* (previously entitled *Fire-Wagon Hockey*) by Andy O'Brien and *The Stanley Cup Story* by Henry Roxborough.

David McKay Company, Inc. for excerpt from *The Pageant of Canadian History* by Ann

Joseph R. Smallwood for excerpt from *Peril and Glory* published 1966 by High Hill Publishing House.

Southam News Services for excerpt from "We Really Love Uncle Sam. We Have to Love Him" by Charles Lynch published in *The Canadian Magazine* 1972.

Arthur H. Stockwell Ltd., for excerpt from *Oh! Canada* by H. C. Cox.

The *Toronto Star* Syndicate for permission to reproduce cartoons by Macpherson and Barron.

The *Toronto Sun* and Peter Worthington for excerpt from a July 27, 1972 column "Jingoism Vs. Patriotism." Also for excerpt from a column by Lubor J. Zink; and for cartoons by Yardley-Jones and Donato.

Bill Trent for excerpt from an article in *Weekend Magazine*, November 21, 1970.

The University of Toronto Press for excerpts from *Canadians and Foreign Policy* by F. Alexander © 1960; *Roots and Values in Canadian Lives* by Jean-C. Falardeau © 1960; *The Social Credit Movement in Alberta* by J. A. Irving © 1959; *Next-Year Country, A Study of Rural Social Organization in Alberta* and *Words and Occasions* by Lester B. Pearson © 1970.

The *Vancouver Sun* for a cartoon by Leonard Norris.

Thomas Van Dusen for excerpt from *The Chief*.

The Viking Press, Inc. for excerpt from *Canada—America's Problem* by John MacCormac. Copyright 1940 by John MacCormac, renewed © 1948 by Molly MacCormac.

Western Producer Prairie Books, Modern Press, Saskatoon for excerpt from Of Us and the Oxen by Sarah Ellen Roberts.

Every reasonable effort has been made to trace ownership of copyright material. Information will be welcomed which will enable the publisher to rectify any reference or credit in future printings.